Crime
Law
and
Society

Crime
Law
and
Society

by Frank E. Hartung
WAYNE STATE UNIVERSITY

DETROIT   WAYNE STATE UNIVERSITY PRESS   1965

ACKNOWLEDGMENT

To E. P. Dutton & Co., Inc., for permission to quote from When We Were
Very Young, by A. A. Milne; copyright, 1924, by E. P. Dutton, renewal ©
1952 by A. A. Milne; and to Methuen and Co., Ltd., for the extended permission covering the British Commonwealth excluding Canada.

Grateful acknowledgment is made to the Ford Foundation for financial
assistance in the publication of this book.

To my wife, Rosemary

Contents

Preface 9

Introduction 13

1 The Sociological Theory of Crime 15
Differential Association 15
Crime as Social Disorganization 19
Frustration, Crime, and Delinquency 25

2 Crime, Sociocultural Learning, and Symbolism 37
Symbolic Communication in the Learning of Criminality 37
Role of the Group in the Learning of Criminality 47

3 Crime, Sociocultural Learning, and Symbolism:
Urban Delinquency 53
Vocabulary of Motives and Self-Conception 53
The Delinquent Subculture 55
Rationalizations 62
The "Good Boy" 84
The Numbers Racketeer 88

4 Rural and Hinterland Delinquency 93
Similarities in Rural and Urban Delinquency 93
Social Class and Rural Delinquency 99
Sociocultural Setting of Rural Delinquency 102
The Delinquent as Hedonist 108
Self-Conception of the Rural Delinquent 118

5 Differential Association and the "Atypical" Offender 125
The White-Collar Thief 125
The Compulsive Criminal 136

6 Reason and Responsibility: the Social Movement of
Mental Health 167
The Respectability of Irrationalism 167
A Confusion of the Experts 173

7

7 Crime as Mental Illness   181
Psychiatrists and the Law   181
Concept of the "Irresistible Impulse"   190
"Irresistible Impulse" and the Law   201

8 Individual Rights and the Rehabilitative Ideal   219
The Juvenile Court and Other Agencies   219
The Attempt to Predict Delinquency   244
Some Significant Positive Trends   251

Notes   265

Index   311

Preface

One of the great pleasures of my professional life was the privilege of teaching at the University of Alberta and the University of Saskatchewan in 1958 and 1959. I was therefore more than delighted when former Dean F. C. Cronkite of the College of Law, University of Saskatchewan, honored me by inviting me to deliver the W. M. Martin Lectures for 1962, and was happy to accept. Yet my delight in the invitation was mixed with some reservation because of my being without professional qualification in the law, particularly when following lecturers whose eminence in that field is so widely recognized.

In mitigation of that temerity I can plead that the topic I chose —crime—is one on which laymen, under the Anglo-American system of jurisprudence, are expected to make decisions, and which therefore must be presumed to be within their competence. I can also plead that there is an increasing interest in criminological and correctional matters in Canada. In 1953, Chief Justice Martin, in whose honor the lectures were established, presented the *Report* of the Royal Commission to Revise the Criminal Code of Canada. Since 1956 there have been other *Reports*, on capital and corporal punishment, the law of insanity as a defense in criminal cases, the principles and procedures followed in the remission service of the Department of Justice in Canada, and on the criminal law relating to the criminal sexual psychopath.

There has also been an increase in the number of Canadian universities offering courses in criminology and corrections. In some, the courses are offered in academic departments, usually sociology; and in others, by professional schools, usually the college of law or the school of social work. Several Institutes of Criminology and Corrections have also been established. The professional upsurge of interest and the founding of the *Canadian Journal of Corrections* in 1958 occurred almost together. While the question as to whether there are distinct disciplines of criminology and corrections is still debated by people professionally interested in them, there seems little doubt that those two areas of concern have become permanently established components of the Canadian intellectual scene.

I wish to thank former Dean F. C. Cronkite and the Benchers of the Law Society of Saskatchewan for the invitation to present the Martin Lectures. In addition, I must thank Dean O. E. Lang and the faculty of the College of Law, particularly Professor D. Colwyn Williams, for completing the arrangements. They and their wives, as well as the Saskatoon Bar and the Law Society of Saskatchewan, through their gracious and generous hospitality made the entire period of our stay in Saskatoon memorable to both my wife and me. I should also thank Mr. J. M. Cuelenaere, Q.C., president of the Law Society of Saskatchewan, and Mr. C. H. Schmitt, Q.C., of the Benchers and the Saskatoon Bar, for their kind remarks. My wife and I must express our appreciation for the graciousness of the Honourable Mervyn J. Woods, M.B.E., Q.C., B.A., L.L.B., Supreme Court of Saskatchewan, and Mrs. Woods.

I must also thank Professor Richard E. Du Wors, head of the department of sociology, for suggesting my name to Dean Cronkite. Professor Rudolf A. Helling, head of the department of sociology of the University of Windsor, facilitated research necessary to the lectures. Professor Robert L. James, head of the department of sociology of the University of Alberta, made it possible for me to deliver several lectures at that university, and to have the benefit of several departmental discussions on a number of ideas in the field of social psychology.

The terms of reference of the Martin Lectures specify that they should be in the interest of legal scholarship at the College of Law and the maintenance of the rule of law in Canada. The Benchers, the College of Law, the Saskatoon Bar, and the Law Society of Saskatchewan will judge whether or not those terms were met. It is my hope that, in addition to meeting them, the lectures, as well as this book, will also have furthered the cause of reason, which is coming under increasing attack, especially in the law and in psychiatry—although more so, it seems, in the United States than in Canada at the present time.

The Martin Lectures of 1962 are the basis of this book, which includes much material that was not and could not have been part of them. There are, for example, many references to books, articles, and papers published and read in 1961, 1962, and 1963. Chapter 4 and parts of Chapters 3 and 8 were written during the summer and late fall of 1963. Quotations and titles of publications are used in the book in an amount impossible when one is informally addressing an audience. Although it is therefore more formal than the lectures, I have still written somewhat informally and have throughout tried to avoid both catachresis and an excessive use of sociological terms. This seemed necessary to me if the general reader were to find cogent the thesis that the social-psychological postulates of Anglo-American criminal law are both empirically and logically superior to their proposed substitutes discussed below.

My thesis is that sociocultural learning is crucial in the development of criminality. The sociological theory presented is described as a general theory of criminality and crime. It is more than that. It brings together such disparate events as burglary, embezzlement, homicide, numbers racketeering, physical assault, rape, robbery, shop-lifting, vandalism, and white-collar crime. It indicates the fundamental similarity of rural and urban delinquency, and indicates that the same principles of sociocultural learning account for both criminality and lawfulness. It therefore is, or at least aspires by implication to be, a general theory of sociocultural behavior. Some criminologists, in contrast, have been concerned with presenting specific theories to account for specific crimes or types of crimes.

Parts of the book are cast, so to speak, in the form of a dialog between sociology and psychiatry, and between sociology and biology. Although Plato easily won every argument in his dialogs merely because he himself wrote them, in contrast I have tried to indicate the empirical and logical superiority of sociological theory over those theories that compete with it.

I must thank Professors Ralph W. England, Jr., and Michael Hakeem for reading and evaluating the entire manuscript and for offering numerous helpful suggestions of fact and interpretation. Various parts of the manuscript were read by Professors Robert G. Caldwell, Richard Laskin, and Lyle W. Shannon, and by Mr. George Henderson. Their comments were indeed helpful. Dr. Kenneth Polk's invitation to participate in the 1963 Lane County Juvenile Court Summer Institute at the University of Oregon provided the incentive and the occasion to write Chapter 4. All statements of fact and interpretation, however, are, of course, my responsibility. I must also express my appreciation to the Center for the Study of Crime, Delinquency, and Corrections for creating conditions of work that expedited the completion of the manuscript, and to the members of its staff for numerous helpful discussions.

Frank E. Hartung

Introduction

This book will be devoted to two general topics: first, the explication of a general theory of criminality; and second, an evaluation of certain trends in the handling of offenders and non-offenders. The theory is sociological and is in accord with the conception of crime as being deliberate and intentional. The trends to be discussed are those that have resulted in the withering of the concept of responsibility, and some of the consequent corollaries.

A general theory of sociocultural behavior needs two distinct although related and consistent components.[*] First, processes through which individuals come to engage in the behavior must be specified. Experimental testing and development of the theory will be facilitated if those processes are specified in such a manner that predictive statements concerning the sociocultural behavior of given categories of individuals are possible. This is sometimes referred to as a genetic or developmental theory of sociocultural behavior. Second, there must be a statement explaining the statistical distribution of the behavior in time and space. The development of the theory will be facilitated if predictive statements about unknown statistical distributions can be derived from the first statement. The concern with the spatial and temporal distribution of rates is known as epidemiology.

[*] Donald R. Cressey, "Epidemiology and Individual Conduct: A Case from Criminology," *Pacific Sociological Review*, 3, Fall 1960, pp. 47–58.

A complete statement of the sociological analysis of crime and criminality would require the consideration of both epidemiological and developmental aspects. Indeed, it would be impossible to state and develop here in equal detail all the components of the sociological theory of criminality. I have therefore decided to concentrate upon the developmental aspect of criminality in the individual, the aspect that stresses sociocultural learning, placing particular emphasis upon the learning of a vocabulary of motives and a self-conception, each of which is requisite to the other in the learning of criminality. In various places I have indicated that the same social-psychological and sociological processes are involved in the learning of criminality and lawfulness. I have also tried to show that while their cultural contents are different, it is typical for anyone to be knowledgeable in both.

I have not tried, in this book, to present a survey and evaluation of the vast literature dealing with criminal causation; nor can I make any claim to originality, except for the collation of materials. What I have attempted is to present a logically consistent and empirically grounded explication of the propositions that criminality is learned socioculturally and that to commit a crime is to engage in a deliberate act. I have not discussed the problem, What actions ought to be criminal? Even though this is a basic problem that the social sciences, and especially sociology, have failed to attack, it cannot be discussed at this time.

1. The Sociological Theory of Crime

Differential Association

The theory of criminality most widely held in sociology was first explicitly formulated by the late Edwin H. Sutherland.[1] It has been named the theory of differential association. Neither Sutherland nor Cressey, who completed the editing of the fifth edition of the *Principles of Criminology,* should be held responsible for my explication of it, although I think that there are no significant theoretical differences having significant empirical implications between my statement and theirs.

The fundamental proposition in the theory is that criminality is learned in symbolic interaction, and predominantly in small, intimate groups. The content of the learning includes the mastery of techniques, a vocabulary of criminal rationalizations, and criminal conceptions of law, property, and the self. Whether one's conceptions are criminal or lawful—or both, to some degree, as is not unusual—is a function of whether those people and those patterns of thought and action that one observes, or with whom one associates and identifies oneself, conceive of and interpret the law in a manner favorable to its violation or to its observance. It is therefore hypothesized that one will become criminal if his interpersonal relations—including his conversations with himself—present him with an excess of definitions favorable to the violation of the law.

The word "excess," which by itself might seem to imply that lawfulness is a mere summation by lawful experience, suggests that there are two aspects to the process of becoming criminal, namely, the qualitative and the quantitative. Neither has been thoroughly explored through research. Of the (quantitative aspect, it may be said that the influence of association with other people, and with patterns of behavior and thought, on one's own socio-cultural behavior is a function of that association's frequency, priority, duration, and intensity.) Both lawful and criminal behaviors are learned by means of the same symbolic learning processes; and since both lawful and criminal behaviors serve the same general human needs and values, the latter cannot be used to explain the difference in the kinds of behavior. Both thieves and honest people, for example, strive to achieve status; both business-men and racketeers organize in order to secure money and power. Some sociologists have recently helped to popularize the psychological hypothesis that the frustration of ambition ("status frustration") is the basic cause of the several kinds of deviation, including crime and delinquency. Frustration is and must continue to be futile as an explanation because it explains lawful behavior as completely as it explains criminal behavior. (Differential association determines the degree to which one's sociocultural experience advances the learning of conceptions of law, property, and the self by criminal or lawful influences.)

(This is a causal theory.) Any specified condition, in order to be a causal component in the criminality of a person, must so affect his cultural experiences and social relations as to advance criminal influences, and impede lawful influences, on him. Many conditions have been believed to be criminally causative components: home, family, education, income, race, bodily build, psychopathology, and the like. Our sociological theory would also attempt to explain in an integrative manner, why it is that in certain circumstances the above-listed conditions may advance lawful influences and impede criminal ones. According to this theory any component that can be shown to be correlated with crime must be shown to affect one's symbolic learning if it is logically to be conceived as criminally causative. The theory is integrative in that it attempts to bring seemingly diverse factors into one

scheme. Most of Sutherland's critics have ignored this aspect of
the theory. Focusing their attention on the name "differential
association," they have erroneously concluded that "bad companions" encompasses the whole theory. Regrettably, the name has
often been mistaken for the theory. With the label lately given to
it—"a theory of cultural transmission"—such a misunderstanding
might not be as likely to occur.

("Differential association," Sutherland wrote—although not
holding consistently to this usage—should be supplemented by
the concept "differential social organization." *) The latter phrase
conforms to Cooley's conception of contemporary social organization.[2] (The unity of modern society, Cooley showed, is not necessarily the unity of consensus or agreement, but rather the organization that develops from the fact of reciprocal influence or
causation among the several segments of society. By virtue of this
reciprocal influence one event is connected with other events;
thus each results from the whole social process. (Cooley's use of
the term "social organization" to mean the differentiated unity
of modern social life) will be followed throughout this book.
Cooley's classic conception has great empirical and methodological value; it allows crime and delinquency to be conceptualized
as sociocultural phenomena produced, sustained, and perpetuated by the normal operation of the social process, just as ethi-
cally more desirable sociocultural phenomena are produced, sustained, and perpetuated.

The conception of social organization as being a differentiated
unity is an excellent tool in the evaluation of the upper-class
view that crime and delinquency are various kinds of biological
and social pathologies.

The qualitative aspect of the process of becoming criminal can
be studied through the use of social-psychological concepts, par-

* A few years before his death Sutherland was using "differential social
organization" rather than "social disorganization." Both the logical and the
empirical force of his writing point, I think, to the former rather than to the
latter. This puts Sutherland in the most distinguished of company: since at
least the early years of the nineteenth century the differentiated unity of modern
society has been a continuing object of scientific study by a succession of distinguished scholars in anthropology, jurisprudence, political science, and sociology.

ticularly those related to the concepts *symbol* and *self.**("Symbol-ism" refers to the use of language, which has effects pervading all human conduct. "Self" refers to the conception that one has of oneself in relation to others, and also to the system of objects and ideas cherished as one's own.) A critical influence is exerted on conduct through the presence or absence of self-involvement in the given situation. One's conception of self is pervasive in mental activity, giving it unity, coherence, and purpose.

(Glaser has recently introduced the concept "differential iden-tification" into the theory of differential association. It refers to the criminal's and the delinquent's identifying himself both to himself and with certain other individuals or groups.[3] Since the identification of self is a symbolic (linguistic) process, the addi-tional concept "differential learning" can logically and usefully be introduced.† The sociological theory of criminality exemplified in Sutherland's work presents "a conception of crime as a subclass of the totality of all deliberate human action." (Crime is thus to be explained in the same terms as any other kind of deliberate conduct.‡)A leading principle of this social-psychological view

---

* The qualitative and quantitative aspects of experience are not as neatly and sharply separated as this discussion might seem to imply. In the routine of daily life they are most closely twisted, blended, and incorporated. They can, however, be conceptually separated for purposes of study. In science there is a secular trend converting the qualitative into the quantitative by treating attributes as variables. This is not, however, the place to discuss this rather technical point in research, although it can be said that there is a large body of literature dealing quantitatively with self-behavior.

† To avoid possible misunderstanding it should be stated that the reference to learning is to symbolic or linguistic learning, and not to the nonsymbolic learning by animals that is the subject of much intensive and ingenious research in ex-perimental psychology. The latter is exemplified in the work of such students as Clark L. Hull, E. C. Tolman, Harry F. Harlow, and Kenneth W. Spence. Their several theories of learning, based on studies of albino rats, rhesus monkeys, and other species of animals, cannot be extrapolated to human or symbolic learning because there is no psychical equivalence between the human and any other species. For a study of such theories of learning see Ernest R. Hilgard, *Theories of Learning*, 2d ed., New York: Appleton-Century-Crofts, Inc., 1956.

‡ Although many writers have used the term "voluntary" rather than "deliberate," when referring to deliberate actions, and I am one, it seems to me that there are two reasons why this use may be misleading. First, the words are not synonyms. Second, they imply quite different conceptions of the human being and of sociocultural behavior. To refer to our own behavior as *deliberate* stresses its

is that deliberate behavior is guided by the actor in accordance with (1) his anticipation of others' probable responses and (2) the vocabulary of motives that he has developed to explain and to justify his behavior.[5] This view of human conduct is in conformity with what is known concerning the development of the self and self-consciousness. It is being additionally confirmed by researches in crime and delinquency to be discussed later.

There is no implication in the conception advanced here that criminal or delinquent behavior is random, free, uncaused, or undetermined. Quite the contrary. The conception of sociocultural behavior, and therefore of crime, is deterministic because it causally ascribes the actor's anticipations and rationalizations to the content of his sociocultural experiences. It is, furthermore, consistent with the legal conception of crime as wilful, since it emphasizes that a criminal action is deliberate, and results from a decision to act in a certain manner.[6]

This conception of crime is in agreement with a statement made a few years ago by Karl Llewellyn, who for some time had helped in the attempt to develop interdisciplinary inquiry involving law and the social sciences:

> When I was younger I used to hear smuggish assertions among my sociological friends, such as, "I take the sociological, *not* the legal, approach to crime"; and I suspect an inquiring reporter could still hear much the same (perhaps with "psychiatric" substituted for "sociological")—though it is surely somewhat obvious that when you take "the legal" out, you also take out "crime." [7]

Crime as Social Disorganization

It can be seen from the previous discussion that the current sociological analysis of crime and delinquency rejects the motto *facilis descensus Averno* as being demonstrably incorrect. It arrives, in contrast, at the opposite conclusion: crime and delinquency are correctly and most usefully conceived as being a

---

symbolic (linguistic) and hence its intellectual character. To describe it as *voluntary* implies a theory holding the will to be the dominant factor in experience, and behavior to be unimpelled by another's influence, and to be spontaneous and proceeding from the will, as if the will were something substantive "inside" one, propelling him to act, much as the psychiatric "id" is alleged to do.

definite achievement, often the result of years of prolonged effort
and hard work) They therefore require investigation in their own
terms, namely, as sociocultural phenomena.

Delinquency and crime are, however, often conceived negatively, as in the various formulations of "social disorganization."
Sociologists have by no means been the only ones to expound the
hypothesis of social disorganization. They have been joined by
—and have joined—theologians, moralists, social workers, and
others in expatiating on the claim that modern society (most
usually, western civilization) is in a state of breakdown, either
total or partial. Crime and delinquency are explained as being
the result of the breakdown of society as a whole or of specific
institutions in particular. Lawrence K. Frank's *Society as the
Patient* is an example of a book that has helped to popularize the
notion that the social problems confronting a nation or an individual are medical problems, resulting from the breakdown of
society.[8] As we shall see later, the medicalization of social problems is not an unmixed good. The book by Milton L. Barron bears
the cheaply smart title, *The Juvenile in Delinquent Society*.[9]
According to Barron and Frank, it is now possible to indict an
entire society. Clinard writes:

> The urban world is one of anonymity where there are few ties or
> interests to bind a person to others. Urban conditions generally
> do not provide means for getting psychologically "close" to other
> persons. . . .
> Generally speaking, where intimate group participation lan-
> guishes, the incidence of social deviation is high . . . the break-
> down of intimate communication in an urban society lies at the
> center of social problems in that the individual finds that he
> cannot easily communicate with his fellows and thus cannot orient
> his own values or put himself into harmony with the group.[10]

Clinard's notion of the big city is hardly accurate. One aspect
of urban life that is agreed upon by many independent investigators is that involvement with primary group and intimate
relationships on the one hand, or with secondary and impersonal
contacts, on the other, varies according to social class. The former
type of relationship is representative of the urban lower class;
the latter of the middle and upper classes. The fact is, as Mirra

Komarovsky observed some years ago, we have tended to derive our generalizations concerning interpersonal associations—including the family—from studies of the middle and upper social classes.[11] The stereotype of the contemporary urban dweller is that of a man who no longer identifies himself with such a primary group as the neighborhood, who has severed ties with all of his kin except his own nuclear family, who plays with one group, prays with another, joins a third for financial reasons, a fourth for professional reasons, and so on. This stereotype must be revised, because research indicates that it applies to the upper-middle and upper social classes. The urban dweller to whom such a description applies is statistically a minority of the population in the large cities.

Only 32 per cent of the lower-class men in Komarovsky's sample belonged to a formally organized group (including membership in a church club or society, but not a church as such), whereas of the professional men earning $5,000 or more a year (in 1946), 98 per cent belonged to one or more formally organized associations.

All studies of social participation, when social class is taken into consideration, show that the middle and upper classes belong to more formal and impersonal associations through which they participate in affairs of wide social scope, and that the working-class members belong to few, living their life on a predominantly primary-group basis. This applies to the slum as well as to other lower-class residential areas. The most recent study of the worst slum of Toronto refers to the inhabitants' "indifference to secondary associations, which encourage mobility and diffusion of interests," and to their "directness of personal interaction . . . and a concentration on informal primary group, particularistic relationships." [12]

Most of the recent sociological concern with the alleged breakdown of society results largely from the work of Thomas and Znaniecki, who defined social disorganization as "a decrease of the influence of existing social rules of behavior upon individual members of the group." [13]

This definition has been adopted in practically all of the textbooks dealing with social problems, published since 1918. A num-

ber of writers, including many sociologists—who should have
known better—have adopted the concept as a major, if not *the*,
explanation of crime. None has succeeded in solving the logical
and empirical problems that are corollaries of the concept. An
analysis of these textbooks, undertaken a few years ago, showed
their level of theoretical abstraction to be so low that they were
hardly more than bodies of meagerly connected facts, marked by
a paste-pot eclectic psychology to provide a rationale for their
facile analysis, and marred by moral judgments presented as if
they were scientifically established principles.[14] Even the textbooks dealing with social problems or deviation convey the impression that the authors are small-town natives pointing with
alarm to the big city as being the sink of iniquity. Mabel A. Elliott,
for example, claims that "displaced" country people in the United
States, unaccustomed as they are to the complexities and stimula-
tions of urban life, "are easy prey to the temptations of crime."
She says further that unpunished criminals and recidivistic prisoners are the real criminals because "they have organized their lives
without reference to social values. They have justified their life-
work . . . on a basis of the material rewards." [15]

Whatever hope there is for reforming the criminal "must lie in
some *conversion of his values*." The significance of the quotation
is not only that her moralism is showing, but also that she has
contradicted herself within two sentences. Another self-contradiction is her statement that "organized crime is one of the amazing
aspects of social disorganization." [16]

Lander's writing exhibits similar logical difficulties. He states,
for example:

> [Certain areas of the city] are characterized by a general social
> instability and weakening of the social controls and norms which
> reflect themselves in a high delinquency rate for all groups.
> . . . One would expect a high delinquency rate in an area
> characterized by normlessness and social instability.[17]

On the next page, however, he says that it would be "erroneous"
to conceive of areas with high rates of delinquency as being
"devoid of norms and group controls," since gangs are "highly
regulatory" of the behavior of their members. Lander's major
logical difficulty in contradicting himself as to the simultaneous

presence and absence of norms is that in studying lower-class life he has committed himself to the upper-class concept, *anomie*. As its sociological popularizer has said, "The term *anomie* has historically referred to the progressive breakdown of norms . . . to normlessness." [18] Lander was thus led to a position that is peculiar, to say the least. In his study of juvenile delinquency in Baltimore, he wrote that he

> found *at least three types of normlessness*. In one area the conflicting sets of norms of different ethnic groups gave rise to a lack of external control.
> In another area normlessness arose, not because the norms were conflicting, but because the community was so completely disorganized that there was a complete absence of social consensus.[19]

Lander then described the third kind of normlessness that he had discovered, "in which there was not a conflict of norms, but a very stable and completely criminal set of norms. The normal form of behavior was to be a criminal. The norms were highly organized, but they were not the accepted norms of society at large." [20]

(The social disorganizationists and pathologists conceive of crime—as well as the other social problems—as resulting from the failure, the breakdown or the disintegration (all three terms are used) of society as a whole, or of specific institutions.) Society is "sick" or "delinquent," and the individual, particularly the juvenile, is its victim. This is an old man's conception, namely, the notion that today's morals have degenerated while yesterday's were advanced and refined. An excellent if not wholly convincing example of the old man's conception of delinquency is to be found in the statement of Judge Samuel Leibowitz to the United States Senate committee investigating juvenile delinquency:

> Well, what has happened to this great country? . . .
> Senator, you will agree with me and every right-thinking man that is not a fool will agree, that there has been a deterioration of the moral climate in our country. You see it all over. The old things that were tried and true when you were a kid and I was a kid, that is all gone by the board. If it is old, it is dirty; if it is old and tried and true, it has to be discarded.[21]

The old man's conception reminds one of the search for the Golden Age of the past. It is a secular statement of the biblical mythology of the Fall, popularized in sociology largely by the Chicago School of sociology. It has its parallel in theology, as exemplified in the statement by the Roman Catholic Bishops of the United States, entitled "Unchanging Duty in a Changing World." [22] The Bishops described what they called "the present moral deterioration" as being a basic evil, rather than "a mere temporary relaxation of standards." They claimed that:

> Ignorance of moral principles and the rejection of the very notion of morality are on the rise today and threaten to undermine our nation and its most sacred traditions. The evidences of our moral decline are everywhere to be seen: In the alarming increase in crime, particularly among the young; in the sensational treatment of violence and sexuality in literature, on the stage, screen and television; in the disclosures of greed and cynicism in government, labor and business; in the stubborn continuance of race prejudice and injustice; in the multiplication of divorce and the rapid disintegration of the family; in a harsh and pagan disregard of the sacredness of human life concealed under the mantle of science.

A viewpoint very similar to, if not identical with, that of the bishops has been expressed by the director of the Bureau of Investigation of the United States Department of Justice. In response to the question as to what has caused the (supposed) increase in the rate of crime among youth, J. Edgar Hoover is reported as replying:

> For one thing, there is a steady decline of parental authority. Moral standards, too, have declined in the home and the community. Because of adult delinquency, young people are not being given the proper guidance.
> Public indifference to organized vice has made it easy for the salesmen of the criminal empire to reach young people with obscene material, narcotics and other evils which weaken their character.
> Television and movies, I think, must also share part of the blame. The highly suggestive and, at times, offensive, scenes, as well as the frequent portrayal of violence and brutality on television screens and in motion pictures, are bound to have an adverse effect on young people.[23]

Written with eloquence but without evidence, the bishops'

statements as well as Hoover's call to mind one of the questions that many students ask about the allegations of social disorganization: "If the United States (or some other country) is in fact so disorganized, why doesn't it collapse overnight?" Reference to one trend in research will be helpful in evaluating the claim that social disorganization and moral deterioration are abroad in the land. Much, if not almost all, of the recent criminological (etiological) and correctional research has found social disorganization and its related concepts unnecessary, unworkable, and erroneous.

That research does not find that people are today being progressively freed from social constraint, being thus free to act at random or at fancy. It does find that in a heterogeneous society the constraining influence of one value-system may be substituted for another, and that individuals characteristically are possessed by more than one value-system. (One of its important conclusions is that social control is not diminished in a heterogeneous society.) Even the allegedly most disorganized and most deteriorated slum has been shown to be marked by social organization and value-systems, just as are the residentially more desirable sections of the city. This research is, in part, based on the conception of social organization as consisting of the organization of differences, which was referred to previously.

Frustration, Crime, and Delinquency

(One widely accepted conception of the cause of delinquency is that it results from the continually frustrating conditions of lower-class life.) One must be careful in discussing this idea because it seems to be based on a sincere and determined humanitarianism. Anyone who opposes it may be charged with being cruel, sadistic, medieval, reactionary, illiberal, rightist, and opposed to progress. There is no need to document once more the difficult conditions of social existence under which a large proportion of the people live. A physically miserable life is no new phenomenon in even the cities of the western world. Even so, many of those in the United States who are alarmed over the alleged but undemonstrated large increase in the rate of crime and delinquency since the end of World War II seem to think that human misery was invented by Herbert Hoover, practically eliminated by Franklin D. Roosevelt, and restored by Dwight D. Eisenhower.

It is sufficient to point to the criminal history of only two nations to refute that idea, namely, England and the United States. Criminal gangs have existed in England for centuries and in the United States since the colonial period. There is a continuous history of established crime in England since before the time of the Elizabethan underworld. American cities such as Boston, Charleston, South Carolina, New York, Philadelphia, and New Orleans have a history of criminal gangs reaching well back into the eighteenth century. Others, such as Chicago, have a criminal history almost from the date of their founding.

It is surely no news to state that much of mankind has lived in misery and that crime and delinquency are well established components of culture. But the repetition is necessary because so many of the people who want to help the miserable and deviant seem unable to place today's social problems in either their historical perspective or their contemporary cultural matrix. It has been properly said that "Delinquency is a social institution in the big city. That is why it is so difficult to come to grips with it." [24] Contemporary methods of handling criminals and delinquents seem futile and perhaps cruel and callous only when viewed from today's perspective, ignoring the bloody history of punishment.

When viewed in historical perspective, today's handling of criminals in western Europe, in North America, and elsewhere, seems much more humane than that of previous centuries. Law and order have increased, gangs and corruption have decreased, the safety of the seas, the streets, and of the person and property have increased. Adult gangs today tend to develop into large-scale bureaucratic business enterprises, which want no violence—except when necessary. The streets of London and New York City are immeasurably safer today than they were in 1800. I say this even though members of youthful gangs in the latter city killed at least eleven boys and girls during the first nine months of 1959, and at least one hundred during the decade of the 1950's; and even though the New York City Youth Board during the two months of July and August, working directly and indirectly with 115 youthful gangs, averted 192 incidents that might have resulted in tragedy for those involved, from a mere beating to murder.[25]

Having demonstrated, I hope, my own humanitarianism and concern for progress, I shall now consider some aspects of the hypothesis that delinquency results from frustration, and particularly from what some students term "status frustration." That hypothesis is negativistic in its assumption that delinquency results from the breakdown or the malfunctioning or the normlessness of some segment of, or the entirety of, the social system. A typical statement can be found in the report of a Governor's Committee of the state of Michigan: "Many marginal delinquent pupils become frustrated as a consequence of their school failure." [26]

Another example is provided by a survey of the school children in grades 3 through 8 in the public and separate schools of Windsor, Ontario:

> The social delinquent is typically male and from the lower or working class. His motivation may be understood as a reaction against a society which on the one hand sets up middle class goals as the proper aspirations of all children—wealth, a prestigeful occupation, college education—but on the other hand allows little opportunity for the lower class child to achieve these goals.
>
> His delinquent behavior is thus typically a striking back against the standards and values of a middle class society. He lies, steals, destroys property—the values of honesty and respect for property are flouted. He is tough, disrespectful to adults. He is loud and noisy. He is not remorseful after his misdeeds.[27]

The report states further that because school and school work are symbols of what he is reacting against, the "social delinquent" performs poorly in school. Of the 92 pupils classified as "social delinquents" by the report, the schoolteachers rated 13 per cent "good" on their school work, 38 per cent "fair," and 49 per cent "poor." The report nowhere takes into consideration that fact that lower-class boys tend to have average to less-than-average marks in school just because, coming from the lower class, they have a lesser interest in school and more modest ambitions than pupils from the middle and upper classes.

Sometimes the hypothesis that frustration leads to delinquency includes the observer's moral values, disguised as an objective description:

> Delinquents, more often than nondelinquents, come from homes broken by death, divorce, or desertion or homes lacking in understanding, self-respect, stability, affection and moral standards. Frequently their homes are economically as well as emotionally deprived.[28]

(Sometimes the hypothesis concerning the relationship of frustration to delinquency is dramatically stated in the form of the "two strikes theory.") Judge Leibowitz, quoted previously, said:

> A child brought here [New York City] to live in crowded slums begins life with two strikes against him. Our tenements teem with thousands of families squeezed into rooms unfit for human habitation.
>
> . These are the people exploited by the slumlords who grow richer on exorbitant rentals. In thousands of cases the New York City Department of Welfare foots the bill by paying fantastic rents for rat-infested, disease-breeding tenement flats. Such hovels exist because we have been coddling and pampering and protecting their slumlord owners. Rarely, if ever, does the offender go to jail. Suspended sentences and small fines are handed out right and left. . . .
>
> Last year (1958) the taxpayers expended the staggering sum of $41 million in New York City for the support of 54,000 illegitimate children living in our slums . . . we are supporting them in the most wretched and degrading environment which prevents the moral development of the child. . . .

Judge Leibowitz then described a visit to the slums, in the company of the Mayor and the members of a grand jury:

> We stopped off at a place on Throop Avenue which is in the Bedford-Stuyvesant section, and we entered the living quarters of a family of six. What were the living quarters?
>
> It was a room about 10 by 12. There wasn't a window in the place. There was no lavatory or bathroom. There were holes in the walls and there was just one bed in the premises, a single bed. Listen to this:
>
> Four boys, three of them slept on this one bed with the mother, and during . . . the night the mother would have to sit on the bed with a stick to beat off the rats that came from the holes in the wall, the little dump.

The father slept on the floor and the youngest boy slept in the baby carriage. The place was a firetrap. If ever a conflagration started there they would be burned like rats before the fire engines could respond. . . .

Now, these are the conditions in New York.[29]

(Judge Leibowitz cast considerable doubt upon the validity of his "two strikes" theory)when a few minutes later in his statement to the senatorial committee he said:

I am [sic] an immigrant boy. I was born in Rumania and came to live here with my parents at four years of age. We didn't live on Riverside Drive. We lived on Essex Street, which is in the very heart of the slums on the East Side up in a two-room hole in the wall on the sixth floor of a tenement.

The toilet was out in the yard. There were no bathrooms. There were no swimming pools. There were no summer camps for kids. There were no recreation centers.[30]

Judge Leibowitz, being both foreign-born and slum-reared had more than two strikes on himself, according to his own criteria. He nevertheless became most eminently successful as a trial lawyer and has a creditable record as a magistrate. Later in this work we will be referring to the class of individual that is an exception to his notion as "college boys." We can at this point be content with the observation—recognized by nearly everyone as unoriginal—that the hypothesized causal relationship between the alleged frustration of members of the lower socioeconomic class, and delinquency, should be subjected to empirical testing. I shall not be advocating the virtues of adversity for other people if I once again repeat the often-stated observation: most poor people do not become criminals and many well-to-do and rich people become crooks.

When educators write for educators, the latter are very likely to take that writing seriously. The work of William C. Kvaraceus has been particularly influential among teachers, as well as others. He, too, propounds the negativistic thesis that frustration leads to delinquency. "There is little doubt," he writes, "that most delinquents, as children of lower status, have been confronted by many more problems of living, have undergone more frustrations . . . than the children of higher status." [31] Kvaraceus thus seems to

ascribe middle- and upper-class values equally to all socioeconomic classes. He regards aggressive behavior as having behind it
"a basic pattern of severe and prolonged frustration." The frustrations "include such factors as excessive poverty, rejection or
insecurity in basic family relationships, membership in marginal
or minority groups, and continuous school failure." So numerous
and prolonged are these frustrations and so common in the lives
of delinquents, Kvaraceus believes, that many social workers tend
automatically to look for them on the principle that wherever
there is aggression (delinquency) there must be an underlying
frustration. He asserts that the pattern of aggression is pre-
dominant in delinquency: "Looking into the backgrounds of
delinquents there is the common history of severe frustrations." [32]

[In evaluating the hypothesis of the causal relationship between
frustration and delinquency there are at least three things that
can be said.]

((1) Delinquency should be conceived as a positive thing. It
should be conceived as being a definite achievement. Many children work more or less diligently at being delinquent,) since it
requires practice to become, say, a fairly successful shoplifter or
burglar, or even a jackroller. "Frustration" works an injustice on
the perseverance, hard work, ingenuity and enterprise of many
juvenile delinquents—at least as far as the career delinquent is
concerned. It requires years to produce a good delinquent.

((2) The theory states incorrectly the relationship between
delinquency and failure in school. The delinquent tends to fail
in school because he is delinquent or is in the process of becoming
delinquent. He is, furthermore, likely to be uninterested in school
to begin with because he comes from the lower socioeconomic
class. An example of the latter point is provided in a study of
children in the third through the sixth grades in a school on the
west side of the central school district of Detroit. There was a
total of 528 pupils in four grades, with 99 in the sixth. Of the
latter, 80 were retarded in their reading from one to four years;
11 read at grade level, and 8 read from one to two years above
grade level. Of the 80 who were retarded, 29 were one year
behind in their reading, 5 were two years behind, 26 were three
years behind and 20 were four years behind. These figures

indicate that in the sixth grade the latter had difficulty in reading a second grade reader. They ranged in age from about eleven and one-half years to about fourteen and one-half. A visit to the homes of the pupils revealed a marked lack of intellectual resources. This does not refer to the fact that practically all of the fathers, when the family was intact—or the men in the household—were in unskilled or semiskilled work, or that the mothers were in domestic service or comparable occupations. Lower class "college boys" also have parents in such occupations. It refers rather to the lack of books in the home, with the almost universal exception of a dusty Bible, and to the presence of pulp magazines and "comic" books, read equally by children and adults. It refers also to the uses of leisure time: watching television, drinking at home or in the corner bar, "hanging" with the street corner gang, and the like. The professionally trained observer, judging these matters on the basis of his moral values, could well summarize what he saw in the statement that there are almost no constructive leisure time activities for either adults or children.

(It should be added that "failure in school" and "delinquency" are not synonyms.) While practically all delinquents are some kind of failure in school, not all, and not even most, of those who fail in school are delinquent. It can safely be said of Detroit that tenth grade pupils in schools in the central school district are typically retarded three years in reading, though not typically delinquent. It is difficult for them to read at the seventh grade level. Detroit is by no means unique in this respect. Some years ago Mort and Featherstone secured data on promotional practices of 36 school systems, representative of American urban school systems. They reported that 47 per cent of the pupils in the tenth grade were retarded, in the school systems with semiannual promotions. That percentage provides no information concerning the degree of retardation, that is, whether retarded by one or more semesters. They also found that the percentage of pupils retarded increased from the first grade, to the sixth grade, and to the tenth grade.[33]

We said above that the delinquent fails in school because he is delinquent or is becoming so, and also that he is initially uninterested in school. The lack of interest may find expression in several forms, one of which is truancy, by definition an act of delinquency. It may also express itself in the classroom, as any teacher will recognize who has taught for more than three consecutive days in a school where the pupils come predominately from the lower class. We can set aside for the moment the legal point that any given truancy is by definition a delinquent act. A number of studies dealing with truancy, misconduct in the classroom, and retardation have been published. These studies show that while retardation, misconduct, and truancy have a high statistical correlation, once they begin one of them may be a cause of or a result of the others. Each is the meat upon which the others feed. Powell's study of children retarded in reading supports this hypothesis. Of a sample of 400 children retarded in reading, 200 children, selected at random, were given individual help in reading; the other 200 received no such help. Only 4 per cent of those given help in reading were sent to an "ungraded room," as compared to 20 per cent who received no such help.[34] (The label "ungraded room," is not in universal use in American school systems. Regardless of the euphemistic names given them, such "rooms" or "classes" are composed of boys so obstreperous in school as to present extreme behaviorial problems to the teacher.)

Since the proportion of boys in "ungraded" classes who become delinquent, as compared with the proportion of other boys with the same general background who become delinquent, is unknown, the following terms cannot be said to be synonyms: "retarded," "truant," "behavioral problem," "delinquent," or whatever special name a given school system may give to similar categories of pupils.

Continuing research of the type undertaken by Powell and others, extended as a result of the sharper definition of the relationship between performance in school, the social-class influencing of ambitions, and the influence of the neighborhood and the delinquent subculture, is certainly needed.

The problem of school withdrawal is different from that of delinquency and therefore a detailed discussion of it is not relevant here. When withdrawal occurs at or beyond the legal minimum age, which is sixteen years in most states of the United

States, it is not illegal. One may question the child's or its parents' judgment, but such withdrawal is not legally actionable. The school dropout has become a "social problem" even though a greater proportion of children are graduated from high school than ever before. In 1900 about 7 of every 100 ninth grade pupils was graduated four years later. By 1930 the number had increased to about 50, and in 1963 it was about 66.

The dropout has become a social problem for reasons independent of the school and largely independent of his subsequent involvement in delinquency. One reason is the increasing number and proportion of young people. In the 1960 decade some 27 million children 10–18 years of age will pass through American schools. It is estimated that 7.5 million of them will be dropouts and that 2.5 million of the latter will have had less than eight years of formal education. Until recently the dropout had been counted on to fill a rather large demand for unskilled labor. The possibility of such employment has been radically reduced in the past few years. Automation and other technological change is the second reason why the dropout is a social problem: ". . . the essence of the dropout problem is not so much the number or proportion of dropouts as that the world to which they seek entrance has drastically, and rather incredibly, *changed*."

There is an increasing tendency to make "dropout" and "delinquent" synonyms. But various studies, from Bridgeport, Connecticut, to Seattle, Washington, show that while a greater proportion of dropouts than of in-school children is delinquent, about 65 per cent to 75 per cent of the former are lawful. Perhaps the main, if not *the*, reason why there is relatively more delinquency among dropouts than among in-school children is that both school withdrawal and delinquency are highly concentrated in the lower social class.[35]

(3) The hypothesis "frustration leads to delinquency" is an upper-class interpretation of lower-class life. The upper-class observer—a university professor, for example, a social worker, or a psychiatrist—may note something of the difficulties and characteristics of lower-class life: the relative lack of education and income, low-status occupations, housekeeping that ranges from neat to filthy, housing that ranges from adequate to slum, the broken

homes, the obscene and ungrammatical speech, the frequent lack
of personal hygiene, and the like. In noticing these things he
may ask himself, "How can the lower class possibly help being
frustrated? It is no wonder that their children are delinquent."
(Such a view completely ignores the research establishing that
there is a great difference between the social classes in respect
to their aspirations, with a significant part of this difference relating to the value placed upon education.) The lower class just
simply does not define the value of school and higher or collegiate
education in the same degree and manner as do the middle and
upper classes. Studies of social class and stratification dealing with
aspirations show that a significant portion of the lower class has
no realistic idea of moving up the social ladder. The boys who
have no such aspiration have been classified as "corner boys."
The boys who do aspire to move upwards are "college boys," and
there is a large proportion of them.[36] It seems as though socialization in the family is as effective for the paths it blocks as for the
horizons it opens. The corner boys do not have a vision of an
exciting future, in an occupation which will raise them socially
and tend to great success; and which can be entered by means
of the proper education. Indeed, according to a staff psychiatrist
of New York City's children's courts, there are some schools in
which it is "physically dangerous for a schoolchild to try to
behave and learn." [37] That is undoubtedly an extreme situation.
Still, it is typical that

> A lower-class corner boy can undergo a forced exposure to the
> sentiments and concerns of middle-class schoolteachers for ten
> years of his life without really investing much of himself in the
> experience. Even while in class, his mind and heart are out on
> the corner with the boys, a corner where academic achievement
> is of little consequence and confers no status, and he marks time
> until he is sixteen when he can leave school and push the difficult
> ten-year interlude out of his consciousness.[38]

The school as an institution and its individual teachers cannot
possibly hope to overcome the influence of class culture, whether
lower, middle, or upper. Some psychiatrists, psychologists, retired
university presidents, social workers, sociologists, and others have
often criticized and calumniated schoolteachers. They charge that
middle-class teachers attempt to force their middle-class values

upon lower-class pupils, who cannot accept them, act on them, or achieve them, and who therefore fail in school and then, being frustrated, become delinquent, narcotics users, sexual offenders, retreatists, or some other kind of problem. An untold number of schoolteachers has come to believe this peculiar doctrine since 1928, when a formal basis for it was laid by Wickman's often referred to, infrequently read, and methodologically questionable *Children's Behavior and Teacher's Attitudes.*[39]

An unsophisticated classification of lower-class boys, the categories of which are not necessarily mutually exclusive, is as follows:

A. College Boys:
    1. Those who try and succeed in rising socially.
    2. Those who try and fail to rise socially.
B. Corner Boys:
    1. Stable lower class
    2. Delinquents:
        a. Transitory: delinquency is and remains a game. Become stable lower-class adults.
        b. Career delinquents: delinquency changes from a game to a livelihood. Tend to become criminals as young adults.[40]

The two categories of corner boys are not mutually exclusive; there is a solid empirical basis for assuming that the customary set of activities of the adolescent street corner group includes some violations of laws and ordinances. Most of these violations center around assault and theft of various kinds: the gang fight, automobile theft (often for a "joyride"), assault on an individual, mugging, petty pilfering and shoplifting, and purse-snatching. Furthermore, to engage in cultural practices comprising essential elements of the total pattern of lower-class culture automatically violates certain legal norms. The culturally "demanded" response to certain situations recurrently engendered within lower-class culture automatically involves the commission of illegal acts.[41] There are, as we shall see, common characteristics of culture and delinquency as they can be observed in cities in at least the countries of Canada, England and the United States.[42]

It can be said, in summary, that crime and delinquency are

correctly and most usefully conceived of as being positive achievements.)A number of sociological criminologists have made the point that criminal behavior is human, or sociocultural, behavior. Since the same sociocultural processes are shown to produce both the criminal and the lawful person, the sociological and social-psychological analysis of crime and criminality is methodologically superior to other theoretical conceptions. It brings the widest range of human behavioral phenomena within the scope of a single theory, making it unnecessary to invent specific pathologies to explain specific kinds of disapproved behavior. The title of one study, "Their Achievement is Delinquency," is a succinct statement of much of the research upon which this theory draws.[43]

2. Crime, Sociocultural Learning, and Symbolism

The following pages present a genetic or developmental explanation of criminality, placing particular emphasis on the learning of a vocabulary of motives and a corresponding self-conception. It is admittedly incomplete in that it is limited to an elaboration and elucidation of three propositions with a common theoretical base, the assumption that a criminal act will be performed when a situation appropriate for it, as defined by the actor, is present.* Propositions 1 and 2 are the subject of the present chapter; Proposition 3 will be introduced in the chapter following.

Symbolic Communication in the Learning of Criminality

1. *Criminality is learned socioculturally in the process of symbolic (linguistic) communication, including one's conversations with oneself.* This basic proposition asserting a positive behavioral process underlies the following ones. A person has achieved something when he has learned to perform certain actions; the

* Everyone familiar with Edwin H. Sutherland and Donald R. Cressey, *Principles of Criminology*, 5th or 6th edition, will recognize the three propositions as having been drawn from the first four propositions of that book, on pages 77–79. As indebted as I am to Sutherland's statement of the propositions, I must assume the responsibility for their elaboration here. As I said previously, it seems to me that there are no significant theoretical differences between my elaboration and the complete statement of the theory in the above work; and, in a positive sense, my elaboration is in agreement with the complete statement of the theory.

fact that some performances are condemned according to a given legal or moral code does not in any manner or degree lessen the achievement of being able to perform.) Negatively stated, the proposition implies two things relevant to the present discussion. (First, it implies that criminality is not innate.) This may seem so trite as to be obvious and hardly worth stating or repeating; but considering the tenacious hold that hereditary theories of crime have upon the mind, the proposition that crime is learned cannot be obvious. The theory of the "born criminal" is still with us, and in a more virulent form than that propounded by the Italian psychiatrist, Cesare Lombroso.

In the last third of the nineteenth century and through the first decade of the twentieth, Lombroso and his disciples argued vehemently for the proposition that the criminal is born a criminal, that he is an atavism, namely, a primitive man living in civilized society. The bodily traits of the criminal, he said, were the physical traits of primitive man; the born criminal was not responsible for acting as he did. Dissecting the skull of a famous brigand, who might be compared to our own John Dillinger, Lombroso observed what he thought were certain anomalies of the brain, and was particularly impressed with a depression situated "precisely in the middle of the occiput as in inferior animals, especially rodents." The vision came to him that criminals are hereditarily determined:

> This was not merely an idea, but a revelation. At the sight of that skull I seemed to see all of a sudden, lighted up as a vast plain under a flaming sky, the problem of the nature of the criminal—an atavistic being who reproduces in his person the ferocious instincts of primitive humanity and the inferior animals. Thus were explained anatomically the enormous jaws, high cheek-bones, prominent superciliary arches, solitary lines in the palms, handle-shaped or sessile ears found in criminals, savages, and apes; insensibility to pain, extremely acute sight, excessive idleness, love of orgies, and the irresistible craving for evil for its own sake, the desire not only to extinguish life in the victim, but to mutilate the corpse, tear its flesh, and drink its blood.[1]

Lombroso also resorted to epilepsy—which he believed was hereditary—as a secondary explanation of crime. In reporting on the dissection of the skull of another criminal, he described himself as having another flash:

It flashed across my mind that many criminal characteristics not attributable to atavism, such as facial asymmetry, cerebral sclerosis, impulsiveness, instantaneousness, the periodicity of criminal acts, the desire for evil for evil's sake, were morbid characteristics common to epilepsy, mingled with others due to atavism.[2]

Lombroso, the psychiatrist, described the vision that he had experienced—and it was surely a widely-encompassing vision. It was of the type which, when experienced by other people, often results in their being brought to the psychiatrist for treatment. He claimed that there are certain physical stigmata, open to visual inspection by the initiated observer, enabling him to detect the born criminal on sight! The following characteristics necessarily appear in the criminal type:

> Prognathism, abundant woolly hair, scarce beard, usually brown and dusky skin, oxycephaly, obliquity of the eyes, small size of the cranium, development of the jawbones . . . receding forehead, huge and ansated ears, analogy between the sexes, and muscular weakness. These symptoms, added to the observations gathered in the course of post-mortem examinations, draw the European criminal close to pre-historic man and the Mongol.[3]

A man was a born criminal if he possessed four or five of these stigmata, and a woman if she had only three or four. A woman needed fewer stigmata in order to be a born criminal than did a man, Lombroso held, because she was organically (hereditarily), emotionally, and intellectually inferior to man to begin with.*

The psychiatric explanation advanced by Lombroso explained the criminal as being caused by a neurological pathology. He focused attention on the criminal's anatomy and alleged heredity and conceived human beings as being basically irrational. For, if a criminal cannot, by virtue of his heredity and bodily constitution, help acting as he does, then by logical extrapolation the lawful person cannot help acting as he does, by virtue of *his* heredity and bodily constitution.

Although Lombroso and his adherents encountered a continu-

---

* The Lombrosian notion of the inferiority of women (which is at least as old as Plato and Aristotle) is continued in contemporary psychiatry in the Freudian notion that women are genetically, intellectually, and emotionally inferior to men. Freud changed his mind about many things during the course of his life, but not his conviction as to the inferiority of women.

ous opposition from many criminologists and psychologists in many countries, his conception of criminality as pathological exerted an enormous international influence, and succeeded in impeding the development of criminology for at least fifty years. Even though he died in 1909, his ideas—just as erroneous today as when he first published them in 1876—still are widely held, although not in American criminology, however, for about sixty years. The immigration law of the United States, enacted in 1922, is based in part on the psychiatric conception of the neurological pathology of criminals and of those people who comprise the other social problems. Lombroso's influence is still considerable in South America, as well as in Asia and Europe. In Italy, it seems that nothing has happened anywhere in the world of criminology since Lombroso's death. His conception of the born criminal has been perpetuated by psychiatry in the notion that every human infant is a born criminal. The broadening of the conception of only some people being born criminals to everyone being born a criminal is one of the contributions of psychoanalysis to the study of human behavior. Thus the nineteenth century psychiatric conception of crime as being a genetically pathological phenomenon —rather than a cultural and social phenomenon—is with us today.

The first systematic test of Lombroso's hypothesis that there exists a definite physical type of criminal was not published until 1913, when Charles Goring brought out his now well-known work, *The English Convict*.[4] Goring, a medical officer in the English penal system, worked with Francis Galton and Karl Pearson. Part I of his book constitutes a statistical comparison of anthropometric measurements of several significant segments of the criminal and lawful population of England and Scotland:

1. Habitual with nonhabitual criminals.
2. Criminals with students of Cambridge University.
3. Criminals with students of Oxford University.
4. Criminals with students of the University of Aberdeen.
5. Criminals with the staff of University College, London.
6. Criminals with the patients in a general hospital.
7. English convicts with Scottish insane and criminals.
8. Typical [random?] samples of convicts and soldiers.

(Goring stated that he found no evidence confirming the existence of a physical criminal type, such as hypothesized by Lombroso and his followers.) His statement on this conclusion is forcefully put:

> In the present investigation we have exhaustively compared, with regard to many physical characters, different types of criminals with each other, and criminals as a class, with the law-abiding public. From these comparisons, *no evidence has emerged confirming the existence of a physical criminal type, such as Lombroso and his disciples have described.* Our data do show that physical differences exist between different types of criminals: precisely as they exist between different types of law-abiding people. But, when allowance is made for a certain range of probable variation, and when they are reduced to a common standard of age, stature, and [socioeconomic class—my paraphrase, F. E. H.], these differences tend entirely to disappear. Our results nowhere confirm the evidence, nor justify the allegations, of [Lombrosians]. . . . In fact, both with regard to measurements and the presence of physical anomalies in criminals, our statistics present a startling conformity with similar statistics of the law-abiding classes. The final conclusion we are bound to accept . . . must be that *there is no such thing as a physical criminal type.*[5]

At the same time that Goring in England was systematically testing the hypothesis of a physical criminal type, William Healy in the United States was investigating the alleged inheritance of criminality. Goring and Healy worked independently of, and, it seems, unknown to each other. After making detailed studies of the family backgrounds of a large number of delinquents in Chicago, and relating these background items to the possible etiology of each delinquent, Healy and his associates were unable to find evidence to support the hypothesis that there is an inheritance of criminality or of a criminal tendency.[6]

Although criminologists in the United States accepted the conclusions of Goring and Healy—and of other investigators not named here—some students in other disciplines did not. In the late 1930's Ernest A. Hooton, a physical anthropologist on the faculty of Harvard University, sparked a revival of Lombroso's hypothesis of the physical type of criminal.[7] There are five leading principles in Hooton's books. (1) Criminals differ physically from lawful people. (2) The differences indicate the physical inferiority of the criminal. (3) The indicated physical inferiority is the primary cause of crime. (4) Physical inferiority is inherited. (5) A basic solution of the problem of crime must be based on the elimination of the physically inferior stock. Sociologists and most anthropologists reject Hooton's conclusions and his work on both empirical and methodological grounds.[8] Three other recent investigators advocating the hypothesis of the physical type of criminal are W. H. Sheldon and Sheldon and Eleanor Glueck, although the Gluecks are much less adamant about physical typology than Sheldon. The late Edwin H. Sutherland, during a sudden and seemingly irresistible impulse of leniency wrote the following of Sheldon's consitutional psychology:

> The futility of this study in constitutional psychology should have been obvious in advance from the previous failures of analogous studies. Sheldon adds himself to the list of Lombroso, Kretschmer, Hooton and others who have attempted to demonstrate a physical difference between criminals and non-criminals. *Unfortunately, the administrators of research funds can be seduced into wasting many hundreds of thousands of dollars on such projects even after the results of previous studies have been repeatedly shown not to be worth a nickel.*[9]

Goring's testing and consequent disproving of the psychiatric hypothesis that an hereditary neurological pathology is the cause of crime is one of the great achievements in criminology. Even though many people in many countries still believe in the hereditary or instinctual origin of crime and delinquency, Goring and Healy—and their associates in research—not only made possible but logically necessary the jettisoning of the notion of the "born criminal."

In my opinion, Goring should have stopped, in *The English Convict,* with his demonstration of the impossibility of distinguishing physically between the criminal and the lawful on the basis of a visual inspection. Most of the physical "differences" between criminal and lawful people to which Lombroso devoted his time were on that part of the anatomy visible beyond the end of the sleeves and above the neck. In late nineteenth century Italy not many square inches of skin were open to such inspection. When anthropometric measurements were taken, the subsequent tabulations revealed differences between the means of the dimensions of criminal and lawful people that were stated in millimeters! As an example, Lombroso found that the average length of the inner side of the middle finger of prostitutes was 70–74 mm. In "normal women," he said, "the average is similar." The length of the outer side of the middle finger of prostitutes was 80–84 mm.[10]

Lombroso never troubled himself to indicate the manner in which the inner and outer lengths of the middle finger of women were causally related to prostitution or to chastity. And, of course, since he measured the prostitutes while they were in prison, he never measured the size of any of their customers. Since there is a continuity in physical characteristics—such as height, weight, length of the inner and outer dimension of the middle finger, pigmentation, and the like—the typical result of all such measurements shows that the criminal and the lawful are the same. This is what makes a physical distinction between them always difficult and impossible. It is what is referred to as "overlapping."[11]

It may be that (Goring) thinking his invalidation of the psychiatric hypothesis was merely negative, concluded that he should give a positive cast to his work through presenting a different explanation of criminality. (Whatever his reasons, in the second part of *The English Convict* he formulated the famous, erroneous, and vicious hypothesis of feeblemindness: The criminal is feeble-minded and is criminal because of and on account of his feeblemindedness.) He conceived criminals to be organically deficient and described them as "unteachable, unemployable, a nuisance to themselves and to everyone else . . . (and they) . . . can hardly fail, in the long run, to swell disproportionately the criminal ranks." The feebleminded offender, he said, is

> one who is found to possess low degrees of general intelligence; or to hold extreme disregard for truth, for opinion, and for authority; or to be unteachable, unemployable, profligate, lazy; or to display marked preferences for undesirable company; or to be very impulsive, excitable, restless, uncertain, passionate, violent and refractory in conduct; or to be careless in business, neglectful in responsibility, false and malevolent in speech, filthy in habits, and nearly always inebriate.

. . . the one vital mental constitutional factor in the etiology of crime is defective intelligence.[12]

One can say of Goring that he was an upper-class statistician committed to an individualistic psychology. He surely had no appreciation of the idea that the prison, like any other institution, is a small community. Goring's theory of feeblemindedness is all the more remarkable because he used no standardized test of intelligence. Intelligence tests had at that time not yet invaded England.

A similar theory was advocated by the "mental testers" in the United States for more than a generation. This hypothesis was dedicatedly diffused throughout the elementary school systems after 1910, by Henry H. Goddard, Lewis M. Terman, and their followers.[13] Terman's *The Measurement of Intelligence* (1916) helped to fasten the hypothesis of feeblemindedness upon the United States and many other countries. Both popular and professional psychological thought accepted Terman's work. The invention of the United States Army Alpha and Beta tests of intelligence in World War I, and their subsequent publication— the army had for several years classified them as "secret"—did more than cement the grip upon the thinking of psychologists that the average mental age of the American people was about thirteen years. The results of performance on the Stanford-Binet and United States Army tests of intelligence were used—both by professionally trained psychologists and others—to disseminate and perpetuate racialism among both the educated and the lay population.

The tests were submitted to a severe logical and empirical evaluation in 1922 by Charles Horton Cooley and A. L. Kroeber. In the second edition of his *Human Nature and the Social Order* (1922), Cooley showed that the results of the tests could more parsimoniously and reasonably be explained by differences in language, family life, education, and occupation, than by heredity. Cooley had, in fact, in the first edition of this work shown that intellectual growth is altogether a sociocultural process.[14] There was thus no scientific basis for the contention of the "mental testers" in the period 1910–40, and even today in England, that their instruments measured the hereditary capacity to learn.[15]

In the first edition of his *Anthropology* (1922), Kroeber showed it to be not surprising that an illiterate twelve-year-old Negro boy from the rural southeastern United States, or a recently arrived Italian boy of the same age, should perform at a markedly lower level on a paper-and-pencil test written and administered in English, than a native-born boy of the same age who had been reared and educated in the public school system of Detroit. Kroeber went even further and contended that the native-born student *must* perform at a higher level. Mental testers rejected Kroeber's proposition. Terman went so far as to claim that a linguistic difficulty in reading English was irrelevant to a pupil's level of performance on the Stanford-Binet test! "As a matter of fact," Terman alleged in arguing that the lower class is hereditarily inferior, "limited acquaintance with the language employed in the examination [the Stanford-Binet test] does not put the subject at great disadvantage in many of the tests." [16]

The Stanford-Binet is, of course, printed in English, and the teachers give the directions to their pupils in English. Surely no one can accuse Terman and his followers of having taken into consideration the social psychology of the situation in which such tests are given.

This discussion can be terminated by referring briefly to two important analyses of the studies of feeblemindedness. (Sutherland and Leslie D. Zeleny found no significant difference between prisoners and the general population in respect to mental deficiency;) Vold's findings, in a more recent study, are similar. [17] The hypothesis in question gradually came into disrepute after the publication of the studies by Sutherland and Zeleny, and has for some decades not been seriously considered by criminologists, in the United States, at least, as a significant factor or variable in crime and delinquency. [18]

(To summarize briefly, the biological theories of criminality depending on "original nature" have failed to meet empirical, experimental, and logical tests of validity and are therefore dubitable. [19]) There is no place for them in social psychological and sociological criminology. The biologists, physical anthropologists, psychiatrists, psychologists and—I am sorry to have to add— sociologists advocating such theories have not demonstrated what the biological factors are that supposedly operate in criminals and delinquents but that do *not* operate in lawful people. The fundamental fault with the biological and other physical theories of crime is that they attempt to test biological hypotheses with sociocultural data. Beginning with Goring, Goddard and Terman, "mental testers" classified literally hundreds of thousands of boys and girls as "feebleminded" or "moronic" with no attempt whatever to obtain neurological data, and untold numbers were committed to institutions because of low performance on a pencil-and-paper test. That this has for some years no longer been the practice in commitment emphasizes that theories of sociocultural behavior have serious consequences.

To test biological hypotheses with human behavioral and cultural data is just as reasonable as to investigate the physics of gases by studying the behavior of swarms of people. When people are "released from under pressure," as when leaving a church, mosque, or synagog after a service or a theater after a play, they can be observed to swarm around the exits, much as molecules of gases swarm around the top of an opened container. A physicist could well complain against the illogic of the analogy. To assume that biological data can explain sociocultural conduct is equally, though perhaps less clearly, illogical.

The second negative implication of the proposition that criminality is learned socioculturally can be stated briefly. The person who is not already trained or knowledgeable in crime does not invent it. Criminals appear to be about as adaptive or as inventive, and about as conservative, as other categories of people. First, they learn the present techniques for the committing of offenses. Second, they continually modify these techniques when necessary, in order to commit the same kinds of offenses. Examples come readily to mind, such as the development of bank robbery and burglary from the 1870's to the 1930's; its relative decline, and the "moving in" of "amateurs" after 1945. The dialectic of interaction, between bankers and law enforcement, on the one hand, includes the invention of safes and vaults, the adoption of nitroglycerine and the oxyacetylene torch, on the other, and so on.[20]

Other examples can be found in the progressive mechanization of the police force and criminals: the short wave radio, the development of "scientific crime detection" or "criminalistics" in police departments, and the attempt to professionalize the police. All of this parallels the development of bureaucracy among criminals as vice and rackets become larger and demand the application of the methods of big business if the rackets are to remain profitable and relatively nonviolent.

Mechanization of both police and criminals can be seen in their utilizing of the horse, bicycle, motorcycle, automobile, airplane, and helicopter. These developments and the bureaucratization mentioned in the previous paragraph are results of the development of organized crime that came with the advent of prohibition in the United States. Criminal gangs centering on St. Louis, Missouri, were the first to use armored automobiles and airplanes for bombing, in their attacks upon each other, in the first half of the decade of the 1920's.

The use of radar is another good example of this dialectic of adjustment. Radar was developed by English scientists shortly before the start of World War II, for use against the enemy. Radar is now well established as a means legally used by police to catch speeding motorists. It is now being used by the public to catch police radar traps. It detects the radar trap's presence in time to alert the motorist and allow him to pass the waiting police at the legal speed. Thus the normal course of events has occurred. When the police develop a method to apprehend offenders, the offenders develop a method to neutralize the police action. Thousands of motorists in the United States purchased anti-radar devices in the latter part of 1961. Also as part of the normal course of events, the police are striking back at the negation of their radar traps, and attempting to have the radar detectors declared "illegal equipment" on privately owned motor vehicles. They have already succeeded in a number of cities and in several states.

Role of the Group in the Learning of Criminality

(2. *The learning of criminality occurs predominantly in small, intimate groups.* Reference here is made primarily to the family and to the play group, peer group, or gang—the three terms are often used interchangeably—and to the neighborhood. Even in the sections of the city with the highest rates of delinquency the family appears very seldom to have a Fagin-like quality as far as the parents are concerned. The children of the family may and probably do exert a greater influence toward delinquency than do the parents, in a high-delinquency neighborhood. The processes of learning criminality and lawfulness are basically similar in that the latter also occurs predominantly within small groups, the members of which are intimately known to one another.

Negatively stated, this proposition means that the impersonal media of mass communication play a relatively unimportant part in the genesis of criminality in the individual. The mass media of communication are the press, radio, screen, and television. It must be admitted, however, that we have no experimentally derived knowledge of their specific functioning in the orthogenesis of crime. It can be observed that some children after watching a gangster movie, play at being gangsters, and that some other children, after watching a romantic movie, play at being gangsters.

There is no lack of "expert" opinion concerning the supposed effect of the mass media in causing, or influencing children toward, delinquency or conformity. The thousands of pages of *Hearings* and *Reports* of the committee of the United States Senate assigned to investigate juvenile delinquency are replete with the opinions of experts, which, as a matter of course, usually contradict each other. The state of expert opinion may be illustrated by citing the views of two psychiatrists, each equally qualified professionally in terms of training, experience, publications, and by recognition of the profession, as experts in the field of child psychiatry. Dr. Lauretta Bender and Dr. Frederick Wertham have expressed themselves as to the effect of comic books upon the psychical well-being of normal, neurotic, and pre-neurotic children. Since the furor over the supposed consequences of the reading of comic books has subsided while that over television continues unabated, the psychiatric experts' opinion of comic books can perhaps be more objectively evaluated.

Dr. Wertham, in giving evidence before the Committee on the Judiciary, United States Senate, stated it to be one of his conclusions that there is no such thing as a good comic book. Answering the question "Are there any bad effects of comic books?" he replied: ". . . on this subject there is practically no controversy. Anybody who has studied them and seem them knows that some of them have bad effects." He added that there is a "good deal of controversy" as to how far-reaching "these bad effects" are. His opinion was based on extensive clinical research conducted by himself and his associates in clinics and in public and parochial (separate) schools. No one versed in clinical research, he said, would claim that comic books alone are the cause of juvenile delinquency. He then said:

> It is my opinion, without any reasonable doubt, and without any reservation, that comic books are an important contributing factor in many cases of juvenile delinquency.
> There arises the question: What kind of child is affected? I say again without any reasonable doubt and based on hundreds and hundreds of cases of all kinds, that it is primarily the normal child.
> . . . It is senseless to say that all of these [children] who get into some kind of trouble with the law must be abnormal or [that] there must be something very wrong with them.
> As a matter of fact, the most morbid children that we have seen are the ones who are less affected by comic books because they are wrapped up in their own phantasies.[21]

Dr. Wertham's professional judgment, then, is that comic books cannot be good for children, that they may have deleterious effects, and that those adversely affected are normal children. The opinion of Dr. Lauretta Bender, senior psychiatrist in the psychiatric division of Bellevue Hospital, differs from Dr. Wertham's. She believes that there are good comic books. Furthermore, she observes which ones a child in her waiting room will use, and uses this observation in her diagnosis.

Dr. Bender gave the following in evidence before the Senate committee:

> As I say, I have found one of the best methods in my experience to examine children is to get them to tell me their favorite comic book and to relate it and then analyse the material. . . .
> The Chairman: If Superman could have that influence, what sort of influence do you think that picture there, called "Crime Suspen— [sic] Stories," would have?

Dr. Bender: I can tell you why. This would have nowhere near. Superman represents an instinctive problem that we are all born and grown [sic] up with, that we can fly—after all, we can fly now; we couldn't before—and that we can carry on all kinds of scientific investigations, that we can stop crime, which Superman does, and that we can have a good influence on the world, and that we can be protected by the powerful influences in the world which may be our own parents, or may be the authorities, or what not.

Mr. Beaser [associate chief counsel]: It is your considered judgment, then, that Superman has been a good influence?

Dr. Bender: A good influence.[22]

In effect, what Dr. Bender gave in evidence, is that Superman is a good influence on children because he teaches them that justice can be achieved by individuals violently taking the law into their own hands, according to their own standards of justice. Dr. Bender for a long time was on the editorial advisory board of Superman Comics, being paid $150.00 per month. She said in evidence, "My duties on the editorial advisory board are to be consulted by them whenever they wish to consult me. . . . I also helped them work out their first code." [23]

Dr. Bender has provided an excellent example of the proposition that contemporary psychiatry has created man in the image of the mental patient. While still giving evidence to the senatorial committee she testified that the result of supplying children with "crime" or "horror" comics to read would be minimal, and also, that there is no such thing as a normal child:

. . . if you want to ask me what I think the result would be [of exposing children to "Crime Comics"], I think it would be minimal. I think that many of the children would be bored with them, I think that many of the children would refuse to read them and the more sophisticated would say, "So what, I have seen stuff like that before."

Mr. Beaser: But you do not actually know, Doctor?

The Chairman: You are talking about normal children, though?

Dr. Bender: There is no such thing as a normal child.

The Chairman: There is not?

Dr. Bender: No.

The Chairman: That is your medical opinion?

Dr. Bender: That is my medical opinion.[24]

Despite her unqualifiedly stated medical opinion Dr. Bender had saved herself, about ten minutes previously, from taking the logically absurd position that there are *no* normal children on the basis of whose conduct abnormality in other children could be established, when she said in evidence that she based her opinion on "the comics, as I have known them and worked with them through these years and the kind of emotionally [disturbed] children that I have known and worked with, and my own three normal children. . . ." [25] Both the members of the committee and its associate chief counsel were kind enough not to call Dr. Bender's attention to her self-contradiction.

The state of expert opinion in respect to the cinema and television is the same as that regarding comic books.[26] The thousands of pages of the *Hearings* and *Reports* of the committee of the United States Senate investigating juvenile delinquency are replete with contradictory statements,[27] unsubstantiated opinions,[28] moralisms paraded under the guise of scientifically established principles of behavior,[29] and an outmoded and erroneous social psychology.[30] The committee held hearings for several years, traveling thousands of miles to take evidence from qualified and unqualified persons in cities from the Canadian to the Mexican borders, spending about one million dollars in doing so. The result of this mountain of labor and money was a pusillanimous, controversial report that not even all the members of the subcommittee would sign.[31]

The truth is that there is no experimentally validated knowledge concerning the specific functioning—as to manner and degree—of the mass media on specific forms of behavior. It can be said, however, that the spokesmen for the mass media cannot have it both ways. In public defense the spokesmen for the television industry have denied that television can be shown to have any direct causal effect on behavior—specifically, the effect of driving children to delinquency and adults to crime. But when selling time for commercial advertisements they must and do argue that watching it has direct and measurable effects on specific kinds of behavior. There is no end of good descriptive and other observational studies in books and the learned journals. That kind of study enables us only to estimate how many of different types of people—by sex, age, education, and so on—watch what types of programs at what hours and for how long.

⎧Even without experimentation it is possible to conclude that the mass media, at least in the United States, have no *direct* causal connection with crime and delinquency.⎫Those agencies have had a growth since 1900 many times greater than the population. Indeed, most people in the United States today—the great majority was born since 1920—do not know what life is without the cinema, radio and television. If those agencies did in fact have a *direct* causal connection with crime and delinquency, we should logically expect an increase in the rates of crime and delinquency somewhat commensurate with their expansion in American life. Practically the total population, in short, should by now be habitually and hopelessly criminal. What is found, however, is a relative constancy in the rates of crime through the decades. At least, there is a constancy as revealed by analysis of available statistics.

The impersonal agencies of mass communication may be of importance in two ways. First, they communicate the fact of crime to everyone. No child five years of age in the United States who can hear, read, or see can remain ignorant of the dramatic and insidious nature of crime. And the children soon scorn the moral "Crime does not pay." It is true enough that the bad guy dies in the last minute of the half-hour program, just in advance of the fifth set of commercials. This does not fool the children, for by about seven years of age they already know that the only reason the bad guy "got it in the end" is that he was just a bit more stupid than the not-quite-moronic sheriff. Second, a child may be social-psychologically prepared to accept the invitation to delinquency when he becomes a member of a group that is already engaging in delinquencies, or becomes friendly with another, already-delinquent child.

3. Crime, Sociocultural Learning, and Symbolism: Urban Delinquency

Vocabulary of Motives and Self-Conception

(The foregoing chapter argued that (1) crime is learned socio-culturally through symbolic (linguistic) communication and that (2) the learning of criminality occurs predominantly in small, intimate groups) The reader is asked to keep these two propositions in mind as we undertake analysis and discussion of the third:

(3. *The learning of criminal conceptions of thought and action with respect to the law, the person, and property includes the learning of both* (a) *a vocabulary of motives for the committing of crime; and* (b) *a self-conception that allows the individual to admit his criminal acts to himself without damage to his conception of himself as being a worthy person*(Also included is the learning of techniques for the committing of offenses, but limitations of space will allow analysis only of the learning of a vocabulary of motives and a self-conception.

The present analysis of the process of criminal learning can most appropriately start by referring to a topic discussed briefly in the first chapter(The hypothesis that "status-frustration" leads to or is conducive to delinquency was described as being a negativistic approach to the problem of causation. That hypothesis can be summarily stated as follows. Behavior that fails to conform to middle-class values is dysfunctional. (At times, it seems to me, there is the implication that one's behavior *should* conform to

53

middle-class values.) Dysfunctional and nonconformist behavior is the resultant of status-frustration and is forced on the individual because he occupies a lower-class position in a social structure that tends to preclude his attaining the desirable middle-class goals. Only some lower-class members are able to achieve middle-class goals. Merton's outline of this hypothesized process lists four types of dysfunctional deviations in behavior, namely, innovation, ritualism, retreatism, and rebellion. Delinquents and criminals are classified as "innovators," a term which is misleading because it is not used in its established meaning. There is no innovation in that "innovation," and the "innovators" do not innovate, except in the very limited manner that we mentioned briefly in referring to the modifying of techniques for the committing of old offenses. It is necessary, in order to understand crime and delinquency, to realize that they are long-established components of culture and social organization, and that the individual criminal or delinquent does not invent his crimes.

A reading of the literature, both psychological and sociological, dealing with status-frustration reveals, among other things, that the authors seem to have forgotten the existence of the old-fashioned social process, *competition.* One can at least state objectively that competition is not referred to in the most often quoted works of the status-frustrationists. This is true even of the book officially sponsored by the American Sociological Association.[1]

One cannot, of course, substitute the scanning of a book's index for the study of its contents. There is no doubt, however, that those who advance the hypothesis of status-frustration to explain delinquency have minimized the study of competition as a social process; in so doing they have maximized the concept and study of conformity. They have not, in their methodology, systematically studied the process of competition and conformity, and decided on the basis of scientific criteria that competition has disappeared from human society and been replaced by conformity. Competition has simply been ignored on the basis of an arbitrary and unannounced decision. Conformity has been elevated to the top position of the social processes on the basis of the same kind of arbitrary and unannounced decision.

A particularly apt illustration of this is found in the work of

Cloward and Ohlin. They have widened the scope of the notion of dysfunction. In their refining of Merton's dysfunctional category "retreatism," they discuss the topic, " 'double failure' and drug use." They postulate that retreatism may, in given cases, result from the fact that access to illegitimate means is limited by barriers existing in the social structure. The "double failure" of such persons results from socially limited access to both legitimate and illegitimate means. They hypothesize: "It is our contention that retreatist behavior emerges among some lower-class adolescents because they have failed to find a place for themselves in criminal or conflict subcultures." [2]

One cannot help wondering if the old criminal custom of muscling-in has fallen into complete and utter desuetude. One concludes from a study of the literature dealing with status-frustration that the authors of that literature conceive of criminals and delinquents as being wholly passive subjects of external agents. Like billiard balls, they are acted upon rather than acting. And, just as billiard balls are not responsible for their movements, criminals and delinquents, in the hypothesis of status-frustration, are not responsible for their actions. We thus seem to have another statement to the effect that man's behavior is basically irrational.

We can now indicate why it is that to become a delinquent is a positive achievement.

The Delinquent Subculture

Studies concerned with the content of criminal learning have to a great extent been devoted to describing and analyzing delinquent subcultures and, in recent years, trying to account for their existence. It is my opinion that two of the best of the older works are Shaw and McKay, *Social Factors in Delinquency*, and Thrasher, *The Gang*.[3] If the former were to be written today rather than in 1931, it probably would have a somewhat different terminology, its empirical material would be more contemporary, but its conceptual organization would not be fundamentally changed even though it might be formulated differently. Its conclusions would very likely be the same.

Three of the worthwhile contemporary statements of the conception of the delinquent subculture are by Cohen, by Cohen and Short, and by Short.[4] In the work by Cohen, the delinquent subculture is presented as a lower-class, urban, male culture that inverts, turns inside-out, or stands on its head the value system of middle-class society. The values of the delinquent culture thus stand in an almost point-to-point opposition to those of the dominant middle-class culture. Cohen lists three characteristics of the delinquent subculture as being nonutilitarianism, maliciousness, and negativism. Concerning the last, he says that the delinquent subculture is not only a design for living that is in conflict with the norms of "respectable" society, but also that it seems to be defined by its negative polarity to the norms of the larger society. The delinquent's conduct is correct, Cohen tells us, precisely *because* it is wrong according to the norms of the larger culture.[5]

Cohen's discussion of the supposed nonutilitarian character of this delinquency is, at best, ambiguous, and comes close to being self-contradictory. "There is no accounting in rational and utilitarian terms," he writes, for the danger faced and the effort expended in stealing things that are often destroyed or given or thrown away. "Store-hopping" is an example. A gang of boys will enter a store and each will steal something; say a ball or a flashlight. They then go to another store, where the stolen articles are surreptitiously exchanged for other articles. They continue this game until tired of it and will then destroy, or discard, give away, or throw away the last series of stolen articles. Cohen's claim that this behavior is "nonutilitarian" and "irrational" is a judgment passed by an upper-class professional observer. This seemingly senseless behavior can be accounted for in rational and utilitarian terms, as Cohen himself admits when he says of this kind of shop-lifting, that "stealing 'for the Hell of it' and apart from considerations of gain and profit is a highly valued activity to which attaches glory, prowess and profound satisfaction." [6]

Cohen's last statement is undoubtedly correct. One can add that store-hopping also provides practice in developing the manual and observational skills necessary in successful shoplifting, as well as assisting in the learning of criminal habits of thought with respect to property and the self. Since prestige, as evidenced by the admiration of his fellows, is achieved through these acts of daring and skill, the boy is helped to develop a conception of himself as being at one and the same time a crook and a worthy person. The conclusion that delinquency is irrational if it is financially nonutilitarian from the view point of an upper-class observer, is in keeping with the psychiatric trend constantly to expand the scope of irrationalism in human behavior. When one understands what the boys are doing, *from their viewpoint*, the delinquency becomes deliberate and purposive and can be described as being rational, as Cohen himself states.

Many students of delinquency have observed, over the years, that much of it is not financially motivated, even among the poor:

> while older offenders may have definitely crystallized beliefs about profitable returns from anti-social conduct, it is very clear that in childhood and earlier youth delinquency is certainly not entered into as a paying proposition in any ordinary sense.[7]

Tappan has observed that "the juvenile property offender's thefts, at least at the start, are usually 'for fun' and not for gain." [8] (McKay has concluded that "in its early stages, delinquency is clearly a form of play.") McKay showed that delinquency and recreation have a number of qualities in common, with delinquency taking the place of recreation for many boys.

The notion that delinquency, or much of it, is "senseless" is widely held by middle-class and upper-class people. What some of them regard as even more disturbing than the "increase in the number and savagery" of delinquencies "is the fact that more and more of the young people who get into trouble seem to act without understandable motive or provocation, and to feel no noticeable guilt for what they have done." [9] Cohen believes that the maliciousness marking juvenile delinquency is "even less" rational than the supposedly irrational stealing for fun. The teacher and her rules, he says, are not merely something onerous to be evaded; they are to be flouted. There is a keen delight in terrorizing good children, in driving them from playfields and gymnasiums for which the gang itself may have little or no use, and, in general, "making themselves obnoxious to the virtuous." [10]

It is a kind of behavior engaged in by gangs in Canadian cities, also.[11]

The malice can be readily illustrated:

> We did all kind of dirty tricks for fun. We'd see a sign, "Please keep the street clean," but we'd tear it down and say, "We don't feel like keeping it clean." One day we put a can of glue in the engine of a man's car. We would always tear things down. That would make us laugh and feel good, to have so many jokes.[12]

> One time . . . four or five of us boys went to an apartment just being built, took a whole wall of cement down. We took a chisel and knocked down hundreds of cinder blocks . . . We went to old houses, broke windows . . . In one house we found a big victrola. We threw it down the stairs, we broke the chandelier. We didn't steal anything, just broke things . . . I had to do it so they wouldn't call me chicken.[13]

A middle-class or upper-class observer may insist on labeling such behavior "senseless," and reject the reason for it that the boy supplied in the last sentence quoted. I must insist, however, that from the viewpoint of the boys involved, their actions were deliberate, conscious, and reasoned. The mere fact that we disapprove some behaviors, or reject the motivations supplied us by the actors, or both, is no warrant for calling them "senseless" or "irrational" or "nonutilitarian."

Many analysts of lower-class culture have held lower-class culture and lower-class behavioral patterns to be deviations from middle-class culture and behavior patterns. They have studied the whole of society as if all social classes were possessed of the same cultural system and the same set of values. Such an analysis ignores two things: (1) Lower-class people in general and delinquents in particular know of the middle-class system of values, even if they do not accept it. (2) Lower-class children undergo a process of learning lower-class culture; and those who become delinquent learn the culture of delinquency, which, among other things, involves to some degree rejecting the conventional moral code and to some degree only neutralizing it.[14]

It is appropriate to discuss here the learning of a criminal vocabulary of motives, and the neutralizing of some aspects of the conventional moral code. There is good evidence for the conclusion that many, if not most or all, youthful delinquents do experience guilt when they begin their delinquencies and for some time after that. This is illustrated by the case of a boy whose petty pilfering and burglary started shortly after he was about seven years old:

> One day while we were passing a fruit store [Joseph] picked up an apple while nobody was looking and continued to walk past the store with the apple in his hand. He performed for me in like manner quite a few times and nothing would do but that he must teach me to do the same thing. That was the first time I ever stole anything . . . as Joseph came to a box of fruit he took some fruit and walked on. He motioned to me to do the same thing . . . as soon as he would pick up a piece of fruit I was supposed to do likewise. It took lots of practice and he had to set many examples before I could at last gain enough courage to follow suit.
>
> [One] morning . . . he took me to a pool room that was not yet open, and merely made the fact known that we were to enter it by means of a hole in one corner of the plate-glass window. . . . Joseph wanted me to crawl in first, but I lacked the courage. So he had to crawl in first himself. After he was inside he had to do a lot of coaxing and motioning in order to get me to follow him.
>
> . . . the shoplifting experiences were alluring, exciting, and thrilling. But underneath I knew that I was a kind of social outcast when I stole. But yet I was in the grip of the bunch and led on by the enticing pleasure we had together. There was no way out. The feeling of guilt which I held could not overbalance the strong appeal of my chums and shoplifting.[15]

One illustration cannot, of course, be taken as a demonstration, but the point is that many who have worked with children beginning their delinquencies have heard similar comments. Boys, even those less than ten years old, soon learn the correct answers to give when they are caught, and their statement, "Yes, I know I ought to be ashamed," becomes a minor manipulative technique. But not all such statements are manipulative, particularly not, I hazard, when first made by the boys.

Juvenile delinquents do not necessarily dislike, hate, or consider as hypocrites, or as natural enemies, the entire population in the upper classes. They frequently accord admiration and respect to lawful persons, and may resent illegality being charged against those important to themselves in their immediate environment;

they may particularly resent illegality being charged to heroes in the areas of sport and entertainment.

There is also good evidence that juvenile delinquents often distinguish sharply between those categories of people and objects that may be attacked and those that should not be. The range of potential victims seems limited by considerations of kinship, friendship, social class, ethnic group and race, age, and sex. A good illustration is found in Thrasher's description of the "Itschkies," a juvenile gang in Chicago, composed of Jewish boys. Jewish drunks enjoyed immunity from being "rolled" or robbed by the Itschkies. Sykes and Matza indicate that while this may seem obvious, its implications have not received sufficient attention. One implication is that this selection of victims indicates the wrongfulness of their offenses to be widely recognized by delinquents.

The experiencing of guilt, the according of respect to lawful persons, and the selection of victims all indicate that typically the juvenile delinquent knows the conventional moral code and what is in general demanded by it in the way of conformity. This applies to career delinquents—those who make the transition from delinquency as a game to delinquency for gain—as well as to transitory delinquents or "bad boys"—those who do not go beyond delinquency as a game. Their actions thus do not fit the conception of people who have turned the conventional (or middle-class) code inside out, so as to act on the basis of a point-to-point reversal of its demands. As we will attempt to show, they do fit the conception of individuals who to some extent have been educated according to the conventional code, are still in the process of being educated in the value system of lower-class culture in general and introduced to the criminal and delinquent aspects of lower-class culture in particular. Among other kinds of evidence, this proposition is confirmed by the published researches of Walter B. Miller and his associates, dealing with the social organization, culture and daily activities of street-corner groups. They studied a group in Boston known as the Junior Outlaws, which was one of a set of age-graded subdivisions of a larger street-corner aggregate known as the Outlaws. The Junior Outlaws consisted of a core group of eighteen white Roman

Catholic boys between the ages of fourteen and sixteen years. They were near the center of a range of behavior from highly delinquent to negligibly delinquent. In studying them for a period of several years in their natural habitat, a number of identifiable personal qualities or forms of behavior were isolated. One cluster consisted of qualities and behaviors that the boys recognized as prestige-conferring for adult reference groups. The cluster included: respect to women, qualities such as lawfulness, regularity in attending school, and cleanliness and industriousness. Concerning their conception of conventional values, Miller writes:

> several qualities defined by the boys as concerns of groups outside their immediate cultural milieu, were always referred to in a mocking, derisive manner; concern over cleanliness, industriousness, lawfulness, or school regularity was seen as a sign of "squareness" or lack of sophistication. However, little real malice or animus characterized such expression. These values of adult groups were seen as rather laughable and "square" but of relatively insignificant import. This mode of reference indicated that the Junior Outlaws were well aware that these characteristics were seen as important by outside groups, at the same time affirming the fact that they themselves were using quite different criteria of estimability . . . the lower class cultural milieu itself generates and transmits emphases on strength, fighting prowess, toughness, and the quest of risk, all of which may achieve fulfillment in certain forms of crime. . . . the cultivation of competence in individual and collective aggressive action is a highly functional component of the role of the lower class male.[16]

Miller's comments are relevant to two programs developed by the Detroit Board of Education that were based at least in part on the realization that lower-class socialization is as effective for the paths it blocks as it is for the horizons it opens. The first, operative during the late 1930's, was called the General Continuation Training Program. Its purpose was to enable unemployed lower-class persons between 18 to 25 years of age to overcome two marked handicaps, according to middle-class standards:

(1) They possessed "inappropriate" skills (especially the young men), referred to in the above quotation from Miller, *et al.*, as "fighting prowess, toughness, and the quest of risk." Anyone who expects physical aggression in interpersonal relations is prepared to meet it with a ready resort to fists and weapons, and who on

his own initiative engages in such aggression will find it difficult to "relate to people" in the peaceful manner required in practically all occupations except for those sports that entail physical contact.

(2) The young people were distinctively handicapped by a lack of "appropriate" social skills and an inability in the playing of roles. They were to be taught good grooming, how to enter a room and be seated for an interview for a job, how to answer questions politely, how to complete an application for a job, and the value of sound habits of work (which indoctrination, being wholly verbal, involved no actual work). A middle-class young person will, in general, from the elementary school forward, learn such things as a matter of course.

The program was discontinued after passage of the Selective Service Act and the beginning of World War II, which solved the problem of unemployment—not permanently, however. The Detroit Board of Education began its Job Upgrading Program on April 25, 1949, and has continued it to the present. It is designed to help unemployed lower-class high school withdrawees of 16 to 20 years of age overcome the same two types of handicaps that marked the generation of the 1930's. They tend to possess the inappropriate skills of physical aggressiveness in interpersonal relations and lack the appropriate peaceful skills, including facility in changing rapidly and easily from one role to another. Bordua's conclusion of some years ago is valid today: "Long-term involvement in the 'free, undisciplined' street life with money at hand from petty theft and with the days devoted to play was not exactly ideal preparation for the humdrum life of the job." That conclusion applies to corner boys in general, whether or not they have been members of persistently delinquent gangs.

Rationalizations

Sykes and Matza use the concept "techniques of neutralization" to indicate the process of reasoning in which the boy engages before he commits his delinquency, or after it, or both. It emphasizes that delinquency, being purposive in one way or another, results, in part, from the way in which the individual conceives of himself in relation to others. I must add that it also implies that lawful behavior results from the same process of rationalization, but with a different vocabulary of reasons being employed. This conclusion is in keeping with the social-psychological analysis of motivation. The following discussion will show, I hope, that the juvenile delinquent and the adult offender are engaging in deliberate action accompanied by reasoning, and that they are therefore rational. This analysis presents a very different conception, therefore, of the juvenile delinquent and the criminal from that presented by psychiatry, which tends to view them as being emotionally disturbed or mentally ill—to use terms often regarded as synonyms.

An individual is not culpable and therefore not legally punishable if he can prove the absence of criminal intent in the act he committed.[17] Much delinquency is based on what is essentially an unrecognized extension to crimes, in the form of justifications for deviance that are held valid by the delinquent but denied validity by the criminal law and by society at large.[18] These justifications comprise a vocabulary of motives. The delinquent learns them from a number of sources, for they are abundantly supplied by the community, as we shall see. They are thus sociocultural products and not individually invented. In social-psychological analysis the term "motivation" refers to the process through which an individual, as a participant in a group (or perhaps by himself through sociocultural action such as reading or thinking) symbolically (by means of language) defines a situation as calling for the performance of a particular act with, symbolically, more or less expected consummation and consequences.[19] Motives, then, are linguistic constructs organizing actions in particular situations.[20] They are rationalizations of acts, or symbolic constructs, which not only organize the acts in particular situations, but make them recognizably recurrent in the life-history of any group or individual. The pattern of recurrence is part of what is referred to as the group's culture and part of the individual's self. The use of these motives can be examined empirically, as we shall presently indicate.

The reader may have noticed that the psychiatric meaning of "to rationalize" is radically different from the historically long established social-psychological meaning. The former means that one advances plausible or socially conforming reasons for his conduct, as a substitute for the supposedly true and socially unacceptable reasons. The "true" reasons, psychiatry also claims, are "in" the actor's unconscious (wherever may that organ be?) and therefore unknowable to him but discoverable by a psychiatrist. The psychiatric meaning thus enables one to disregard and to discredit the conclusions and motives of other people. Kenneth Burke has said of the psychiatric meaning of rationalization that "as people tend to round out their orientations verbally, we sometimes show our approval of the verbalizations by the term 'reasoning' and our disapproval by the term 'rationalizing.'" [21] But in social psychology the symbolic constructs applied by an individual to his own behavior in a given situation are motives. The complete process in which these verbalizations are used is motivation.

It will be seen later that the social-psychological conceptions of motivation and rationalization are important in the understanding of the allegedly "senseless" actions that are supposed to comprise "compulsive" crimes. It is therefore appropriate to emphasize in the present discussion of juvenile delinquency that a person acts because he has already rationalized, and that the rationalization is his motive. The psychiatric notion that rationalization is "merely" an *ex post facto* justification of action resulting from "deep-seated and unconscious motives" is erroneous. It not only disregards the reasoning that precedes the act, but denies that it occurred.

Some vocabularies of motives are more systematized and widely held than others. When an individual—say, a juvenile delinquent —draws upon the rationalizations of his group, he will observe himself as conforming because the rationalizations that he shares with the others support and sanction him in his actions. This comforting experience of conforming applies of course, to other people, including the lawful. One may also suppose it to be the experience of all or practically all of the forty-five executives from the twenty-nine corporations who were defendants in the Incredible Electrical Conspiracy, for violation of the Sherman Anti-Trust Act, including, according to *Fortune's* account, "men in the highest echelons of the corporations." [22] Judge J. Cullen Ganey, chief judge of the United States District Court of Philadelphia, referred to "the company man, the conformist, who goes along with his superiors and finds balm for his conscience in additional comforts and the security of his place in the corporate setup." If the corporate executives had acted on the basis of the rationalization "All businessmen are crooks," a rationalization that seems not to be widely held by businessmen, they would perhaps not have experienced the support and sanction that they evidently did.

One can also speculate that the conspirators apprehended late in 1961 in the province of Ontario for the sale of uninspected and contaminated meat drew personal comfort from the fact that they were acting in concert. They could not have acted on the basis of the maxim that a number of legitimate small meat-packers have expressed to me, "Anybody who sells uninspected meat should be forced to feed his own family with it."

We can therefore say, in the case of juveniles who are learning delinquency, that the disapproval they would otherwise apply to their own conduct, and the disapproval that they believe others would express, can be neutralized in advance by the use of one or more of the rationalizations provided by the delinquent vocabulary of motives. Through this means a delinquent can (a) remain committed to the conventional code but so qualify its moral imperatives that violations of them are not only "acceptable" but "right," and (b) not seriously endanger his own self-conception. It is well known that many, if not most, delinquent children do not progress from delinquency as a game to being career delinquents. It may very well be that a major reason for this is that the boys are possessed by conventional norms. Perhaps research can provide a valid answer. These rationalizations, as Sykes and Matza state, comprise a significant component of Sutherland's "definitions favorable to the violation of law." We shall discuss five of them.

First, *the denial of responsibility*. This rationalization seems to be the most frequently resorted to by delinquents, one reason being, perhaps, that it is so firmly a part of the professional ideology of many people in authoritative positions who handle delinquents: social workers, juvenile-court judges, psychiatrists and other employees of the court, probation officers, and the like. The denial of responsibility asserts that delinquent acts are due to agencies beyond the control of the individual. The delinquency, it may be asserted, is the result of such things as being a member of a minority group, living in a slum with inadequate housing, having a broken home or drunken parents, bad companions, and lack of recreation. Judge Leibowitz' "two strikes" theory, previously cited, is an illustration of the kind of statement through which a delinquent can deny his responsibility for his actions: ". . . we are supporting them [children and families] in the most wretched and degrading environment which prevents the moral development of the child . . . A child brought here [New York City] to live in crowded slums begins life with two strikes against him."

The delinquents do not, of course, express themselves in such correct English. Their speech is typically ungrammatical and vulgar, but in their slogan—with the obscenities removed—"I couldn't help it," and similar expressions, one can discern the self-conception advanced to the person in authority. It is a conception of themselves as billiard balls. Helpless subjects of agents that knock them around the billiard table, they are acted upon rather than acting. It will have been recognized that this rationalization repeats some of the psychiatric, psychological, and sociological theories advanced to explain delinquency. If the boy does not know the juvenile version of the mechanistic explanation of his misdeeds the first time he is in juvenile court—"I couldn't help it"—he will have learned it by the second time. He plays back to the social worker the explanation that the social worker originally advanced, the explanation that relieves the delinquent of his responsibility. Virginia P. Held provides an excellent illustration in the rationalization, "It's not my fault":

> "A 15-year-old boy came here the other day," Dr. [Melitta] Schmideberg told me, "with a handful of clippings that said that delinquency is the fault of the parents, and that parents should talk with and try to understand their children. He said his parents didn't understand him, so it wasn't his fault that he held up a store." Another delinquent blamed his mother, saying she was impossibly neurotic: she made him straighten up his room. "One would like simply to laugh at these cases," Dr. Schmideberg said, "but one can't, because they have unfortunately become quite typical." [23]

As the psychiatrist Plant says, "Juvenile delinquency is a thing that happens to an individual, not a thing that he does." This conception is reinforced when the boy is repeatedly told by those in legal authority, "We are here to help you." The juvenile court was invented, in part, just for that purpose: to help the juvenile, and not to blame, punish, or hold him responsible. When the delinquent can present a conception of himself as an innocent victim of evil forces, he can steal without danger to his self-conception, while at the same time not having to reject the conventional moral code. Respectable society has told him, "It isn't your fault because you couldn't help yourself."

An illustration of this type of thinking may be drawn from a juvenile-court hearing that I attended in one of the more populous counties of Iowa, in July 1963. The complaint alleged that a twelve-year-old boy had stolen several purses, removed the money, and then thrown them away. A fourteen-year-old girl was also involved, but she had only acted as an overseer and had taken none of the money. Both children were in the courtroom, as were the boy's divorced parents, the county probation officer, and the woman who was to receive the boy when he was placed in her foster home. The judge began by praising the boy's appearance and smile, saying that he could go far in life if he continued to have such a winning smile. "You are a good boy," he said, and proceeded to question him about the theft. The boy, to judge from his frequent smiling, was pleased indeed to hear himself praised so fulsomely.

After a few moments of silence and in the presence of the two children, the judge verbally excoriated the boy's parents. When they were divorced, he said, they were thoroughly selfish and thought only of their own bodies (he had himself granted the divorce in August 1962). They ought to be ashamed of themselves and be horse-whipped, and if the state law allowed it he would have a whipping post erected in the courtyard and do the whipping himself. He forced the mother to admit that she had had sexual relations in her home since the divorce and that she was now pregnant out of wedlock. He said, further, that he was going to declare the boy a ward of the court, not because he was delinquent but because he was a dependent and neglected child from an unfit home, repeating the charge of "unfit home" loudly and emotionally three times. In reply to his questions, the mother said that she was twenty-seven years of age and had six children, the oldest of whom was the twelve-year-old boy presently in court. He then said she was a good-looking woman, but that while she was good-looking now she would be old tomorrow; if she did not mend her ways, she would lose everything and wind up in the gutter before she was thirty. He then repeated his comments about horsewhipping and the parents' shameful behavior. He then told both parents twice that they were responsible for their son's thefts, that the boy was not, and that therefore they should be ashamed.

The judge then told the boy that he was a good boy, that he had friends—namely, himself (the judge), the probation officer, and the woman who was to be his foster mother. He then threatened the parents with jail if they bothered the foster parents, told the boy once more that he was a good boy, announced that the session was over, and walked around the table with his right hand extended to shake hands with the parents, which neither parent wanted to do. At the end of the hearing the boy was still smiling.

During a conversation with the probation officer the next day I commented on the judge's remarks and asked, "Does he usually talk that way to the parents when their children are present?" She replied, "No, he has several speeches, and he talks that way only to those parents who deserve it." She added that the mother had "come by her immorality honestly, so to speak," because *her* mother had been pregnant out of wedlock when she was fifteen years old.

Perhaps in ten years that twelve-year-old will say and believe, as the young man in the Iowa State Reformatory said in effect, "The reason why I commit evil is because my father was evil":

> Well starting at an early age I was living in B———, Iowa with my mother, father & 15 Brothers and Sisters which was 9 Boys and 7 Girls and we were in hard times and my dad and two Brothers worked on W. P. A. Makinng about $110.00 a month and my Brothers were married with small familys and all we got to eat was what the W. P. A. workers and familys were issued which wasn't very much and my older Brothers and myself had to steal food in Order for the family to live and we even stoled milk so we could fed the smaller Babys. we didn't have enough clothing for

all of us to go to school each day so we would change off wearing clothes so we could all get at least 1½ to 2 days a week in school. And soon after some of the girls got married and left home and the Boys as well and so that left me and My younger brothers to help out at home so I had to quit school to Help my dad make a living for the rest of us kids and if we did do everything we were Beat and I mean Beat not whipped And we were brought up to fight with every one who said a word wrong to us I am pretty sure that if I or any of my brothers would of come from a family of 5 or 6 we would of had had a better chance of Being like we wanted to Be able to complete school had plenty of clothes and shoes on are feet and Not Been treated so mean and made to do wrong things I am now seving a five year sentence which I Believe and always will Believe I got it from Being treated like i was treated at home my dad is responseable for my wrong and all my Brothers wrongs . . . I am suffering from the wrong rearing I had at home. . . .[24]

The young man's disclaimer of responsibility for his crimes is matched by the one reported by Dr. William Glasser. While eating lunch with five newly admitted inmates at the Ventura School for Girls, one girl said, "Doc, you know why I'm here—it's because I'm emotionally disturbed." The other four also claimed that they needed help because they were emotionally disturbed, and that was why they were committed. In relating how the girls then admitted that they were incarcerated because they had violated a criminal law, Glasser described what he and Dr. G. L. Harrison call "reality therapy," which they contrast with "conventional therapy." In discussing the girls' claim of "emotional disturbance," Glasser writes:

What this example illustrates is how the application of modern psychiatry, psychology, sociology, and criminology is understood by these delinquent girls and most children in trouble. It is a function of the effect of our whole psychotherapeutic profession that these girls feel they are basically emotionally disturbed and what they did is much less important, because it is only a part of a deep emotional disturbance over which they have little control. They feel that they are psychologically upset and therefore not particularly responsible for their behavior.

This is not something they would be aware of on their own. The have learned that to get along well in a modern, treatment-conscious institution, this is the most comfortable attitude to take.[25]

Both Glasser and Harrison "disagree completely" with both the conception of the child as emotionally disturbed and the assumption that the child's understanding of his unconscious conflicts will lead him to rational behavior:

> . . . this is most obvious with delinquent children, that just the opposite will occur. The more they are convinced by traditional therapy that they are disturbed and have good reason to be so, the worse they will act in or out of custody. There is nothing in the traditional therapy which leads to responsible behavior, only the vague hope that understanding one's actions will motivate one in the right direction.[26]

Traditional therapy, Glasser concludes, is ineffective because it never puts the responsibility for disturbed behavior or thought processes on the patient; and indeed, it does just the opposite:

> Its stated purpose is to remove the responsibility for the behavior from the patient and place it on his unconscious conflicts, conflicts caused by parents, environment, society, or usually a combination of all three. The argument is that a child never takes narcotics because he consciously wants to, it is because his unconscious conflicts left him desperately in need of the feeling of security that narcotics provide.
>
> Thus, in the words again of my lunch companions, "it is because we are emotionally disturbed that we're in trouble." Carried a step further, the up-to-date delinquent child expects the therapist to ask "why?" It's part of the therapy game and when the traditional therapist complies it is as if the child never really broke the law. What happened didn't really happen, it is only a surface manifestation of an unconscious conflict.
>
> There is nothing in the traditional therapy which presents the patient with the responsibility for his actions, there is no personal responsibility even implied. The present reality is less important than the reasons why he got into trouble. In working with delinquent children this is a serious handicap. Relieved by the well-meaning therapist of the responsibility for their actions, they often react with violent behavior, partly in an effort to be helped now, rather than to be dragged through disturbing memories which both incite and justify their activities.
>
> In his eagerness to be accepted and to help, the traditional therapist emphasizes that the patient has little responsibility for what he did as long as he understands why he did it, but the patient, unfortunately, interprets this as meaning "I have no

responsibility for anything I do that is wrong because I have problems."

There is nothing in the concept of traditional therapy which will help him to stop except the hope that reason and understanding will prevail. . . . the inclusion of traditional therapy in an institution which previously had no psychiatric treatment program often leads to acting out, discipline breakdown, increased emotional upset and conflict between the old personnel and the new traditional therapists.[27]

Reality therapy, as presented by Glasser, is the opposite of conventional therapy. It never excuses any conduct, past or present, directly or indirectly, by asking "Why?" or by seeking the reason in the unconscious. It ignores the unconscious completely, and works only with the conscious and present situation.

We always ask *what*, we never ask *why*. We will say to a girl who breaks an institutional rule, "What did you do?" We ask this even if what she did was obvious, because, accustomed to the traditional way and expecting us to ask *why*, she has already dismissed what she really did and formed an excuse, an excuse which relieves her of the responsibility for what she did.[28]

Reality therapy thus never asks, "Why did you do it?" because to do so is to admit that there may be an excuse. The child is held primarily responsible regardless of what causes his bad behavior. There is never any intimation that psychiatric treatment relieves him of the responsibility for what he has done. He is held accountable to his own principles for what he does. It is assumed —which is rarely if ever the case in conventional therapy—that he has a workable set of principles, standards, or values. The delinquent, Glasser believes, knows right from wrong, and good from bad in some absolute way for himself. Glasser is at one with sociology when he maintains that, no matter how severe the personality disorder is, when removed from a situation in which excuses are accepted, the boy has adequate standards: "We have never met anyone who lacks adequate standards." [29]

This is in accord with the experience of Redl and Wineman, who report that "the strength of the conscience may vary from child to child but *we have never seen a child in whom it is totally absent*." [30]

The assertion that reality therapy is an effective treatment for delinquents has yet to be tested. There are at present no departments of psychiatry in medical schools or schools of social work that train graduate students in its practice and theory, and it may be years before any do. Even so, it surely bolsters the sociological analysis of the denial of responsibility. It presents clinical, empirical evidence that the delinquent transforms the scientifically based and authoritatively presented reasons explaining his delinquency into excuses and justifications for it. One can generalize and state that there seems to be a continual tendency for reasons to be used as excuses and justifications.

Second, *the denial of injury*. The delinquent may rest the matter of whether his actions were wrong on the point of whether or not anyone was unquestionably hurt by them. This, of course, is a matter of judgment, and of interpretation. He may say that he "borrowed" an automobile and had no intention of stealing or stripping it; he just wanted a joyride. "After all," he may say, "I didn't wreck it, and it isn't damaged and I didn't even empty the gas tank. So, who's hurt?" The police very often recognize the distinction made by the delinquent, and the complaint will be "Unlawfully Driving Away an Automobile," rather than a complaint of automobile theft. Vandalism, especially when committed against the property of an impersonal agent—say, a corporation of an absentee owner—may be defined as "fun," or as "having a good joke."

If the delinquent can break the relation between what he did and its consequences, he does not have to judge himself adversely and can reject the otherwise expected adverse judgments of respectable, lawful people. It must be said that society at large presents the delinquent with many reasons for using this rationalization, just as it does for the first: "Providing there is not serious injury to property, the American public tends to view pranks with a kind of careless tolerance, probably because most American males were once participants in this kind of activity." [31]

Whether a given action is vandalism, good clean fun, or just a lark, seems to depend, in large part, on time, place, and social context. In the past that is beyond the memory of, perhaps, most of my readers, it was permissible "skylarking" to overturn farm wagons or outhouses on Halloween, or to dismantle a farmer's wagon and reassemble it on the roof of his barn. But today the overturning of a truck is "malicious destruction of property." There was often widespread vandalism in college towns on the evening of a "homecoming" football game, or after the victory of the home team over a hated rival—or after its defeat. Liberty Street in Ann Arbor, Michigan, and State Street in Madison, Wisconsin, have in the past been the victims of such good, clean, and expensive destruction by the students at the two universities. Occasionally, a few students were placed on probation. Had that destruction of property, and the rioting, been the work of the "town" youth, rather than of the "gown" youth, it would without question have resulted in a demand for stricter enforcement of the law, a call to stop the mollycoddling of delinquents, and an effort to re-establish the woodshed as a place for punishing the deserving delinquent or youthful criminal. This distinction between the good, clean fun of college boys and the vandalism of delinquents is also made in England:

> the party of public schoolboys who damage property during a "rag" are behaving very differently from the street corner gang who smash street lamps or shop windows "just for the fun of it". . . . The mores of the Public School community allow and even encourage such explosively expressive behavior and the scholar's participation in its restricted setting, whereas the casual destructiveness of promiscuous gangs has no such social approval to sustain it.[32]

There is probably no college fraternity that does not have its traffic signs, stolen from the municipality and the state, and its laboratory equipment—stolen from the college's laboratories in a completely selfish disregard of the other students. But this is defined as "good, clean fun," and not as larceny. The newspapers and magazines make much of the physical and sometimes savage attacks in which juvenile gangs sometimes engage. Perhaps a stir should be created over that violence. Those same newspapers and magazines will not, however, devote the same amount of time to the brutal, corporal attacks of upper-class college students on freshmen. Hazing is not as brutal as it used to be; one still learns, however, of an occasional homicide. A recent case that comes to mind is that of a young man killed while being initiated into the fraternity of a university in southern California, in 1959. He had been forced by his brothers [sic] to swallow a piece of oil-soaked liver that lodged in his throat; he choked to death. His life might have been saved had his "brothers" not lied to the internes on the ambulance that was called, as to what his trouble was. No sanctions were imposed on the other students involved; yet, had this happened in a gang of boys from the other side of the tracks they would very likely have been charged with either negligent or nonnegligent manslaughter. (If they were of juvenile-court age, and the judge refused to waive jurisdiction to the criminal court, the complaint would be the same, but they could be found to have "committed a delinquent act," and then be subject to the juvenile court's sanctions.)

About two weeks after the above event, two freshmen at Michigan State University, in East Lansing, were involved in a hazing "incident." They had been kidnapped near the campus on Saturday night, November 7, 1959, by six or seven fraternity members who forced the two into an automobile and drove them about fifty miles northeast. There, on an unlighted side road, they were undressed, bound, and spattered with red, black, yellow, and brown paint and shellac; tape was placed over their eyes and mouths, and they were then abandoned. One victim was able to chew through the tape covering his mouth, and then managed to chew through his companion's bonds. They were taken to a hospital by a motorist who passed their way. No charges were brought against the young men who perpetrated the kidnapping and the assault. In some states it is a capital offense to commit bodily harm on the person who has been kidnapped.

Sororities and fraternities have been prohibited by law in the public high schools of Michigan since 1911. Some high schools have allowed the formation of what are called "social clubs," as a substitute. The social clubs are in addition to the usual high school activity clubs. In January of 1962 the principal of Redford High School in Detroit announced that social clubs were thenceforward to be banned at that school.

The principal blamed cruel and brutal hazing and the practice of beating unwanted members, for the ban. He had received repeated complaints of hazing from parents, students, and ministers. "It was so bad," the principal was quoted as saying, "that I dreaded coming to school on Thursday mornings because I knew there would be a flood of calls about the meetings held the night before. Parents were supposed to supervise the meetings but I discovered that many of them were not supervised." He further said that it was difficult to identify the boys who were the subjects of brutal hazing. It was not only that they were frightened of a subsequent beating. They were more "scared" of being known as "crybaby" or "chicken" to their fellow students. A number of boys who were beaten went to their ministers for help, rather than to their parents or to the school's administration.

Since the social clubs at Redford High School were not permitted to blackball any students assigned to them as members, the older members resorted to beating unwelcome new members with a paddle until they quit. This practice was ungrammatically but picturesquely referred to as a "swat-out." The "swat-out" could not be ignored when public attention was called to it. Late in January 1962, a swimming instructor asked the principal to come to the swimming pool. Two of the boys "were black and blue from their waists to the backs of their knees." The banning of the "social" clubs followed.

No attempt to identify the assailants of the boys was reported. The admission of injury and the denial of injury thus depend partly on the respective social class of the victim and his assailant; and also partly on the context in which the crimes or delinquencies are perpetrated. To repeat, the rationalization, *the denial of injury*, shows that the community supplies its members with a host of motivations, and free of charge.[33]

Third, *the denial of the victim.* The moral disapproval of self and of respectable people that can be expected for delinquencies may be neutralized in advance by insisting that the misdeed was not wrong in the given circumstances. In this rationalization the delinquent reverses the positions of himself and his victim. The victim, it may be insisted, "had it coming to him"; so the injury is rationalized as being nothing more nor less than a just punishment, and, if anything, less than the victim really deserved. Sykes and Matza list some types of victims who may be "justly" punished on the basis of this motivation. Assaults on homosexuals are not only justified by delinquents on this basis, but the police seem often to condone such attacks, if not actively to approve them. A fifteen-year-old boy in Chicago described briefly how the four members of his gang "pulled off our trick in a slick way":

> West Madison Street and vicinity was a rather dark section of the city, so it was easy to strongarm. . . . There were a lot of homosexuals and we played our game on them. We would let them approach one of us, usually me, because I was so little and they like little fellows, and then I'd follow him to his room or to a vacant house to do the act. My pals would follow us to our destination and then we'd rob him.[34]

Other types of victims who are "justly punished" because "they had it coming" are members of minority groups who have "gotten out of their place," the "crooked" store owner, the unfair teacher, and the harsh principal. Lawful society provides the delinquents with a store of respectable examples of lawbreakers who are held in high esteem. Robin Hood and Zorro are two. It will be recalled that the psychiatrist, Lauretta Bender, described *Superman Comics* as being "good," because Superman righted wrongs and imposed "just punishment" outside the law, according to his conception of justice. The National Association for Better Radio and Television, in its Tenth Annual Survey of Children's Programs, classified "Superman" as the "Most objectionable":

> The essence of Superman is violence to those whom he thinks deserve it. He is permitted to commit crimes under the pretense of imposing punishment. He is immortal and has powers beyond any physical, natural, or religious law. Clark Kent as Superman shows up at just the right time and the right place to fight for "truth, justice and the American way." There is no division between reality and fantasy. Crimes are solved because, and only because, a reporter can turn into an extra-terrestrial investigator. Murder, kidnapping, and other crimes make this an outstanding example of exploitation of children, serving them poisoned mental food, to make sales and money. A most distasteful program.[35]

Examples are by no means confined to fiction and folklore. Many members of the lawful community will on occasion "justly punish" members of minority groups who are "trying to get out of their place." During 1963 thousands of Negroes were arrested in the United States while attempting to exercise their constitutional rights. Many were beaten, some seriously, and others assaulted. Some were murdered. Arson, dynamiting, and other forms of vandalism were committed on homes, churches, and places of business. It was necessary in several situations to mobilize United States marshals and part of the military. Most of the instances in which lawful citizens resorted to the rationalization, the denial of the victim, occurred in the former Confederate states of the southeast. An example from a northern state is provided by Dearborn, Michigan, a satellite of Detroit. In the fall of 1963 a home was ruined by a crowd of white vandals who thought that it had been sold to a Negro family. The Dearborn police did not interfere, and its mayor praised them for their "fine work" in maintaining order. The home had been purchased by a white family; the company moving their furniture in had Negro employees.

The existence of these victims and the use of this motivation show once again that delinquency, like lawfulness, is selective, ordered, and sociocultural, rather than unselective, random, and individualistic. This is so, regardless of the race, nationality, religion, or personality of the delinquent,—all of which further shows that delinquency involving vandalism, theft, and physical assault is deliberate and willful. It is therefore erroneous to describe the vandalism and bodily assaults committed by teen-age hoodlums as "senseless," and as having "no purpose, no rhyme, no reason," as many psychiatrists, social workers, psychologists, policemen, sociologists and other people do. It is correct to describe them as being often malicious, savage, and vicious.

Our repugnance for some of the delinquents' actions and our inability to conceive of ourselves as committing them should not lead us to accept the erroneous and misleading hypothesis of the irresistible impulse or compulsive crime.

Fourth, *the condemnation of the condemners*. This is the phrase used by Sykes and Matza, whereas McCorkle and Korn refer to *the rejection of the rejectors*. Both phrases refer to the same rationalization, which focuses attention on the motives and behavior of those who would morally disapprove of the delinquent's action.[36] Those who would condemn, disapprove, or reject him, the delinquent may argue, are hypocrites, motivated by spite, or are themselves undetected criminals or delinquents. The forms of this rationalization reported by Dr. Melitta Schmideberg from her questioning of delinquent children are commonly heard: "When I ask them why they were sent [to training schools or to jail], they tell me the judge didn't like them, or their lawyer was no good, or the jury was rigged. Almost never do they say, 'I stole' or 'I shot a man. . . .' " [37]

The present rationalization, in common with the first three, is supplied in one or more forms by, and confirmed by, the larger society. Thus, the delinquent may say that the police are corrupt and brutal. Despite the remarkable professionalization of police departments since about 1930, including many state systems, there is enough corruption to give a degree of validity to the assertion. It is no secret that in the United States this conception of the police is widely held in all segments of the population. The municipal police in the United States have, in fact, come to the point at which their effective functioning is dependent upon their developing a positive conception of themselves among the general population. They are confronted by no problem more pressing and serious. It is admittedly very difficult to solve when members of police departments, widely separated geographically, are themselves revealed as being burglars.

The delinquent's use of this rationalization is facilitated by newspaper reports of widespread crookedness on the part of retail grocery store operators, service establishments such as watch and jewelry repair, radio and television service and repair, automobile garages, and the like. These assist the adolescent in adopting the rationalization "Everyone has his own racket." This reaches its finest flower among (1) the young narcotics addict who claims that everyone is an "operator" who is always "shooting the angles" (except the Square John, who is so stupid that he works at a regular job); (2) the convict's ideal of the "real man," who knows that there are only two kinds of people: the "suckers" who work, and the "smart guys" who "skim it off the top"; and (3) the honest policeman who believes that "everyone has larceny in his heart."

The world of the delinquent and of the juvenile-becoming-delinquent is also populated—according to the boys—with teachers who always have their pets; with hypocritical male probation officers who are lushes (excessive drinkers), or who are having extramarital sexual affairs with female probation officers or policewomen; with the homosexual Boy Scout master and the like. The juvenile is assisted in coming to believe and to use this rationalization, "Everybody's got it in for me," or, "He's worse than I am," by respectable organizations and lawful individuals in positions of authority. Thus—with no attempt on my part to evaluate or deny the validity of their assertions—organizations ranging from the United States Department of Justice to the National Association for the Advancement of Colored People often assert and confirm, or attempt to confirm, the existence of various kinds and degrees of discrimination. The newspapers, including the Negro press, also report this as a matter of course.

Some professional people also confirm the delinquent's rationalization "They're just picking on me," "Everybody's against me." Anyone with experience in dealing with delinquents and near-delinquents soon learns that he must guard against the boy's attempt to manipulate him through the use of the verbalization "They're picking on me." But there are some professional people who never learn this lesson. Bruno Bettelheim is one who seems, on the basis of his own words, firmly to believe that every delinquent does in fact and in actuality believe his jaundiced rationalization, "Everybody's against me; I didn't have a chance." In giving evidence before the Committee on the Judiciary, United States Senate, he said, ". . . we believe that basically every delinquent is an individual who is convinced that society has not given him a fair break, that society is against him, that he hasn't gotten [sic] a chance to succeed, he feels very much degraded." [38]

The boys regard as fair game for "conning," or manipulating, any adult representing the lawful world who takes them at their own word, as Bettelheim seems to. But the boys, as I have tried to show, begin early to learn the "scientific" explanations for their behavior that they acquire from their peers, from the mass media of communication, and from the professional and semi-professional persons with whom they come to have dealings. The song, "Gee! Officer Kruppke," in *West Side Story,* is an excellent example of delinquents' mastery of the psychiatric, psychological, and sociological theories of juvenile delinquency.

Bettelheim had much more to say in justifying the delinquent's use of the rationalization "They're picking on me." He said, concerning a boy with a stick in his hand:

> Let there be a plate glass window unexpectedly, it is too bad for the window, but there we already come to very fancy business because if he is a poor kid and he gets picked up, he probably won't be punished, but he might be booked. But if it is a rich man's son, you know, he doesn't get booked, and that isn't only true for plate glass windows. . . . That is true for stealing cars, that is true for major acts of crime, and the delinquents of our big city know there is a great difference when they are picked up on the West Side of Chicago and one of our fancy suburbs.[39]

He further developed the psychoanalytic statement of the delinquents' condemnation of the condemners:

> . . . the court process against juvenile delinquency is [not] the best way to rehabilitate them, but it is a miserable way when all delinquents know whether they are subject to the punishment by the court or not depends on the parental pocketbook; or influence, because you see, youngsters have a much finer sense of justice. . . . we definitely have two classes of justice, and if you are a rich man's son and have all the other breaks in your favor, good food, and good housing and, hopefully, a good home, and what have you, and you commit a delinquent act, you get a psychiatrist as a reward, and very often, "Well, we are going to provide psychiatry for the boy," so he gets psychiatry [sic] services as a reward, and the poor boy who has none of these advantages is sent to St. Charles, and the youngsters know that. . . .[40]

No one would want to be so unrealistic as to claim that a completely even-handed justice is dispensed in the legal system of any country. But the refutation of Bettelheim's conception of the police and the courts, accepting as it does without question the criminal's and the delinquent's claim of absolute and unremitting injustice perpetrated against the poor, downtrodden and exploited masses, would be merely tedious rather than difficult. It is sufficient to note that Bettelheim's statement is one kind of respectable and lawful source from which the delinquent derives the rationalization for his offense, "The cops are picking on me."

It is thus necessary to indicate that some professionally trained people justify the delinquent's use of the motive "It isn't fair and they're only hypocrites anyway." (One more example will be sufficient. Gibney's *The Operators* depicts the American nation as being a population most of which falls into one or the other of two classes. One class is composed of individuals who are Operators. They thrive on immoral, unethical, and illegal practices. The second class is composed of individuals who are Corruptibles. They are either already receiving unethical or illegal gains from the Operators or are eager to do so. Gibney contends that Americans today live in a climate of fraud, a "Genial Society" that practices the corruption it hypocritically condemns and secretly applauds the shunting of the ethical precepts that it professes to believe and practice) Gibney writes that "our national future is being misshaped, far more than we realize, by the witless optimist gulled into phony stock purchases, by the two-bit chiseler padding his outsize expense account, by the corporate dodger who writes off his Florida yacht as a business expense [and by] the influence peddler who tampers with legislation." [41] He discusses "retailers who shortchange their customers, advertising men who misrepresent their products, income-tax cheats, expense-account wizards and stockmarket sharpers." By the time one finishes reading the book, he may be convinced that the "real man" convict is correct in saying that there are only two classes: the smart guys who skim it off the top and the suckers who work. One may also conclude that the delinquent is justified in using the motive, "Everybody's got his own racket, and those squares [lawful people] are only hypocrites, anyway."

(Fifth, *the appeal to higher loyalty*. The delinquent may violate the moral demands of the larger society, and neutralize the expected moral condemnation by appealing to a smaller group in the community. He may claim loyalty to his brothers, or to a friend, or to the corner gang) The occasional necessity of having to choose between the demands of the law, on the one hand, and the claims of fraternity or friendship, on the other, is by no means confined to the delinquent. As Sykes and Matza observe, this theme has long been recognized both in literature and social science as a fairly common problem. Both the criminal and the lawful adolescent and adult know that one must "never squeal on a pal." Nobody, it seems—not even the police who use them—

loves an informer; or depending on one's particular view, a squealer, a rat, a stool-pigeon, or a courageous, patriotic citizen.

The delinquent confronted with choosing between the law and a friend is in a situation familiar to many. To decide in favor of his friends enables him to violate the conventional code without rejecting it. This acceptance and negation is a property common to the other rationalizations. The delinquent is unusual only in that he is perhaps able to appreciate the fact that his action in behalf of his small group is a justification for the violation of the larger society's norms. This, however, is only a distinction of degree between the delinquent and the lawful person.

The vocabulary of motives discussed above is a presentation in academic language of what delinquent boys say, and of what boys who are becoming delinquent are learning to say. It is a translation of the ungrammatical, vulgar, and often colorful speech that can be heard in their conversation in the streets and alleys, and in formal and informal interviews and discussions. They may say, "I couldn't help it," "I didn't really hurt anybody," "He had it coming," "Everybody's picking on me," or "I did it for my friend." These expressions are, in social-psychological terminology, definitions of the situation. They are learned from family, friends, social workers, juvenile-court employees, psychiatrists, and others; and from newspapers, the cinema, radio, and television. They are criminal conceptions of thought and action. Their mastery requires time and practice. This is why we have said that it is a positive achievement to become a delinquent. The boy learns reasons for committing delinquencies and also a conception of himself in relation to others that enables him to admit his offenses to himself without damaging his own self-conception.

The above discussion has not evaluated the truth or validity of the delinquent's motives, nor has it evaluated the twofold classification of the American population into Operators and Corruptibles. The distinction between criminal and lawful people is not as sharp as the latter seem to want to believe. Even so, it is unlikely that there will ever be an empirical verification of the criminal's "everybody has his own racket," and the honest policeman's "everybody has larceny in his heart." The discussion has indicated that (1) delinquents learn a number of motives for the committing of delinquency and (2) the stock of motives exists as habits of thought held by professional people and the general public, as well as by delinquents.)

Habits and patterns of thought and the learning of those patterns by delinquents have been emphasized. Association with given individuals has not been emphasized. As we have shown, lawful people as well as criminals and delinquents can be and sometimes are involved in a young person's learning to be delinquent. Patterns of action have also been emphasized, rather than patterns of personal association. This is an important point in understanding both the types of offenders already considered and those to be discussed subsequently.

There is good evidence that the delinquent's use of the vocabulary of motives is inclusive in the sense that the motives may be innervated in situations not defined as delinquent by the juvenile but in which he may nevertheless believe that others may impute guilt to him. We may quote from Redl and Wineman in this connection, although their thesis cannot be presented in detail here:

> We want the basic mechanisms described here to be considered applicable to a much wider range of situations, even to such where the word "delinquent" in its original meaning loses its sense. That means that what we described here under the title of defense techniques of the "delinquent ego" are actually techniques of defense anywhere, *whenever an ego makes up its mind to stick to impulsive demands or to its pathology against changes which the educator or clinician is trying to bring about.*[42]

We have tried to show that the vocabulary of motives consists of rationalizations in the public domain, that delinquents make use of them, and that therefore their motivations are sociocultural rather than individual in origin. Under the metaphorical caption, "The Strategy of Tax Evasion," Redl and Wineman discuss some "common techniques" very often used by delinquents to neutralize the adverse judgments that they think others and they themselves (through their conscience) would pass concerning their conduct. Their conception of the "common techniques" is quite different from that of the "techniques of neutralization" previously discussed, although the two seem to be similar. They explicitly reject the conception of "verbal skill" in arguing with society's representative of responsibility and guilt, and hold that the common techniques constitute a "system of delusions" invented by the delinquent in order to talk himself out of the demands of his own conscience.) Their "fairly cursory list of such tax evasion from guilt feelings" includes:

Repression of own intent.
He did it first.
Everybody else does such things anyway.
We were all in on it.
But somebody else did that same thing to me before.
He had it coming to him.
I had to do it, or I would have lost face.
I didn't use the proceeds anyway.
But I made up with him afterwards.
He's a no good so-and-so himself.
They are all against me, nobody likes me, they are always picking on me.
I couldn't have gotten it any other way.[43]

Research among Ohio prisoners reveals that the delinquent's use of the vocabulary of motives extends to situations and conduct not defined as delinquent by the juvenile, and also confirms the use of the motive, denial of responsibility. In analyzing the criminal's vocabulary of motives, John P. Clark has shown that the more powerless an offender conceives himself to be in relation to his environment, the more likely he is to hold agencies other than himself responsible for his misdeeds. Those who commit offenses against the person are especially prone to assign responsibility to such agents as luck, a bum rap, a vindictive wife, a harsh judge, a lousy lawyer, or "other things." [44]

The "Good Boy"

I have indicated how the theory of differential association accounts for the learning of delinquent patterns of thought and action. The same theory may be used, in reverse, so to speak, to account for the fact of nondelinquency, for the existence of "the good boy," who, in an area high in delinquency, does not develop a criminal vocabulary of motives and a corresponding self-conception. Dinitz and Reckless addressed themselves to the question,

What is the process through which nondelinquent boys in areas high in delinquency, remain nondelinquent?[45] They found the major differences between the two classes of boys to be in self-conception, in type and content of interpersonal relations, in contacts with and/or conceptions of officials, school, home, parents and in choice of companions.(Dinitz and Reckless suggest that a socially appropriate or inappropriate conception of self and others is a major factor in influencing a youth away from or toward delinquency. This hypothesis should help to explain not only delinquency and the "good boy" in high-delinquency areas, but also the delinquent youth in the low-delinquency area.)Dinitz and his colleagues use "socially appropriate" as defined in the sociocultural context of neighborhood and social class. They commit themselves, in their research, to the social-psychological system presented in these essays. Their work shows, in brief, that the conventional adolescents in areas with high rates of delinquency learn a vocabulary of motives requisite to their role as lawful persons.

The most extensive and methodologically resourceful study of the self-conception of delinquents and nondelinquents, with reference to differential association, has been conducted by Voss.[46] His problem was to explain the differential involvement in delinquent behavior of children of Hawaiian and Japanese ancestry. His subjects were seventh graders in the public schools of Honolulu. These children are at opposite poles with respect to delinquency. The Hawaiians provide the great majority of officially classified delinquents and residents of training schools. The rate of delinquency among the Japanese, by contrast, is very low; as a result they are rarely institutionalized as delinquents.

Voss employed the technique known as self-reporting. In an interview in which anonymity of response was assured, the juveniles completed a questionnaire that provided information on such matters as trivial and serious offenses; conceptions that the juvenile thinks his parents, teachers, and others have of him; and various conceptions that he has of himself in relation to others. "Delinquent behavior" was defined in terms of the juvenile's behavior as reported on the anonymous questionnaire. "Differential association" was defined as a sociocultural process by means of which individuals have differential access to delinquent and/or conventional norms through interaction with others and through contact with various aspects of culture and society. "Delinquent self-conception" was defined as the product or result of the juvenile's acceptance of the conceptions of others defining him as delinquent. Conventional, or "nondelinquent self-conception" was defined as the product or result of the juvenile's acceptance of others defining him as conventional. "Nondelinquent" is of course the more often-used term, but it seems to me that "conventional self-conception" imparts a positive cast to being lawful, which the negative concept "nondelinquent" does not.

The purpose of the study was to test the hypothesis that the differential involvement of the Hawaiian and Japanese adolescents in delinquent behavior could be explained at least partially in terms of differential association and self-conception. The data supported the hypothesis that adolescents who conceive the expectations of others in conventional or nondelinquent terms report significantly less delinquent behavior than do those who conceive these expectations in terms of delinquency. The data indicated that a socially appropriate or conventional self-conception insulates an adolescent against delinquency. The Japanese, who reported significantly less delinquent behavior than the Hawaiians, have a significantly greater frequency of conventional self-conception. The Hawaiians, who reported significantly more delinquent behavior than the Japanese, have a significantly greater frequency of delinquent or "socially unacceptable" self-conception.

The concept "insulation against delinquency" is used here as referring to an ongoing sociocultural process marked by the actor's acceptance of conventional or nondelinquent norms, and by conformity to the expectations of significant others who uphold and engage in conventional or nondelinquent behaviors. "Vulnerability to delinquency" can be conceived of as the same kind of process but marked, in contrast, by the actor's tendency to accept delinquent norms, and to conform to the expectations of significant others who uphold and/or engage in delinquent behavior. The use of the verb "to accept" rather than "to receive" is deliberate. While both mean "to allow something to come to one," "receive"

ordinarily implies passiveness, whereas "accept" implies a measure
of approval and assent. (This is in keeping with the conception,
already stated, that the learning of delinquency and lawfulness
is a positive process in which the person involved participates
actively.)

Voss raised the question whether a delinquent self-conception
precedes delinquent behavior or is a product of it. I suggested
previously, in discussing the vocabulary of motives, that the
learning of delinquency and of lawfulness is a complex process of
symbolic communication and differential association, in which
motives, self-conception, and habits of thought and action develop
together in such a way as generally to be requisite to one another.
One must agree with Voss that data obtained at one period of
time, relating to a given panel of adolescents, are inadequate
to the task of providing a definitive answer. Perhaps such an
answer could be provided by a longitudinal study of panels of
children selected according to relevant criteria.

One example of such a study is Scarpitti's investigation, four
years later, of the "good boys" in a high-delinquency area who
were subjects in Dinitz and Reckless' original study in Columbus,
Ohio, in 1955. Of the original 125 good boys, 103 were located
in 1959; of these 99 were still in school although most of them
were more than sixteen years old. Only four of the 103 had come
to the attention of the police or juvenile court—once each—who
considered the incidents trivial. The fourth boy was placed on
probation. He had driven his neighbor's automobile without permission early one morning, to deliver his newspapers. The study
confirmed the 1955 predictions that the boys would remain lawful.
They still assessed themselves, their parents, teachers, and schools
favorably. They continued to isolate themselves from delinquents
and predicted lawful behavior for themselves, as did their teachers. They did not self-report any appreciable violations. In brief,
they continued to define themselves as good boys and were so
conceived by others, in spite of remaining, for the most part,
in areas with high rates of delinquency. (The study confirms the
conclusion that once a favorable or conventional self-conception
has been developed by a preadolescent, with respect to parents,
friends, school, and the law, it seems to be as difficult to modify

as is a delinquent self-conception: "In view of their relatively stable and cohesive families, the continued interest in and supervision of their activities by their parents, their school aspirations, and isolation from purveyors of delinquent values, it may be predicted that the good boys will persist in their law-abiding behavior." [47]

Differential association and self-conception were taken as the independent variables in Voss' study, and self-reported delinquency as the dependent variable. This is also the relationship between differential association, self-conception, and delinquency that has been implicitly, if not explicitly, basic to my previous discussion. As to the relationship between differential association and self-conception—disregarding delinquency for the moment—my discussion has held differential association to be the independent variable and self-conception the dependent variable. That will be taken to be the relationship between them in my subsequent analyses of the thief in the white collar and of the compulsive criminal. Voss concludes: "Self conception helps to explain differential response to the confrontation of delinquent patterns of behavior. The findings suggest that differential association is a more fundamental process underlying delinquent behavior than is self conception." [48]

The Numbers Racketeer

Whereas Scarpitti investigated the "good boy" in the process of developing into a lawful adult, Roebuck has studied other nondelinquent boys, who developed into criminal adults, professional racketeers who, as far as criminal records reveal, were not themselves juvenile delinquents; who avoided juvenile delinquents and gang activities; who defined stealing, fighting, and violence as being outside their style of life; and who were especially concerned with remaining free of arrests and contacts with the police. In an interesting and ingenious research he has compared the life histories of sixteen Negro numbers men, including their pattern of arrests, with those of 384 other felons imprisoned in the District of Columbia Reformatory in Lorton. He obtained data on 33 selected social and personal characteristics. [49]

The statistical analysis revealed that the numbers racketeers differed significantly from the 384 other felons in 25 of the 33 characteristics. These data, as well as the qualitative data, indicate that the Negro numbers man differs in some respects in both degree and kind from other criminal types in terms of theoreti‐ cally relevant social-psychological experiential components. There is a significant similarity or sameness, also, with respect to the learning of a vocabulary of motives.

(The numbers men, unlike most of the other criminals in the study, were reared in what a middle-class observer could describe as "adequate" homes.)Their families were supported on the earn‐ ings of the fathers, and there was no criminality on the part of fathers, siblings, and other relatives. Only two came from families in which the mother was dominant. Fifteen of the sixteen rack‐ eteers came from the Negro middle class. All were reared in non-slum neighborhoods by respectable parents; twelve had graduated from high school and three had attended college; ten stated that one or more of their siblings had attended college; fourteen stated that their parents had steady, nonlaboring jobs; and all mentioned having friends and family connections among professional and semiprofessional people. These statements were supported by the admission summary materials in their folders, as well as by their records of correspondence and visitors. They had all received numerous friendly letters and visits from Negro professional and businessmen while incarcerated. The men pre‐ sented themselves, says Roebuck, as respectable, middle-class people who were church-goers, home-owners, and fathers. "They were well-poised, confident, and self-satisfied. In short, they seemed to relate well and to have well-integrated personalities." [50]

Other aspects of their experience are theoretically relevant to the motivation and rationalization of their racketeering. The fol‐ lowing is of course a brief and tentative statement and makes no pretense to being a complete answer.(The great similarity of the numbers racketeers to the boys discussed previously is in their dependence upon and use of culturally supplied vocabularies of motives.)The respectable and legally authoritative people who, among others, are sources of the delinquents' motivations, dis‐ approve of the young people's proscribed behavior. It is also disapproved by the mass media of communication, which condemn racketeering as well. In contrast, the numbers racket was more than passively accepted by the respectable adults who were significant to the racketeers when they were boys and adolescents. They were reared in homes and neighborhoods that were not only tolerant of the racket but in which it was played openly. Parents and parents' friends and acquaintances played it, and some of their in-laws and neighbors derived their livelihood from it. In the presence of the boys they talked of "close misses," "hits" (a "win"), and the "killing." The last is a financially large "win"— enjoyed by a friend of a friend but never by oneself or by one's own friend. They were thus reared in a cultural milieu in which it was an institution that, while defined as criminal by the law, was defined by the local community as being "not really criminal." In late adolescence the racketeers turned to drinking, gambling, and dancing as recreation. Earlier, they had begun dating and engaging in promiscuous heterosexual relations. They did not conceive of what they did as being reprehensible or illegal. The role of the "sport," the "smoothie," and the "big spender," which was tied in with their form of recreation, began to intrigue them. They became interested in "sharp" clothes, developed expensive tastes, and engaged in what they described as "high living." They were surreptitious in these matters because of their desire to please their conventional parents. During their adolescence they avoided juvenile delinquents and gangs, and eschewed stealing, fighting, and violence.

As young adults they admired the men already in the racket whom they met through their families or friends and acquaintances in the neighborhood. They considered some of those racketeers to be outstanding successes in their field. Material success and the way of life of the numbers racketeer that went with such success appealed to them; consequently, Roebuck infers, they rationalized away the illegal aspects of the numbers racket and entered it as a "business pursuit." [5] The conception of the numbers racket as a business is widespread among numbers players, both white and Negro; thus when the young adults entered the racket as numbers writers, they were making use of a well-established rationalization. When interviewed in prison the racketeers still defined it as a business; some had been in it for years and were at the top of their numbers ring.)

There is empirical evidence that the urban Negro middle class has in part accepted the numbers racketeer, perhaps because of his money and influence. The racketeers in Roebuck's study fall into the category that Frazier has called "the new black bourgeoisie":

> The black bourgeoisie is also being recruited from the successful underworld Negroes, who have gained their money from gambling, prostitution, bootlegging and the "numbers." The old upper class in the Negro community erected an impenetrable barrier between themselves and the Negroes who represented the "sporting" and criminal world. Since such Negroes were generally able to handle more money than the majority of Negroes, they always constituted a threat to the respectable way of life cherished by the old middle classes. As a result of urbanization, which upset the old class structure of the Negro community, the "sporting" and criminal elements began to acquire a dominant position among Negroes.
>
> With the emergence of the new black bourgeoisie, the standards of consumption which the "sporting" and criminal elements are able to maintain have become the measure of success among the black middle class. The standards which they set are emulated by Negroes in the professional classes—doctors, dentists, and lawyers, and even teachers as far as they are able to do so. But more important still, in order to secure the money necessary to maintain these standards, Negro professional men engage in the same "rackets" as the successful Negro in the underworld.[52]

At one time, Frazier writes, the Negro middle class regarded the numbers racket as a lower-class form of gambling and largely restricted themselves to betting on horses. With the emergence of the new Negro "society," however, "playing the numbers" has become respectable. This is not strange, since some members of "society" derive incomes from the racket. "Therefore, it is not unusual for Negro professional men and their wives to play the 'numbers' daily. Even the wives of Negro college professors are sometimes 'writers' or collectors of 'numbers' for the 'numbers racket.'"[53]

Frazier's analysis of the rise of the new Negro middle class, and the life experience of the Negro numbers racketeer, are in conformity with each other. A diligent student of the Washington scene since becoming chairman of the department of sociology of Howard University in 1934 until his recent death, he may well have known some of the subjects of Roebuck's study.

One point will become evident, I hope, from both the preceding discussion of delinquents, "good boys," and numbers racketeers, and from the following discussions of rural and hinterland delinquency, and of white-collar and compulsive criminals. (The learning of criminality is much more complex than is implied in the various theories of pathology. This applies to the entire range, from the hereditary neurological pathology of psychiatry to the status-frustration of sociology. The following comments, which extend the previous analysis, attempt to do justice to that complexity.)

4. Rural and Hinterland Delinquency[1]

Similarities in Rural and Urban Delinquency

The existence of a criminal and delinquent culture and social organization in urban areas seems definitely to have been established. A crucial question is whether there is a rural criminal tradition. The studies we have cited by Albert K. Cohen, Solomon Kobrin, Henry McKay, Walter B. Miller, Clifford Shaw, and others present the orthogenesis of delinquency explicitly and exclusively in an urban idiom. Even Clinard and Eastman seem to explain rural and village delinquency as being a result of the contamination of the virtuous countryside by the spreading miasma of urban crime. It is appropriate to observe the similarities between rural and urban delinquency sufficiently to indicate that rural delinquency is not an exception to the sociological theory.

Three kinds of evidence attest the existence of a rural criminal tradition. First, there is a fairly large body of folklore and unconfirmed assertions, some of which is perpetuated in textbooks of criminology. Second, there are many qualitative or descriptive studies, a large number of which have been published by the several state and local historical societies. They deal with such topics as the James and Dalton gangs, the gangs in Indiana and southern Illinois, and vogues in villainy in the ante-bellum slavery states. Third, there is accumulating a body of quantitative studies guided by some type of theory. Examples are the Lane County

(Oregon) Youth Study Project, directed by Kenneth Polk and D. R. Rinehart, the Vermont Rural Youth Project, directed by Jerome Himelhoch, and the study of rural, village, and urban offenders in Iowa by Harold D. Eastman.)

My concern is with processes and not primarily with rates. Although many writers assert that urban areas have significantly higher rates of delinquency and crime, the problem is still open, so to speak, because rural areas have never been studied in any degree comparable to the minute and almost microscopic examination of cities. Esselstyn's study of the county sheriff is a case in point. He found that the ideal sheriff, as a social type, was a mature man with a good reputation and a knowledge of farming. Experience in law enforcement was considered unnecessary; interpretations of the law were very broad, being controlled by local custom. The sheriff had a high tolerance for certain types of lawlessness: the conduct of agriculture was outside the law.[2] This situation confirms one of Sutherland's views on white-collar crime, namely, that some of favored groups' business practices, even though probably illegal, fail to stimulate legal proceedings. England's conclusion is that in towns in which the police force ranges in size from one to about seven men, the "city fathers" largely determine what laws and ordinances will be enforced, and against whom.[3]

(Differential law enforcement in small cities may result in lower official rates, as exemplified in Hollingshead's study) The adults in Elmtown, he discovered, recognized that boys and girls in their middle teens may play one or the other of two major roles, namely, that of the pupil or that of the young adult. High school students are held by adults to play the former role, withdrawees from high school the latter. Pupils are ascribed the status of older children; they are regarded as being dependent and not responsible for their conduct. Parents, school authorities, and the leaders of voluntary organizations devoted especially to adolescents are held to be responsible for what these children do, "from hour to hour, day to day." The withdrawee, since he has entered the world of work, is regarded as an adult by the same people who define his age-peers in school as being dependent children. And the withdrawees, predominantly from the lower social class, in spending their leisure time, behave as many lower-class adults do:

The nightly search for excitement by speeding, shooting firearms along the river roads, drinking, picking up girls, gambling, with now and again a fight, brings many of these young people face-to-face with the law. Pleasure-bent youths violate the mores, if not the law, almost every night, but they are not overly interested in the consequences of their acts. Actually they seldom think about this aspect of their behavior until they find themselves in trouble. This does not occur often, for they seldom commit offenses serious enough to bring them to the attention of the police or the sheriff. When they do, the differences which adults attach to the roles played by the withdrawees in comparison with high school students become clear. The police, and adults in general, assume that parents, often the school, are to blame when a student is apprehended for violation of law. However, when a withdrawee of the same age commits an offense of the same nature officials hold him responsible. The deliberate protection-of-the-pupil policy which fails to place responsibility on the student who violates the law, in contrast to the application of adult judgments to the withdrawee, before he has developed a sense of personal responsibility for his behavior, results in a very much higher incidence of official delinquency in the out-of-school series than in the in-school one.[4]

One consequence is that the crude rate of delinquency, computed on the basis of adjudications of delinquency, differs significantly between the two categories. The rate for high school boys in social classes III through V (V is the lowest) was 9 per 1,000. The rate for withdrawees in the same social classes was 165 per 1,000. The girls in the three classes who were withdrawees had a rate of 104 per 1,000. No rates were available for the high school girls. Only one, in social class IV, was the subject of a complaint, which was dropped without further action.

During the Sixth Annual Juvenile Court Institute, held on the campus of the University of Oregon in August 1963, it was stated that barely one-third of the contacts that policemen of the city of Eugene had with juvenile delinquents come to a hearing in the juvenile department of the court. A comparable assertion was made in July 1963 by an official of Johnson County, Iowa, who stated with a good deal of pride that "most" of the delinquent children in that county were "handled unofficially by the police."

The statement was in conformity with Eastman's observation in Iowa ten years earlier:

> One significant factor in the whole problem of rural crime is the application of informal sanctions by local authorities when offenses involve local people who are well acquainted with the boy or his family. Just how extensive are such practices is difficult to say. The data gathered [in this study] indicates that rural boys are dealt with informally several times before formal steps are taken to "correct" their behavior.[5]

Rural and urban delinquency are, then, alike with respect to differential law enforcement, informal or unofficial decisions by police and others prior to decisions at the juvenile-court intake desk, the overlooking of actions that are probably delinquent, and the giving of a "second chance" (or more), all resulting in the official rates being less than those that the demonstrable incidence of known delinquency would probably give. This seems to be the situation in Canada, also, if one can judge from a study for which incomplete data were available. Juvenile-court practice in the use of informal procedures varies from province to province and from time to time. At one extreme, a formal charge is laid in every case in which a delinquent act is alleged to have occurred. At the other, formal charges may be withdrawn in any case in which the appearance of the juvenile in court might be damaging to him or to his family. Zay attempted to ascertain the number of supposedly delinquent children who were handled informally, but only thirty-six courts supplied figures. If their practice can be taken as an indication of the general practice in Canada, then for every three cases involving a formal hearing, four are dealt with informally as "occurrences," and are not registered. Zay observes:

> Delinquency cases handled in an informal way are not included in the tables published by the Dominion Bureau of Statistics, because no information is available about the children involved and because many courts do not report occurrences. . . . it seems that many courts find it difficult to differentiate between official registration of cases and keeping statistical records on juveniles that have been dealt with in one way or another.[6]

Rural and urban crime are basically alike in another important aspect. Crimes against the person are equal or nearly equal in rate. Several of the significant studies of rural offenders, however, explicitly excluded such offenses, and included only offenses against property. No hypotheses were advanced in the studies concerning "any necessary connection" between urbanism and such offenses against the person as:

> murder, manslaughter, assault, and rape. . . . Such crimes are often due to individual personal situations, often of a fortuitous character. . . . Crimes of personal violence are found with some frequency among many primitive peoples and rural offenders generally have a high proportion of these crimes, in some instances, such as rape, almost equal to urban rates. Property offenses like burglary, larceny, robbery, and embezzlement involve the acquisition of things, a process which does not necessarily have any personal or fortuitous situation behind [it].[7]

Several comments can be made concerning the exclusion of offenses against the person from the study of rural crime and delinquency. First, the researchers thereby estopped themselves from studying the one type of offense admittedly found in equal or nearly equal rates in both rural and urban areas. They therefore could not investigate a very important problem: Are the sociocultural processes that commit one to the value of violence in interpersonal relations the same in rural and urban areas? If they are not, wherein do they differ? Fortunately, the Lane County Youth Study Project and the Vermont Rural Youth Project, previously mentioned, do include all delinquents who commit offenses against the person.

Second, the reason advanced by the previous researchers for excluding offenses against the person from their study of rural delinquency is unsound. The assertion that an offense, either against the person or against property, is spontaneous cannot be proved, the hypothesis of spontaneous behavior being in fact untestable. It is merely another form of the "irresistible impulse" of psychiatry, to be discussed in detail later. Neither researcher presented any evidence that the behavior described as "spontaneous" was either instinctive or uncaused. When one reads their examples of supposedly spontaneous actions, those actions are, in their own words, deliberate. Two instances will be sufficient.

The crime I done was a few miles from home. Perhaps I would of done it anywhere, as I had to be at a certain place at a certain time. I wanted to go to a dance, and my folks would not give me any money, so I really didn't care what I done. I had a car, but it was getting fixed and I didn't have the money to pay for it, so I stole my neighbor's car, just to show my folks I was not scared. I told them I was going to do it, but they didn't think I would. I have never thought about any crime as far as that goes. Like breaking into a place is way out of my line. I always was honest. My father is one of the best citizens. I consider him one of the best in that county. The boys I went with never stole anything. *I never had any experience stealing cars.* Guess it don't take any practice. *When a boy I would use dad's car without asking him,* but he didn't care. *Sometimes he didn't like it very well, but he always got over it somehow.*[8]

The italicized parts of the above quotation are relevant to our point. The assertion, "I never had any experience stealing cars," is contradicted by the admission, "When a boy I would use dad's car without asking him." Perhaps he thought that the neighbor would "get over it somehow" when his car was stolen, as his father had. The point is that he had had practice in stealing automobiles, but his father never complained to the police about it, as his neighbor did. Eastman wrote of rural offenders that:

First offenses [were] *spontaneous occurrences.* . . . When offenders ran out of gas, for example, or money, or were seeking "new experiences" a crime was committed. *There appeared to be no real intent to commit a crime* nor recognition of the need to drive a considerable distance to accomplish that end. Travel seemed to be involved indirectly as gas or money . . . was needed either to travel further or to return to the home community. . . . *The important thing considered by the individual was* not "how far away from home" should an offense be committed, but "*where, among all the places I know, can I best succeed*" in a criminal venture.[9]

Here, again, the earlier claim of spontaneity is negated by the later showing of deliberate conduct.

To exclude offenses against the person from the study of rural crime is a mistake because the use of violence in interpersonal relations is as sociocultural in rural as it is in urban areas, and is not to be conceived of as spontaneous, individualistic, or pathological. Some of the evidence indicating the reasonableness of the hypothesis that interpersonal violence is sociocultural will be presented in our subsequent analysis of the concept of the compulsive criminal. One reference will therefore have to do here, from the observation of one of my colleagues with a great deal of experience in research in small-and medium-sized midwestern cities, including the study of delinquency. Born, reared, and educated in rural Iowa and small cities in Iowa and northwestern Illinois, he concluded, in July 1963, on the basis of his extensive experience, that "there is a definite commitment to the use of violence on the part of rural and small town people, especially in the lower class." Our later analysis of interpersonal violence will support his conclusion.

Canadian statistics reveal a pattern similar to that of the United States. The rural and urban rates for homicide, family offenses, and malicious offenses against property are almost the same. Physical assaults and sexual offenses appear to be nearly equal. The rural rate exceeded the urban for motor vehicle offenses. One student has challenged the conclusion that during the development of the Canadian wheat frontier and the new industrial cities, "juvenile delinquency was almost wholly peculiar to the city." Ferns writes:

> Speaking as a participant observer, who lived as a child for six years in a Canadian prairie farming community and for nine years in a prairie city, I can contradict this statement. In my experience, the behavior of farm children is characterized by more violence, sadism, vandalism, vice and bloody-mindedness than the behavior of city children. The difference is simply that in the wide open spaces, adults notice delinquency less and condone it more.[10]

Social Class and Rural Delinquency

Delinquency and interpersonal violence are highly concentrated in urban areas according to social class, sex, age, and, in some cities, race. A similar concentration seems to characterize delinquency in rural and hinterland areas, and small cities. One must be tentative here because of the relative neglect of social class in studies of rural crime and delinquency. The two studies of rural Iowan offenders referred to previously, for example, are largely silent on the matter of social class. My conclusion is that their subjects were, on the whole, from the lower social class. This inference is based on Clinard's statement that his 200 subjects had "some high school education," a reading of Eastman's study, discussions with some of the upper-echelon staff of the Iowa Men's Reformatory at Anamosa and with several past and present probation officers in Johnson County, a study of the records of a sample of juvenile delinquents of that county, and discussions with two colleagues at the State University of Iowa qualified in theory and research in crime, delinquency, and corrections. But it is a tentative conclusion.

The relative lack of concern with social class in relation to rural delinquency may be a function of the idea that "the concept of social stratification . . . runs counter to a basic rural value, that of a high degree of equality among the people of a community." [11] An investigator who, without realizing it, himself accepts that value could have his observations unwittingly so affected that he might not observe the significance of social class in his research. There is some evidence that rural communities tend to be stratified according to the same principles that operate in urban areas. [12]

Recent research into rural, hinterland, and small-town delinquency finds it to be predominantly male and associated significantly with lower social-class membership. Polk, in the Lane County Youth Project Study, found that:

> There appears a dominant *economic theme* in the delinquency and school withdrawal of these hinterland youths. . . . not only are the "trouble-prone" youth found at the lower end of these traditional economic measures, they are also more likely to think that opportunity for advancement is "not very good." Furthermore, other data show that these youngsters are economically vulnerable once they drop out of school, since at the time of the survey 38 per cent of the drop-out male population was unemployed, and those who were employed were by and large in low income, low status positions. [13]

Himelhoch, in Vermont, also reported a concentration of delinquency among lower-class youths in the rural and hinterland areas covered in the Vermont Youth Study:

The rural delinquent subculture is usually characterized by a loosely organized, non-exclusive, sporadically delinquent group which has a shifting membership which draws upon a larger population of youth who are mostly, but not always, of lower-class backgrounds.[14]

The relationship between social class and delinquency found in these two studies seems to conflict with an opposite finding in other recent studies of delinquency in rural areas and small towns. In the latter studies anonymous questionnaires were administered to high school students. In their responses the students admitted to the fact and frequency of various misdeeds. Their responses are held to be "a measure of self-reported delinquency in the home and community." Some of the self-reported offenses on one questionnaire are:

1. Did things my parents told me not to do.
2. Minor theft (compilation of such items as the stealing of fruit, pencils, lipstick, candy, cigarettes, comic books, money less than $1, etc.).
3. Told a lie to my family, principal, or friends.
4. Used swearwords or dirty words out loud in school, church, or on the street so that other people could hear me.
10. Major theft (compilation of such items as stealing auto parts, autos, money over $1, bicycles, radios and parts, clothing, wallets, liquor, guns, etc.).
28. Hung around the railroad tracks and trains.
36. Attacked someone with the idea of killing them [sic].

One tentative conclusion of the research was that the patterns of delinquent action might be "dramatically different" from what they were previously thought to be. But there is no empirical basis for accepting this conclusion.[15]

The findings from various studies, indicating that delinquency in small towns and rural areas is both significantly related to and not significantly related to social class, are not contradictory. They tap different sources of data. The self-reported or confessed delinquencies involve conduct that has been judged only by the high school pupil who completed the questionnaire. The other type of research, in contrast, deals with delinquency to which the community has reacted through some of its designated agents. Thus the two types of research deal with different bodies of information. This is a point already made in some of the "self-report" studies themselves.[16] One may ask, in addition, how often such actions as those listed in the first four items, above, would likely bring a boy to the intake desk of a juvenile court.

(Community studies of small cities have consistently revealed, over the years, a uniform pattern of concentration of delinquency and delinquents in the lower social class.[17] One must conclude, then, on the basis of the available data, that the patterns of rural, hinterland, small city, and urban delinquency have in common a concentration in the lower social class.)

Sociocultural Setting of Rural Delinquency

(A number of studies present empirical evidence for the conclusion that rural and hinterland juvenile delinquency and young adult crime, in common with urban, start and continue in a sociocultural setting.)This is revealed in the young offenders' knowledge of their communities, membership in groups that committed trivial or serious thefts, and the approximate age at which they began to engage in certain types of activities.(Speaking negatively, one can say that the rural and hinterland young offender is not individualistic in committing his offenses.)

This lack of individuality is shown in Eastman's study, in 1954, of offenders in Iowa. Young adult offenders in the reformatory in Anamosa indicated that they did not travel to other communities in order to be anonymous. They were, in fact, wary of going outside their own community because they would not know what to expect if they were caught.(They thought that the success of their ventures depended in great measure on their personal knowledge both of the place or person to be victimized, and the methods of operation of the local police. An essential part of a delinquent's or criminal's self-conception seems to be his belief in his ability to avoid detection and thus to outwit the police as well as the intended victim.)This component of the self-conception, Eastman concludes, must arise from at least a minimum knowledge of the community in which the offender intends to operate as an offender. The subjects of his study had such knowledge.

(It seems inaccurate in most cases to refer to the young rural offender's association with a group of boys as "gang" activity, even though practically all offenses were committed with one or more companions.) Eastman's data were not detailed enough to enable one to decide whether the basis for the association was specifically related to the commission of some offense, or whether the offense grew out of some activity in school or some other special interest in the community. Nevertheless, the data showing the membership of offenders and nonoffenders in groups committing theft shows that rural boys, in terms of percentage, approximated the degree to which urban boys were members of such gangs. It may therefore be concluded that the phenomenon of "gang-like" groups has in some measure become a part of rural life.) The control groups of nonoffenders with rural, village, and urban residence were less often members of such groups, in a statistically significant degree. The data thus do not support the hypothesis that the rural offender is characteristically individualistic in his offenses. The data also do not show a downward progression of membership in gang-like groups, with the greatest rate of membership among the urban and the least among the rural offenders. The same patterns are revealed in the data related to offenders and nonoffenders who committed serious thefts in association with other boys, except that there was an even greater difference between offenders and nonoffenders.[18]

(The age at which boys became members of groups, or associated with boys who stole, showed the same pattern for rural, village, and urban offenders and nonoffenders. The offenders started their associations and their memberships at a significantly earlier age. Again, there was no downward progression with the urban offenders showing the greatest proportion joining in the earliest years and the rural having the greatest proportion joining in the later years. Instead, the urban and rural boys were closely similar.) In addition, the rural, village, and urban boys began certain behaviors at about the same ages, and at an earlier age than that reported by the nonoffenders: the first truancy, smoking, drinking alcohol excessively, gambling seriously for money, and heterosexual relations. One cannot, of course, make anything behaviorally significant of "early" smoking. And, since data as to specific ages is not available, this must remain a qualitative statement. The relatively earlier gambling, drinking, and sexual experience of the offenders is, however, in conformity with other studies of lower-class youth. To cite only one example, Hollingshead reported this behavior in his study of Elmtown.[19]

Eastman's data lead to the conclusion that the rural offender has had associations with and been a member of gang-like groups at an earlier age and more often than the rural nonoffender, and that he has committed both trivial and serious offenses more often, and probably has started to engage in certain other morally disapproved kinds of conduct at an earlier age. There remain to be considered explicitly the matters of the existence of and participation in a delinquent subculture, and the social participation of the delinquent.

"Delinquent subculture" and "social participation" have often been misconceived as being separate and distinct concepts and processes. That misconception, I suggest, is a cause of much of the confusion in the literature dealing with social disorganization, status-frustration, alienation, and delinquency in general. It will be recalled that the first chapter described the social participation of upper-class and professional people as occurring to a great extent through formal and secondary associations, whereas that of the urban lower class was said to occur predominantly on the basis of primary relations. Whether primary or secondary relations predominate in one's life, or whether both are engaged in to some degree—which is typical for perhaps much of the population—there is still social participation. And, significantly, there is social participation whether one is a member of conventional or unconventional social organizations, or of both.

The point seems to be simple but is, in fact, complex. To the extent that one participates in the delinquent subculture one is precluded from participating in conventional social organizations; conversely, to the extent that one participates in conventional social organizations one is precluded from participating in the delinquent subculture. The respective participations are thus reciprocals, corresponding to each other by being complementary.

(The understanding of both delinquency and lawfulness has been impeded by the failure to realize that "participation in a delinquent subculture" is not the same as "no social participation.") It is surely trite to state again that delinquency and crime do not occur in a sociocultural vacuum. Although trite, it is just as surely not obvious to anyone who can write or believe—or both— that from more than 20 per cent to about 40 per cent of offenders "have participated in no community organizations" because they have been members of delinquent cliques or gangs rather than members of a 4-H club or a Boy Scout troop. It expresses an upper-class sociologist's value as if it were a scientific statement of fact. We shall refer to only a few of the many works showing that legally and morally disapproved conduct occurs in a social setting in rural and hinterland areas.

(We can begin by showing briefly that the rural and small-town juvenile delinquent and young adult offender—in common with their urban counterparts—participate significantly less in conventional community organizations than do their lawful peers.)Eastman found that about 60 per cent of his rural offenders belonged to no traditional community organization, and that the other 40 per cent had belonged to one or two. Of the rural lawful control group, 77 per cent belonged to one or two, and 23 per cent to from three to five. He reported comparable figures for offenders and controls from villages and urban areas. In addition, offenders had not been leaders in those organizations to which they had belonged, as measured by length of time of membership and offices held. (The offenders remained members for brief periods only; none was elected to an office.[20] Polk found that the troublesome youth of rural and hinterland Lane County are less likely to participate in school organizations than the lawful. They seemed to believe that they had been rejected by the lawful youth. Perhaps as a consequence of not participating they think that they are not close to the "center of things," and are more likely to agree that "there are a few who control things" in school and that "the rest of us are left out in the cold." In revealing the rejection of some of the values held by the lawful, the troublesome youth are less likely to agree that high grades in school confer high status among males.[21]

The lower-class pupils in Elmtown's high school also decided that "there are a few who control things," and that "the rest are out in the cold," although not in those exact words. The correctness of their judgment is confirmed unquestionably by the data of *Elmtown's Youth*. The cliques of middle- and upper-class pupils excluded those of the lower class. The latter were discriminated against by the staff, from the superintendent of schools down, at the same time that they were subject to the other educational disadvantages of their position in the social-class system. Some students would describe them today as being "alienated from society." That description may or may not be correct; the noun "alienation," now popular with many students of contemporary American society, is a word of variable meaning. What is important here is the social process involved, not a semantic discussion of a changeling word. The lower-class pupils in Elmtown's high school were involved in the social process of reciprocal rejection. Themselves rejected, they rejected their rejectors as well as some of the rejectors' values. One consequence was their nonparticipation in the school's organized activities and a marked tendency to withdraw from school before graduation. Their conclusions about "the few who control" and "being left in the cold" can surely be accepted as being realistic appraisals of their position in the social system. The lower class also did not participate in organized religious activities, even according to Hollingshead's very liberal criterion of attendance at *at least one* church service, Sunday School class, choir practice, or other religious gathering between September 1, 1941, and May 31, 1942. The percentages attending parties attended by young people's groups, by class, was: Class II, 77; Class III, 42; Class IV, 20; and Class V, 4. "Organized social affairs are not an important trait in the activity pattern of the typical adolescent of Class IV or Class V." [22] The lower-class youth of River City displayed the same pattern of nonparticipation in the organized social activities of school and church. [23]

It has been found, in community after community, that the great bulk of organized, conventional social activity is carried forward by a small minority: "Community studies, virtually without exception, have shown that membership and participation follow a kind of J-curve, in which a small proportion of the population is highly active in many associations while the great majority remains passively on the side lines." [24] The studies cited above seem to be no exception. They enable one to be rather specific about two categories of nonparticipants. Juvenile delinquents and young adult offenders are integrated into the *conventionally* organized community life to a significantly lesser degree than are nonoffenders, as measured in terms of participation in conventional community organizations. They are also integrated into *unconventional* or *criminal* or *delinquent* social organizations to a significantly greater degree than the nonoffenders. Some students of delinquency and crime are prone to misread that pattern of participation. Thus they write of "nonparticipation in community organizations," or claim that "the impersonality in the lives of farm and village offenders seems to be due to a lack of general participation in community life." Two points should be made concerning this.

First, there is a failure to take into account the fact that the life of the urban delinquent is overwhelmingly on the basis of primary, personal relationships. One can, in fact, develop the thesis that criminal and delinquent organizations *must* be based on primary relationships. The participants must be known to each other in order to be able to trust one another. The secondary relationships that mark formal organizations—and to which correctional and other professional people belong in such great numbers—are by definition precluded for delinquent and criminal organizations. Rackets (sometimes called "criminal syndicates") and other forms of organized crime especially must be organized on the basis of primary relations. That is why it is so difficult for the federal Bureau of Narcotics to plant its agents in the narcotics racket. It is also one reason why first-hand research on the criminal community is so difficult to conduct.

Second, "lack of participation in *conventional* community life" is transformed into "lack of participation in community life." The crucial adjective "conventional" is omitted and the delinquents and criminals are then classified as "normless," "alienated," "anomic," or "mentally ill," and their neighborhoods as "disorganized" and "unable to exert control"—a misinterpretation that is of venerable age. It is almost as if students of human society are unable to bear the thought that some people belong to unconventional organizations. They in effect assert that members of the unconventional groups are proper targets for such epithets as "anomic" or "mentally ill."

There is no need to pursue further the point that the unconventionally-acting member of an unconventional organization (as judged by the observer) is just as much a member of the human community as anyone else. Indeed, we showed that Eastman's own data disproved the hypothesis that the rural offender is individualistic in committing his offenses. This discussion will, I hope, help to emphasize the analytical value of the conception of contemporary society as being a differentiated unity. The use of the concepts of differential association and differential social organization tend to keep one constantly aware of the fact that groups with somewhat differing cultures (goals, practices, and values) compete and conflict with one another. One tends always to ask the question, "Is there one group or are there some groups?" One is therefore less likely to confuse "nonparticipation in the conventional" with "nonexistence."

The Delinquent as Hedonist

Many similarities in patterns of conduct of rural and hinterland delinquents are reported in studies in widely separated parts of the country. The Vermont Youth Study described the misbehaving boys as "hedonists" rather than "delinquents" because their conduct, even though often illegal, was not seriously delinquent. The essential purpose of the group seemed to be pleasure-seeking, rather than violation of the law or defiance of authority. Their most frequent delinquencies were buying, furnishing, and possessing alcoholic beverages, which is illegal in Vermont for anyone less than twenty-one years of age. Usually associated with drinking were the next most frequent offenses: fighting (with fists only) and reckless driving. The boys boasted of drag racing, "peeling rubber," and playing "chicken," a game in which drivers race towards each other, the one who first swerves out of line to avoid the head-on collision being the derided "chicken." The boys less often jack deer, steal inexpensive goods, and commit vandalism. On a typical evening a boy with an automobile will collect some of his friends; they will ride around "to see if there's anything going on." They may visit some neighboring city or town and buy liquor to be drunk in the car by the roadside or in a barn dance parking lot. They may attend one of the barn dances that are held regularly most of the year. The places that are most appreciated by the boys are "Way down in the country, nobody to follow you, nice big parking area," where drinking and sexual activity with the girls they have picked up may be engaged in in relative privacy.[25]

(The delinquents said that they liked to do things that are against the law, and to violate rules laid down by the school.) They preferred gambling to working, and enjoyed joking, sleeping, drinking beer, playing pool, and necking. They did not want to study in school, to speak more grammatically, or to think more clearly. They preferred good clothes to high grades, and cars to small children.[26])

The hedonists' conduct is quite similar to that described in more detail for the withdrawees from Elmtown's high school.[27] Youthful rural offenders in Iowa reported traveling to other towns in groups in order to drink, pursue girls, and skate. Reports of such activities, given during interviews, indicated that the delinquent rural boy did regularly associate with a given group but that the interests of the group were primarily recreational rather than criminal. The group engaged in a great deal of vandalism in which there was no expectation of financial gain; but the boys did not regard it as vandalism, and Eastman himself refers to it as "what may be called 'destructive' play." They can be compared with Himelhoch's hedonists and the trouble-prone delinquents of Lane County who think that "stirring up a little excitement" confers status among males. Many of the property offenses of the Iowan youths were committed in order to have money to buy something or to go somewhere as a part of the group. Farm boys, particularly, reported committing thefts so as to be able to travel to a nearby town or to pick up a girl friend. The offense of many of the farm boys that led to commitment was automobile theft in which the goal was not the stealing of

the car but the entertaining of a girl friend. Obtaining the necessary money, or automobile, or suit of clothing, seemed to be
incidental to the goal, which might be a girl, a dance, or a
drinking or skating party, or some combination of these.

(When other boys accompanied the offender on such adven-
tures—and there were almost invariably from one to three others
—the offender did not conceive of his companions as accomplices
but as friends who, in a sense, went along for the ride with their
own girls, and who would help with the car if necessary. The
boys did not regard such assistance as being criminal behavior.
When they were asked about the equal guilt of their accomplices,
almost all of the farm boys responded by rejecting the concepts
of "accomplice" and "equal guilt." [28])

The rural and hinterland delinquents seem, in brief, from northern Vermont to western Oregon, to enjoy themselves in their
delinquency. It is a form of recreation that provides excitement
and confers status. They are similar to the young urban delinquent in this respect, as described by such students as Shaw and
McKay, Tappan, Thrasher, Walter B. Miller, and others. They
stand in sharp contrast to the delinquent as depicted in much if
not most of today's literature in psychiatry, psychology, social
work, and sociology. He is held to be status-frustrated, doubly
defeated, unconsciously guilt-ridden, pathological, and mentally
ill. He is held to hate himself in what he does, does not want
to be a delinquent but cannot control his irresistible impulses,
and would really much rather behave as and have the same
values as the middle class, because his rejection of that class is
really not a rejection at all but a reaction-formation. It may be
recalled that in the first essay I partially developed the thesis that
such a conception of the delinquent is incorrect. The findings of
the studies of the rural and hinterland delinquent support that
thesis. Eastman has given a succinct summary of what to do and
what to enjoy when away from home, according to Iowan rural
delinquents of about fourteen or more years of age: "When asked
to tell what he did on these short trips to a neighboring state,
community, or large service center, the usual reply was, drink,
fuck, play pool and roller skate." [29]

In discussing the existence of a rural and hinterland delinquent subculture, it is necessary to refer to two points made in the first and third chapters. The hypothesis of a delinquent subculture that inverts the values of the conventional middle- and upper-class culture was found inadequate and therefore rejected, through the analysis of the concepts of social disorganization and status-frustration. I also indicated the complexity of the process of learning delinquency, and categorized it, hypothetically, as linguistic or symbolic learning with at least three components. First, the lower-class child learns the conventional code and what is in general expected by it in terms of conduct. Second, he also learns the values of, and the conduct expected by, lower-class culture. Third, the youths who are, or who are becoming, delinquent are also learning the values of and the conduct expected by the delinquent subculture. It is appropriate to make this point explicitly for rural and hinterland delinquency and delinquents.

Some studies have postulated the existence of an adolescent subculture rejecting adult culture in general, as an expression of the rebellion of adolescence. It is as necessary to reject this postulate as it is Cohen's less inclusive one, and for the same reason, namely, that it is infirmed. Some may think "infirm" too strong a verb. If it is, then the most that can be said for the postulated "rebellious youth subculture" is that the evidence is contradictory and confusing and does not warrant the hypothesis being taken seriously. The hypothesis implies that there is a qualitative sociocultural discontinuity between adolescents and adults without answering the further question, Why is it, then, that American society or any similar society can remain in being? A former president of the American Sociological Association has described the period of adolescence as one of "compulsive independence of antagonism to adult expectation and authority." [30] Ernest A. Smith has published an analysis that "is largely descriptive" and that "to a great extent consists of a *projection* of both fact and interpretation derived from a wide range of literature." In discussing the topic, "Youth Culture as a Distinct Culture," he writes:

> Youth culture enforces a conformity upon its members, which is intensified by the withdrawal of youth from adult socializing

institutions . . . and by the resulting secrecy, which acts as an obstacle to the supervision and control of adults over youth activities. From this secrecy, there arises the series of conflicts between youth culture and adult culture that is characteristic of the American society.[31]

In a work definitely superior to that of Parsons and Smith, (Coleman summarizes his general point by stating:

> In sum, then, the general point is this: our adolescents today are cut off, probably more than ever before, from the adult society. They are still oriented toward fulfilling their parents' desires, but they look very much to their peers for approval as well. Consequently, our society has in its midst a set of small teen-age societies, which focus teen-age interests and attitudes on things far removed from adult responsibilities, and which may develop standards that lead away from those goals established by the larger society.[32])

One wishes, however, for the sake of his thesis that Coleman's data allowed an unequivocal interpretation, and can only comment, "But our children still marry, have children, work, play, worship, and so on, and American society still remains in being." As another example, Coleman used the design of an empathic study in ascertaining what parents want for their children, and what children think their parents want for them: A states what he wants for B. B states what he thinks A wants for B. The overwhelming majority of parents said they wanted their sons to be brilliant students in school, and a smaller majority wanted this for their daughters.) But a larger majority of boys and girls thought that "both parents would be very proud of me" if they made the basketball team or cheerleader, than if they were made an assistant in the biology class. Significantly, however, the great majority of children thought that both parents would be "very proud" of *both* achievements. Coleman also writes that scholastic achievement is very important to girls in high school: "Motivated as they are to conform to the demands of parents and teachers, they work harder in school . . . and are, on the whole, more oriented to 'doing well' in scholastic matters than are the boys." [33]

All studies of empathy, in addition, reveal a degree of discrepancy in the role-playing of A when compared to the role-taking of B. There is no indication that the difference between what parents wanted for their children and what children thought their parents would be proud of, is any greater than the discrepancy in role-playing and role-taking than would be found for other categories of the population. The above points do not allow one to infer that there is a general discontinuity in significant values between the parents and the children in Coleman's study.

The data on social participation, cited previously, are relevant here. All of the studies referred to, regardless of residence of their subjects, showed a high, consistent, positive correlation of social participation with social class. Members of the middle and upper class, both adults and children, participate in conventional social organizations to a significantly greater degree than do members of the lower class, whether adults or children. All of the community studies, furthermore, reported a differential commitment to education, according to social class, for both adults and adolescents. It is of course well known that the number and proportion of voluntary withdrawals (dropouts) from high school are highly concentrated in the lower class. Patterns of voting of adolescents, as revealed in mock elections in schools, have been found to be strikingly similar to those of adults, according to social class.[34]

The study of occupations also reveals a continuity between generations, by social class. One of the best single predictors of a youth's general occupational category as an adult is that of his father. Race, religion, ethnic derivation, and occupation, according to social class, are the best predictors of who will marry whom. Marriages that cross races are comparatively rare in the United States, even among those in the professions.

Elkin and Westley found "many similar patterns of behavior" in a suburb of Montreal and in Elmtown. In both cities the upper-middle-class adolescent spends much of his time outside of school in supervised activities. The parents know the families of their children's associates and influence them to drop "undesirable" friends. The children are taught to be grammatical in speech, polite in speech and behavior, and to avoid physically aggressive conduct. Hollingshead concluded that the children of the middle and upper classes "are guided by the parents along lines approved by the class cultures with remarkable success." [35]

There are of course differences of culture and conduct between adolescents and parents. One can speak of an adolescent culture with reference to such matters as a distinctive dress, a language or argot, interests in popular music and dances; in favorite movie, singing, and television personages; and in sports; and secrecy in learning such components of adult culture as smoking, gambling, drinking, and sexual relations. That culture is not a myth, as Elkin and Westley claim. But neither is it in rebellion against adult culture, whether the adolescents are of the upper, middle, or lower class.

One can conclude, on the basis of the available evidence, that there is a greater discontinuity in significant values between social classes than there is between the two contiguous generations (parents and adolescents) of any given social class. This seems to be the situation in Green Mountain Town, in northern Vermont. The more delinquent adolescents conceived of their parents as sanctioning or at least as tolerating many values of the delinquent subculture, and particularly, those favoring immediate gratification of desires, and a negativistic evaluation of the standards of respectable adults. By contrast, the lawful adolescents reported that their parents teach a moral philosophy that includes worldly asceticism, the control of impulses, hard work, peer-group popularity, making a good impression on others, and achieving status through conformity:

> For example, their parents approve much more than the delinquents' parents the boy who works hard, saves for college, always obeys, and is popular with the other boys. Similarly, they are much more enthusiastic about the girl who works hard for grades, is active in her church youth group, is good-looking and knows how to dress, and is popular with the other girls. Regardless of whether they are well-behaved or badly-behaved, Green Mountain Town teen-agers agree with their parents rather than rebel against them. Perhaps the delinquents are conforming to delinquent parental models or their permissive parents do not restrain them. Similarly, the well-behaved adolescents appear to be conforming to moralistic, other-directed, status-oriented parents.[36]

Although Eastman's study did not include adolescent-parent relationships, it did show that there was significant contact between the rural Iowan offenders and some components of criminal culture. The rural offenders had both a higher rate of arrest than the urban offenders and a higher rate of contact with prostitutes. Eastman interpreted the more frequent resort to prostitutes as being a function of rural life in the sense that opportunity for contact with the opposite sex was limited by patterns of work as well as residence. Perhaps the lower-class school withdrawees of Elmtown had an advantage over the lower-class rural youth. The young Elmtowners liked to boast that they would get "what they could, where they could, and as cheaply as they could." By this they meant pick-ups, not prostitutes. Pick-ups were on the street, in a tavern, a hangout, the skating rink, the dance hall or the theater.

Eastman suggests that the higher rates of arrest and greater frequenting are one means by which rural individuals and groups come to define their activities as "criminal." Since prostitution is an important component of the criminal culture, the patronizing of the professional prostitute by the young rural offender is significant. It brings him into direct and intimate contact with criminal patterns. Such contacts, Eastman states, constitute differential association of the most intimate kind. It is "increasingly difficult," he concludes, to continue the claim made in previous years that the rural offender had little or no contact with urban criminal culture.[37]

The studies in Iowa and Vermont do not reveal what Cohen and Short call "the parent male subculture." This has been described previously: nonutilitarian, malicious, negativistic, versatile, and marked by short-run hedonism and group autonomy. They call it the "parent" delinquent subculture because, they assert, it is probably the most common variety in the United States, and also because the characteristics listed above seem to constitute a common core shared by other important variants. I do not want either to repeat my previous analysis of Cohen's view or to anticipate my subsequent comments on the differences between "rural" and "urban" delinquency. It is nevertheless necessary to state that the high degree of organization often found in urban delinquency is only in varying degree to be found in rural and hinterland delinquency.

Polk refers, and properly in my opinion, to a "troublemaking" subculture among rural and hinterland youth. Empey, however, uses the concept of "parent delinquent subculture" in referring to Utah County:

> Despite the fact the Utah county is not a highly urbanized area, when compared to large metropolitan centers, the concept of a "parent" delinquent subculture has real meaning for it. While there are no clear-cut gangs, per se, it is surprising to observe the extent to which delinquent boys from the entire county, who have never met, know each other by reputation, go with the same girls, use the same language, or can seek each other out when they change high schools. About half of them are permanently out of school, do not participate in any regular institutional activities, and are reliant almost entirely upon the delinquent system for social acceptance and participation.[38]

In presenting the characteristics of "troublesome youth" in Lane County, Polk concluded that there is evidence of a sub-cultural theme of delinquency in the county:

> While there are no "gangs" as we use the term to apply to the group behavior of metropolitan slum delinquents, data are found here which show some commonly held norms and common patterns of behavior among delinquents which are different from non-delinquents. Trouble-prone youth were much more likely to indicate friendship with youth who have "been in trouble with the police." They are more likely to think that "stirring up a little excitement" is status-conferring among males, and they are more likely to spend evenings with friends than with family or in organized activities. Furthermore, data from the Juvenile Department show that among males in the typical year, around three-fourths of the referrals will have a companion involved in the offense. Each of these pieces of information supports the notion that there is an important social context of delinquency in the hinterland. It should be pointed out that this is a male sub-culture and that delinquency in Lane County is predominantly a male phenomenon.[39]

A number of the significant similarities between rural, hinterland, and urban delinquency and delinquents have been indicated. But similarity, even if described as "essential," is not synonymous with identity. Indeed, sociocultural systems being what they are, there is neither an empirical nor a logical basis for expecting identity of systems differently located in socio-cultural time and space. There are quantitative differences in delinquency in rural, hinterland, and urban areas. There also are, as we have indicated, the basic sociocultural features of differential association and differential social organization, regardless of area. The immediately preceding quotation from Polk's work is representative of this double aspect of basic similarity and quantitative difference.

(Polk's statement refers to one of the features of rural delinquency that one quickly observes as being highly typical. Rural and hinterland youth rarely form the type of delinquent gang that is given so much publicity in the metropolitan areas, particularly the slums. Polk referred to "troublesome youth," Empey found that "there are no gangs, per se," Eastman referred to "gang-like" activities, Hollingshead referred to "cliques" that became "gangs" when the members became delinquent, and Himelhoch referred to "hedonists.") Loomis and Beegle discussed the great importance of clique and friendship groupings in rural areas, and asserted that their existence has been neglected by sociologists. There is a great variety of these groups, and they are known by different names: set, neighbors, group, friends, bunch, and so on. Such groups act in many ways, some lawful and some unlawful.[10] Whatever the situation in rural sociology may have been in 1950, contemporary research in rural delinquency surely has taken cognizance of delinquent rural cliques.

A few highly organized gangs "in somewhat modified form" will be found in rural areas, according to Himelhoch. Perhaps Empey had such groups in mind, in his reference to the "parent" delinquent subculture in Utah County. The rural delinquent subculture in northern Vermont, however, is usually marked by a loosely-organized, nonexclusive, sporadically delinquent group which has a shifting membership drawing upon a population of youth who are largely but not exclusively members of the lower class. They are somewhat different from the rural delinquent groups in Iowa. Eastman reported relatively little turnover of membership in the latter. They are homogeneous in the sense that they share common behaviors, values, and occupational goals. "It is this homogeneity that seems to provide the frame of reference within which the group operates." It may be hypothesized that each member learned criminal conceptions of self, law, and property through what they had in common.[41]

Self-Conception of the Rural Delinquent

Some of the differences in self-conception held by delinquents and by "good boys" in urban areas with high rates of delinquency were listed in the previous chapter. Some of the differences between the "career" delinquent and the criminal violator of financial trust will be indicated later. It is therefore appropriate to indicate here some of the differences in self-conception between rural and urban delinquents. In common with other aspects of rural delinquency, there is comparatively little empirical material dealing directly with this topic. However, at least two of the research projects now in progress will supply a good deal of empirical data.

The hypothesis was advanced [in the second previous paragraph] that rural Iowan delinquents learned criminal conceptions of self through participating in a social system the members of which had common behavior, values, and occupational goals. One should logically expect, at least in part as one consequence of the less developed criminal and delinquent subcultures in rural and hinterland areas, that the delinquents and young adult criminals of those areas would have a comparatively undeveloped criminal conception of property, person, and the law. There is, however, so little direct data that one must be quite tentative.* We are told, for example, that rural Iowan

* The meaning of "comparatively undeveloped criminal conception of property, person, and the law" will be specified more fully at the end of the subsequent discussion of the thief in the white collar.

There is at least one compelling reason why the hypothesis of the difference in self-conception between rural and hinterland, and urban delinquents is presented as being very tentative and quite incomplete. The rural and hinterland studies considered here have "decent" people as their subjects. There is no attempt whatever to include the gangs that developed in midwestern rural areas during the century after the end of the Civil War. The Midwest, which claims to be typical of the United States, has produced some notably ruthless gangs. Those from southern Indiana and Illinois, and from Kansas and Missouri, are examples. In addition, some of the Civil War states presently (late 1963) have organizations composed of some white people devoted to the denial of certain constitu-

delinquents had comparatively frequent contacts with prostitutes. There is, however, no information on the frequency of contact—if any—with other components of criminal culture. The absence of association with other criminal patterns would, according to our hypothesis, tend to impede the development of a conception of oneself as a criminal. No narcotics addicts or marijuana smokers were mentioned in any of the rural and hinterland studies referred to above. This also indicates a less developed criminal subculture. One consequence is that none of the delinquents or young adult criminals could become narcotics addicts or marijuana users.

There seems also to be no consistent pattern of "progression" in rural and hinterland delinquency and youthful crime. Such a pattern would include moving from occasional to habitual and from trivial to serious offenses, the learning of a vocabulary of motives and more or less constant companionship with other delinquents, and a change from delinquency regarded as a game to delinquency regarded as a means to gains, with perhaps some type and degree of specialization. Neither Clinard nor Eastman found evidence that criminal specialists developed in Iowan rural areas, who, because of their maturity in crime, their contacts with criminal culture or their self-conception as criminals, selected and became skilled at the commission of the more complex crimes, as contrasted to stealing what could be had for the taking, at presumably the least risk and the greatest assurance of success. Clinard reported several self-conceptions. A delinquent may think of himself as basically a "good boy" who has in fact done nothing more than to make a mistake from a technical or legalistic viewpoint, or he may think of his actions as being isolated transgressions, or he may regard himself as "tough," "antisocial," or "criminal." "Farm boys" were reported to have conceptions of themselves as being wild and reckless. Urban offenders with more criminal and delinquent experiences, in contrast, referred to themselves as being hard, tough, criminal, mean, and no-good.[42]

---

tional rights to Negroes through the deliberate violation of court decisions by means that include the threat of and the actual use of force, even to the point of murder. No material is included here concerning those people's self-conception. They live in both rural and urban areas.

There were some changes, in time, in the offenses committed by Iowan youth, even though no "career line" from delinquency to crime was found. First arrests typically were for minor offenses, involving either the boy's car or drunkenness. Second and third arrests, in contrast, were for suspicion of burglary or larceny, or the like. In a number of cases the boys were guilty of forgery several times but on each occasion were allowed to repay the money without the application of formal sanctions. When it was learned that gasoline could be pumped, after closing time, at a certain service station, or that a certain farmer had enough cattle so as not to miss a calf or two, or that a relative against whose account a check had been written was satisfied with a promise and restitution, they were victimized to the extent that the boy was arrested and warned for the last time. The delinquent groups had no name, as urban gangs often do, and no "code" of belonging through having to engage in some kind of offense.[43] In brief, crime and delinquency were accepted by the members of the groups, rather than demanded.

The rural delinquent, in common with the urban, tends to develop a self-conception that allows him to admit his delinquencies to himself without damage to his self-esteem. Vandalism provides an example. The fact that it is often free of accompanying larceny helps to confirm the delinquent's conception of himself as being only a prankster. Some students of delinquency have interpreted vandalism, when not accompanied by larceny, as being nonutilitarian and irrational. But I have already indicated something of the rational and functional character of larceny-free vandalism. The Vermont delinquents' self-conception seems to be very favorable. They were previously referred to as hedonists, and none of them wanted to be anything but himself. They unanimously agree as a group as to the personal qualities that they admire. It is most important to be friendly, good-natured, and loyal. It is equally important to be a good automobile driver, a good dancer, a good fighter, and able to "hold liquor." Each hedonist thought that he himself possessed all these qualities. They tend not to interpret their experiences as being frustrating. When asked to estimate their chances of achieving their goals in career and marriage, they replied "Good." [44]

There are other differences between rural and hinterland, and urban delinquency. One that is quite evident but not necessarily superficial is the difference in distance traveled by the offenders. An untold number of young people in Manhattan and Brooklyn, and the south side of Chicago, including lawful children, have not, throughout adolescence, been more than a few city blocks away from their birthplace. The distances traveled by rural and hinterland youth in such states as Illinois, Iowa, Minnesota, Oregon, Utah, and even Vermont are in striking contrast. They think nothing of driving a 25- to 35-mile radius—and even more—night after night, "to see if something's doing," or "just for the Hell of it," or often for "excitement and girls." The lawful adolescents, still in high school, differ in that they take such drives for a publicly stated objective such as "a hamburger and milk shake" on school-dance nights, weekends, or other nights that are not "school nights."(There is no concept of "turf" or "territory" as is sometimes found with urban gangs. And not all urban delinquents, by any means, are as confined to limited areas as are those gangs that have a "turf.") The delinquents in and around Los Angeles are examples.

Rural and hinterland delinquency seems to retain its character as a game and as a means to excitement, when compared to much urban delinquency. It can in this respect be compared to the delinquency of the young urban offender, but not to that of the "career" delinquent who makes the transition to delinquency as a means of income. Its recreational and exciting quality, and the lack of progression in delinquency and crime, are of course related to each other. These, in turn, will at least in part account for the tendency of rural and hinterland delinquency to be less serious than urban. Some studies, at any rate, report this. In River City, for example, of the 114 offenders, more than 40 had only one contact with the police. Their offenses included such petty things as truancy, speeding, faulty automobile brakes, and breaking windows or street lights. They could be described as "naughty." Another one-third of the 114 had more than one contact with the police, for offenses that were definitely of minor seriousness.[45]

(Himelhoch described his hedonists as having "a relaxed attitude" toward their delinquencies: ﴾"The things we do, they're wrong, actually, but we don't carry them too far, we take it easy." Several of them named the chief of police as a person whom they would ask for advice or help if they had a problem, even if it did not concern the law.[46] One can hardly imagine a policeman being asked for help or advice on a personal problem by the subjects of Shaw's life-histories, or by the members of the gangs more recently studied on the south side of Chicago, or in Manhattan and Brooklyn. Indeed, the police of practically any large city in the the United States and Canada would probably welcome as substitutes for their own delinquents those from northern Vermont. Polk also reported that Lane County "hinterland youth are charged more often with the minor but troublesome offenses, and are officially handled in a more lenient fashion than one would find in the courts of a large metropolitan center." [47]

The Lane County youth may be more leniently handled, but before one can generalize—and Polk does not—that juvenile courts in metropolitan areas are harsher, well controlled research is necessary. It is likely that there are variations in dispositions among the juvenile courts in the less populous counties, as there are variations in sentences from one criminal court to another. It is my opinion, based on the reading of some cases and discussions with knowledgeable people in Iowa, that in at least some Iowan counties the dispositions of juvenile cases may be harsher for the same offense than in Wayne County (Detroit, Michigan) juvenile court, or in the Lane County Juvenile Department.

The large cities differ in degree from one another with respect to various aspects of delinquency. No other city in the United States, for example, can equal New York City in the matter of fighting gangs. Rural and hinterland areas also differ in degree from one another as well as from urban areas. A good example is the commission of offenses against the person which in general are equal or nearly equal in rates in rural and urban regions. Some rural areas seem to have a lower rate of such offenses. It will be recalled that Vermont delinquents used only their fists when they fought. The records of the Lane County Juvenile Department reveal that the committing (and reporting) of dangerous offenses of bodily harm are "virtually nonexistent in this hinterland community, and the incidence of burglary and auto theft is lower than in large metropolitan areas." [48]

In brief summary it can be said that rural, hinterland, and urban delinquency and delinquents are the same kinds of socio-cultural phenomena, that the concepts of differential association and differential social organization are validly applicable to all three, and that there are quantitative differences between them. In short, they are essentially the same, and their differences from each other are thus of degree and not of kind. I shall try to show in the following pages that this proposition also applies to the white-collar thief, often known as an embezzler, and to the supposedly compulsive criminal.

5. Differential Association and the "Atypical" Offender

The White-Collar Thief

The development and the use of vocabularies of motives are by no means confined to some juveniles learning to be delinquent and some others learning to be lawful. The same process characterizes both the criminal and the lawful adult, and may be observed with particular clarity in the adult offender commonly known as the "embezzler." Before analyzing the sociological research dealing with this type of offender, we shall find it useful, by way of comparison, to see him through the perspective of a recent popular study, *The Thief in the White Collar*, by Jaspan and Black.[1] According to the claim made on the dust-jacket of the book, Jaspan is one of the foremost management consultants in the United States, president of Norman Jaspan Associates, management engineers, and of its "fact-finding" division, Investigations, Inc. His firm's clients include many large and small manufacturing, service, and retail establishments; and his firm operates throughout Canada and the United States. With hardly more than one exception the cases in the book were drawn from the files of his firm. It may be that the book was written for business firms and the potential embezzlers whom they employ. Jaspan does establish one thing beyond question, to judge from his interpretation of his firm's experience; embezzlement has become endemic in American business. White-collar employees, both rank-and-file, and supervisory and executive, steal about four million dollars from their employers every working day. More than one billion dollars was stolen in 1960. The United States Department of Justice's *Uniform Crime Reports* shows that in 1960 American police departments reported that burglars, pickpockets, robbers, and automobile thieves stole only 570 million dollars worth. Jaspan estimated that as of today employees of banks have embezzled between ten million to twenty-five million dollars still to be discovered. Such estimates are statistically worthless because they cannot be checked.

When I first began to read *The Thief in the White Collar*, I decided merely to sample it here and there, because it seemed, at first glance, to be only another hastily—which is to say, badly —written book. I had not read very far in it, however, before it became fascinating. As a result of his company's experience in finding that such things as embezzlement, the theft of goods, kickbacks, and cheating on expense-accounts are so common as to have become an integral part of the culture of business, Jaspan has a message for employers. Even though never explicitly stated, it is perhaps the more forcefully communicated for being implicit. The message is: pay your employees adequately or your niggardliness will cause them to embezzle; treat them decently and ascertain their personal problems or your indifference and ignorance may cause them to embezzle; always distrust both them and the security personnel whom you hire to check on them; conduct your own personal and unannounced checks on your security personnel. Mr. Jaspan never asks or considers the question, Who will check on the honesty of the employers?

This book may serve an end never intended by its authors. By their sympathetic interpretation of the embezzler they may help to perpetuate the vocabulary of motives employed by such people since time out of mind. Their conception of *cause* constitutes, in my judgment, a vocabulary of motives for the committing of embezzlement! It seems to me, for example, that in the first pages of the book Jaspan provides a white-collar formulation of two often-repeated motives used by delinquents, and also by adults who commit serious crimes. He asserts not only that "everyone has larceny in his heart," or that "everyone has his own racket," but also (p. 12) that "most people will try to cheat on their income tax if they think they can get away with it." He presents no supporting evidence. Perhaps he had his own clients in mind. We read (p. 101) that a Mrs. Burton was possessed by an "irrational hunger" for "conspicuous consumption," the "same senseless desire that we all have."

In addition to learning that crooks and honest people all have the same senseless desires and motives, the man or woman contemplating embezzlement may take heart when reading of "the fact" that "chance and luck are responsible for the detection of most white collar thieves." [2] An interesting project would be a comparative study of vocabularies of motives according to social class and education. It will be recalled that delinquents make use of *irresponsibility* and *a higher loyalty*. They present themselves as being subjects moved around by agencies beyond their control, such as the slum, a broken home, a drunken mother or a worthless father; or they might claim, "I did it for a friend." Jaspan presents these two motives to the embezzler in a more elegant and esthetic form. "The Honest Crooks" of his fifth chapter "have in common the fact that circumstances over which they had no control forced them to commit their dishonest acts." We should understand "the forces that drive" the white-collar thief. [3] Continuing the discussion with reference to the white-collar accomplice in crime, who also is an "honest crook," Jaspan notes that "there is often a mitigating circumstance, for the individual he is protecting usually is a close relative, friend or loved one."

The creation of a role that the potential embezzler can enact frees him of responsibility, supplying further motivation for his offense. In this instance the role is that of a sick person and— as everyone knows—the sick person is not responsible for his sickness. Thus we are informed that a thief by the name of Jean "couldn't help herself. She was a kleptomaniac." [4] If Jaspan were familiar with the psychiatric literature he would know that the diagnosis of kleptomania depends at least as much on what goes on in the head of the psychiatrist as on what goes into the pocket of the thief. White-collar crime, we are told, is a disease; perhaps "it may be possible to detect the first symptoms of the disease, and perhaps, in many instances even prevent the original infection." [5] The medical metaphor is misleading, even if it does help a man to talk himself into being a thief. Jaspan seems to take it literally. We are informed (p. 154) that "horses, cards and dice have become the largest single causative factor in white collar crime." On the next page we find that "gambling is a disease, the causes of this bacillus are numerous. . . . The bacillus of this disease, of course, feasts on a ready supply of cash." Jaspan even quotes from a bank teller in grammar typical of a third-grade street-corner boy, "It got like a disease." That quotation, of course, presents the embezzling bank teller as the passive subject of an active agent that he could not control. Six pages later gambling has grown so large that "it is a national disease." "The Insecure Executive" (the title of Chapter 7) will be interested in the motivation supplied to John Russell Cooney: "The cause of his thefts was the promise of a salary raise that was fulfilled too late."

It seems to me that Jaspan and Black understand neither Sutherland's conception of white-collar crime nor Cressey's analysis of the violation of financial trust. Sutherland studied white-collar crime as perpetrated by businessmen in the conduct of their *business* and not of their *personal* affairs. Jaspan makes no reference to this conception and type of white-collar crime. Perhaps the reason is that the United States Department of Justice may investigate Jaspan's employers (that is, his firm's clients), whereas Jaspan investigates their employees.[6]

Cressey's book, *Other People's Money*, is a study in the criminal violation of financial trust. Where Cressey's book is scientific and analytical, Jaspan and Black's is sympathetic and moralistic, and may contribute to the criminal's vocabulary of motives.*

Cressey's research on the criminal violation of financial trust is of great significance for both a general theory of criminality and for a general theory of human, or sociocultural, behavior. The theory of differential association has been attacked on sev-

---

* The comments on Jaspan's book are concerned with the validity of its analysis. While they indicate that the book may provide motivation to potential embezzlers, that is not relevant to its evaluation. The logico-empirical validity of a theory, and the actual or potential uses made of that theory, are two quite different things. The scientific evaluation of a theory can, as a matter of course, be concerned only with validity, and not with possible misuse.

eral grounds. One of the criticisms is that some types of criminals are exceptions to it. Two of the supposed exceptions are (1) persons such as embezzlers, with no previous criminal record and no known past or present criminal friends and (2) murderers, nonprofessional shoplifters, and persons who commit crimes of passion under emotional stress.[7] These two classes do not, in my opinion, constitute exceptions to the social-psychological and sociological analysis of human conduct. One great merit of that analysis is that it makes possible the bringing within the purview of a single theory the widest range of sociocultural behavior. It renders unnecessary the postulation or invention of pathologies in order to explain morally disapproved behavior. It cannot, however, account for cases of strict liability and negligence which, Jerome Hall has suggested, should be excluded from the rules of criminal law.

The legal category "embezzlement" does not, Cressey found, refer to a homogeneous class of criminal behavior, because of variations in the definitions of legal terms from one state to another. He developed the concept "criminal violation of financial trust" to refer to a homogeneous class. Two criteria must be met in order for a given case to be included. First, a person must have accepted a position of financial trust in good faith. This criterion is practically identical with the legal definition that the "felonious intent" in embezzlement must be formulated *after* taking the position. Second, the person must have violated that trust by committing a crime.[8] The central problem of Cressey's research was to ascertain whether a definite sequence or concurrence of events is always present when the criminal violation of trust occurs and never present when that violation is absent, and the correlated problem, to explain genetically the presence or absence of those events. Cressey formulated the following hypothesis, which he subsequently tested and confirmed:

> Trusted persons become trust violators when they conceive of themselves as having a financial problem which is nonshareable, are aware that this problem can be secretly resolved by violation of the position of financial trust, and are able to apply to their own conduct in that situation verbalizations which enable them to adjust their conceptions of themselves as trusted persons with

their conception of themselves as users of the entrusted funds or property.[9]

The nonshareable financial problem was so defined by the violator. Another person might not have defined it thus. A, for example, could lose a considerable amount of money at the race track daily; but the loss, even if it constituted a personal problem for him, would not be defined by him as being a nonshareable problem. For B, however, the financial problem created by his loss would be defined as nonshareable. He would thus find it impossible to discuss the problem with his wife, best friend, or employer. People may have nonshareable problems of a nonfinancial character, for example, whether or not to obtain a divorce. Such nonfinancial, nonshareable problems are usually not solvable by obtaining more money either legitimately or through the violation of financial trust. Thus not all trusted persons who have nonshareable problems become trust violators; but according to the present research and theory, all criminal violators of financial trust have what *they* define as nonshareable financial problems. All of the situations involved in producing nonshareable financial problems were concerned with either status-seeking or status-maintaining activities. Since, however, status-seeking or -maintaining seems to be universal, engaging in these activities does not differentiate the trust-violators from non-violators.[10]

In addition to defining a financial problem as nonshareable the violator of trust must identify his position and knowledge *to himself* as providing the means of solving it. He must also apply certain motives to his own conduct that will allow him to use this means. The identification of the opportunity for trust violation and the development of motivation occur together.[11] The realization by the violator that he can solve his problem criminally is indicated by his use of such phrases as "it occurred to me," or "it dawned on me," that the entrusted funds or property could be used personally. Trusted persons know that positions of trust can be criminally violated, even when they have no nonshareable financial problem, and so do most other adults. I have already referred to a small part of the literature dealing with fraud and embezzlement in particular and white-collar crime in general.[12] In many cases of trust violation, the people trained to discharge the routine duties of a position have at the same time been trained in the skills necessary for the violation of trust. The technical skill necessary to the violation is the same technical skill necessary to hold the position in the first place. When violators perpetrate their criminal violations, they do not depart from ordinary occupational routines in which they are skilled. Thus, "Accountants use checks which they have been entrusted to dispose of, sales clerks withhold receipts, bankers manipulate seldom-used accounts or withhold deposits, real estate men use deposits entrusted to them, and so on." As an example Cressey quotes from an accountant who "never even thought of stealing" the money that passed across his desk outside of normal routine. "It was a matter of routine with me; I simply followed out the routine I had every day." [13]

If a person in a position of financial trust defines his financial problem as being nonshareable, realizes that he can solve it illegally, and at the same time applies to his own conduct verbalizations enabling him to adjust his conception of himself as a trusted person with his conception of himself as a user of the entrusted funds, he will violate that trust. When these three components are in conjuncture, the criminal violation of trust will occur; when any one of them is absent there will be no such violation.

This hypothesis makes use of the social-psychological theory of motivation mentioned briefly in the discussion of the development of a vocabulary of motives by delinquent boys and boys who are becoming delinquent. The process through which the criminal violator of financial trust develops and uses motives is basically the same process through which the boys proceed. The adult violator uses a language enabling him to conceive of the violation of trust as being essentially noncriminal and also as either justified or as irresponsible behavior over which he can exert no control. Cressey uses the term "rationalization" to refer to this use of language by the violator. As we indicated previously, this use of the term emphasizes that the behavior in question is deliberate and purposive and in part results from the way in which the actor conceives of himself in relation to others. The rationalization is the actor's motivation, as we said before, and this applies to the criminal violator. His motive is a linguistic construct organizing his behavior in a particular situation. The use of the motive makes his behavior intelligible to himself. Its use may or may not make his behavior understandable to others, depending on whether they accept or reject his vocabulary of motives. If they accept his rationalization they will define his behavior as "understandable," even if they disapprove of or condemn it, and even if they may think him "stupid," or "not very smart." If others reject the criminal violator's rationalization, they will define his behavior as "unintelligible," or "senseless," or "impulsive," or "unmotivated."

Significant rationalizations were always present *before* the criminal violation of financial trust in all the cases in the study now being discussed. It was often found that the rationalization was abandoned after the violation was discovered. The trusted person can violate his trusted position because he is able to rationalize. The use of these rationalizations in trust violation is not separable from their sources. Just as the delinquent boys were able to draw upon the cultural store of motives, the trust violators "discovered" or "rediscovered" the cultural store of motivations sanctioning trust violation and applied them to their own conduct. The trust violators thus came into effective contact with cultural patterns of thought and action. Association with other criminals was unnecessary, and, as Cressey has said, could not be demonstrated. He has suggested the following definitions of situations calling for the violation of financial trust, and thus amounting to justifications for the crime: "Some of our most respectable citizens got their start in life by using other people's money temporarily." He quotes from Alexander Dumas' *The Money Question,* "What is business? That's easy. It's other people's money, of course." "In the real estate business there is nothing wrong about using deposits before the deal is closed." "All people steal when they are in a difficult position."

The trust violator gives a personal touch to the above rationalizations: "My intent is only to use this money temporarily so I am 'borrowing,' not 'stealing' "; "My immediate use of real estate deposits is 'ordinary business' "; "I have been trying to live an honest life but I have had nothing but troubles so 'to Hell with it.' " [14] In applying motives such as these to his behavior, the violator of financial trust may have some comfort in the knowledge that reactions by others to "borrowing" in order to solve a nonshareable problem are very different from their reactions to "stealing." Thus, like the delinquent drawing upon the rationalizations of his peers and the larger community, and like the business executives in the electrical industry conspiracy mentioned above, the trust violator can observe himself as being "all right" because the rationalizations upon which he has drawn sanction and support him in his actions.

(The criminal violator of financial trust is a man who almost by definition has had no criminal record, no known criminal friends and associates, and who for a greater or lesser number of years has been well established as a respectable member of his community. And still he becomes a criminal. As I have tried to indicate above, this does not constitute an exception to the theory of differential association. The violator of trust is involved in the sociocultural process from the beginning to the end of his crime. Starting with his having learned his occupation socioculturally, he has encountered a financial problem. By linguistic means—a conversation confined wholly to himself—he has defined his problem as being nonshareable. He cannot even discuss it with his wife! The definition of his problem is based upon his system of values, and upon his conception of himself in relation to others who are significant to him—"What *will* they think of me?"—and his values and self-conception are purely sociocultural.)

Through the continued private use of language he informs himself that he knows how to solve his problem. By the same means he draws upon cultural resources in the form of motives applicable in his situation, finds a vocabulary of adjustment, and criminally violates his position of financial trust. Through his private conversation he has "conned" or talked or verbally manipulated himself into a situation in which he can perpetrate his crime.

(Physical contact with others already criminal is therefore not always necessary to the development of criminality in a given individual. It seems, however, that effective contact with appropriate sociocultural sources and processes, in the form of patterns of thought and action, is always necessary. This type of offender's criminality is learned socioculturally, in the process of symbolic communication, including his self-conversations.)

It will have been noticed that the criminal violator of financial trust and the career delinquent have one thing in common: Their criminality is learned in the process of symbolic communication, dependent upon cultural sources for patterns of thought and action, and for systems of values and vocabularies of motives. The criminality and the life-history of the two types of offenders is, however, quite different. The delinquent who engages in delinquency as a financial means is most likely to be a more completely developed criminal than the trust violator. A boy who is reared in an area with a high rate of delinquency might have a well developed pattern of criminality, Sutherland and Cressey say, "by age twelve or fourteen." Some might object that twelve years is a bit too young, and it could be that one should set the years at twelve to sixteen, or fourteen to sixteen. But whatever the range of years, the significant fact is that by about twelve to about sixteen years such a boy is criminally developed in the sense that criminal conceptions of law, person, and property have been accepted by him as values upon which to act.

Such a boy is deliberate in committing his crimes: he plans how to perpetrate them, plots possible escape routes, and soon learns to consider securing immunity if caught. If his precautions are inadequate—as they often are—his apprehension and subsequent possible detention and commitment to a juvenile correctional institution do not constitute crises for him. He does not like detection or detention but he can accept them as part of his life, an occupational hazard, so to speak, "just as a newsboy who has made what provision he could against the rain takes the rain as a part of his life." He may, and in fact often does, gain in prestige among his peers if he is committed to a correctional institution. In addition, the career delinquent of sixteen years of age is likely to have had about five to six years, and it seems in many cases as much as about eight years, of active and intensive experience with other delinquents. If the boy is on the way to becoming an adult burglar or robber, there is considerable evidence to show that his delinquency has had a typical development: from trivial to serious offenses, from a game to a livelihood, and from membership in a loosely organized boy's gang to a rather tightly organized gang of adolescents.[15] In those years he will have engaged in a wide range of offenses. Usually they begin with petty pilfering and truancy, and proceed to such offenses as shoplifting, purse-snatching, strong-arming, robbery, and burglary.

The career of the trust violator is quite different. First, as we said before, he is most likely not to have had a previous record, even though typically he is middle-aged when detected. Second, his education, occupation, residence, friends, and leisure-time activities usually set him in a social class higher than that of the delinquent. Third, even though his crime is deliberate and he attempts to avoid detection, he fails to plan for the securing of immunity if caught. Fourth, even though he may be three or four times as old as the career delinquent, his arrest constitutes a serious crisis for him that he cannot take in his stride. His arrest and conviction, and the attendant publicity, are a disgrace to him. He loses status even though some segment of the community may sympathize with him without condoning what he did. The trust violator is therefore typically not as fully developed a criminal as a sixteen-year-old delinquent is likely to be.

The career delinquent and the criminal violator of financial trust are like and unlike each other in ways significant to our further discussion. They are similar in that both are dependent upon and make use of culturally supplied vocabularies of motives. They are different in that the delinquent makes use of a more systematized and widely held vocabulary of motives openly and explicitly discussed and accepted by his peers. At least one important motive—the denial of responsibility—is also widely accepted by persons in positions of legal authority who use that motive to explain the delinquency of the boy. Furthermore, the conception of cause and effect that marks mechanistic theories imparts to this motive the respectability and persuasive power of science. The delinquent has a relative psychical advantage in that his motivation is constantly validated by other, significant people. Knowledge that he is conforming to acceptable motives helps him to justify his delinquency to himself. Policemen, reporters, parents, and newspapers confirm the delinquent's motive when, in a case involving adolescent offenders from the middle class and upper class, a parent says, "I don't understand why he stole;

my boy had everything he needed." [16] Those boys have no motive
that is acceptable to respectable society; hence, their delinquency
is described as "having no cause," or as "senseless," or as "unmotivated."

Because the delinquent is conforming to an acceptable and
independently validated motive he does not have to contend
with his conscience very much. This state of affairs is one reason
why he is sometimes described as "displaying no remorse." Another and perhaps major reason is that "displaying no remorse"
is an interpretation made by an examiner. The criminal violator
of financial trust, in contrast, does not find such a constant validation in his personal experience. He has only himself and the impersonal cultural source of his motivation. The sanction for his
behavior is not systematized and not as widely accepted as the
delinquent's. The trust violator is therefore not as emancipated
from his conscience. When apprehended he may experience great
shame and guilt through rejecting his previous criminal rationalization, and agreeing with respectable society that what he did
was criminal.

The Compulsive Criminal

The relative lack of support and sanction from others, and the
accompanying shame and guilt of the violator of financial trust
are important in understanding another type of offender, the so-
called compulsive criminal. (Compulsive criminals include those
classified as pyromaniacs and kleptomaniacs, those who commit
"crimes of passion," and the murderer who "just blew his top.")
The compulsive criminal also makes use of unsystematized cultural motivations that are learned in a more or less prolonged,
private self-conversation, the assumptions and conclusions of
which are not evaluated in conversation with other people. Since
he does not talk to others about his being a compulsive criminal,
there is no way for him to validate, modify, or reject the assumptions and conclusions that he applies to himself; and he continues to play the role of "compulsive criminal" or "compulsive
person," perhaps even while despairing of himself for being one.
Many people who will accept a scientific analysis of behavioral

patterns—both of thought and action—as being developmental will refuse to accept a rational analysis of what they consider to be compulsive behavior. They may accept the above analysis of the juvenile delinquent, and may consider it as perhaps holding true for the criminal violator of financial trust; but they will reject it when applied to the kleptomaniac and the murderer. "These behaviors," some of my friends have told me, "are irrational and pathological, and scientific explanations do not and cannot apply to them." Others have said, "When it comes to kleptomania and murder it is necessary to call in the doctor—the psychiatrist." That conclusion, I suggest, is incorrect. The remainder of this chapter will develop the thesis—although by no means completely—that the behavior of compulsive criminals is validly subject to social-psychological and sociological analysis.

Those who insist on an explanation in terms of some pathology may cite a particularly horrible murder as an example of their position. There are murders that are horrible and repugnant, and their occurrences, infrequent as they are, demonstrate that differences between theories of human behavior may be of the greatest practical importance. They are not merely interesting but insignificant differences of opinion between professors. A recent example of such a murder in Detroit will illustrate this point. A twenty-one-year-old man murdered a woman who was a stranger to him. He had stopped at her home to see her daughter, who was not there. She allowed him to enter and to telephone her daughter, with whom he talked briefly. As he was leaving, she said something to him about not going to walk to the door with him. He thereupon struck her in the face, attempted to strangle her, seized her sewing scissors, and stabbed her forty-three times in the head and body, pulled her sweater over her shoulders, removed her slacks, and then left the house. He is quoted as saying, "in an emotionless monotone," to the police:

> "I just blew my top. I punched her four or five times in the mouth and knocked her down. . . . Then I grabbed a pair of scissors and started stabbing.
> "I went into the bathroom and washed my hands. I don't remember anything else that happened." [17]

One cannot say that social-psychological analysis can as yet answer all questions concerning compulsive crime. It seems to me that there are two reasons why it is necessary to attempt to analyze the so-called compulsive criminal as having proceeded, through the process of symbolic communication, to develop a motivation that enables him to act as he does. The first reason is scientific and theoretical, with practical implications. That reason is the tendency of science to attempt constantly to bring within the scope of a single theory all known instances of the same class of phenomenon. Cressey must have had this reason in mind when he wrote that the theory of differential association "describes the processes by which one becomes a 'compulsive criminal' as well as it describes the processes by which one becomes a 'non-compulsive' criminal. 'Compulsive criminality, as traditionally described, is not of such a nature that it is necessarily an exception to the differential association theory." [18] I agree completely. "Compulsive behavior," as traditionally described, is here classified as "sociocultural" and "symbolic" behavior, and therefore validly to be subjected to social-psychological analysis. The claim that it is biological or instinctual behavior, or that it is a response to biological or instinctual stimuli is rejected. All psychology is either biological or social, and the psychology of human behavior is social. [19]

The second reason for a social-psychological analysis of the compulsive criminal is expedient and practical, and has theoretical implications. If the social-psychological explanation of criminality is not given—and repeated and repeated—there will be no logical or theoretical ground on which to halt the drive of psychiatry for the complete elimination of the concept of responsibility. That drive is already powerful in some countries, especially, it seems to me, in the United States. Lady Wootton's statement on this matter is in my opinion correct:

> once we allow any movement away from a rigid intellectual test of responsibility on McNaghten lines, our feet are set upon a slippery slope which offers no real resting-place short of the total abandonment of the whole concept of responsibility. All the intermediate positions . . . have shown themselves to be logically quite insecure. Already in many countries, amongst which England must now be included, the first steps down this slope have been taken; and the possibility cannot be dismissed that the relaxation

of definitions of responsibility which is already in progress is the beginning of a process which, in the remoter future, is destined to result in the total destruction of the concept itself.[20]

An *argumentum ad hominem* may be advanced to explain, at least in part, why some people will accept a rational explanation for many types of crime—and lawful behavior as well—but insist upon an explanation in terms of pathology for "compulsive" crimes. Some crimes, particularly some murders, are so savage, horrible, and repugnant that a person reading only a partial description finds it impossible to imagine himself in the role of that murderer. In discussing with some of my colleagues the murder of a woman by a man who was a stranger to her, I was told the following. "I just cannot understand it. If he had just strangled her, that would be one thing. But he stabbed her 43 times. Why? There must be something wrong with him." Another said, "Look at how many times he stabbed her. That's senseless. He's a maniac. He must be crazy." Another said that it is possible to understand how Eichmann, as a member of the Nazi hierarchy, could "go along" with the collective decision and organize the murder of millions of people. "That was an organizational matter; he issued his orders from a desk physically remote from the gas chambers and he couldn't hear the pleadings of the children," I was told, "but the murder of that woman was an individual matter. Eichmann was taking orders and giving orders but this man just acted on his own impulses. How could he stab her so many times? Maybe his expression 'I blew my top,' is just a naïve way of saying what happened inside him. It just isn't reasonable."

Those comments were made by people who, by virtue of professional training and extensive personal experience, have a sophisticated view of human behavior, and who are not given to classifying behavior as "senseless" just because it is different or bizarre. But, in common with humane people generally, they could not conceive of a situation in which they could be so brutal and savage, and therefore they concluded that the social-psychological concepts of motivation, role-taking, and role-playing, and identification were not applicable.

The suggested explanation as to why some sociologists and many others refuse to apply their own theories to "compulsive" crimes is, I have admitted, *argumentum ad hominem*. Even so, it is intended as an impersonal statement calling attention to the values that respect the dignity of the individual and that hold human life in great esteem, and is by no means intended to be derogatory. I further suggest that those—including the professionally trained—who insist on a pathological explanation have had a life experience significantly different, at least as far as interpersonal relations are concerned, from that of the supposedly compulsive criminal who "blows his top" and then murders. That probable difference in life experience can be stated in the following hypothesis.

Such a murderer will be found (a) to have engaged previously in physical violence in interpersonal relations, including the beating of women; or (b) to have had such violence as a major part of his fantasy-life; or (c) most probably to have engaged in both actual and fantasied violence. Negatively speaking, such a person is not controlled in his behavior by the moral injunction against the use of violence in interpersonal relations. Positively speaking, he has learned violent patterns of thought and action.

The testing of the hypothesis would require, among other things, an empirical investigation of each seemingly "unmotivated," "senseless," or "explosive" homicide, including those that have "no incentive at all," or that seem to result from "trivial" incidents. Homicides resulting from psychosis would of course be excluded. The homicidal psychotic, it is generally agreed, may exhibit reasoning of a high order. The reasoning will be based on premises that can be demonstrated to him to be false; nevertheless, he will be able to advance reasons for the homicide that he committed. Such *a psychotic will not advance the rational plea,* "I blew my top." He will, on the contrary, claim preventive self-defense, or that the victim "had it coming," or some other, comparable circumstances.

Discussing the hypothesis, Michael Hakeem includes the comment that:

The hypothesis that murders of this type are explainable as normal behavior and in the terms of social psychology, has not even been investigated in those terms. The people most competent to investigate it have failed to conduct research on it. They have excluded it from any consideration of theirs by yielding to psychiatric theory. They have in effect said, "We don't even have to investigate it. It has already been answered by the doctors."

If such murders lie in the bailiwick of medicine, which medical specialty should be called on? They cannot be psychiatrists because psychiatry is the only medical specialty that does not have a part of the body with which to deal. Neurologists? Have they adduced empirical evidence that connects such behavior with neurological lesions of dysfunction?

If it is "disease" it is an amazing disease. It ends with the one symptom, in this instance, killing the woman. What other symptoms are there? Conversing with a mother who has been dead for twenty years, mistaking a broomstick for a rifle, eating excrement, or not knowing what a policeman is? Even a pimple on the skin has more symptoms than does this sickness which is said to be so devastating and total that the person kills another human being against his will.

Let us assume that the young man who killed a woman with a pair of scissors were placed with a group of non-killers. Could the expert on this kind of sickness identify him, and select him from among the others *without knowing what he was accused of having done?* [21]

Psychiatrists may well agree that the hypothesis is correct. Zilboorg says that:

> Except for totally deteriorated, drooling, hopeless psychotics of long standing, and congenital idiots—who seldom commit or have the opportunity to commit murder—the great majority and perhaps all murderers know what they are doing, the nature and quality of their act, and the consequences thereof, and they are therefore "legally sane" regardless of the opinions of any psychiatrist. [22]

But mere agreement, however personally pleasant it may be, is scientifically inadequate. What is needed is empirical testing. There is an extensive body of empirical data that make it reasonable to entertain the hypothesis seriously. Guttmacher states that some psychiatrists are loath to accept the conclusion that a large proportion of criminals, particularly recidivists, are psychiatrically normal. When one argues the point, they say, "But surely, nearly all murderers must be sick individuals." It seems to Guttmacher, however, that

> in dealing with these questions, consideration should be given to

statistics on the racial incidence of crime. For example, in 1957, the homicide rate for Negroes compared to whites in Baltimore was eleven times their incidence in the population. I know of no study, however, indicating a greatly higher psychiatric morbidity rate for Negroes than for whites.[23]

Guttmacher is correct in directing attention to differences in rates between the races, in studying murder in the United States. It is not in itself sufficient; social class and sex must also be considered, as well as social organization and culture.[24]

Wolfgang made a complex study of patterns in criminal homicide in Philadelphia from January 1, 1948, through December 31, 1952. Criminal homicide includes murder, voluntary (nonnegligent) and involuntary (negligent) manslaughter. There were 588 such homicides for which 621 persons were taken into custody. Although criminal homicides are for the most part not the result of prolonged planning, research nevertheless discloses regularities and patterns. Negroes and males involved in homicide far exceed their proportions in the general population. Rates for these two categories are many times greater than for whites and females. The rate per 100,000 by race and sex of offenders reveals the following rank order: Negro males (41.7), Negro females (9.3), white males (3.4) and white females (0.4).[25] The association between race and homicide is statistically more significant than that between sex and homicide, although Negroes of either sex, and males of either race, are positively associated with criminal homicide. This is in conformity with the findings of other studies conducted in the United States.

A recent study of criminal homicide in Cuyahoga County (Greater Cleveland, Ohio), from January 1, 1947, through December 31, 1953 found differences in the rates for Negroes and whites similar to those in Philadelphia. The "most conspicuous fact" of the distribution of criminal homicide is its geographic and racial concentration. Of 462 persons formally charged during the above period, 76.4 per cent were Negroes; the remainder were white. About three-fourths of the criminal homicides occurred in about 10 per cent of the county's population and in about 0.6 per cent of its area.[26] Furthermore, this concentration correlates with the residential distribution of social class. One must take care, in interpreting the significance of these rates, not to attribute to *race* what should properly be attributed to *class.* Many years ago, for example, Goring showed that among the English, "Crimes of violence to the person . . . are committed mainly by the lower classes."[27]

The age period 20–24 predominates among offenders, with a rate of 12.6 per 100,000; the median age is 21.9 years. The importance of race in respect to age is "striking," Wolfgang says,

> in view of the fact that the *lowest* 5-year age-specific rates for Negro males and females are similar to or higher than the *highest* of such rates for white males and females, respectively. Although males of both races more frequently commit criminal homicide during their twenties than during any other period of life, Negro males in their early sixties kill as frequently as do white males in their early twenties.[28]

A few of the reasons for rejecting biological explanations of crime were discussed in connection with the three propositions elucidated in Chapters 2 and 3. We need not, therefore, indicate now why a biological or hereditary difference between Negroes and whites is inadmissible as an explanation of the differences in rates. Wolfgang properly sought for the explanation in the variant conditions of social existence.[29] Despite recent changes in the residential distribution of urban Negroes and whites, Negroes generally are still subject to residential restrictions that contain them largely in the older, physically deteriorated neighborhoods marked by poor housing, high density of population and overcrowding in the home. Judge Leibowitz' dramatic description of the slums in New York City may be recalled here. There is considerable evidence for the conclusion that "many central cities of the great metropolitan areas of the United States are fast becoming lower class, largely Negro slums." Wolf has concluded that "there is no evidence that racial segregation in private housing has declined."[30]

Regardless of how depressing and difficult to endure the physical conditions of existence may be, they are not directly relevant to an understanding of behavior and differences in the distribution of behavioral phenomena in the several sections of the social structure. What is directly relevant is the social organization and subculture of social class, with its accompanying system of values, which has already been discussed to a certain degree. The overwhelming majority of Negroes are members of the lower class. Some estimate that in certain metropolitan areas the proportion is as much as 95 per cent. Miller estimates that in the United States "in 1940, about 80 per cent of all Negroes were culturally lower class in contrast to about 40 per cent of whites." [31] This situation contributes to the widespread fallacy of attributing to *race* certain behavioral patterns (crime, illegitimacy) which in fact are attributable to *class*. A significant component of lower-class culture is

> a system of values that often condones violence and physical aggression from child-rearing processes to adult interpersonal relationships that sometimes end in criminal slayings. To a lesser degree, whites in the lower socioeconomic classes as well as Negroes become part of this *subculture of violence* and participate in criminal homicide. [32]

The absence or presence of a previous police record, the number of times arrested and the type of crime charged in the arrest are of direct relevance to our hypothesis concerning the murderer. Of the 621 offenders involved in homicides in the five-year period in Philadelphia, almost two-thirds had a previous record. Of the 588 victims, almost one-half had a previous record. Proportionately more *male victims* have a previous record than have *female offenders*. A male offender with a previous record is more likely to have a record of offenses against the person. With a record of offenses against the person he is more likely to have a record of a serious assault, such as aggravated assault or assault with intent to kill. Wolfgang's statistics show that *"a larger proportion of* [criminal homicide] *offenders with an arrest record have a record of aggravated assault than of all types of property offenses combined.* [33]

The data of this study suggest a conflict between the dominant middle-class values and the lower-class values of the subculture of violence. Miller has specified six focal concerns of lower-class culture: trouble, toughness, excitement, smartness, fate, and autonomy. The first three necessarily involve lower-class persons of both sexes in interpersonal physical violence. [34] Wolfgang hypothesizes that the more complete the integration of the individual into his subculture the greater the likelihood that his behavior will often be violent. Miller's work confirms the hypothesis, as do also some of the other works mentioned in this chapter. It thus appears that "there is a direct relationship between rates of homicide and the degree of integration of the subculture of violence to which the individual belongs." Wolfgang has observed that:

> . . . the significance of a jostle, a slightly derogatory remark, or the appearance of a weapon in the hands of an adversary are stimuli differentially perceived and interpreted by Negroes and whites, males and females. Social expectations of response in particular types of social interaction result in differential "definitions of the situation." A male is usually expected to defend the name and honor of his mother, the virtue of womanhood . . . and to accept no derogation about his race (even from a member of his own race), his age, or his masculinity. Quick resort to physical combat as a measure of daring, courage, or defense of status appears to be a cultural expression, especially for lower socioeconomic class males of both races. When such a culture norm response is elicited from an individual engaged in social interplay with others who harbor the same response mechanism, physical assaults, altercations, and violent domestic quarrels that result in homicide are likely to be common. The upper-middle and upper social class value system defines and codifies behavioral norms into legal rules that often transcend subcultural mores, and considers many of the social and personal stimuli that evoke a combative reaction in the lower classes as "trivial." Thus, there exists a cultural antipathy between many folk rationalizations of the lower class, and of males of both races, on the one hand, and the middle-class legal norms under which they live, on the other.[35]

What is "trivial" is of course a matter of judgment, and in arriving at such judgments we hardly ever list for ourselves the criteria that we employ. Although we could, if necessary, specify some criteria for deciding whether an event is "trivial" or "serious," we most often, it seems to us, "just know," and do not recognize the cultural-class basis of our judgment. "It just stands to reason," we say, "that a bottle of beer is no reason for one man to kill another," when we read of an incident like the following:

D was sitting on the bed in his room. V, D's friend of many

years, entered the room and headed for the refrigerator. D said: "Where are you going?" V replied: "I'm going to get me a beer out of your refrigerator." D retorted: "Nobody gets no beer out of my ice box unless I tells him to," whereupon V whirled, pulled out a knife, and said: "The Hell with you and your ice box, too." D reached under the mattress, pulled out a pistol, and shot V three times, killing him instantly. D admitted having had "a couple beers." Test of V's blood revealed he had been drinking, but was not intoxicated.[36]

It is perhaps the failure to recognize the cultural component of our judgment as to what is "obvious" to us that leads a professionally trained observer—as well as many other reasonable people—to conclude that "many of the most brutal homicides seem to be without incentive of any kind." [37] Whether or not an observer will conclude that behavior he has witnessed in another is "without incentive of any kind," and made in response to a circumstance that is "trivial" or of "great magnitude," will depend on *how the observer and not the subject* defines "trivial," and also upon what incentives he will accept as being operative. Judge Jackson, for example, has observed that in Cuyahoga County (Greater Cleveland),

> Aside from those homicides which were in conjunction with another felony, such as robbery, rape, burglary, etc., our own observation in the courts is that the circumstances igniting homicides in the majority of cases are trivial. Such things as anger over nonpayment of a loan of small amounts [sic], even as low as fifty cents, jealousy, arguments while under the influence of intoxicating beverages, minor disputes of an inconsequential character in which tempers flare, predominate.[38]

Judge Jackson's comments are almost a tailor-made illustration of an upper-class interpretation of lower-class life in terms of the value system of an upper-class observer. He further obliges us by furnishing examples in the next paragraph of upper-class moralisms concerning lower-class life:

> These [homicides] suggest a certain amount of immaturity—the kind that results from a low economic status and very little education—a minimum of self discipline. Along with this is a very noticeable lack of profitable use of leisure time. Many of the homicides occur in or near drinking or gambling establishments

and other non-uplifting or non-cultural places. Other homicides are found where persons are cooped up in overcrowded housing.[39]

How comforting to be able to believe that all the things approved by one's moral code are psychologically and sociologically sound, and that all those that are disapproved by it are psychologically and sociologically unsound.[40] It is significant that many of the students of crime and delinquency who are aware of the existence of culture and social organization, and who appreciate their influence on the behavior of the individual, have on the whole little trouble in avoiding such moralisms. If one wants to understand a phenomenon scientifically, it is necessary to study it in its own terms. Crime and delinquency are sociocultural phenomena, forms of behavior that result from the routine functioning of the normal sociocultural processes. They must therefore be studied in sociocultural terms, and methodologically conceived as existing in their own right. They are not ethical, moral, or religious phenomena. Indeed, as long as lower-class forms of social organization, such as the family and the adolescent street-corner group, are conceived to be deviant or pathological forms of the middle-class family and the Boy Scout troop, preventive efforts based on that conception are doomed to failure in advance. As long as crime and delinquency are conceived to be immoral manifestations of middle- and upper-class moral values, they will be misunderstood and programs based on that conception that are designed to "prevent and rehabilitate" will be doomed to failure in advance.

There are other indications of the validity of the concept, *subculture of violence.* Those categories of people who in Philadelphia had the highest rate of criminal homicide were the ones who also had the highest rates of forcible rape, aggravated assault, and recidivism. Short's excellent discussion of the aleatory factor in delinquency is relevant here. In his study of adolescent gangs in the South Side of Chicago, he uses the concept "aleatory" factor to refer to situations which, in particular behavioral episodes, contribute to involvement in delinquency, but which, in and of themselves, are independent of delinquency.[41] Such behavioral settings seem to be found disproportionately in the lower class. The following are illustrative:

1. The high incidence of guns to be found among lower-class adults is a part of many behavior settings and guns become at times behavior objects as well. Guns often are "borrowed" by the boys, and we have recorded instances in which parents have enjoined their children to "keep the gun handy" when they [the parents] are not at home, or to bring the gun along for protection when meeting at a bus stop a parent who is returning from work or shopping.

2. The "milling" character of life on the street is a characteristic of many lower class communities. Indeed, a great deal of lower class life takes place in the street and in other semi-public settings.

3. "Toughness" has been commented on as a "focal concern" within lower class culture. Physical violence is a means of settling disputes in the "normal" interaction of lower class males, particularly.

4. There is a high consumption of alcohol in public—on the street, at "quarter parties" particularly among adolescents, and in taverns and pool halls—especially within the lower class.

5. The tendency to distrust all "outsiders" beyond one's own intimate associates, to exploit each situation to one's personal advantage and to assume that others are similarly motivated has been found to be widespread among persons at the bottom of the social and economic ladder in a variety of cultures.[42]

Short illustrates something of the manner in which these aleatory components of behavioral settings may be conducive to physical violence in interpersonal relationships:

> Elements such as these combine often to enhance the prospects of a high incidence of delinquency within lower class communities. Thus, the "milling" character of life on the street and the use of violence as a means of settling disputes combine to produce a higher exposure of lower class youngsters to the possibility of becoming involved in such disputes. Add to this the higher incidence of carrying guns in lower class culture and the possibility of more dangerous situations becomes clear. . . . The numerous "accidental" shootings and deaths attendant upon bar-room brawls may be cited as examples of some of these.[43]

Miller, Short, Wolfgang, and others thus find that ready access to weapons may be thought by one person to be essential for protection against others in his milieu who act in a similarly violent manner. In a situation where each expects this of the other, the carrying of a knife, gun or other weapon becomes a collective symbol of one's expectation of violence and one's willingness to engage in it. Wolfgang finds a parallel in front-line combat during warfare, when a situation of "it-was-either-him-or-me" arises. There are similar conceptions and reactions among participants in homicide, he found in his study of offenders. The situation is not unlike that of combat, in which "two persons committed to the value of violence come together, and in which chance often dictates" who will be the slayer and who the slain.[44]

Some of the data on justifiable homicide constitute additional confirmation of the reasonableness of my hypothesis. At common law, justifiable homicide is an intentional killing either commanded or authorized by law. It includes the killing of an enemy during war, the execution of a legal sentence of death, an unavoidable killing in arresting a felon or in preventing his escape, and a killing necessitated in lawful self-defense in which the killer was placed in imminent peril of death or of great bodily harm. The following discussion will be concerned only with justifiable homicide committed by police officers. It will also be confined to the 1950's. One reason for this limitation is the changing pattern of the killings committed by police. The overall pattern for the United States since about 1940 is that of a declining rate.

The reasons for the lesser number of killings by the police are not relevant to the present discussion. Some figures, however, may be of interest. For the period 1952 through 1955 justifiable police homicide comprised 3.2 per cent of all homicides, not including accidental and negligent homicides. In 1920, they comprised 26.6 per cent of the homicides in Detroit and 31.5 per cent of those in Chicago. The violence of that civil war has greatly abated.

Robin's analysis of justifiable police homicide tends to confirm our hypothesis. He analyzed the figures for Philadelphia and nine other cities for the period, 1950–60. His study shows that the concept of violence must be extended to the victim-offenders who were killed by police in the discharge of their duties. The study shows the same general pattern with respect to social class, race, age, and sex that is revealed in the analysis of criminal homicide. There were 32 justifiable homicides in Philadelphia in the eleven-year period. One of the victims was a machinist, one a shoe repair man, and the other 30 were unskilled. Although their average age was 27.6 years, 16 were less than 24 years of age. None was a woman.

Most of the victim-offenders had an official record of violence. Of the offenses presumably committed that resulted in their death, 24 were of Class I: 5 burglaries, 9 robberies, 7 larcenies, 2 assaults with intent to kill, and 1 aggravated assault and battery. Of the others, 3 were disorderly conduct, 4 were violations concerning concealed weapons, and one man was merely being questioned. Seven of the men fled, and 25 resisted arrest; 19 of the latter committed aggravated assault on the officer. Twenty-four of the victim-offenders had a previous police record, with an average of 4.9 charges, and an average of 2.1 Part I charges. Twenty-two had served at least one prison term, and had a previous record of violence.[45]

In the years 1950, 1955, 1956, and 1957, there was a total of 963 justifiable homicides reported in the United States. There were almost no female victims: 959 were men. Seven-eighths were Negro. There were 350 justifiable police homicides reported in the period, 1950–60, in ten selected cities.[46] Although data on social class and previous criminal record are unavailable except for Philadelphia, the pattern as to race, age, and sex is as given previously. Of the 269 decedents for whom race was given, 61.7 per cent were Negro. None of the 350 was a woman. One-half were 20 to 25 years of age, and about 8 per cent were more than 45. There was a large variation between the cities. Chicago accounted for about 55 per cent of the killings, and had the second highest rate of justifiable homicide. The resort city of Miami had the highest annual rate (7.06 decedents per 1,000,000 inhabitants). Its rate was about twenty times that of Boston (0.4).

It seems reasonable to infer that the pattern of justifiable homicide in Philadelphia can be generalized. (In summary, then, one can infer that the *victims* of justifiable homicide are predominantly participants in the subculture of violence.)

The studies by Miller in Boston, by Short in Chicago, and by Wolfgang in Philadelphia are studies of members of one social class—urban lower class—dealing with one another. When two people of the same class who are committed to the value of violence encounter each other, each knows or believes that he knows what to expect. When only one of the two is committed to that value, the second party—say, a middle-class person—may not know what to expect. That is not relevant for the violent person, who brings his values with him, so to speak. It is thus that a trivial comment by the middle-class person may call forth a combative response on the part of the other, to whom quick resort to physical violence is a cultural and therefore normal expression.

One lower-class man can shoot and kill another lower-class man, a friend of years, and then say, "He shouldn't ought to have said that about my ice box." Or, a lower-class man can beat and brutally stab to death a woman who was a stranger to him, and then say, "She shouldn't ought to have said that." His subsequent plea, "I just blew my top"—which is an upper-class and professional motive, and therefore acceptable to an upper-class person such as a psychiatrist—should not be allowed to stand in the way of an investigation by the police. My hypothesis is, it will be recalled, that he will likely be found to have learned and practiced his violence more or less frequently before committing his present criminal homicide.

Many humane people, we suggested previously, believe that because a person has committed a particularly revolting act, say, cannibalism, he must be mentally ill. He must therefore, they continue, be held irresponsible and placed in a hospital for the insane. The repugnance one experiences at such an action, we also said, should not be allowed to stand in the way of an objective investigation even though the murderer or someone else claims that the killer is mentally diseased. Some years ago a man who had committed many cannibalisms in and around New York City was examined by psychiatrists. Some classified him as insane, some as sane; he was finally held to be sane and then executed.[47] Another cannibal from rural Wisconsin was also examined, intensively and extensively, by psychiatrists during the entire period of quarantine. Their diagnoses also were conflicting. They finally decided—on the basis of expediency, it seems, rather than of psychiatric diagnosis—that he was insane and therefore irresponsible. He was committed to the Wisconsin hospital for the criminally insane. When I visited that hospital in Waupun during the summer of 1960 I saw him in one of the open wards. Someone with some kind of sense of humor had given him an appropriate work assignment: he was waiting on table.

A more compelling example of the mental normality of a murderer is that of Adolf Eichmann. The evidence produced at the Nuremburg trials showed that the mass murders and cruelties committed by the Germans were not for the utilitarian purpose only of eliminating opposition to German rule, but were "part of a plan to get rid of whole native populations." That evidence was in the center of the trial of Eichmann in Jerusalem. Hannah Arendt concluded that the three judges of the Israeli court displayed conspicuous helplessness when confronted with the task of understanding the criminal that they had to judge. They refused to accept the prosecutor's obviously mistaken description of Eichmann as being "a perverted sadist." They also refused to accept the inconsistent case presented by the prosecutor. The latter wanted to try Eichmann as "the most abnormal monster the world had ever seen" and, at the same time, try in him "many like him," and even "the whole Nazi movement and anti-Semitism at large." First, if there are in fact, "many" Eichmanns and if Nazis and anti-Semites "in general" are also Eichmanns, then the Adolf Eichmann on trial in the dock at Jerusalem could not be abnormal, no matter how monstrous. Second, it could have been very comforting indeed to believe Eichmann to be an abnormal monster, even though Israel's case against him would have collapsed under this belief. One can hardly ask for the attention of the entire world and gather correspondents from all over the earth merely to display an abnormal and therefore irresponsible monster in a bullet-proof cage of glass. As Dr. Arendt says:

> The trouble with Eichmann was precisely that so many were like him, and that the many were neither perverted nor sadistic, that they were, and still are, terribly and terrifyingly normal. From the viewpoint of our legal institutions and of our moral standards of judgments, this normality was much more terrifying than all the atrocities put together, for it implied—as had been said at Nuremburg over and over again by the defendants and their counsels— that this new type of criminal, who is indeed *hostis generis humani*, commits his crimes under circumstances that make it

well-nigh impossible for him to know or to feel that he is doing wrong.[48]

The statement that the new criminal—the enemy of the human race—commits his crimes under conditions that make it almost impossible for him to know or to believe that he is doing wrong, fits 1963 as well as it does 1940. Sane people in the United States in 1960, in discussing the thermonuclear strategy known as "credible first strike capability," speak of sixty million Americans killed as an "acceptable price." Herman Kahn says that no American with whom he discussed the matter, and who was serious about it, "believed that any U. S. action, limited or unlimited, would be justified—no matter what our commitments were—if more than half of our population would be killed in retaliation." Credibility, in the context of thermonuclear strategy, "depends on being willing to accept the other side's retaliatory blow." It is important to know, Kahn says, "that a war in which the U. S. made the first strike would result in more favorable conditions for us than would the wars that are generally considered." [49]

The general staffs and heads of government of, at least, England, France, (Western) Germany, Russia, and the United States have planned for thermonuclear war. Perhaps one should add Canada, China, Israel, and the United Arab Republic to the list of countries whose governmental heads and chiefs of staff deliberate the use of thermonuclear aggression. The citizens of their respective countries on the whole think of them as being patriotic and as legitimately engaged in protective planning for national and international security. They are not regarded as criminally insane.

The previous discussion has several times referred to the great differences in the rates of violent crimes between Negroes and whites in the United States. Savitz has asked the question, Should any study touching on the sensitive area of minority groups and crime be undertaken at this time? His answer is an explicit "Yes," even though, as he remarks, some think that such research would have an adverse effect on the present state of "racial" relations. Perhaps such objectors fear that the conclusions would contradict their humanitarian beliefs. But one whose intellectual convictions are scientifically grounded need have no such fear. He would be able to show that racial variations in the rates of crime and delinquency are explicable in terms of socio-cultural data, and not by biological data. To sociologists, at least, investigations of this matter are necessities, both to evaluate contemporary conclusions and theories, and to provide an empirical basis for their refinement. It can be said that science is on their side.[50]

Eames asked an even more basic question: Should there be any collection of criminal statistics according to race? He discussed a number of reasons why there should. (1) The data are necessary in order to continue research relating to the basic problem of causation. (2) The data can be used to test the hypothesis of a direct causal relationship between race and crime. (3) It would advance the investigation of the epidemiology of crime. (4) It could be used to test the hypothesis that there is discrimination in the procedures of handling offenders. (5) It could test the simplistic theories of Negro criminality; for example, that poverty is the basic cause of Negro criminality, or that status-frustration is its basic cause. (6) It could be used in estimating the future needs for correctional institutions.[51]

Some have been unwilling to accept the fact that one class of people may have a greater rate of arrests and convictions than another. Reid has said that any attempt to conceal or disguise the fact of differential rates is a serious indictment of a society that wants to eliminate legally punishable behavior.[52]

The examples of the one lower-class man who shot an old friend, and of the other who murdered a stranger, return us to the social-psychological conception of motivation. That conception, it will be recalled, refers to the process through which a person, as a participant in a group—or perhaps by himself as a result of engaging in reading or fantasy—defines a problematic situation as calling for the performance of a particular act. A motive is a construct that organizes actions in particular situations. The organization of that action, it should be explicitly stated, may be so rapid as to seem instantaneous, both to the actor and to a possible observer. The rapidity of an action does not by itself indicate the absence of cognition and reasoning.[53] The temporal aspect of any human act is in itself no ground for concluding that interpretation, inference, and reason were absent from the act.[54]

The individual classified or diagnosed as being a "compulsive criminal" or as having been forced to action by an "irresistible impulse" is playing a role. He is, specifically, playing the role of a compulsive person. He has defined himself as, or *he has identified himself to himself* as being compulsive or having a compulsion. He has learned from various sources that there are compulsive individuals who cannot control their behavior because of their compulsions. The existence of such persons has been postulated in medicine and psychiatry for several centuries. In recent years psychiatry has become strident in insisting that there are such people. Psychoanalytic psychiatry could not, in fact, exist without its basic postulate that everyone is possessed by unconscious impulses that are beyond his control. The former "PN" (psychoneurotic) discharge from the American military service has helped to increase the number of people who believe in the existence of this type of person. Other sources of the belief are of course such things as books, learned journals, and popular magazines, the radio, press, television, cinema, and personal conversation.

In short, the social role of compulsive criminal is firmly established culturally even though the actual or corporeal existence of such a person has never been established scientifically. The compulsive criminal of today can in important respects be compared with the Christian witch of the fifteenth through the seventeenth centuries. The witch had a broomstick to carry her lands away. The compulsive criminal has his irresistible impulse to carry his behavior beyond his control. The cultural existence of the witch was not the invention of the "best" people, the most highly educated of whom were the priests, but her perpetuation was insisted on by them. The compulsive criminal is not the invention of today's "best" people, namely the psychiatrists, but his perpetuation and an increase in his numbers is insisted on by them. To believe in witches became a test of one's religious faith and orthodoxy of thought, because to *dis*believe in them publicly led to one's being burned at the stake. To believe in compulsive criminals has today, among some people, become a test of one's mental health and correctness of thought, because to disbelieve in them publicly can lead to one's being classified as in need of psychiatric treatment, and as being immature or irrational, or as being backward, outmoded, medieval, and archaic.

Present knowledge does not supply us with all the variables influencing our commitment to our various identities and motives, but it does enable us to propose that the process involves symbolic learning. A crucial aspect of the entire process is the learning of the pronominal system. When a person is able to use the first, second, and third person pronouns so that he habitually refers to himself as "I" or "me" or "my," and to his possessions as "mine," he has become an object in his own experience, and has been able to distinguish between himself, other people, and all other objects. He has become self-conscious, and able to identify himself in the various roles that he plays.[5] In order to play a role he must observe himself on the basis of another person's presumed viewpoint. By indicating to himself the probable reactions of others to himself he observes himself as an object. This is the process through which he identifies himself to himself as being a particular kind of object, which, in personal terms, means that he defines himself as being a particular kind of person. He then performs the role appropriate to the kind of person that he has identified himself as being. The vocabulary of motives employed in the enactment of the role is part of this process of self-identification. One must learn to identify oneself differently in a variety of different situations, and to discharge the accompanying different roles, some of which may be in conflict with each other. One's statement to oneself of who and what one is determines the role that is played in a particular situation.

During the course of a day, for example, I can in different situations identify myself as a father, husband, voter, professor —or visiting lecturer. The motives employed in the discharge of each role will be appropriate to my different self-identifications. The "compulsive" criminal engages in the same process of self-identification, role-playing, and motivation. His motive and identification will be requisite to each other. A woman, for example, may in a certain situation—say, while shopping in a department store—identify herself as a kleptomaniac. A kleptomaniac, she knows, is a person who is seized by an uncontrollable impulse to steal. Since she knows (that is, has identified herself to herself) that she is a kleptomaniac, she knows that she cannot control her impulse to steal. Her rationalization is: "I am a kleptomaniac. A kleptomaniac is a person who has an irresistible impulse to steal. Therefore I cannot resist my impulse to steal." Her behavior in certain situations is organized by her identification of herself to herself by means of the concept "kleptomania." The kleptomania (shoplifting) may be engaged in again and again. A psychiatrist might describe this as "compulsive repetition." But as we suggested above, it is the *repetition* of behavior that makes possible the discernment of *patterns* of behavior. John Dewey showed long ago that habit is a dynamic demand upon the individual for a given kind of behavior in a given kind of situation. Repetition, therefore, reveals a symbolically learned habit, and not a compulsive or psychopathic state. Where is the individual who has not experienced the compelling influence of habit? I have suggested elsewhere that a request to distinguish logically between "compulsion" and "habit" may be embarrassing to a psychiatrist.[56]

The particular manner in which a person informs himself that he is "compulsive" is related to his subsequent behavior in at least two ways. First, he may decide—we do not know for what reasons this can happen—that the compulsive role and its appropriate rationalizations conflict with his identification of himself in another role—such as property owner, father, or responsible citizen. He most likely will deny in the latter role that he engaged in the first role, which has now become unacceptable. He may say, "I wasn't myself then, I was drunk," or, "I was sick when that happened." Sometimes one who has pleaded "compulsion" may later find that role so unacceptable that he will reject it completely. Second, his continued identification of himself as a compulsive criminal may reveal that he abhors himself in that role. The abhorrence may result in an anonymous plea for help. One example is a brilliant student of the University of Chicago who wrote on the mirror of the dressing-table of one of his victims, with her lipstick, "Stop me before I kill again."

The compulsion is conceived of as if it were an irreducible atom of behavior which, when a person has "it" "in" him, will

inexorably "come out," as one's fingernails "come out" regardless
of one's wishes. It is not only the individual who "has" a compulsion, and the general public who conceive that compulsion
to be an irreducible atom of behavior. The conception is firmly
established in psychiatry, which regards it variously as being a
basic drive or need, or an instinct; or as a derivative of a basic
drive or instinct. Since psychiatry does not conceive the "compulsion" to be sociocultural in origin, a psychiatrically oriented
individual is unlikely to recognize it as being a result of sociocultural experience.

A person who plays the role of a compulsive criminal, such as
a kleptomaniac cannot, as the career delinquent can, make use of
a systematized vocabulary of motives openly accepted by and
discussed with his peers. His conception of himself as "compulsive" therefore cannot be validated by the consensus of others.
His conception of himself is dependent upon his continued private
self-conversation and contact with the impersonal cultural sources
from which he obtained the conception in the first place. He
cannot have the comforting assurance that the delinquent has in
his delinquency, namely, that he is conforming to group norms.

It seems, however, that in recent years the compulsive person
is better off than he used to be, because the role of the compulsive—while still not respectable—is being advocated by some
of the most respectable people. I have already mentioned the
propagandistic character of some psychiatric publicity. The Group
for the Advancement of Psychiatry is in the forefront of this. It
is being advocated by the American Law Institute through its
proposed Model Penal Code. It is, in addition, espoused by some
judges and numerous attorneys. Lady Wootton stated it well
when she said:

> the range of intelligible motives is itself modified by new knowl-
> edge and new attitudes. Thanks to the popularity of psychiatric
> notions, the urge to steal for stealing's sake begins to find its place
> among the recognized, if not indeed the "normal" motives for
> theft; for the conception of the normal is itself defined by "lin-
> guistic constructs." With the invention of the term "kleptomania,"
> a sociological role is established for the previously "motiveless"
> thief. No longer compelled to plead that he "doesn't know what
> made him do it," he can now at least explain his own conduct. "I
> did it," he says, "because I am a kleptomaniac"; and, "I did it,"

says the poor man, "because I was hungry." The analogy is complete.[57]

It is my hypothesis that research will reveal that in the past decade in the United States the statement "I was drunk" has been superseded by "I just blew my top," "Something snapped in my head," "I just cracked up," "The tension was too great for me," "I broke down," "I blew up," and similar ungrammatical and misleading physical metaphors that are taken literally.

In the preceding discussion I have tried to show that "temporary insanity," the "irresistible impulse," and the "compulsive" acts of kleptomania and incendiarism, and the like, are motivated by the same social-psychological processes as other sociocultural actions. Employing the social-psychological meanings of the concepts *self, motivation, rationalization, role-playing* and *identification,* I have tried to show that supposedly compulsive crimes have a motivational and developmental history, that they involve and require the use of language, and that they therefore do not constitute exceptions to behavior that is deliberate. Temporary insanity, irresistible impulse, and compulsive act are therefore in this analysis not valid grounds for exculpation. They are not valid grounds for holding a person irresponsible.

It should be stated emphatically that this applies as much to the sexual offender as it does to the thief (kleptomaniac) and to the arsonist (pyromaniac). It makes no difference whether by law the sexual offender is classified as a "sexual psychopath" or "criminal sexual psychopath," or whether he is known by the newspaper terms, "sex maniac" and "sex fiend." Social psychology has shown long ago that for human beings there is no direct, immediate, or instinctive sexual need-reduction.[58] A sexual thought, a sexual feeling, or sexual relations depend on a process of rationalization in which a man concludes that a given "female" is a member of a certain category and tends *then* to react toward her both with the behavior appropriate to one of her class and his interpretation of the current situation. The rationalization, or process of reasoning, through which a man identifies a "female" as being of a given class, as well as his interpretation of the then current situation, precede whatever overt sexual gesture toward her that he may make.

For a man, therefore, a woman is not just any "female" whatever, but a child, a girl, or a woman; or a sweetheart, wife, sister, mother, or other relative; or a friend or stranger, toward whom he acts in accordance with certain pre-established patterns of behavior. A man, consequently, never immediately mounts the nearest female or female-like object, not even in the extreme case of the forcible rapist, because his behavior also is selective. Indeed, one should not say, "even in the case of the forcible rapist," but rather, *especially not* in the case of the forcible rapist, because his behavior is very highly selective. It is selective, first, in that he chooses a noncommercial heterosexual outlet rather than one of the other possible outlets. The others are prostitution, homosexuality, bestiality, and narcissism. His behavior is selective, second, in that he seeks a victim at a place and time such that he will likely not be caught, and plans to escape when finished. The fact that he most usually is caught in no way detracts from the selectivity of his act. Thus the forcible rapist, even if he is colloquially known as a "sex maniac," is like the accomplished sixteen-year-old delinquent in that both engage in deliberate behavior after a process of rationalization. The forcible rapist and the rape-murderer, as revolting as their crimes may be, are not to be held irresponsible merely because the revulsion that others experience might lead them to seek for a pathological explanation.

Earlier, I said that the conception of the compulsive criminal is well established culturally, but that his existence has not been established scientifically. It may well be that everyone who has at some time in his life succumbed to a desire to do something against his better judgment, will disagree with the statement as to the nonexistence of compulsive acts. The postulate of the irresistible impulse does not in any way refer to such common experiences. There seem to be genuinely compulsive acts, whose existence is attested to by clinical evidence,[59] and by the culture of childhood. Psychiatrists have shown that those genuinely compulsive acts are limited to such harmless and individual actions as excessive handwashing, counting windows, prolonged testing of a door to insure its being locked, always stepping up a curb or a flight of stairs with the left foot first—or perhaps the right, and avoiding stepping on cracks in the sidewalk. "Step on a crack and break your mother's back." One recalls the care with which Christopher Robin walked on the sidewalk:

> Whenever I walk in a London street,
> I'm ever so careful to watch my feet;
>   And I keep in the squares,
>   And the masses of bears,
> Who wait at the corners all ready to eat
> The sillies who tread on the lines of the street,
>   Go back to their lairs,
>   And I say to them, "Bears,
> Just look how I'm walking in all
>   of the squares." [60]

The legal issue of the concept of "irresistible impulse," Hall says, is the commission of serious harms. Wertham has stated in a vigorous and forthright manner his conclusion, as a psychiatrist, that there is no foundation for the concept of the irresistible impulse "in the facts of life or science:"

> There is with one exception no symptom in the whole field of psychopathology that would correspond to a really ungovernable or uncontrollable impulse. That exception is an obsessive-compulsive neurosis. . . . Yet compulsions play no part in criminal acts. . . . It can be stated definitely and flatly that compulsions are always unimportant and harmless acts. A patient may have to count the windows of a room of a building, he may have to wipe off the doorknobs with his handkerchief (for fear of germs), he may have to avoid stepping on the cracks of a pavement, he may have to leave the elevator on the twelfth floor and walk to the thirteenth; but he never has to commit a truly compulsive criminal act. . . .
>
> In the whole literature of psychoanalysis there is not a single case where a violent act, homicidal or suicidal, constituted a symptom in an obsessive-compulsive neurosis. It is therefore always bad psychopathology to speak of a compulsive murder or a compulsive suicide.
>
> The medico-legal theory of the irresistible impulse is advocated only by laymen and by psychiatrists who are scientifically not sufficiently oriented. It lends an air of scientific literalness and accuracy to a purely legal definition without any foundation in the facts of life or science.[61]

The practice of using unscientific criteria in classifying the compulsive criminal was established many years ago in psychi-

atry. I am referring to the work of Isaac Ray, the most prominent
and influential American psychiatrist of the nineteenth century.
His widely used book, *A Treatise on the Medical Jurisprudence
of Insanity,* was printed in its fifth edition in 1871, more than
ninety years ago. He wrote that the offenses to which a person
with an irresistible impulse "may be moved are murder, theft, or
incendiarism. Instances of an irresistible propensity to steal,
unaccompanied by any intellectual alienation, are related on good
authority and are by no means rare." He then cited cases in
which the diagnosis of "irresistible propensity to steal" was based
on the upper-class position of the female shoplifter and on pity
for a lowly female servant.[62] The only evidence cited for the
existence of the irresistible impulse was the act of thievery that
is itself to be explained by the hypothesis of the irresistible impulse. Ray stated explicitly that the diagnosis of shoplifting as
being kleptomania is indicated if the thief is a respectable, upper-
class person:

> Where the propensity to steal is manifested in a person whose
> moral character has previously been irreproachable, and whose
> social position and pecuniary means render indulgence in this vice
> peculiarly degrading and unnecessary, his plea of having com-
> mitted the larceny while deprived, in a measure, of his moral
> liberty, deserves to be respectfully considered. If the object stolen
> is of trifling value, or incapable of being turned to any purpose of
> use or ornament . . . there can scarcely be a doubt that the plea
> should be admitted.[63]

Ray showed that he was gallant as well as a gentleman by
adding another to the above criteria of exculpation and irresponsibility. He said, "especially if, in addition, the individual be a
woman in a state of pregnancy," her plea of an irresistible propensity to steal should be admitted. Isaac Ray would have been
quite at home in contemporary psychiatric diagnosis: he was by
no means the last student who mistook the beliefs and values
of his social class for scientific principles. Since delusions are
false beliefs regarding the self, can one properly suggest that
such investigators are suffering from delusions? They believe
themselves to be scientific in that they proclaim (and, sometimes,
"discover") and apply scientific criteria and principles, when in

fact they are repeating the values of their social class. Redlich's conclusion, that "many statements about health in the fields of psychiatry and organic medicine are value judgments," applies to the past as well as to the present.[64]

A crucial problem of the concept of irresistible impulse, perhaps *the* crucial problem, has both methodological and empirical aspects. It can be briefly stated: What empirical evidence is there, *other than the act in question,* for the existence of the postulated irresistible impulse? None of Ray's cases present any evidence other than the act itself. And, in common with most contemporary reporting of cases, it is difficult to decide where, in the recital, fact, interpretation, and speculation begin and end, so closely are they interwoven and incorporated.

Contemporary psychiatrists are no more able to solve this problem than Ray was. Some Canadian psychiatrists have found no irresistible impulse, according to their evidence given before a royal commission investigating criminal law in relation to the sexual psychopath:

> Dr. R. R. Prosser said in evidence before us that one cannot determine lack of power to control. Dr. R. L. Whitman [a psychiatrist of the University of British Columbia] said that he has never tried to distinguish between uncontrolled and uncontrollable impulse. Dr. J. N. Senn, Superintendent of the Ontario Hospital . . . said that he did not believe in uncontrollable impulses, he believed impulses were just uncontrolled.[65]

Chief Justice McRuer said, in a summary statement, "Psychiatrists find it difficult to distinguish between an uncontrollable and an uncontrolled impulse." [66]

The beliefs and values of the examining psychiatrist's social class continue even today to influence the classification of kleptomania. A poor person, Cressey has observed, might think that the act of stealing by a middle-class person, not being based on financial need, must be due to "greed" or "compulsion." A middle-class person might believe that of an upper-class individual whose income far exceeds his own. "If all psychiatrists were poverty-stricken the proportion of shoplifters called 'kleptomaniacs' probably would be much higher than it is." [67] An erroneous assumption in this conception of kleptomania is that all other thefts are financially based and to that extent can be rationally understood. Thus the economic status of the observer, today as in Ray's day, is significant in determining whether or not another individual is in "financial need" and, consequently, whether she is a thief or a kleptomaniac. It seems hardly fair to call a well-to-do thief a kleptomaniac just because she is well-to-do.

In his classic statement Issac Ray said that "if the object stolen is . . . incapable of being turned to any purpose of use or ornament . . . there can scarcely be a doubt that the plea" of irresistible impulse should be admitted. An example of the continued use of this unscientific criterion is found in Alexander and Staub. They did not classify as kleptomania the theft by a physician of medical books and instruments. They made a very fine distinction between his thefts, for he had also stolen porcelain figures. They said of the latter, "The theft of the porcelain figures which were new and actually of no value is more in the nature of a kleptomaniac act." [68]

Alexander has an interesting interpretation of the theft of a microscope. He says that "by way of displacement, the possession of a scientific instrument (the microscope) became charged with the affect of the infantile peeping lust, which is a special manifestation of one's incestuous drive." Since, according to psychoanalysis, everyone has—or had—an emotionalized "peeping lust" while a small child, one wonders whether it finds expression in various types of activities that require peering into things: the use of a microscope, telescope, or binoculars, or "peering" into the unknown as experimental scientists and explorers do, and as detectives and psychiatrists do.

The third edition of the *Psychiatric Dictionary* finds stealing to be sex-linked.[69] It cites Hugo Staub, who regards stealing as essentially a female problem. This conclusion is in keeping with the disregard of empirical evidence in the psychiatric literature dealing with kleptomania. *Uniform Crime Reports* for 1960 shows 359,612 men arrested on charges of robbery, burglary, larceny and automobile theft. It also shows only 41,333 women arrested for the same offenses.[70] Since, for every *one woman* arrested on these charges there are *nine men* arrested, the assertion of the editors of the *Psychiatric Dictionary* must be reversed:

stealing is essentially a male problem. It is methodologically interesting to note that that dictionary's definitional essays on kleptomania and pyromania cite no empirical works. There is reference to two speculative works of about fifty years ago.

In discussing the social-psychological theory of motivation, self-conception, and roles, we have depicted the individual's learning and mastery of those behaviors as being a positive achievement. It is through learning them that he is able to participate in the sociocultural systems of which they are attributes. Much of the individual's behavior—delinquency, in this instance—although always engaged in by him, is thus an attribute of sociocultural systems. Many students of crime and delinquency fail to consider this. Eleanor Glueck speaks of children as being "vulnerable to delinquency"—perhaps as Achilles' heel was vulnerable to an arrow?—and of the "common denominator" of the many types of delinquency as being "aggressive antisocial behavior." [71] But we have tried to show that this behavior is well established *socioculturally*. When the individual learns it, and engages in it, he is in a reciprocal relationship with his society, and contributes his mite to the perpetuation of that behavior. Cartwright has summarized this conception in his statement that behavioral characteristics such as aggression or cooperation *"are properties of groups and of the relationships between people."* [72]

One important implication of the social-psychological theory of human behavior should be indicated here. Sociocultural participation precludes the development of certain self-conceptions, just as it makes others possible. An example is provided in connection with homosexuality—which, when engaged in in the United States, Canada, and many other countries, by young adolescent boys is considered as delinquent and deviant in the extreme. Perhaps only the use of narcotics would be considered by most people to be more deviant. Reiss described the sexual relation between "delinquent peers" and "adult queers," and advanced a sociological explanation for its social organization.

> This transaction is one form of homosexual prostitution between a young male and an adult male fellator. The adult male client pays the delinquent boy prostitute a sum of money in order to be allowed to act as a fellator. The transaction is limited to fellation

and is one in which the boy develops no self-conception as a homo-sexual person or sexual deviator, although he perceives adult male clients as sexual deviators, "queers" or "gay boys." [73]

After analyzing the "Norms Governing the Transaction," Reiss shows that the norms of the adolescent gang that govern the peer-queer transaction also function to prevent boys in the peer-queer society from defining themselves as being homosexual:

> The prescriptions that the goal is money, that sexual gratification is not to be sought as an end in the relationship, that affective neutrality be maintained toward the fellator and that only mouth-genital fellation is permitted, all tend to insulate the boy from a homosexual self-definition. So long as he conforms to these expec-tations, *his "significant others" will not define him as homosexual;* and this is perhaps the most crucial factor in his own self-defini-tion. The peers define one as homosexual not on the basis of homo-sexual *behavior* as such, but on the basis of participation in the homosexual *role,* the "queer" role. The reaction of the larger society, in defining the *behavior* as homosexual is unimportant in their own self-definition. What is important to them is the reactions of their peers to violation of peer group norms which define roles in the peer-queer transaction. [74]

Reiss's study is a cogent confirmation of the theory that motives, self-conceptions, and roles are attributes of sociocultural systems and of relationships between people.

6. Reason and Responsibility: the Social Movement of Mental Health

The Respectability of Irrationalism

A development of the past sixty years or so, of considerable importance to the country as a whole and to the law and sociology in particular, is the according of a constantly increasing respectability to irrationalism. It is especially the highly educated and the intellectual who in the past few decades have achieved an enormous increase in the kinds of behavior classified as irrational. A corollary is a decrease in the kinds of behavior classified as rational. This development has been accompanied by violent attacks on the concept of reason and by attempts to eliminate the concept of culpability and to replace it with the concept of exculpation. The latter have been successful to an undetermined degree. They have recently been described by a former president of the American Psychological Association as "our retreat from reason":

> Modern psychology . . . has shattered this picture of man [as a rational being] by calling attention to the power of unconscious and irrational forces in him, so that his claims to rationality are superficial and his intellect is in reality at the service of blind impulses, inherited from the past or instilled in earliest childhood.[1]

Kingsley Davis showed, in 1938, that mental hygiene is a social movement rather than a scientific development.[2] Barbara Wootton has shown that mental health in England, so far from being scientific, is just as much a social movement in that country as it is elsewhere. When the loquacity, emotionality, moralism, and verbiage has been "laboriously sifted" from the literature of mental hygiene, one can discern the recurrence of certain themes: "Mental health tends to be equated with happiness, preferably of a 'higher' order, with vigour, with the full use of capabilities, with integration in the sense of freedom from conflict within oneself, and with harmonious adjustment to the environment." [3]

More than twenty years after Davis' study, the mental health movement was continuing to propagate middle-class ethics under the guise of science.[4] This conclusion is based on a content analysis of publications issued by several national life insurance companies, several corporations, the New York State Department of Mental Hygiene, the Public Affairs Committee, Inc., and the National Association for Mental Health. The prototype of the mentally healthy person and the prototype of the middle-class person are shown to be in many respects equivalent to each other. It is hence not to be wondered at that when psychiatrists and other clinicians interview and otherwise "examine" lower-class children, especially delinquent boys, they conclude that the boys are "emotionally disturbed" or "mentally disturbed" in some form and to some degree.

Professor John Seeley, of Ycrk University, has recently shown the mental health movement to be in many respects the functional equivalent of religion in the system of traditional middle-class values.[5]

The sphere of the rational has been drastically reduced in sociology also. The area from which reason has been evicted is classified as *nonrational* by a former president of the American Sociological Association.[6] Davis' work is an example of what is sometimes referred to in sociology as "action theory." He presents his analysis of what he calls "the problem of rationality" as being scientific, objective and amoral. A study of his writing on the topics of rationality and religion reveals, however, something quite different. In common with some other functionalists and action theorists, Davis has a moralistic, technological, and upper-class approach to the problem of rationality. The rational, to him, consists only of the selection of the most efficient and knowledgeable (unignorant) means, free of normative restrictions, to an empirical and sharply defined or unhazy end.[7]

Davis' position lays a heavy burden indeed upon rationality, because his discussion shows that he conceives the rational to be also the errorless! Normative restrictions on conduct, according to his position, are another constant source of the nonrational because they limit the number of ends from among which one may choose. Society is inherently and necessarily the cause of this nonrationality, Davis says, since its continued existence requires obedience to a system of rules of conduct. Thus, if murder is the most efficient means to a legitimate end (money, for example), and if one refrains from it because to murder would violate one's conscience, one is nonrational.[8]

Many people will undoubtedly discern in these two examples of alleged nonrationality—the absence of error and the observance of morality and the law—a very unusual meaning of rationality on Davis' part. Surely most people would agree that, (1) to entertain the thought of murder (or of force or fraud) as a means to a legitimate end; and then (2) to reject it as a possible means just because it is wrong constitutes taking thought on the matter and reaching a decision on the basis of reasoning. And reaching a decision in this manner, most people would also undoubtedly agree, is an example of the rational. If a man deliberately chooses to conduct himself according to some norm rather than doing what he personally would prefer, he is rational even if he does not particularly care for the consequences.

The supposed efficiency of a means is, indeed, totally irrelevant to the problem of ascertaining the presence or absence of reason. In relation to the problem of rationality, as Davis formulates it, the concern with the greater or greatest degree of efficiency is a function of social class, or of ideology, but not of science. The position represented by Davis is that of a mid-twentieth-century, upper-class, professionally educated individual. The president of a trade union who is involved in negotiating a contract with management, and who has to contend with certain problems resulting from automation, could well have a different conception of efficiency.[9]

The positions represented by Davis in his analysis of the mental health movement and of the problem of rationality illustrate the difficulty that the sociologist—or any scientist, for that matter—has in being continuously objective in his work. Davis demonstrated the social-class origin and chauvinism of the mental health movement, but failed to observe them in the approach of action theory to the problem of rationality.

(Action theory confines rationality to the relation of means to ends; and conduct that cannot be fitted into the "means-end" scheme is not rational. "Rational thought," Davis writes, "refers to the application of means to ends; it cannot determine the ends themselves." [10] He has, of course, the semantic right to define rationality in the way he does, just as another person has the right to specify one result of that definition. To restrict the scope of the rational to such small quarters is to perform an act of conceptual surgery that excises the greatest part of rationality from human conduct and society.) It is comparable to defining an iceberg as consisting only of that portion of its ice that protrudes above the sea. It decreases the sphere of rationality by truncating all that does not fit into the particular means-end scheme of action theory. It has been shown that the process of observation has an inherently cognitive component. But that rationality is denied when it is restricted to the application of means to ends.

That viewpoint is at least as old as Aristotle's *Ethics* (VI, ii). "Intellect itself," he wrote, "sets nothing moving." The arguments advanced in support of this view are much the same today, according to Ginsberg, as when Aristotle stated them. They consist partly of definitions of reason or intelligence which from the beginning restrict its possible bearing on conduct; partly of the type of distinctions made between means and ends in the analysis of purposive conduct; and partly of a faculty psychology that assumes that cognition and orexis function independently of each other and that it is possible to ascertain just what each by itself does in human conduct. (Our subsequent discussion of the integrative and disjunctive theories of the self will consider briefly the position of faculty psychology in contemporary psychiatry.)

All theories that base motivation on instincts or unconscious impulses hold that reason is subordinate and secondary to these postulated instincts or unconscious impulses. One example will be sufficient to illustrate this. William McDougall was perhaps the most influential psychological proponent of the instinctivist doctrine during the first third of the twentieth century (Freud's conception of instinct was radically different from McDougall's). The prime movers of all human conduct, he wrote, are the instincts:

> directly or indirectly the instincts are the prime movers of all human activity; by the conative or impulsive force of some instinct (or of some habit derived from an instinct) every train of thought, however cold and passionless it may seem, is borne along towards its end, and every bodily activity is initiated and sustained. The instinctive impulses determine the ends of all activities and supply the driving power by which all mental activities are sustained; and all the complex intellectual apparatus of the most highly developed mind is but a means towards these ends. . . .

Writing a book is presumably a complex intellectual activity of a highly developed mind. McDougall never stated which instinct had the end of writing a book. But of course, if the writing of a book were merely a means—a means, say, to a reputation in one's profession—then the end would be that of the instinct of self-assertion. "The function of reason," McDougall asserted, "is merely to deduce new propositions from propositions already accepted." He asserted of reason that "To create a desire is beyond its competence; it can only direct pre-existing tendencies towards their appropriate objects." [11]

McDougall's statements concerning the instinctive basis of conduct were never sustained by biological (or in today's terms, genetic) evidence, but only by discursions. That is also true of contemporary psychiatry. From the publication of Freud's earliest writings to the present, no biological (genetic) evidence has been adduced to confirm the hypothesis that human conduct is instinctively determined. The evidence, rather, confirms the sociological conclusion that our conduct is sociocultural in character.

McDougall correctly referred to the social psychology propounded in this book as being an intellectualist doctrine. In rejecting that "doctrine" and in supporting his own, he wrote that "Unless . . . the [instinctivist doctrine] is the purely fanciful construction of a diseased brain [that] intellectualist doctrine is radically false." [12] Many people in the behavioral sciences thought that a number of McDougall's theories were unsound. But no one other than he, as far as I have been able to ascertain, ever suggested that his own theories were the "construction of a diseased brain." There has been no need of the concept of instinct as explanatory of human conduct since the publication of John Locke's *An Essay Concerning Human Understanding* in 1690.

In considering the distinction between means and ends, it is difficult to comprehend why action theory's view, which restricts reason or deliberation to means, has seemed self-evident to so many for so many decades. It can be granted that in daily activities one takes many ends as given and is concerned only to select the most efficient means to achieve them. Given agreed ends, it is often necessary to resort to the use of reason with respect to them. Members of a union, for example, must decide whether an increase in wages and other benefits are sufficient to warrant the sacrifices entailed by a strike. Or it may be necessary to choose between different ends. A young married couple, for example, may have to choose between having the number of children they want, which will entail living in an older house in a less desirable section, and having a lesser number of children, which makes possible living in a newer house in a more desirable section. College students have, in general, decided to seek a "better" job later rather than a "good" job now. Their decision is at least in part a result of their parents' decision to value education highly and to have their children engage in "constructive" leisure time activities. It may also be necessary to decide whether different ends are or are not compatible. Our later discussion of the juvenile court provides an example. There we ask if the freedom of the individual and the necessity for order in society can be reconciled, and answer in the affirmative.

We can surely reason on all these and similar matters and do so more or less systematically. As Morris Ginsberg has said, perhaps what is intended is not that we cannot reason about ends but rather that our reflections about them can never culminate in demonstration, and that our doubts with respect to them cannot be resolved by the same sort of inquiry that we undertake in deliberating about means. In this there is some truth, but it does not justify the assertion that ends fall entirely outside the scope of reason.[13]

As another example of the excision of rationality, one can cite Davis' claim that "Religious beliefs, however, are obviously non-rational," and that "religious ends represent a constant source of nonrational conduct." [14] In this way, action theory's solution of the problem of rationality effectively conceals the greatest part of reason in man's life. It has the result of continuously presenting a partial and distorted conception of man, culture, and society as being complete and accurate. Since Davis failed to list the criteria of the obvious, it is not possible to discern the "obviously" nonrational character of religious beliefs. Religion reveals to many people, including atheists, the consequences of reasoning; superstition is not lacking in reason merely because it reasons from false premises. The analysis of religion developed by the great anthropologist, E. B. Tylor, could not arrive at the conclusion that man is basically irrational or nonrational because, as that analysis showed, the process of the formation of custom is itself rational. Taking perhaps the extreme case, Tylor showed that the principles involved in the formation and development of superstition are fundamentally rational:

> Few who will give their minds to master the general principles of savage religion will ever again think it ridiculous, or the knowledge of it superfluous for the rest of mankind. Far from its beliefs and practices being a rubbish-heap of miscellaneous folly, they are consistent and logical in so high a degree as to begin, as soon as even roughly classified, to display the principles of their formation and development; and these principles prove to be essentially rational, though working in a mental condition of intense and inveterate ignorance.
>
> [We must] look dispassionately on myth as a natural and regular product of the human mind, acting on appropriate facts in a manner suited to the intellectual state of the people producing it.[15]

A Confusion of the Experts

The conceptual blinders worn by action theorists when examining the character and role of the rational "prevents them from taking an entirely clear view of their own milieu." [16] Sociological analysis, in contrast—as I tried to show previously—conceives rationality to be pervasive in human conduct, so that the individual human being can properly be described as self-conscious and rational in even the most routine of daily affairs, and to be an active agent in his own conduct. Anyone who follows that sociological analysis will find it impossible to engage in a practice quite common in psychiatry, clinical psychology, social work, and, I am sorry to say, sociology. I refer to the practice of accusing people of being irrational or nonrational only because their conduct is less efficient than we claim that ours would be in the same circumstance, even though we have been unable to agree on the definition of efficiency, and have no means of measuring its greater or lesser degree. Another form of the same practice is to accuse others of being irrational or of having a mental disease when they engage in conduct that we disapprove or do not understand, or when they commit some error in reasoning.

There are at least two reasons why it is in the interest of science that the practice should immediately be abandoned. First, there is no agreement as to what mental health and mental disease are. For a demonstration of the state of prolonged and utter confusion in the very definition of "mental health" and "mental disease" one can turn to the volumes published by the Joint Commission on Mental Illness and Health. The Joint Commission was established by action of the United States Congress in 1955, with an appropriation of $1,410,600. An additional $132,427 was obtained from private sources, making a total of $1,543,027. Its mandate was "to survey the resources and to make recommendations for combatting mental illness in the United States." The personnel of the Commission itself, its officers and staff, and also its advisory committees and consultants, included persons eminent in psychiatry, public health, education and the behavioral sciences. Ten extensive surveys were undertaken, of which six have been published to this date, including the last of the ten, which summarizes and interprets the previous books. One would think that, with all that money, time, qualified personnel, and ten books, the Commission would know what "mental illness" is, so that, under the terms of the Congressional mandate, it could be combatted. This is not the case.

The first of the ten volumes is devoted to the problem of defining mental health and mental illness.[17] One can only conclude, after reading the monograph, that whether a person is mentally healthy or mentally diseased does not depend on his own psychical state. It depends, rather, upon the respective social classes to which he and the examining psychiatrist belong, the psychiatric school of which the latter is a discipline, the values that he holds, and the system of morals that controls him. In fact, the advisory panel that worked with Professor Jahoda could not even agree with her as to whether we should be primarily concerned with mental health or mental disease.

The mental confusion of the experts revealed in Jahoda's work can be found in the other volumes as well. One example will have to be sufficient here. The Staff Director of the Joint Commission, Jack R. Ewalt, M.D., wrote, in his "Staff Review" of the fourth of the ten volumes, that *there is no general agreement among the experts on what constitutes mental health or mental illness;* mental health means many things to many people—to some, the absence of mental illness, itself often ill-defined." [18]

Barbara Wootton has shown that the English, no less than the Americans, literally do not know what they are talking about when they refer to mental illness, that a person would be in good mental health according to one conception, in disturbed mental health according to a second, and quite obviously seriously mentally ill according to a third.[19]

The second reason for discontinuing the *ad hominem* accusation that a person is irrational or mentally ill when we disapprove his behavior or do not understand it, can be stated briefly. Psychiatrists are divided on the crucial issue as to whether there can in fact be such an entity as mental disease. The suggestion made some years ago, that the term "mental disease" should be abandoned altogether, has periodically been repeated.[20]

Szasz has shown that modern psychiatry—the study of so-called mental diseases—began when, under the authority of Charcot, the "malingerer" was reclassified as "hysteric." Freud accepted this reclassification although he offered neither empirical evidence nor logical reasons for preferring the category "hysteria." Szasz concluded that this reclassification contains the major logical and procedural errors in the evolution of modern psychiatry. First, error lies in the socioethical elevation of the sufferer from the rank of malingerer to the rank of patient. This was not itself a neurological discovery nor the result of such a discovery. It was a humanitarian social reform, and can be compared with Pinel's liberation of the incarcerated from their chains, the removal of venereal infection from the list of disciplinary diseases among military personnel, and Dr. Guillotin's invention. Second, error lies in that the reclassification led to obscuring the similarities and differences between organic, neurological diseases and phenomena that only resemble them. The differences are in the empirical findings on physical, laboratory, and post-mortem examinations.[21]

Modern psychiatry deals with behavioral disorders, or, to use the concept that Szasz prefers, "problems in living." During the past nine decades vast numbers of occurrences have been re-classified as "mental illnesses." "We have thus come to regard phobias, delinquencies, divorce, homicide, addiction, and so on almost without limit as psychiatric illnesses. This is a colossal and costly mistake." [22] For one thing, it has undermined the principle of individual responsibility, upon which a democratic political system is necessarily based, by (a) assigning responsibility for undesirable or disapproved behavior to the "mental disease," and by (b) depriving the offender (patient) of his constitutional civil rights by reclassifying the crime as "mental disease" or "delin-quency" and substituting the decision of the psychiatrist for that of the jury. The politically reactionary consequences of modern psychiatry, which in some respects return us constitutionally almost to the Roman Catholic Inquisition, the Star Chamber, and the pre-French Revolution period, can be seen in the United States in the juvenile courts and to a lesser degree in the sexual-psychopath laws of the various states. This statement applies to a lesser degree to England, and to a markedly lesser degree to Canada. But there is good evidence that this trend is accelerating in Canada. The psychiatrization of behavioral problems can no longer be considered as liberal or progressive, as many psychi-atrists like to claim.[23]

Redlich also calls attention to the crucial question as to whether there can be *mental disease*: "The word 'health' is used loosely in everyday psychiatric practice and in the literature, and this looseness reflects our ignorance." [24] The critical but unsolved problem in the definition of mental health and mental illness is to develop criteria that are not social norms. Redlich believes that most psychiatric propositions about normal and abnormal behavior contain normative judgments:

> the question as to normal or abnormal usually turns out to be a question about good or bad. Some of the most quoted statements, such as the one by Menninger, are definitely value statements. . . . Many value statements in the field of mental health have been made by middle-class psychiatrists and were addressed to and understood by middle-class people only.[25]

Menninger's often quoted, value-laden, and saccharine definition of mental health is:

> the adjustment of human beings to the world and to each other with a maximum of effectiveness and happiness. Not just efficiency or just contentment—or the grace of obeying the rules of the game cheerfully. It is all of these together. It is the ability to maintain an even temper, an alert intelligence, socially considerate behavior, and a happy disposition. This, I think, is a healthy mind.[26]

The authors of the mid-Manhattan study of mental disease also mistook their upper-class conception of what a decent upper-class person is, for a scientific definition of mental health. They used Thomas A. C. Rennie's criteria:

> Independence of action, thought, and standards . . . freedom from undue anxiety, freedom from crippling inferiority and guilt feelings, from excessive egotism, and from competitiveness and unbridled hostility . . . concern for others, a respect for differing religions and ethics, and appreciation of one's own liabilities and assets . . . the assumption of adult responsibilities [including] the obligation to find and sustain a satisfying job, to recognize the need for play and rest, and to find satisfaction in one's role as an individual in relation to family, social, and civic life . . . the establishment and maintenance of a home . . . loving and giving to mate and children . . . a capacity to accept illness, disappointments, bereavements, even death and all that which is largely beyond our control [as well] as our own make-up and individuality, the perfection and imperfection of self and others, success and fail-

ure, sportsmanship, and the social comparisons which we call advice, criticism, and authority . . . a philosophy of objectivity about the past and a vision of creative opportunity for the present and the future . . . the capacity to create and participate in a consensus based on understanding others and on making one's self understood.[27]

That conception of mental health reads as if it were an inspirational talk given to a troop of upper-class Boy Scouts, or a Sunday school sermon, or an address to the luncheon meeting of the local Rotary Club. The authors of the work claimed that 81.5 per cent of their mid-Manhattan population was in measurable degree mentally ill; and that disproportionately more lower-class people were more mentally diseased than the middle and upper classes.[28]

Heinz Hartmann has protested against making synonyms of "social," "good," and "mentally healthy," on the one hand, and "antisocial," "bad," and "mentally ill," on the other. In discussing the history of psychoanalysis, he wrote, "I think we will agree that so far no concept of mental health which could be considered generally valid and definitive has emerged out of that great wealth of factual knowledge and theories." He then referred to

a trend in our civilization which makes an objective approach to this aspect of our problem more difficult than it had been before: the psychological differences between health valuations and, for example, moral valuations are radically discarded. One does not call people, or actions, "good" or "bad" or "social" or "antisocial," but indiscriminately "healthy" or "sick." The very interesting question of what are the empirical connections between what we actually call healthy and actually call good is disposed of by definition. This . . . is bound to create confusions in the evaluations of mental health. It promotes a greater arbitrariness in those valuations because it burdens the concept of mental health with a great many extraneous valuations, moral or even political.[29]

⟨The scientific study of human conduct and human society is difficult. One of the greatest pitfalls is that of mistaking one's own personal, social class, or national values for scientific principles.⟩ The preceding discussion has laid the basis for the following consideration of the conception of crime as being mental illness. Before doing so, however, I must make one point explicit. One might infer from my use of "mental illness" in the previous and following pages that I conceive it to be an entity, that is, a lesion of some type that can be discovered as a lesion in a physical disease can be discovered. I intend no such implication and, in fact, reject the medical analogy(Speaking in social-psychological terms, "mental illness" refers to a class of behavior, namely, to the kind of sociocultural behavior that, when judged according to middle- or upper-class values, results in the subject being classified as mentally ill) People engaging in such behavior have "problems in living," to use Szasz's expression.

That class of behavior does not include what the old-fashioned and now somewhat quaint psychiatric category listed as psychotic. An example is the man who claims that he is Napoleon and acts as if he does in fact think himself to be Napoleon. Even a member of the lower class would agree that such a man could be crazy (psychotic). But such people constitute only about one-tenth of one per cent of those whom psychiatrists now classify as mentally ill. The following discussion thus is not based on the assumption that mental disease is an entity such as some kind of lesion. It is based on the assumption that mental disease is sociocultural behavior that is classified according to certain unstated values used by the observer. It is necessary to use the term "mental disease" because the conception of its being an entity is discussed.[30]

7. Crime as Mental Illness

Psychiatrists and the Law

When crime is due to a mental disease, the individual, under Anglo-American law, is in a condition that exculpates him. Many students have asked the question, How far can certain theories of the origin of criminal behavior, both adult and juvenile, be applied without undermining the concept of responsibility? It should be clear, as they state, that general acceptance of the idea that no one is responsible for what he does would lead to chaos.

Responsibility for the promulgation and wide public acceptance of the notion of crime and delinquency as a mental disease must be assigned primarily to developments in psychiatry and the law during the past several decades. Social work and clinical psychology are responsible to a lesser degree. Some sociologists have accepted the notion in recent years; indeed, the most rapidly growing area of interest in sociology is called "medical sociology." As these several arts are applied in the juvenile court, and to a much lesser degree in the criminal court, one can discern their basic philosophy of man and human society.

That philosophy can be briefly stated. The model of man and society that it employs is a combination of the billiard table, the jungle and the mental patient. The individual is likened to a billiard ball that is knocked around the table by forces beyond its control. This is, of course, a familiar and highly respectable metaphor, and is by no means the exclusive property of psychiatry. As we have already seen, delinquents very soon learn to conceive of themselves in this manner. Whether they in fact believe it, or use it as a manipulative technique, or do both, is still moot⟨ Psychoanalytic psychiatry postulates instincts as man's motivating agencies, with the vicissitudes of one's instincts during the first six years of life largely determining what one will be and do. The individual is thus conceived as a basically irrational creature.⟩

It seems—if I may be permitted a parenthetical comment—that no Christian or Jew can believe in that psychiatry or in the social-casework philosophy of the juvenile court without accepting a set of beliefs in basic and irreconcilable conflict with his religion. One of the important trends in psychiatry today, at least in the United States, is the forming of close working relationships with the clergy. There can be no objection to this, and it seems to be based on members of both professions wanting to help those in distress. One wonders, however, how familiar the members of the clergy are with the conception of the human individual, family, and society revealed in some of the basic psychoanalytic literature, such as Freud's *Totem and Taboo* and *Moses and Monotheism*.

Freud never claimed to have discovered the fact that in some families the members love one another and that in other families the members hate each other. What he did claim to have discovered was his own version of the relations of love and hate between parents and children. He also advanced some reasons to explain why his postulated details of the family drama had remained unknown until he published them. Freud postulated that infants are born with two sets of instincts: (1) the death or hate instinct, and (2) the life or love instinct. The first, he wrote, is more powerful in determining one's conduct. In more detail, he wrote that the male child is born (1) unconsciously hating his father and wanting to kill and eat him; (2) unconsciously loving his mother sexually, desiring not merely maternal affection from her, but complete sexual intercourse, with her subsequently bearing his child, and desiring also to engage in sororal incest;

to which some of Freud's disciples have added (3) wanting not merely to nurse, but to suck his mother's breasts, to engorge them, to scoop them out, to consume them completely, and indeed, to eat his mother.[1]

Freud was not so specific concerning the instinctive equipment of the girl, although he did claim that she instinctively wished her mother to be dead, to have complete sexual relations with her father, and in due course to bear his child.[2] Freud discussed the little girl's "need to do away with the superfluous mother and to take her place" with the father. A little girl, he continued, "takes an older brother as a love-substitute for the father," whereas "A boy may take his sister as a love object in place of the faithless mother." Freud did not mean that the mother has been sexually faithless to her husband; her little son, according to Freud, regards her as being sexually faithless to *him*, her son, just because she does continue conjugal relations with her husband. In the psychoanalytic picture of the Oedipus complex the son's hatred of his father and his death-wishes against him become explicit, and "the affection for the mother declares itself with the intention of possessing her as a woman." All of us, Freud continued, "and not only neurotic persons" have as "the path of normal development" this "perverse, incestuous, and murderous" passage.[3]

When one thinks of a maiden being seduced the action is usually attributed to some man, either young or old. According to Freud's "The Psychology of Women," the love that a girl has for her mother turns to hate at about the age of six years when she realizes that the first person to have seduced her was her own mother.[4] It is also claimed that "in every normal marriage" two unconscious tendencies can be observed in the father. First, the husband endeavors to decrease his wife's affection for her son because of his unconscious recognition of its incestuous origin. Second, "in every satisfactory marriage," in addition to the husband's sexual love for his wife, "there exists . . . as well a homosexual tendency towards his son." Part of this homosexual tendency, it is alleged, was directed originally to the man's own father and only later was transferred to his own son.[5] One who reads Reik's work, in which this conception of family life is stated, will find no empirical evidence adduced in support of these contentions.

(Freud claimed further, and once again with no evidence, that the human infant has an instinctive and unconscious sense of guilt due to his alleged instinctive desires for patricide and maternal and sororatal incest. The guilt is said to plague one throughout one's life, and to be the basis of the general, pervasive, and endless anxiety that everyone is supposed to experience, and which can lead to neurosis.)

I suggest that this creature of the Freudian imagination has not in fact been encountered by anyone, and is totally foreign to human experience generally. Not all psychiatrists, by any means, subscribe completely to the above viewpoint, which is sometimes described as "orthodox Freudianism." I further suggest that some do adhere fully and that some others adhere largely; and still further that many accept the conception of instincts as being not a postulate but a biologically and behaviorally established fact. Since instincts are by definition hereditary, the individual is conceived as having his conduct determined by internal forces beyond his control. (I have said nothing in the past few pages concerning repression and the unconscious.) The sociological conception, by contrast, is that of a being who is basically rational because he is able to reach a decision through the use of reason, and who is therefore responsible.

The contemporary art of psychiatry is heavily indebted to Freud. One of his most significant contributions was to lay the basis for the theoretically indefinite expansion of its scope. When he was able to indicate phenomena in himself, in his friends, and in the more grossly disturbed, that were identical or highly similar, (he destroyed the wall between the normal and the abnormal.[6] Without intending to diminish Freud's importance to the social movement to equate "normal" and "abnormal," one should not give him too much credit for it) The belief that there is "only a thin line" between genius and madness is quite old, and is by no means confined to psychiatrists. The great neurologist, Sir Russell Brain, for instance, recently stated that a genius is not necessarily mad, and that he believes only a few of them are in fact mad.[7] John Dryden expressed this notion very well in *Absalom and Achitophel* (1681):

> Great wits are sure to madness near allied,
> And thin partitions do their bounds divide.

According to Redlich, psychiatrists who followed Freud's think-ing on this matter abandoned the island of psychiatric disease "and thus were engulfed in the boundless sea of human troubles rather than in problems of diagnosis and treatment only." [8] What is perhaps the most explicit statement that the concept *mental disorder* is broader in scope than the concept of other diseases has been made by Harry Stack Sullivan.

His theory of mental illness can be described as "inclusive," in the sense that it subsumes the boundless sea of human troubles. He defines mental disorder as disturbed or inadequate self-other relationships. Mental disorder, in his conception, ranges from forgetting the name of a person whom one is about to introduce, or, from whom one is about to request a favor, to being chronically psychotic. This conception means, of course, that in a country with the population of the United States there is a myriad of mentally disordered people.[9]

Perhaps the most inclusive as well as the most useless defini-tion for distinguishing between mental health and mental illness has been advanced by Hollingshead and Redlich. They are, respectively, a sociologist and a psychiatrist. For them, "mental illness is defined socially; that is, whatever a psychiatrist treats or is expected to treat must be viewed as mental illness." They state explicitly that "the conventional conceptual scheme of dis-ease is not applicable to mental disease." They then continue, and reveal one methodological reason why psychiatrists find such a disproportionately large number of mentally diseased in the lower class, and so few in the upper class. They state that the working rules of psychiatry are practiced in ways that are con-nected implicitly with class status. They regard a person's social-class status as being the independent or *antecedent* variable, and the diagnosis of his illness and the treatment prescribed for him by a psychiatrist, as being the dependent or *consequent* vari-ables.[10]

The position of the segment of contemporary psychiatry hold-ing crime and delinquency to be diseases can be summarily stated: the criminal is sick, not evil. A few examples of the many available from prominent psychiatrists will suffice. William Alanson White, one of America's most distinguished psychiatrists, conceived crime as being the result of unconscious determination. He conceived man as being a born criminal, and the unfolding of his life cycle necessitated the repression of his unconscious, evil desires that would be injurious to society. A crime, White wrote, is "conduct which for some reason or other has escaped the control of the individual or of society as stamped into the pattern of the Super-ego systems in the forms of beliefs, traditions, customs or what not."[11] Criminals are defined by White as those who,

> being of defective development or through illness or otherwise, have had their capacities for the more difficult requirements of the complex social group more or less impaired, and who consequently tend to lapse to these more primitive, simpler, direct ways of reacting, which, because they are to the disadvantage of society and tend to the disruption of the bonds that hold it together as a functioning unity, are regarded as criminal and as calling for punitive measures.[12]

Reaction formation, according to White, underlies the demand for punishment and retaliation. Most criminal conduct, he says, lies

> very close to the desires of the average person . . . and because they are easily stirred to action, and we have that within us which makes us feel . . . that we should not yield to them . . . we resent their activation. This activation means that we must bring to bear our efforts at controlling them very definitely and strenuously. This is an uncomfortable process and we resent the person who thus adds to or increases our discomfort. And so it is understandable how the average person will turn with hate against the person who, as it were, discovers the weak point in his armor.[13]

Abrahamsen asserted, without presenting confirming evidence, that criminals and delinquents, as well as most other people, were mentally disturbed and in need of psychiatric treatment: "In all my experience I have not been able to find one single offender who did not show some mental pathology. . . . The 'normal' offender is a myth."[14]

Alexander and Staub conceive crime as resulting from the combination of an austere conscience and an unresolved Oedipus complex. The criminal's severe conscience produces in him an unconscious sense of guilt. He holds himself guilty because of unconscious tendencies, never actually discharged, that go back to his early childhood "and which mostly emanate from his Oedipus complex." The criminal "ties his unconscious guilt" for his fratricidal and patricidal tendencies to a much less serious offense, for which he is punished, and the punishment relieves his guilt for his unconscious murderous tendencies. The authors then distinguish "neurotic" and "normal" criminals. In the next paragraph this distinction is discarded through the claim that "both conscious and unconscious motivations operate in *all* human beings." Through their repeated assertions that there are "unconscious motivations in all behavior," they succeed in presenting man in the image of the mental patient, an image that is reinforced through their repetition of the psychiatric claim that crime is a medical problem.[15]

Bromberg claimed that everyone is possessed by unconscious criminal impulses. He postulated "antisocial impulses which are completely buried slumber deep in the minds of everyone." We are restrained from acting on these impulses because of the "powerful forces within us—the conscience, and the equally powerful institutions within our social structure: morality, religion, law, and attitudes like that of 'common decency.'" The difficulty that the criminal faces is that "the forces of control have never been under his domination, either because unconscious impulses were too strong or his conscience [superego] was too weak. . . ." Bromberg concluded that the present system of legal punishment is marked by "unconscious prejudices of everyone toward lawbreakers."[16]

Benjamin Karpman postulated that "criminal behavior is an unconsciously conditioned psychic reaction over which [criminals] have no conscious control." He also advanced the argument that criminals are "in every respect" mentally sick and that it is "unreasonable" to punish them:

> We have to treat them as psychically sick people, which in every respect they are. It is no more reasonable to punish these individuals . . . than it is to punish an individual for breathing through his mouth because of enlarged adenoids, when a simple operation will do the trick.

Karpman recently started the publication of a journal devoted to what he called "psychiatric criminology." The purpose of the journal, he wrote, is to "fight for the recognition of the criminal as a very sick person, much sicker than either neurosis or psychosis [sic]." [17]

Karl A. Menninger is also of the opinion that criminals are not really criminals but persons in need of psychiatric treatment. During the past century or so the psychotics (insane) have been studied and treated, whereas criminals have been punished. The message for today, says Menninger, is that criminals are "really" insane and should be given to the psychiatrist rather than to the warden. It is in connection with this argument that Menninger proclaimed psychiatry to be completely unconcerned with justice, which is one of the major concerns of the law. Thus he asked the rhetorical question that psychiatrists have become so fond of quoting, namely, whether "lawyers [must] still continue solemnly to apply medieval stupidities in the name of 'established precedent,' 'public policy,' and other mouthy archaisms?" [18] Menninger, as a representative of the American Psychiatric Association, wrote that "the psychiatrist is not in the least interested in justice, and perhaps even doubts its existence." [19]

The title that Roche gave to his comments on the *Durham* decision reveals his conception of the criminal: "Criminality and Mental Illness—Two Faces of the Same Coin." Several times in his article he writes that criminality and mental illness "are two faces of the same coin." Roche does not confine mental illness to the criminal, but seems to attribute it to everyone as a part of human heredity. He writes:

> All human beings start in life as creatures of instincts that are asocial and self-serving. Our child rearing is intended to modify the instincts for eventual group conformity and mutual security. . . .
> The phenomena of criminality and mental illness are evidence of the insufficiency or breakdown of the built-in controls. . . . Both can be properly regarded as a product of basically similar conflicts unresolved within the limits set by group norms. . . . In this light criminality and mental illness . . . become . . . processes reflecting the breakdown of psychic controls and the release of latent *antisocial drives common to all.*[20]

Mental illness and criminality are in that presentation not identical, but they still cannot be separated from each other because they constitute the head and tail of the same coin. The analogy is confusing. Roche's assertions are ambiguous, in that one cannot decide whether he means that criminality or mental illness, or both, are hereditary. The ambiguity is increased by his peculiar doctrine that "many criminals are compelled to repeat their unlawful acts in order to preserve their sanity, and many law-abiding persons go crazy to avoid crime." Maudsley's original statement of the doctrine is that "crime is a sort of outlet in which their unsound tendencies are discharged; they would go mad if they were not criminals, and they do not go mad because they are criminals." [21]

Psychiatry has been engulfed in the boundless sea of human troubles in England also, although perhaps not to the same degree as in the United States. The renowned English psychiatrist, Ernest Jones, for example, has written that

> By its exploration of the unconscious it [psychoanalysis] has constantly been able to show how various mental processes, such as decisions in behavior, specific interests, ethical attitudes, and so on, in regard to which no determining factor may be visible, have nevertheless been powerfully influenced—and *perhaps altogether determined*—by unconscious factors of which the individual was entirely unaware.[22]

Jones insists that the unconscious is constitutional and begins to work at birth, and claims that "the processes operative in the unconscious represent either the persistence of infantile ones or derivations from them." "Furthermore," continues Jones, "the agencies at work are all conceived of biologically, in terms of innate instincts." He refers to the "genetic study [psychoanalysis] of the development of the mind from biological instincts, all of which are common to man and other animals. . . ."

In using the criterion of efficiency—borrowed from industry, which has been unable to decide on how it is to be measured—in connection with mental disease, Jones shows that English psychiatry also is value laden. He writes that psychoanalysis took as its point of departure a "widespread class of phenomena the common feature of which is inefficiency in mental functioning." [23]

The definition of mental illness as being "inefficiency in mental functioning" is as wonderfully vague and all-encompassing as Sullivan's, namely, disturbed or inadequate self-other relationships.

The above quotations cannot be taken as a census. They are nevertheless representative of the psychiatric conceptions and postulates of crime and delinquency as mental disease, of criminals and delinquents as mentally diseased persons, of all behavior as being strictly determined by the past and overwhelmingly by instinct, and of there being only a "thin line" separating normal, abnormal, criminal, and delinquent people. The quotations are also illustrative of the widespread attack on reason, and of one of its corollaries, the attempt to eliminate responsibility on the part of the individual for his behavior. As Hilgard says, "When what was formerly thought to be moral weakness is interpreted as neurotic illness, the conception of personal responsibility shifts." [24] These conceptions are integral components of the theory of behavior, personality, and society advanced in psychiatry in justification of the attempt to abandon the concept of responsibility and to substitute the concept of irresponsibility.

Jerome Hall has raised a serious question concerning those psychiatric conceptions and postulates. (The assertions that the life of every person is molded during an infancy dominated by the Oedipus complex, that *all behavior is rigorously determined by antecedent experience, predominantly instinctual,* that moral obligation is merely a socially acceptable false pretense, and so on —these can certainly not be accepted as being scientifically established, even if very loose criteria are employed.[25])

Concept of the "Irresistible Impulse"

In psychiatric literature the irresistible impulse has long been conceived by many as a fact to be accepted, rather than as an hypothesis to be tested. The concept of the irresistible impulse is based on the postulate of the disjunction of the self. That theory holds the primary phases of the self to be separate from and to function independently of, one another. The primary phases of the self are cognition, emotion, and volition. Those familiar with nineteenth-century philosophy will recognize the three as the familiar "faculties" believed to be independent of one another. Contemporary psychiatrists have added the notion of the unconscious, by which they mean that the individual has unconscious knowledge, and is impelled by unconscious emotional and volitional forces. Those forces are held to be instinctual in origin, added to by repression, unknown to and unknowable by the subject, and uncontrollable by him.

(The twentieth century has seen the development of the integrative theory of the self. In this theory, which is largely but not exclusively the contribution of social psychology, the primary functions are conceived as coordinate, interrelated, and acting interdependently when the self is involved. Psychiatry accords the integrative theory a verbal allegiance while in practice holding fast to the disjunctive. The disjunctionists believe, in brief, that the self is fractionized, or divided into parts. They seem to accept as a fact the postulate that the several fractions are not equal parts of the whole, since cognition (reason or knowledge) is always held to be the least and emotion and/or volition to be the greatest, and that cognition is subordinate to the other two.)

The disjunctive and the integrative theories of the self can be roughly represented in Figures I and II.

In the integrative theory (Figure I), cognition, emotion, and volition are equal in rank, different in function, and directly interrelated. A serious disturbance in one must therefore have serious consequences for the other two. Even this manner of stating their mutual relationships might be construed as implying that a serious disturbance develops first in, say, behavior, to be followed at an unspecified later time, by a serious disturbance in cognition. No such implication is intended. It is appropriate to refer here to our previous discussion, of the learning of a vocabulary of motives. We referred to boys who engage in delinquency and become "stable lower class" when they abandon delinquency, and to boys who progress to delinquency as a source of income and who contribute largely to the criminal population. We referred also to the "good boy," the thief in the white collar, and to the compulsive criminal. That analysis showed that the development of a vocabulary of motives (cognition), a self-conception of per-

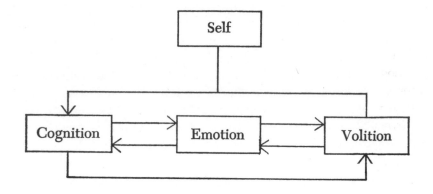

Figure I
The Integrative Theory

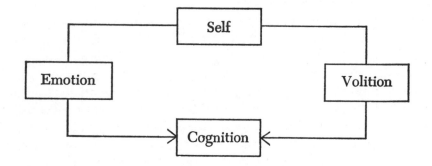

Figure II
The Disjunctive Theory

sonal worthiness (emotion), and delinquent or criminal actions (volition) occur together as a complex process. The phases of cognition, emotion, and volition are therefore separable only for purposes of analysis and discussion.

In the disjunctive theory (Figure II) emotion and volition (behavior) are conceived as being independent of each other, with cognition subordinate to both. The figure also indicates that either emotion or volition may be dominant over the other, but in either case cognition must be subordinate. The proponents of the irresistible impulse—which makes its subject behaviorally and therefore morally and criminally irresponsible—advance this theory of the self.

The irresistible impulse is held by many psychiatrists to be the best or at least a sufficient substitute for the McNaghten Rules, which imply an integrative theory of the self. The hypothesis of the irresistible impulse states that a person can understand what he is doing, can realize that inflicting a serious injury on another person is undoubtedly wrong and grossly immoral but, nevertheless, can at the same time be so impaired in his power to control his conduct that he is "irresistibly impelled" to commit a serious injury. The hypothesis of the irresistible impulse holds, in brief, that (1) cognition, emotion, and volition are separate and discrete from one another in their operations and that (2) one can therefore suffer a severe (pathological) impairment of either emotion or behavior, or of both, without his reason being affected. It is thus that psychiatry has argued for about one hundred and fifty years that a man who is in complete possession of his reason can nevertheless at the same time be mad! Indeed, if one can rely on such a questionable source as Gregory Zilboorg's psychiatric reconstruction of medical psychology, the hypothesis of the irresistible impulse is about four hundred years old.[26]

The crucial problem of the concept of the irresistible impulse is to find empirical evidence of its existence, *other than the act itself*. Neither Isaac Ray in the nineteenth century nor contemporary psychiatrists one century later have been able to solve this problem. Ray gives an excellent example of the reification of the irresistible impulse, in which it is admitted that "almost only the *act*" is diagnostic. One form of murder, Ray states, is that in which "there are no motives to be discerned, the individual being impelled by a blind, irresistible impulse." Discussing twenty-four murderers in the General Prison for Scotland at Perth, in 1862, Ray reports, "In several the intellect was very slightly affected, and almost the only proof of insanity was the *act* itself, which was involuntary, impulsive, irresistible, and scarcely preceded or followed by any disorder of the intellectual functions." [27]

The quotation from Ray's work illustrates the logic of the doctrine of the irresistible impulse. First, the things that men do are classified and named. Second, it is proclaimed that the name explains the behavior. This psychiatric concept thus validates its explanation of social behavior solely in terms of itself! The explanation is as follows. The question is asked, Why do some people commit, for example, arson, larceny, murder, sexual offenses, and lie? The answer is, Because they have an irresistible impulse that forces (causes) them to do so. The further question is then asked, How do we know that they are in fact possessed by that irresistible impulse? The answer is, We know it because they commit arson, larceny, murder, sexual offenses, and lie. The reader will recognize in this the familiar vicious circle of logic, marked by a very small radius.

The doctrine of the irresistible impulse and the disjunctive theory of the self have survived in contemporary psychiatry from nineteenth century phrenology. Ray wrote a laudatory review of Combe's book on phrenology in 1834. He asserted that there is "an original and distinct power for every special end and object of our existence." To this he added the statement that phrenology "lends a powerful support to morality and religion." He apparently "ghost-translated" the fourth and sixth volumes of F. J. Gall's *Sur les fonctions du cerveau et sur celles de chacune de ses parties,* for Winslow Lewis, in 1835. As late as 1879 (less than two years before his death), he wrote to Nahum Capen, Gall's publisher in the United States, that "no storybook was ever devoured with such an abandon of every other thought as was Gall's great work, *Sur les fonctions. . . .*" The thirty-seven faculties postulated in phrenology were held to function independently of each other. It was also held that the faculties overlapped only in that two or more could combine in given behaviors. They were independent of each other in the same manner in which the movements of the right and left hands may be independent, even though, in certain actions, both might be used at the same time. Lange summarized this conception as follows:

> Each organ has its own activity, and yet the activity of all cooperates toward a joint effect. Each organ thinks, feels, and wills for itself; a man's thinking, feeling, and willing is the result of the sum of these activities. In each organ there are various degrees of mental activity. A sensation becomes conception and finally becomes imagination, as the thinking excitability of the organ is weaker or stronger; emotion may become enthusiasm, and impulse may become desire and eventually passion. These activities are related only to the matters that are natural to each organ. "Each mental organ," says one of our cleverest phrenologists, "speaks its own language and understands only the language which it speaks itself; conscience speaks in matters of right and wrong; benevolence only in matters of sympathy, and so on." The more general phenomena result from their union into a whole, such as "understanding," as an activity of the entire thirty-six faculties of thought; they cooperate, however, in the particular individual activities of man, partly in antagonism, partly in support, in modification, and so on, like a group of muscles in the movement of a limb.[28]

Writing at a time when phrenology "attracted the best medical minds in both England and the United States," Lange continued: "One sees at the first glance that this entire conceptualization involves the most shadowy abstractions." He was discussing the assertion that the intellectual and the emotional faculties are independent of each other, and the further assertion that the thirty-seven (or thirty-three, thirty-five, or thirty-six) different faculties postulated in phrenology functioned independently of each other. George Combe, for example, listed twenty-one faculties in his category of "Feelings," and fourteen in the category, "Intellectual Faculties." He considered in detail the question, Whether the mind employs the whole brain as one organ, or whether separate mental faculties are connected with distinct portions of the brain as their respective organs. His answer, as well as that of all other phrenologists, was emphatically in favor of separate and independent faculties. He defined moral (or, partial) insanity as "that state in which one or more faculties of the mind are deranged, while the integrity of the remainder is unaffected."[29]

Ray's commitment to the doctrine of the independently functioning faculties led him to the conclusion that

> While the reason may be unimpaired, the passions may be in a state of insanity, impelling a man . . . to the commission of horrible crimes in spite of all his efforts to resist. . . . The whole mind is seldom affected; it is only one or more faculties . . . whose action . . . is perverted, while the rest enjoy their customary soundness and vigour.[30]

One can see that both Ray and Combe accepted the disjunctive theory of the self. The trial and conviction of Guiteau was a death blow to the concept of moral insanity, even though it was occasionally used into the twentieth century. But it was only the concept, moral insanity, that met its death, so to speak. The disjunctive theory of the self—the doctrine of independently functioning intellectual and emotional faculties—is still alive. It is, indeed, perhaps more viable than when Guiteau was executed. Were he to be tried today before a jury composed of recipients of the Isaac Ray Award, it is most likely that he would be found not guilty by reason of insanity.

One should not interpret these comments about some of the relations between phrenology and psychiatry as being derogatory to either. Phrenology in its early years contributed much to science, and those contributions are widely acknowledged. Philosophy and sociology were certainly among the disciplines affected, not physiology alone. The important point is that, first, an empirically testable theory has been painfully developed in psychiatry, psychology, and sociology, namely, the integrative theory of the self. Second, it has encountered serious competition in the revivified phrenological doctrine of the independence of emotion and instinct from reason. That doctrine, now presented in the form of the disjunctive theory of the self, is experimentally untestable. I may add that whereas phrenology did not rank the intellect and emotions with respect to each other, contemporary psychiatry does.[31] It has revived Hume's assertion that "Reason is and ought always to be the slave of the passions, and can never pretend to any other office than to serve and obey them."[32] As

Sutherland's analysis of the sexual-psychopath laws shows, when a given act is defined as being diagnostic of personality, the services of a psychiatrist are not needed. All that is necessary is proof that the given act was committed.[33]

Some judges and some psychiatrists, during the nineteenth century, rejected the doctrine of the irresistible impulse. In *Commonwealth v. Mosler*, Judge Lewis said, "There *may* be" an impulse that is "incapable of resistance." However, he continued, "this can be recognized only in the clearest cases." [34] Zilboorg, in commenting on Mosler, intended to castigate the judge for stating that an irresistible impulse could be recognized "only in the clearest cases." But what Zilboorg actually did was to state, quite unintentionally, the major empirical objection that has been raised against the doctrine of the irresistible impulse since it was first promulgated: "All this was judicious and good, but *the trouble was and is that the clearest of such cases are* [sic] *very obscure and not easily, if at all demonstrable. . . .*[35]

That "trouble" continues to be the major difficulty today. Even such a dedicated propagandist as Weihofen writes about the plea of "irresistible impulse" that *"the problem of proof is the real riddle* in all these cases." He then continues, in a comment revealing his disregard of scientific method, "It would seem that the solution lies in reforming the method of trying the issue, rather than in rejecting certain defenses merely because they are difficult to disprove." [36]

If an hypothesis in science is to be seriously entertained some empirical or logical grounds—and preferably both—must first be advanced which will indicate that it is reasonable to be serious concerning that hypothesis. The acceptance of the hypothesis is then dependent upon an empirical test that establishes it as being probably or reasonably correct. Its scientific acceptance neither depends on nor results from, as Weihofen claims for psychiatry and the criminal law, the difficulty of its disproof, or from the absence of disproof. The psychiatric and legal proponents, in violation of scientific method, argue in effect that the irresistible impulse does exist, because they refuse to accept the empirical evidence and logical analysis advanced by those who reject the concept. Weihofen and others state in effect, "The irresistible impulse is real and does exist because those who reject it do not disprove it to my satisfaction." This is an antiscientific position.

Dr. John P. Gray, for thirty years editor of the *American Journal of Insanity* (the title was changed to *American Journal of Psychiatry* in 1921) was one of the nineteenth-century American psychiatrists who rejected the hypothesis of the irresistible impulse in his testimony for the prosecution during the trial of Charles Guiteau for the assassination of President Garfield. Guiteau had long exhibited extreme religious enthusiasm, and claimed he acted under the delusion that he had a divine inspiration to "remove the president." According to Alfred Lief's diagnosis (in 1948!), this was "a mission exerting an irresistible impulse." [37] Dr. Gray testified: "Inasmuch as I, in my view, cannot conceive of any moral act . . . without an intellectual operation or mental action accompanying it, so I cannot possibly sever this mental unity." [38]

In today's terminology, one would say that Dr. Gray held to the integrative theory of the self, and rejected the disjunctive theory. It seems to me (about eighty years after Guiteau) that what Dr. Davidson wrote about "psychotic impulse" is wholly applicable to such instances of alleged "irresistible impulse" as Guiteau's:

> . . . one is led to the conclusion that a psychotic defendant is not, by the traditional McNaghten rule and by the general principles of criminal law, responsible for an act which results from a psychotic (insane) irresistible impulse; and that no specific doctrine is needed to spell out such a defense.[39]

Contemporary psychiatry has, of course, added the postulate of the unconscious to the nineteenth century's irresistible impulse. Guttmacher and Weihofen, for example, state that "the *true* kleptomaniacs and the *true* pyromaniacs . . . [are] offenders driven by an unconsciously motivated urge to commit their crimes." Some others who commit "crimes which cannot be effectively resisted" are, it is claimed, most sexual offenders. Guttmacher and Weihofen claim that "in the future, when large numbers of criminals are intensively studied by psychiatrists," many recidivists who commit the less dramatic offenses, such as burglary and automobile theft, "will undoubtedly be found to be victims of morbid impulses." [40] If their prediction is correct, the scope of exculpation and irresponsibility will be indefinitely extended. Most of the 1.4 million to 1.5 million nonviolent serious crimes in the United States reported annually in *Uniform Crime Reports,* appear to be committed by recidivists. The nonviolent crimes are burglary, larceny of fifty dollars or more, and auto theft. They comprise about 85 percent of all reported serious crimes; if robbery is included, then about 90 percent are largely committed by recidivists.

Henry Maudsley was one of the most, perhaps the most, persuasive of the English champions of the irresistible impulse during the last quarter of the nineteenth century. He would no doubt have been amazed at the extensive scope of the above prediction, since he conceived of the conflict between jurisprudence and psychiatry as being very limited. In 1874 he wrote, "Abolish capital punishment, and the dispute between the lawyers and doctors ceases to be of practical importance." [41]

I share the opinion of those who believe that contemporary psychiatric proponents of the doctrine of the irresistible impulse pay hardly more than lip service to the integrative theory of the self, even when they profess to accept it. A few examples will be sufficient for present purposes. Only a few years ago, as Jerome Hall has shown, "irresistible impulse" was the slogan on which the extremist psychiatric critics of individual responsibility centered. [42]

According to Sir Norwood East, perhaps the outstanding feature of modern criminal psychiatry "is the recognition of the emotional rather than the intellectual genesis of crime." [43] It is not only crimes of violence and passion, we are told, that are motivated by unconscious emotional forces, but also such offenses as theft, arson, and fraud. Weihofen states that one's "mental process manifests itself in a tripartite mode—cognitive, or intellectual; conative, or volitional; and affective, or emotional." [44] This seems an adequate statement of the integrative theory; but on the next page he repudiates that theory in favor of the disjunctive. The McNaghten Rules, he says, "fail to take account of the now-recognized fact that all persons—even the normal—are usually more influenced by their emotions than by reasoning."

Again, he writes that a "criticism of the McNaghten rule is that it covers only disorders of the cognitive or intellectual phase of the mind, and makes no allowance for disorders characterized by deficiency or destruction of volition." [45] Sheldon Glueck also holds that a person can be mentally ill without his intellect being affected! In advancing the same kind of criticism as East and Weihofen, he says that the McNaghten Rule "takes no account of the fact that while mental deterioration may not have progressed sufficiently to satisfy the knowledge tests of responsibility, it might yet exist to a degree that has destroyed the subject's control over his instinctive urgings." [46]

Glueck referred in his Isaac Ray Award lectures to what he described as the "devastating" psychiatric criticism of the intellectualist McNaghten Rules: "capacity to assess the nature and quality of an act and its rightness or wrongness can be intact and function as in the case of the average reasonable man, even though a defendant be otherwise demonstrably of disordered mind." The rules are "also too narrow a measure of irresponsibility" because they do not take account of disorders manifesting themselves largely in disturbances of the impulsive and emotional aspects of mental life.[47] It seems to me that Professor Glueck has come to the same antiscientific position concerning the proof and disproof of the existence of the irresistible impulse as Weihofen. He finds it "hard to understand why the majority of the American courts have not extended the test of irresponsibility to include irresistible impulse." [48] Zilboorg unwittingly supplied an explanation when he wrote that the conception of a mental disease in which one's reason or intellect is unimpaired "is a term and a conception not easily accepted by either the scientist or the layman." [49] Jerome Hall gave directly the same kind of explanation when he said that "in the light of existing knowledge and experience, lawyers, judges and intelligent laymen cannot be expected to accept the notion that a rational person may be insane. Yet . . . that is precisely the objective of the extremist criticism of the McNaghten Rules." [50]

Guttmacher and Weihofen advance the same disjunctive doctrine that one can have a mental disease with no effect on one's reason:

But while it is true that the affective, cognitive, and conative processes of the mind are interrelated, certain forms of mental disease may affect one more than the other. A disorder manifesting itself in impulsive acts may affect intelligence *somewhat,* but it is quite possible that the impulsiveness may have reached the point where it can be said that it is "irresistible," and yet intelligence has not deteriorated so much as to obliterate knowledge of right and wrong.[51]

It will be noted that the authors use "interrelation" rather than "integration." The latter means *co-ordination,* and the *interrelation* of the total process of conduct, interpretation, and observation. If they intend "interrelation" and "integration" to be synonyms, they do not describe the psychical processes through which one primary function of the self (either emotion or volition) may be severely disordered to the point of pathology, while at the same time the other function (cognition or reason) with which it fuses may be so unaffected or unimpaired as to remain quite within the realm of reality.

"Irresistible Impulse" and the Law

The discussion to this point has been primarily concerned with psychiatric beliefs and conceptions. They have, of course, a close relationship to legal conceptions. It is not possible to consider here in any detail the large body of legal literature dealing with the concept of the irresistible impulse and the disjunctive theory of the self. That literature is exemplified in *United States v. Pollard* and the fantasia of *Pollard v. United States.* These two decisions illustrate the point that the differences between the integrative and the disjunctive theories are not merely academic. They may have serious practical consequences, namely, freedom or commitment to a mental or correctional institution, or some other sanction such as a fine or probation. The annual report of the Federal Bureau of Prisons for 1961 stated that "in the Pollard case the Sixth Circuit [Court of Appeals] accepted the irresistible impulse doctrine in a landmark decision written by Chief Judge Thomas McAllister."[52] That statement could be taken to imply that Judge McAllister's acceptance of the doctrine of irresistible impulse was an innovation in the federal courts. The implication would be in error because the doctrine has long been accepted in those courts as a defense against the charge of criminal conduct. Perhaps what made it "a landmark decision" is that Judge McAllister went much further in his unquestioning acceptance of the irresistible impulse than did the psychiatrists in the case.

Pollard pleaded guilty in federal district court to three charges of attempted armed robbery of banks insured by the Federal Deposit Insurance Corporation. He had attempted and committed other armed robberies; but, as violations of the criminal code of the State of Michigan, they were not included in the federal case. He subsequently moved to set aside the plea of guilty on the ground that he was insane at the times when he committed the attempted robberies. That move was made after he consulted with his attorney. Judge Theodore Levin, in his decision in *United States v. Pollard,* wrote that

> Admittedly, motivations may be mixed. However, all the facts have clearly established that defendant's criminal activity was planned to meet an extrinsic need by a reasoned but antisocial method. The defendant had financial problems of varying degrees of intensity throughout his life. He had financial difficulties during his first marriage. He was now embarking on a second marriage. He was about to undertake the responsibility of supporting not only a wife and himself, but also four children, three of them the product of his first marriage. In statements given to agents of the Federal Bureau of Investigation admitting his criminal activity, he stated: "Inasmuch as I was about to marry my second wife, I decided that I would not lead the same type of financially insecure life that I had led with my first wife. I needed about $5,000 in order to buy a house. My only purpose in deciding to rob a bank was to obtain $5,000 and if I obtained the money I did not intend to continue the robbing." Defendant's entire pattern of conduct was consistent with this expressed motivation.[53]

Judge Levin accepted Pollard's statement of his motive. It rendered his behavior understandable. But the examining psychiatrists rejected it and supplied him with several other motives, including the crucial irresistible impulse. Pollard, a member of the Detroit Police Department, had experienced a double tragedy about two years before his attempted robberies; his wife and infant daughter were murdered by a drunken neighbor while he was on duty. The psychiatrists explained his attempted armed robberies as follows. (1) Pollard, in their opinion, knew the difference between right and wrong and knew that the acts he committed were wrong. (2) He was, however, suffering from a "dissociative reaction" induced by the traumatic effect of the murders and his belief that he was responsible because his absence from home exposed them to his drunken neighbor. (3) He had an unconscious desire to be punished by society so as to expiate his belief that he was guilty. (4) As a result of his unconscious desire to be punished "the governing power of his mind was so destroyed or impaired that he was unable to resist the commission of the criminal acts." The "irresistible impulse" test of insanity, Judge Levin wrote, has been criticized as inadequate because it is "premised on a compartmentalized approach to personality and thus ignore[s] the fact that man functions as an integrated, unitary being." [54]

The judge was stating his acceptance of the integrative theory of the self and his rejection of the disjunctive theory. In support of his position, he quoted from the writings of prominent psychiatrists. Among the excerpts was Harry Stack Sullivan's conclusion that "the best of psychiatry is still more of art than of science." "For psychiatry," Judge Levin continued:

> what we do is determined by what we are, and . . . all criminal behavior, whether it be the acts of the rapist, the forger, the embezzler, the sender of licentious literature through the mails or tax evasion by a reputable businessman, is evidence of mental disease. But the uncritical adoption of this point of view would completely do away with the concept of criminal responsibility.[55]

The judge found it necessary to reject the psychiatrists' opinion that Pollard unconsciously sought to be caught and punished, and acted on the basis of an unconscious irresistible impulse. Pollard's "entire pattern of conduct during the period of his criminal activities militates against [the psychiatrists] conclusion. His conscious desire not to be apprehended was demonstrably greater than his unconscious desire to the contrary." [56] Judge Levin referred to the following facts. After being caught, Pollard denied engaging in criminal activities of any kind, despite interrogation for more than five hours by officers of the Detroit

Police Department and agents of the Federal Bureau of Investigation. His admission came only after he was positively identified by bank employees. At each attempted robbery, when he thought that he was about to be caught, he escaped. Judge Levin asked one of the psychiatrists to explain the inconsistency between having an irresistible impulse and an unconscious desire to be caught and punished, on the one hand, and escaping at the moment of apprehension, on the other.

The psychiatrist's reply was that "although the defendant had an unconscious desire to be apprehended and punished, when the possibility of apprehension became direct and immediate, the more dominating desire for self-preservation asserted itself." [57] But Judge Levin showed that the defendant's pattern of behavior on May 21, 1958, discloses that "the desire for self-preservation was not fleeting and momentary but continuing, consistent and dominant." What then, asked the judge, becomes of the theory of the irresistible impulse? On that day the defendant attempted the armed robbery of two banks, and contemplated a third, which he did not attempt because he concluded that it was too risky. Looking at the events of that day, the judge said, we are asked to believe the following:

First, the defendant in acting pursuant to an irresistible impulse, selected a bank to rob, entered the bank to achieve that end, and purposely failed in the attempt in order to be caught so as to satisfy his unconscious desire for punishment. Second, in the moment in which the end he sought—apprehension—was imminent, he escaped because of the dominance, at the moment of ultimate accomplishment, of the stronger drive for self-preservation. Third, we must then believe that when the defendant believed himself free from detection, his compulsive state reasserted itself and that he again went through the steps of planning, abortive attempted armed bank robbery, and escape! Fourth, we can add that this same cycle was repeated in two later attempts at armed robbery, on June 3 and June 11, the latter finally leading to his capture after a period of some hours of searching by the police. But, the judge asked, if we accept the above theory, what other psychiatric theory explains the defendant's further conduct after the two attempted robberies in one day?

He planned on that same afternoon to rob a third bank, but finally decided not to because he concluded that its window area was so large that his chances of being caught were too great. If the theory remains the same, then in the latter case the fear of apprehension and punishment tipped "the scales enough to make resistible an impulse otherwise irresistible." [58]

The logical inference was drawn by Judge Levin that the other attempted robberies were undertaken as the result of impulses that the defendant did not choose to resist because, to him, the possibility of success outweighed the likelihood of detection, which is in essence a motivation for all criminal conduct. The impulse being resistible, the judge said, the defendant is responsible for his criminal conduct. He found the defendant guilty as charged.

The doctrine of the irresistible impulse was accepted with no qualification whatever in the decision of the United States Court of Appeals, Sixth Circuit.[59] That decision set aside Pollard's conviction. Written by Chief Judge McAllister, with Senior Judge Charles Simons dissenting, it made greater claims for psychiatry than even eminent psychiatric proponents of the irresistible impulse have made. The examining psychiatrists qualified their conclusions in their reports, which are largely reproduced in the decision. They wrote that "a dissociative state *may* have existed" during the time of his criminal activities and that "his actions *may* not have been consciously activated." He "*may* have been governed by" unconscious irresistible impulses "which *might* have been related to guilt feelings in connection with the death of his wife and child." The report ended: "We readily acknowledge our inability either to marshall sufficient objective facts or formulate a completely satisfactory theory on which to base a solid opinion as to subject's responsibility during the period in question." [60] The judge transmuted the scientifically required, conditional "mays" and "might" into the declarative "was." Pollard *was* suffering from a grave disorder, the judge wrote, "and that disorder *was*, in the opinion of all the psychiatric and medical experts, a dissociative reaction resulting in Pollard's commission of the acts charged *because* of an irresistible impulse." [61]

The judge thereby claimed that a direct causal connection had been established between Pollard's crimes and his alleged mental disease. In addition, he completely rejected the criticism of psychiatry by psychiatrists, stating that "it is unnecessary to consider the disparaging views of certain psychiatric writers." [62] Even Karl A. Menninger, as we shall soon see, admits that psychiatrists may have been irresponsible to a degree, that they have used the term "sickness" too loosely, and that they do not know how to treat the mentally ill in a curative manner.

Judge McAllister rejected Pollard's statement of his motivation, and accepted those supplied by the psychiatrists. The practical consequence of this was that "the court shall direct the release from custody of the appellant [Pollard], the dismissal of the charges against him, and the cancellation of the bond heretofore filed." [63] The decision to dismiss the charges is significant because of at least one thing. No empirical evidence whatever was adduced to sustain the assertion that an irresistible impulse existed or determined the defendant's behavior, other than the very behavior that was to be explained by that impulse! This is nothing but the vicious circle once more, and can be contrasted with the position taken by Chief Justice Dillon of Iowa,

> who said as far back as 1868 that if medical men can definitely establish that a mentally diseased person may know right from wrong in the abstract and yet be driven irresistibly by his disease to commit a criminal act, "the law must modify its ancient doctrines . . . recognize the truth" and permit exculpation when such condition is proved.[64]

The crucial conditions in that passage are of course "definitely establish" and "when such condition is proved." The logic of the vicious circle prevents any demonstration that the conditions ever have been met.

Throughout the statutes and the decisions of the United States courts, Judge McAllister wrote, "it is held that a person who commits a crime under irresistible impulse is insane." [65] An uncontrollable impulse to commit acts charged as a crime, he wrote on the same page, "is insanity of such degree as will relieve the accused of the consequences of the criminal acts." His citation for this was *Smith v. United States*. Smith had been convicted of murdering his daughter, and his lawyer had appealed on the ground of irresistible impulse. In that trial also, and of course in the appeal against the verdict of guilty, no evidence for the existence of an irresistible impulse was adduced by the psychiatrists for the defense except the very murder that they asserted was caused by that impulse. The appellate court accepted completely and without question the assertion of defense counsel concerning the existence and functioning of an irresistible impulse:

> One of the physicians who was examined as a witness on the issue of insanity testified "that he would not say that a man who killed his daughter was *per se* of unsound mind; that the witness believed that at the time the defendant Smith grabbed his daughter he knew what he was doing; and probably appreciated that he was doing wrong"; whereupon counsel for the government propounded the following question: "You say that he did?" A. "He appreciated it . . . he knew the right and wrong, but he was unable to carry it through." Q. "You mean he was unable to carry the right through and refrain from doing the wrong?" A. "Yes." Another physician testified as follows: Q. "Do you think that, at the time he committed that act, he had full recognition of what he was doing, namely, killing his daughter was wrong?" A. "Of course he had the idea, but he was incapable of doing as he would like to do." [66]

In the Smith case—as in all other capital cases in which the irresistible impulse was advanced as a defense—the only evidence cited for the existence of the postulated impulse was the murder that was both explained and exculpated by that impulse. In his decision in *Pollard* Judge McAllister cited *Smith* as a precedent, and broadened the scope of that decision. The decision of the appellate court in the Smith case propounded a legal "modern doctrine" that accepted the phrenological notion of independently functioning faculties as completely as contemporary psychiatry has:

> The *mere* ability to distinguish right from wrong is no longer the correct test *either in civil or criminal cases,* where the defense of insanity is interposed. The accepted rule, in this day and age, with the great advance in medical science as an enlightening influence on this subject, is that the accused must be capable, not only of distinguishing between right and wrong, but that he was not impelled to do the act by an irresistible impulse. . . . [67]

The italicized words in the above quotation are of great significance. They indicate that, contrary to a widely held belief, the
plea of insanity by virtue of an irresistible impulse is by no means
confined to capital or other serious crimes against the person.
Many people seek exculpation for such figures as Smith and
Pollard on the humanitarian grounds of compassion and pity.
They include judges, prosecuting attorneys, and other lawyers
as well as psychiatrists and lay people. One can reject that plea
for exculpation without being either harsh or revengeful, on the
basis of the evidence presented. In both cases, as in any other
meritorious or mitigating case, what is called for is mitigation,
not exculpation, and for this the law explicitly provides. It is at
least in part through the decisions exemplified by *Smith* and
Pollard that the disjunctive theory of the self has become established in federal jurisprudence. With some exceptions, the legal
profession has accepted the theory without examining it. It is, to
repeat, a purely legal-psychiatric theory with no empirical foundation in the facts of life or the method of science.[68]

The purpose and the effect of the disjunctive theory is to elevate
the passions and alleged instincts, and to demean and derogate
reason. The finest expression of this that I have found is a statement by an eminent psychiatrist who suggested that normality
is a mental disease. Glover says, "To repeat: *normality may be
a form of madness which goes unrecognized because it happens
to be a good adaptation to reality.*" [69]

We showed briefly in the earlier chapters that there is an
integral relationship between the developing thought and behavior of the individual. In considering that proposition we
discussed several types of offenders. The thought and behavior
of those offenders were shown to be requisite to each other. In
the social-psychological or integrative theory—from which the
psychiatric deviates radically—there is no possibility of mental
illness without thought, emotion, and behavior being integrally
involved.

Since the primary functions of the self interpenetrate one another, *knowing*, that is, *understanding* moral situations is unlike
knowing or understanding problems in science, and is also unlike
the mere verbal knowing of the rules of etiquette. In moral

situations, tendencies to action are permeated both with knowledge and the warmth of emotion. Mental disorder is therefore a drastic or serious impairment of all three of the primary phases of the self. It is, of course, well known that there may be and often is reasoning of a high order in psychosis. Such reasoning, however, is unsupported by the affect and sensitivity that in normal persons results in an identification with the prospective victim. It is also unsupported by a realistic envisaging of the meaning and probable consequences of a serious attack on him. Furthermore, the psychotic person who does attack another has for some time not had consensual validation of his thoughts through communication with others. One who is psychotic does not, in short, understand the moral significance of his conduct. The normal person who does physically attack another, in, say, a strong-arming, is enabled in part to do so by a vocabulary of motives learned in and consensually validated by active association and communication with others. In addition, neither "emotional pressure" nor emotion, as such, can any more initiate human social conduct than water can run uphill. As we have shown in the second chapter, social behavior results from an appraisal of a situation and a decision to act in accordance with that appraisal. Human behavior thus results from decisions, not emotions.*

In a statement for the Model Penal Code, Dr. Guttmacher indicates his verbal agreement with "the now universally accepted" theory of the integration of the self: cognition, volition, and emotion "are interdependent. One function cannot be affected by disease without affecting others." In the very next sentence,

---

* The above paragraph is an answer to a complaint uttered by Judge Bazelon in his Isaac Ray Award lecture. He lamented the fact that despite the potential breadth of the verb "to know" in the McNaghten Rules, "no court has read it to mean more than 'intellectually comprehend.'" David Bazelon, "Equal Justice for the Unequal," Isaac Ray Lectureship Award Series 5–6, 1961 (mimeographed). Cited in Glueck, *op. cit.*, p. 47. Bazelon seems to want to expand the meaning of "knowing" to include "knowing irrationally" and "knowing emotionally." One is reminded of the sixth meaning of "to feel" given in *Webster's Unabridged Dictionary*, 2d ed.: "To be convinced of emotionally rather than intellectually." Neither the dictionary nor Judge Bazelon, nor any other proponent of the irresistible impulse describes or states how such a remarkable feat can be accomplished.

however, he contradicts his agreement with the integrative, and propounds the disjunctive theory of the fractionized self:

> Certainly, this [integrative theory] is scientifically sound but it is of doubtful practical value since the various functions of mentation are disparately affected in various diseases and in different individuals. The same thing may be said of disorders of other organ systems. Respiratory difficulties are present in cardiac disease but their intensity varies greatly in different pathological conditions and in sick individuals. In many serious psychiatric cases, disorders of the will may be prominent while defects of the intellect are minimal . . .[70]

And later, when commenting on the *Durham* decision, Guttmacher again both rejected and accepted the irresistible impulse:

> The [*Durham*] opinion presents adequately the major faults that modern psychiatry finds in the . . . "irresistible impulse" test[s]. The chief criticism of the rules in the May, 1954 report on "Criminal Responsibility and Psychiatric Expert Testimony," formulated by the Committee on Psychiatry and Law of the Group for the Advancement of Psychiatry can be summarized. . . . [In part] The rules put a false emphasis on intellect, reason, and common sense and underemphasize the emotional pressures that energize behavior. . . .[71]

The last sentence of the quotation completely recovers the irresistible impulse criticized in the first part. Guttmacher's entire thesis must be regarded as dubitable. How is it possible for the theory of the integration of the self to be "scientifically sound" and at the same time "of doubtful practical value"? His position is, at any rate, one that deviates from the theory of the integration of the self, and indicates his rejection of the conclusion that the individual functions as a unitary being.

Guttmacher and Weihofen, through the use of analogy, attempt to equate "integration of the self" with "other organ systems" of the body. But this argument will not be cogent for anyone who has had an introduction to logic, because the fallacy of arguing by analogy is well known. They fail to specify what "organ system" of the personality (there is none!) [72] corresponds to the "other organ systems" of the body.

Continuing his discussion of *Durham,* Guttmacher explicitly calls attention to the disorganized condition of theory and diagnosis in psychiatry today, predicts an increase in the number of criminally insane because of *Durham's* legislation, and states that the possession of a mental disease will more likely depend upon the examining psychiatrist's psychological allegiance than upon the criminal's own mental state:

> There will be uncertainty and differences of opinion as to what constitutes "a diseased or defective mental condition". . . the psychopaths and the severe character neurotics, will still prove to be the difficult cases under the new [Durham] rule. . . . It seems to this author [Guttmacher] that *the new rules will be* somewhat *more liberally interpreted* than the old ones . . . *and, in consequence, the group of the criminally insane will be somewhat broadened. . . . There is certain to be professional disagreement. . . . The training and orientation of the psychiatrist is likely to be the decisive factor. If his orientation is psychoanalytic, he will be more likely to consider cases* with severe character disorders *as suffering from a mental disease."* [73]

In 1957, Philip Q. Roche's *The Criminal Mind* was the American Psychiatric Association's Isaac Ray Award book. Roche's conception of and argument in favor of, the irresistible impulse is the same as Guttmacher's: "many persons act out [sic] as if by some imperative that transcends all common sense and rationality . . . the term 'irresistible impulse' is descriptive of the imperative." [74]

Roche also holds steadfastly to the disjunctive theory that emotion and volition can and do act independently of cognition, when the self is concerned, and that one can therefore be mentally diseased without one's reason being affected:

> The theory of functional unity of mental operations is . . . empirically false. . . . The extension beyond knowledge of right and wrong to "irresistible impulse" provides an exception to the criterion of knowledge. Thus, one knows what one is doing and knows that it is unlawful, yet does it anyway as if impelled in spite of one's knowing. In this is implied some other undefined element of the mind and some alteration of it to effect the control of volition. [75]

Roche, in common with Ray and many others—and including most of the laws on sexual psychopathy—holds that behavior, at least with respect to the hypothesized irresistible impulse, is self-diagnostic:

the idea of irresisitible impulse is actually descriptively closer to what we observe as something real. . . . it has an objective concrete extension in the act, whereas M'Naghten and the notion of knowledge remain in the subjective. . . . the impulse notion is nearer to a real test of responsibility insofar as visible behavior is a guide to the evaluation one can make of the subjective element of crime. The "irresistible impulse" is a demonstration.[76]

If Roche means, by the last sentence in the above quotation, that the observed behavior is a demonstration that the impulse was in fact irresistible, it would be difficult to find a behaviorally and logically more naïve assertion, except, of course, for the literature dealing with the instinctivist doctrine. He is presenting us with nothing less than the old and familiar vicious circle. Roche also shows his acceptance of the disjunctive theory of the self by quoting Maudsley approvingly, who had himself accepted Pinel's earlier version of the doctrine. Maudsley repeated the assertion that "there are many madmen, *who at no period gave any evidence of a lesion of the understanding.*" [77]

Roche, in the best disjunctive tradition, sets "the irresistible impulse [conation and volition]" in opposition to and in successful competition with, "knowledge [cognition]." [78] It may be that Karl A. Menninger's formulation of the proposition that an act is in and of itself diagnostic of personality is the most inclusive statement of that proposition that can be made. According to him, "wrong" (which he does not define) behavior is evidence of the need for psychiatric treatment! He also admits that psychiatrists may have been irresponsible to a degree:

> [It is] my point of view that something wrong [in behavior] be looked at as an evidence of the need for treatment. . . . In an effort to get across to the public that what anyone does, even a criminal offender, is the product of many forces that have caused an unendurable stress in that man, we psychiatrists have perhaps used the word "sickness" too loosely.[79]

The quotation is from Menninger's review of Guttmacher and Weihofen, *Psychiatry and the Law,* and therefore is not to be taken lightly. In the last sentence of the quotation he seems to be taking issue not only with Guttmacher and Weihofen's use of "mental disorder," but also with his own, and that of the members of the Group for the Advancement of Psychiatry.

Menninger says that perhaps psychiatrists have used the word "sickness" too loosely. There is no such qualification in his explicit and open confession that psychiatrists do not know how to treat the mentally ill in a curative manner, and that psychiatrists do not want the responsibility of saying when such a patient is well and can be safely released:

> as to decide what kind of treatment is to be given and who is to administer it, it is certainly an open professional secret that we psychiatrists do not know how to treat such patients [mentally ill] in a curative way . . . and, finally, after an offender has been treated in whatever groping and uncertain ways the psychiatrist may have attempted, what prophet wants to take the responsibility of saying that the patient is well and may be released and will do society no more harm? [80]

Even more recently than Menninger, Roche has admitted that psychiatry cannot establish that a mental illness is the cause of an act, specifically a crime: "if mental illness causes some people to commit crimes, and not others, do we have a reliable method of discriminating those crimes which have no causal nexus with mental illness? . . . the answer is that psychiatry has yet to discover a method." [81]

There are two points here requiring discussion. First, Roche has said that "the notion of knowledge remains in the subjective," referring to psychiatric criticism of the McNaghten rules on the ground that they are incomprehensible because they do not refer to the data and theories with which psychiatry deals. Thus Zilboorg, who was given an Isaac Ray Award, said that the "rules are unintelligible to me." [82] Roche and Zilboorg are among the many psychiatrists who assert their professional inability to understand what is meant by "knowledge of the nature and quality of the act," and who assert further that psychiatry has no means of ascertaining whether a given offender knows right from wrong. Many other psychiatrists, with long experience in dealing with criminals, find the McNaghten rules quite adequate. Jerome Hall has shown that those psychiatrists who reject "right from wrong" as incomprehensible nevertheless accept, as a criterion of normality, the "correctness of the reality-testing" suggested by the psychiatric concept "reality principle." [83] Freud wrote that "a loss of reality must be an inherent element in psychosis . . . the new phantastic outer world of a psychosis attempts to set itself in place of external reality." [84]

Alexander and Healy write that "this more far-seeing attitude of controlling intelligently the instinctual demands in accordance with the requirements of the given external situation is the reality principle." [85] Hall shows that this reality principle can be equated with the prevailing legal test. First, both the McNaghten rules and the reality principle assume the existence of an outer world. Freud wrote, "Let us, moreover, bear in mind the great practical importance there is in the capacity to distinguish perceptions from mental images. . . . Our whole attitude toward the outer world, to reality, depends on this capacity so to distinguish." [86] Second, both assume the existence of "nature-events" and "social events" that occur in that world.[87] Third, both assume the possibility of knowledge of that world. Brill writes, ". . . we use the term *ego* where is commonly meant the intellect." [88] Fourth, both correlate changes in functioning in that regard with "mental abnormality." Freud said that "neurosis does not deny the existence of reality, it merely tries to ignore it; psychosis denies it and tries to substitute something else for it." [89] Fifth, both indicate that there are methods by which the "knowledge of the outer world can be tested" [90] and that this is the function of the intelligence.[91]

Hall observes that the "reality-principle" has been defined in almost the very words of the McNaghten Rule, as "the comprehension of the true nature of an object." [92] There are, he continues, various disciplines concerned with people and their mutual relationships, and the suggestion may be ventured that

> even a slight acquaintance with the literature of philosophy indicates that the authors of the McNaghten Rules achieved a vast improvement over both Erskine and Freud in avoiding the use of the term which has perhaps as good a claim as any to being the vaguest of all words, namely, "reality." Whatever the criteria of scientific psychiatry may require, it is not unlikely that those who know that term to be pregnant with the limitless equivocations of hundreds of years prefer the simpler language of the McNaghten Rules.[93]

The sophistry in the psychiatric criticism of the legal conception of human behavior as intellectual, and in the claim that psychiatrists have no means to ascertain whether or not a man knows right from wrong, is demonstrated in Hall's point-by-point equating of the psychiatric "reality-principle" with the Anglo-American legal conception of the intellectual character of human behavior.*

The second matter of interest in the contemporary psychiatric conception of the irresistible impulse is the self-admitted incompetence of psychiatric knowledge. Since this incompetence is admitted by those very psychiatrists who are the most vocally insistent on changes in the fundamental law, the admission of inability to treat, to rehabilitate, and to discharge from custody should not be mistaken for modesty. Psychiatry has succeeded, in the past few decades, in reversing scientific procedure in its plea for irresponsibility and the irresistible impulse. Weihofen, we saw previously, wants the plea accepted because he claims that it is difficult to disprove. Scientific procedure, in contrast, demands that empirical evidence and logical force are needed if an hypothesis is to be seriously entertained.

There are instances of nonpsychiatrists who seemingly accept this psychiatric platform. Grünhut, for example, correctly states that "Criminal responsibility for the act committed as well as comprehension of the punishment imply a certain standard of normality." [94] He then suggests that "on this subject, the law must take counsel from the psychologist and the physician." Grünhut's assertion, I respectfully urge, is erroneous. It is within the competence of anthropology, social psychology, and sociology to establish the normality of sociocultural conduct. Grünhut's ultimate sentence in the paragraph from which I have quoted will receive the assent of most criminologists and lawyers who hold to the Anglo-American principles of the criminal law: "But in the end it is legal rules that must determine the criteria of criminal liability."

---

* It can, I suppose, be shown that any discipline is self-contradictory if quotations from the qualified writers of a discipline—of the same period of time—are properly arranged. But the immediately preceding discussion shows only that psychiatrists are unaware of the fact that at times they unconsciously refute the fundamental psychiatric postulate that the individual is basically irrational and therefore irresponsible.

Weihofen claims that "whether or not knowledge of right and wrong may coexist with a lack of power to do the right and resist the wrong would seem to be a question for psychiatrists, and not judges, to decide." [95] Guttmacher and Weihofen, with the academic imperialism that so often marks forensic psychiatry, dogmatically proclaim: "Whether a truly irresistible impulse can exist is a question for psychiatrists rather than judges to decide." [96] The proclamation is wrong on at least three counts. First, no one art, nor its practitioners—social workers, clinical psychologists, psychiatrists and the like—can "decide" the answer to the question. This is because an answer that is empirically and logically sound can be derived only from experimentation. It cannot come merely from the clinical observations and the phrenological philosophy of man that today constitute the only bases for the irresistible impulse. It is necessary to agree with Jerome Hall's conclusion on this matter:

> A theory has only that degree of validity which supporting facts confer upon it, and the writer [Jerome Hall] must acknowledge that he knows of no book, article or report of clinical data which even makes a serious effort to establish the validity of the "irresistible impulse" hypothesis. If the like question were raised regarding, e.g., immunization or diabetes, a vast amount of supporting fact would be immediately adduced. No reason appears why psychiatrists should claim an exemption from the ordinary canons of scientific proof.[97]

Second, there are neither empirical nor logical grounds for concluding that the psychology of modern penal law must be replaced by a psychiatry that has admitted it cannot establish mental illness as the cause of a crime, that it does not know how to rehabilitate the mentally ill, and that psychiatrists do not want the responsibility of having to decide when a "mentally ill" person should be released from custody. These are surely crucial matters, since they involve the lives, liberty, and property of untold numbers of people.[98] It has been insisted that what psychiatry has to offer the law must be carefully appraised. One reason is that it has thus far been largely oriented to individual therapy.[99] E. L. Thorndike has aptly made the point: "Dealing as it does mainly with human behavior, the law very likely has more to teach psychology than to learn from it. The law has had a long history and very able students and practitioners." [100]

One can properly substitute "psychiatry" for "psychology" in the above quotation.

Third, role theory, as developed in social psychology, is logically and empirically superior to the psychology of contemporary psychiatry. This is particularly and especially true in accounting for the behavior that psychiatry asserts must be explained by its postulate of the irresistible impulse. One of the significant ways in which sociology and social psychology are superior to psychiatry is that they include the widest range of sociocultural behavior within a single theory, and without having to invent pathologies in order to explain various types of immoral and undesirable behavior. Biology, psychiatry, and psychology, as well as sociology, have invented a number of pathologies in attempting to explain disapproved and undesirable behavior, especially crime. But, as the famous sociological theory of differential association demonstrates, such pathologies are wholly superfluous in the analysis of sociocultural behavior.

Several years ago Jandy analyzed some of the problems common to social psychology and psychoanalysis. His conclusion, still correct today, was that the latter had much to learn from social psychology:

> On the nature and development of the human mind and self, we still think that social psychology . . . gives a more adequate theoretical explanation than does psychoanalysis. Psychoanalysis can learn much from social psychology. We have shown that many problems of the self can be approached without resorting to the biological determinism of instincts or to mystical conceptions of the self. [101]

8. Individual Rights and the Rehabilitative Ideal

The Juvenile Court and Other Agencies

Much of the force of the social movement of mental health is encountered when one enters the juvenile court. The changing fate of the criminal and the insane can be taken as a rough measure of the extent to which the conception of man as a rational being has been intellectually and practically eroded in the United States. Somewhat more than one century ago, as Lady Wootton noted, criminals and lunatics were not sharply distinguished from each other. Being taken for one another, lunatics were treated as criminals. After some decades of being set off from one another, through being subjected to different judicial procedures and commitment to different institutions, psychiatrists again tend to place them in the same category, except that today the criminal is likely to be diagnosed as being a lunatic.

Kolb is correct in stating that a reversal in conception, policy, and practice has occurred in agencies and institutions dealing with criminals and delinquents.[1] The reversal is continuing but is by no means complete. Summarily stated, it is as follows. Whereas Anglo-American jurisprudence and its related institutions are grounded in part on the postulate that the individual is rational and therefore responsible, the trend—especially but not exclusively, in relation to juveniles—is to conceive the delinquent as being determined in his conduct by unconscious or other impulses that he cannot control. This development can largely be credited to the recent ascendance of psychiatric and social-work philosophy, and to trends in legislation and judicial decisions, rather than to the testing and application of scientific theory. Some sociologists have climbed onto the back of law, psychiatry, and social work in this matter.

In denying responsibility for their own behavior the criminal and the delinquent, as we saw, make use of this conception. One of its corollaries is that they are fit to receive compassionate treatment. The results of the reversal for the people who are the recipients of the treatment have been commented on by attorneys and others. The work of Francis A. Allen is an example. He has shown that the rise of the rehabilitative ideal has been accompanied by measures that conflict, sometimes seriously, with the values of individual liberty in choice and behavior. The obligation to contain power within the limits suggested by a community's political values, he says, has been considerably complicated by the rise of the rehabilitative ideal:

> For the problem today is one of regulating the exercise of power by men of good will, whose motivations are to help not to injure, and whose ambitions are quite different from those of the political adventurer so familiar to history. There is a tendency for such persons to claim immunity from the usual forms of restraint and to insist that professionalism and a devotion to science provide sufficient protections against unwarranted invasion of individual right.[2]

Aldous Huxley, in *Brave New World Revisited*, has subjected to mordant criticism the claim by men of good will that, since their motives are pure and they are extending help, their decisions need not be subject to legal restraint and no appeal against them is necessary: "Like Sir Galahad's their strength is the strength of ten because their heart is pure—and their heart is pure because they are scientists and have taken six thousand hours of social studies."[3]

A recent example is the work by the well-known psychiatrist, David Abrahamsen, *The Psychology of Crime*.[4] The program advanced in this book for the control, reduction, or elimination of crime and delinquency is completely psychiatric. It calls for

(1) psychiatric treatment of delinquents, and of their families, including parents and siblings; (2) a psychiatric screening of schoolteachers, lawyers, and judges; and (3) the creation of a Youth Crime Authority that would "treat" (which is undefined) *prior to his trial* any adolescent arrested by the police: "Upon the arrest of an adolescent this mobile [mental hygiene] clinic would examine him and determine his personality make-up and whether he was dangerous or whether he could be returned to his family." [5] Abrahamsen then states that the Youth Crime Authority would also have the legal right to impose "psychiatric treatment"—which, in common with many psychiatrists, he never defines—upon families with "family tension," which is another concept that he never defines. "Broken families should always be included" in this treatment, and in typical psychiatric manner, there is no definition of the concept "broken family":

> In addition to all this, the Youth Crime Authority would have to take the initiative in a community, for very often *those who most need help will not seek it,* either *because* they are not aware it exists or because of financial hardships or *lack of psychiatric orientation.* The Authority could register as many families as possible, preferably those which are trouble spots because they have already produced a juvenile delinquent, because there is much family tension (broken families should always be included), or because of a poor financial situation requiring support from the community. These are very often the "hard core" families, which are breeding grounds for crime and which show excessive resistance to reform or improvement. Each of these families should be carefully evaluated as to social and ethnical [sic] background, economic status, the number of members in the family and their earning capacity, their emotional and physical health, their emotional attitudes toward one another, and, last but not least, the presence of family tension. If treatment of a family member should be required, contact with these families should not terminate when treatment is over, but should continue over a long period and take into consideration the entire family. [6]

"Family tension" and "broken family" would seem to be whatever the examining psychiatrist would state them to be, as Dr. Abrahamsen makes no provision for an appeal against the decision of the psychiatrist, which thus would be absolute and final. He says nothing about first ascertaining whether the boy is guilty before he is subjected to the psychiatrist's undefined treatment. He seems to take the arrest as being the sufficient ground, and would have adolescents taken into custody even before they had committed a crime or a delinquent act. They would be taken "when they first manifest signs of anti-social behavior." He proposes that a psychiatric staff engage in arbitrary intervention in the lives of families the members of which (1) have not been found guilty of any crime, and (2) perhaps would not even be charged with a crime. Such families, it seems, would be forced to submit to interminable and undefined treatment.

Abrahamsen's psychiatric proposals seem based on the assumption that to be arrested is at the same time to be guilty (I will not here discuss the further assumption that psychiatrists know how to treat arrested persons). But he ignores police practices in the matter of arrest. Hundreds of thousands of people in the United States know from their personal experiences that to be arrested and to be accused is not necessarily to be guilty. *Uniform Crime Reports* lists data received from police departments on twenty-seven offenses. Its "brief definitions of crime classifications" lists the last as "Suspicion.—Arrests for no specific offense and released without formal charges being placed." [7] In 1960 the police departments of 2,446 cities with a population of more than 2,500, and having a total population of only about 73.4 million, reported the following: 126,754 persons were reported arrested in the crime classification, "Suspicion." Of these, 80,387 were white, 45,218 were Negro, 802 were Indian, 43 were Chinese, 8 were Japanese, and 296 were "all others."

"Suspicion," however, is not a crime anywhere in the United States because not one state in the Union makes it a crime to be suspected. Thus a minimum of 126,754 people were arrested and taken into police precinct stations by policemen who wanted to question or otherwise detain them without having evidence against them that would warrant a charge being laid. As Barth says, "nearly every one of these arrests was unlawful; nearly every one was in itself a crime. But the crime is so common that the FBI reported it without so much as a blush or an apology." [8] The practice of illegal arrests has been engaged in by the American police for decades, and has been investigated by various committees and commissions so often that there is now a large bibliography of titles of published works dealing with the matter.

The police of the District of Columbia arrest illegally, not because of "suspicion" but "for investigation." United States Supreme Court Justice Douglas stated that there were 7,367 arrests "for investigation" in the District in 1958, and that every one arrested "for investigation" was subsequently released.[9] There is no crime such as "investigation." Professor Caleb Foote, of the University of Pennsylvania Law School has shown that this is a contemporary and extensive practice. His study was based in part on the annual reports for the years 1953 through 1955, published by the police departments of Baltimore, Boston, Chicago, Cleveland, Cincinnati, Grand Rapids (Michigan), Lincoln (Nebraska), Los Angeles, and San Francisco. He cautiously concludes, "It is probable that many arrests for such minor crimes as vagrancy and disorderly conduct are in fact illegal detentions; how many, we do not know. Perhaps the greatest unknown is the probably very large number of detentions which are arrests in law but which are not so regarded or recorded by the police." [10] Police reports reveal that the overwhelming proportion of people arrested on these pretexts are released without being charged with a crime by the police:

> of a total of 27,146 Detroit suspects whom the police recorded as having been arrested in 1955, 22,477 or nearly 83 per cent were released without being charged. For the last four years the Baltimore reports show the discharge of 95 per cent of those arrested on suspicion. . . . of this total of 9,965 for the four-year period, 9,421 [of those "held for investigation"] were "dismissed," apparently before the preliminary hearing. In Lincoln, Nebraska, out of 187 arrests for "investigation," 184 were dismissed. Cleveland information is incomplete. . . . Of the 25,400 persons "held for investigation by members of the Detective Bureau" during these two years [1953 and 1954], 67 per cent were released without charge.[11]

Police departments will on certain occasions engage in a "dragnet," which is nothing less than the practice of indiscriminate and illegal mass arrest. The police like to refer to this by some euphemism, such as "accelerated program." The dragnet results from police officials, and perhaps the mayor, succumbing to the

hysterical demands of newspapers and radio stations for "action!"
When Negroes are indiscriminately arrested in large numbers,
professional Negro organizations and such bodies as ministerial
associations protest that the police are discriminating against
Negroes. That charge may well be correct, but it is not always
and not necessarily so. Three recent "accelerated programs" of
the Detroit police may be taken as an example. They occurred
late in 1953, 1955, and 1960 subsequent, in each of the years, to
the murder of a young white woman. (I do not recall one that
followed the murder of a Negro woman.) In the 1960 program
more than 1,500 men were arrested within less than three weeks,
in an area centering on the location of the murder. Practically
every one was a Negro. About 40 of the men were detained by
the police in connection with other offenses.[12] In 1955, about
1,620 men were arrested and in 1953 about 1,380. Practically all
were white. Less than three per cent were detained for questioning in connection with other crimes. Considering all three of the
programs, what is revealed is not necessarily discrimination. What
is clearly revealed is the mass violation of constitutional civil
rights by the police.

Liberty is thus imperiled in the United States for the sake of
order. Barth has documented the thesis that a neurotic anxiety
over crime and an almost hysterical demand for order is nurtur-
ing a police state mentality in the United States.[13] The men who
wrote the United States Constitution refused to assign the highest social value to law enforcement. They knew of the English
Star Chamber and the French *lettres de cachet,* and some of them
knew of arbitrary arrest and imprisonment from their own experience, as well as knowing the bloody and corporal manner of
punishment of the previous several centuries. Some of them concluded that the citizenry needed protection from both the law
enforcer and the law violator, and perhaps a greater protection
against the former. The fact that every tyrant in history and
every contemporary dictator found it necessary to engage in
arbitrary arrests confirms the validity of their conclusion and the
soundness of their decision.

It is unlikely that the American people, especially lower-class
Negroes and whites, will ever agree with what seems to be Abra-

hamsen's position: To be arrested is to be guilty, to be guilty is to be mentally diseased, and to be mentally diseased is to be given into the indefinite custody of the psychiatrist.

Considering the hundreds of thousands of people arrested both legally and illegally in the United States, one can imagine the form that Abrahamsen's Mobile Mental Hygiene Clinics would take. They would be a combination of the following units: ambulances, civil defense corps, firemen, hospital personnel, and policemen, all directed by a psychiatrist.

More than thirty years ago the National Commission on Law Observance and Enforcement issued its famous Report No. 11: *Lawlessness in Law Enforcement.* Known popularly as the Wickersham Commission, it stated on the first page of its report that: "respect for law, which is the fundamental prerequisite for law observance, hardly can be expected of people in general if the officers charged with enforcement of the law do not set the example of obedience to its precepts." [14]

And on almost its last page, the commission concluded that criminal actions engaged in by the police had serious consequences for the police:

> The effect upon the *police* is obvious. The third degree, in its nature brutal, must brutalize those who practice it. And the habit of lawlessness on the part of the police cannot fail to lower the dignity of their employment and their sense of that dignity. Their fight against lawless men, if waged by lawless means, is degraded almost to the level of a struggle between two law-breaking gangs.[15]

It seems likely that, since the beginning of 1962, Detroit will have less need of the proposed Mobile Mental Hygiene Squad to examine illegally arrested citizens. George Edwards, newly appointed Commissioner of Police, announced his policy in operating the Department of Police to be as follows: "This department seeks equal protection of the law against all violators. This department seeks the cooperation of all law-abiding people in this city in its efforts on behalf of law enforcement."

The cooperation sought by Commissioner Edwards can be obtained only from a population that has confidence in its police department, from the commissioner to the patrolman. We indicated previously that this is perhaps the most crucial problem confronting municipal police departments in the United States. While it is difficult to modify drastically ways of thinking and acting that are institutionally established, change is not impossible; and it is likely to occur in the arrest practices of the Detroit police. Professor O. W. Wilson was appointed in 1960 as head of the Chicago police department after another particularly shocking revelation of corruption. He has shown in two years that it is possible to effect significant change in a semi-military organization in which corruption has become institutionalized. The crucial question is, How permanent will such changes be?

Commissioner Edwards, in reviewing the first fifteen months of his administration, was of the opinion that the changes in the Detroit police program will be permanent. The program is that of equal law enforcement with improved community relations. He regarded dragnet arrests and the "alley court" as not only unconstitutional but totally impractical. "They defeat the very objectives they are used to achieve," he said, "by decreasing the possibilities of community support for law enforcement." [16]

One may be tempted to think Abrahamsen's proposal ridiculous; there is, however, a tendency of some magnitude to intervene in the lives of certain people—both children and adults— who have committed no offense. The reasons advanced to justify the intervention are usually three in number: (1) The intervenors are trying to help those in need. (2) If there is no intervention, the behavior of the children "is very likely to result ultimately in delinquency, emotional instability, or both. A child exhibiting such behavior will expend a great deal of his mental energy, time, and attention in destructive pursuits; with relatively less efficiency in his other more constructive pursuits." [17] (3) Without intervention the adults will most likely come to, or continue to, live on public assistance, be alcoholics or excessive drinkers, be unemployable, desert their families and form common-law conjugal teams, be criminals, and rear antisocial or asocial children.

An excellent example of such proposed mass intervention is found in the March 1961 *Report* to the Community Fund and Welfare Council of Greater Windsor.[18] By means of a questionnaire distributed to the teachers in the public and separate schools in Windsor, in grades 3 through 8, the Community Fund and

Welfare Council obtained the names of 567 pupils. It was the opinion of the teacher as to "which of the children in her classroom may be 'in trouble' and need special helping services." [19] On the sole basis of a teacher's reply to an impressionistic questionnaire, the *Report* asserted that these children "have serious problems of social and psychological adjustment." With no evidence of delinquency presented and with no adjudication of delinquency by the judge of the juvenile court, it stated that 92 of the boys were social delinquents; and that 77 others were solitary delinquents.[20] Despite the fact that no information concerning sexual delinquencies on the part of girls was requested, and that no such information was provided by the teachers, 31 "prematurely boy-crazy girls" were labeled sexually deviant. The teachers were asked to report gossip about girls. If they had heard gossip about a girl they were asked to place a check mark in front of the statement, "Is the center of reports and rumors about out of school relations with older boys and men (dubious behavior, sex activity)." [21]

The *Report* furthermore metamorphosed the teachers' opinions of the children into diseases that it claimed the children had. And as "next steps" it proposed the construction of an enormous proscription list of hundreds of Windsor families whose privacy would be invaded and who would be placed under continued surveillance:

1. Identify, describe and maintain continuing scrutiny on the *problem families in the community* in which the children are found.
2. *Follow the children* from the time of problem appearance on, observing the course of the *disease* and the effect of services on it.
3. *Coordinate and center* all applicable community services on the family, not on its individual members.
   . . . Treatment should be addressed . . . to the disorganized families which are the *foci of infection;* this way the future incidence of *disease* may be reduced.

There is needed at the outset therefore, a listing of, say, the 500 most disorganized, multiple-problem families of Windsor. To do this, all of the agencies of Windsor—correctional, health, family, relief—must cooperate to identify the *multiple* problem families, to assess the severity of their situations, and to obtain an unduplicated set of names. The names of the [567] children already obtained in this study would be a fine place to start. The withdrawn child at school will now take his place in the family where the father has an unstable work history, the mother is tubercular, the older brother is in trouble with the law.

The problem family listing must be kept up to date. . . . From time to time, perhaps yearly, the agencies should screen new cases and assess them for addition to the list. It should be possible, as *an additional instrument of surveillance,* to maintain an individual spot map of the residential location of these families in the city.

. . . we [must] set up and maintain a *longitudinal* observation on the children. When it comes to the time factor, *social and psychological diseases* are not like most physical diseases. Pneumonia is contracted and runs its course in a few days. The doctor knows within hours whether his treatment is going to work. The diseases we deal with are "contracted" over months or years, and take equally long periods first to be recognized, then to be treated.

. . . new mal-adapting children [should be] added to the list . . .

Finally, . . . in order to overcome the hard shell of resistance to help that these families present, some alteration of the traditional casework approach is called for . . . We are slowly learning that with the "hard to reach" there is needed . . . more outright supervision and management of client's life where needed, more environmental manipulation. . . .[22]

The Community Fund and Welfare Council has started to implement the above proposals. It has hired a highly qualified Social Planning Director. It has not yet, however, established its surveillance list of children and families; and, social agencies being the jealous bodies that they sometimes are, it may be a long time before the list will be completed.

One is impelled to ask some questions concerning the entire survey. Who qualified the teachers to "identify" their pupils on the bases that they employed? Who qualified the social agencies to establish the proposed list? Will a pupil and family be notified that they are to be listed? Is there to be an appellate procedure against being listed? Who qualified the Community Fund and Welfare Council and its employees to attempt to exact conformity to their social values, on the part of all children from all social classes?

The purpose and function of the proposals are to produce conformity, at least in overt behavior if not also in thought, to

the social values on which the survey was based. No child can
be allowed to remain outside its proposals. Conformity is to be
exacted under the guise of extending help and rendering a service. That may be sound social-agency practice and philosophy. It
is not scientific procedure and seems incompletely honest and
hardly ethical. What we are confronted with here is nothing less
than the serious problem of the competence to help.

Although less fortunate persons in our society have some
freedom of choice, they are restricted in many ways as soon as
they are defined as deviants and are thus relatively powerless to
decide to what extent they will be helped and who will help them.
Dr. Shannon has asked what are the criteria of competence to
help: "How may we decide which groups or professions are
competent to deal with the various types of deviant behavior
with which we are concerned, with the behavioral types which
the larger society defines as in need of help?" [23] He suggests the
following:

Positive criteria:
1. The ability to predict human behavior.
2. The ability to modify or control human behavior.
3. The existence of a body of scientific research that tends to
   support the explanation of the professional group in question
   and with which the therapy in question appears to be consistent.
Negative criteria:
1. Existence of a body of research indicating that a group has
   not been able to deal effectively with the behavior in question
   although it may purport to have such ability.
2. Existence of a body of evidence that a group is so torn by dis-
   sension that it cannot be considered to have a unitary approach to the problem behavior.[24]

Projects designed to help people through attempts to minimize
or reduce the incidence of given social problems can be evaluated
as to effectiveness. Such evaluative research, Shannon indicates,
could reveal that no group or profession has demonstrated the
ability to deal effectively with deviant behavior. Research shows
that no program of treatment—using "treatment" as this noun is
used in the several studies—results in a greater improvement than
that which results from merely leaving alone the people with a

behavioral problem. This, of course, means that "the cry for more money, for a saturation approach, is indeed uncalled for." [25] Cressey has undertaken a study evaluating the results of correctional projects or programs designed to control, reduce, or minimize crime and delinquency. His study shows that regardless of what the results of the program are found to be—whether successful or unsuccessful—the personnel who maintain either theoretical or practical interests in the control of crime and delinquency develop a vocabulary of motives that justifies what they are doing.[26] Another study evaluated in detail the effectiveness of a variety of programs designed to deal with juvenile delinquency. The authors conclude, on the basis of their research, that programs designed to control delinquency provide us with no certain knowledge as to how to control it.[27]

At the beginning of this section we referred to Kolb's statement that a reversal in conception, policy, and practice has occurred in institutions dealing with delinquents. One of the important consequences of this, in the United States, is the abrogation in the juvenile court of practically all of the constitutional procedural safeguards of the penal code. Substituted therefor is the conception of that court that makes it a child-guidance agency supported by the compelling power of the state: "... hearsay evidence that is not subject to cross examination, commonly unverified rumor and gossip, become fundamentals of [juvenile] court action." [28] There has been a "wide departure from traditional conceptions of due process in the handling of the child . . . and more particularly . . . irrelevant, prejudicial, and hearsay testimony has become the rule in juvenile court action." [29]

It appears from some evidence in this matter that the Canadian juvenile courts accord much more respect to the young person's rights than do the American. In Windsor, for example, in the juvenile court—located less than five miles south of the Wayne County (Detroit) juvenile court—I can hear only cases of juvenile delinquency. In order to hear cases of dependent and neglected children it is necessary to go to another courtroom, that of the family court.

Tappan has succinctly stated the problem:

I suggest that, in perhaps no phase of contemporary social policy is there greater need for Government to erect—and I think it has failed almost entirely to do so thus far—to erect protections by which the individual with problems may be saved from the ravaging benefactions of his saviors.[30]

Dean Roscoe Pound, one of the most influential persons in promoting the juvenile-court movement, came to compare the juvenile court with the star chamber:

The powers of the star chamber were a trifle in comparison with those of our juvenile courts and courts of domestic relations. It is well known that too often the placing of a child in a home or even in an institution is done casually or perfunctorily or even arbitrarily. Even with the most superior personnel these tribunals call for legal checks.[31]

The similarity of the star chamber and the juvenile court has been noted more recently:

fairness and justice certainly recognize that a child has the right not to be a ward of the State, not to be committed to a reformatory, not to be deprived of his liberty, if he is innocent. The procedure for ascertaining the guilt or innocence of a minor may be [called] a civil inquiry . . . but in substance and form it is a trial—a momentous trial . . . because the defendant's whole life still lies before him. And no matter how trained and experienced a Juvenile Court judge may be, he cannot by any magical fishing rod draw forth the truth out of a confused sea of speculation, rumor, suspicion and hearsay. He must follow certain procedures which the wisdom of centuries have established.[32]

A layman most likely would agree with Judge Musmanno, and could ask, How can anyone disagree with his statement? A majority of the justices of the Supreme Court of Pennsylvania disagreed with it, as *In re Holmes* (1954) indicated. The fact that the United States Constitution and the constitutions of the several states guarantee that none shall be deprived of his liberty without due process of law was not relevant to the justices' majority opinion. That constitutional guarantee, in common with all generalities, is not universal in its application. It applies to traitors, murderers, armed robbers, burglars, and to prostitutes and petty thieves, but not to children in a proceeding in the juvenile court.[33]

Some attorneys, as shown by the quotations from Tappan, are seriously concerned with the manner in which young people are handled in the juvenile court. Another example is the statement given in evidence by Lawrence Speiser, director of the Washington, D. C., office of the American Civil Liberties Union:

> In 1956, a 17-year-old boy had a hearing in juvenile court in Philadelphia on a charge of assault and battery. He was, in effect, found guilty on the basis of a written report of a police officer—supplemented by his equivocal testimony—who said he arrested the boy near the scene and time of the crime. The boy, unrepresented by counsel, protested his innocence and also denied he had been arrested by the officer. The court discounted his protestations and gave the boy an indefinite sentence at a State industrial school.
>
> Friends and neighbors complained to the Pennsylvania branch of the American Civil Liberties Union which provided counsel. Numbers of witnesses were easily found who could testify that they had been with the boy at the time of the crime at a totally different location. It was also discovered through police records, which could have been produced at the first hearing, that the police officer could not have arrested the boy at the time and place in question because he was on desk duty the entire time. The boy was released after a new hearing, after spending 6 weeks of imprisonment.

Speiser then referred to the continuous conflict between the proponents of the juvenile court and those of its critics concerned with the constitutional rights of juveniles. The latter have called attention to "great injustices" that occur in juvenile courts under the rationale "it's in the child's own best interests," and such slogans as *parens patriae* and *in loco parentis*. They contend that many juveniles would not have been deprived of their freedom if juvenile court procedures had accorded them the constitutional rights possessed by adults. Without in any way suggesting the abolition of the juvenile court, they hold that commitment to a "juvenile home," juvenile "training school," or to any similarly named facility impresses a derogatory stigma upon the juvenile. The argument that an adult's constitutional rights have no place in juvenile court proceedings would be more cogent if it could be demonstrated that the state is or can be a better surrogate parent than the natural parents. It is therefore important that the lawful child not be swept into the same pile with the delinquent. There is hardly a more efficient means to embitter a child or an adult than to deprive him of his liberty on the ground that "it's for your own good," if he is in fact innocent of the charge. When a juvenile is in effect charged with the commission of a crime (even though juvenile courts are supposedly civil in nature) Speiser argued that he should have more rather than fewer rights than an adult in the criminal court. This doctrine, he said, has been "clearly stated" by the federal district court in the District of Columbia in the case of *In re Poff* (135 Fed Supp 224 [1955]) as follows:

"While the juvenile court law provides that adjudication of a minor to be a ward of the court shall not be deemed to be a conviction of a crime, nevertheless, for all practical purposes, this is a legal fiction, presenting a challenge to credulity and doing violence to reason. Courts cannot and will not shut their eyes and ears to everyday contemporary happenings.

". . . True, the design of the Juvenile Court Act is intended to be salutary, and every effort should be made to further its legitimate purpose, but never should it be made an instrument for the denial to a minor of a constitutional right or a guarantee afforded by law to an adult. . . .

"Surely a minor charged in the juvenile court with acts denounced by law as a felony does not have lesser constitutional, statutory rights, or guarantees than are afforded an adult under similar circumstances in the superior court. . . .

"In the final analysis the juvenile court is a judicial institution. . . .

". . . it cannot seriously be contended that the constitutional guarantee of due process of law does not extend to minors as well as adults. . . ."

The juvenile court acts were adopted in order to provide for the rehabilitation of the child offender, and to protect him from the stigma and punishment visited upon criminals. The State appears not as the avenger of an outraged society, but as the protector and friend of the child. The rationale is that where parents cannot or do not take responsibility, the State, through the juvenile court system, assumes the parental role. These are good concepts.

When these concepts were adopted, the terminology of the law was radically changed. A child under 18 is not found guilty of a crime and punished by a prison sentence. He is "adjudicated" to be a "delinquent," and may be committed for an indefinite period to a reformatory or a "training school." The judge, of course, may decide that such a drastic measure is not called for, and return him to his home.

Unfortunately, the enlightened concept does not always work out in practice. Being locked up behind bars for an indefinite period is punishment, whatever else it may be. Calling the place a training school instead of a prison does not change the fact. Commitment as a juvenile delinquent is a stigma which can do harm to a child's reputation, despite assertions that it should not be. American Civil Liberties Union knows of many instances where a child's record as a delinquent has been used in other courts or in the newspapers to his disadvantage. These are facts which do not disappear at the invocation of magic words like "adjudication of delinquency."

While American Civil Liberties Union does not hold that juveniles should not be punished, we maintain that no one should be punished by the State without knowing in detail the charges against him, and the source of the accusations. He should have counsel if he wishes, and the opportunity to face and cross-examine his accusers, to call his own witnesses, and not be judged upon incompetent evidence and secret reports. A dissenting opinion in Pennsylvania Supreme Court stated:

"The country today is plagued with considerable juvenile delinquency. The least effective way to solve that problem is to punish indiscriminately the guilty and the innocent. To charge a juvenile with armed robbery and send him off to a reformatory school without legal proof that he has committed that heinous crime is to embitter not only him but all of his companions who will feel that they no longer owe any loyalty to an unjust society." Under our laws, in many jurisdictions, it is easier to convict boys than to convict men.[34]

The American Civil Liberties Union then offered some recommendations designed to protect the constitutional rights of minors in juvenile courts. They included differentiating sharply between delinquent, and dependent and neglected children, defining delinquency so as to restrict it to violations of laws and ordinances, establishing procedures for the arrest, detention, and interrogation of juveniles by policemen, restricting the use made of confessions, and providing for the presence of a parent, guardian, or attorney at the time of interrogation. Separating the adjudication of delinquency completely from the disposition made after adjudication was also recommended. The purpose was to make possible some procedural changes that would give to the juvenile most if not all of the protections enjoyed by adults in the criminal court, while retaining the essential informality of the usual juvenile-court hearing. The changes would result in such things as the full disclosure of the evidence against the juvenile; the application of the rules of evidence so as to exclude hearsay, gossip, the family's history, and the like; confrontation and examination of witnesses; and the prohibition of the juvenile being required to testify against himself over the objections of his parent, guardian, or attorney.

Speiser and the American Civil Liberties Union then pose a question that many people have asked since the juvenile court was established: Shall there be public hearings? The most complete discussion of the several legal and moral aspects of this question is presented in Geis's analysis of publicity in relation to juvenile court proceedings. Geis advances three recommendations:

1. Newspapers should be allowed admittance to juvenile courts, but they should be forbidden by law from disclosing the names of the participants in the hearings.

2. Publication of identifying data about persons in juvenile court hearings should be forbidden by statute in such a manner that the information does not reach the newspapers from sources other than the courts.

3. Every juvenile before the court should be afforded the opportunity of a public hearing if he so desires.[35]

Similar recommendations have often been made in the past.[36] The necessity of striving for their implementation is to be found partly in the fact that, in those juvenile courts operating as social agencies, there may be little practical difference in the way in which delinquent children, on the one hand, and dependent and neglected children, on the other, are handled. A boy's status may, for example, be changed from "delinquent" to "neglected" during a hearing. The change may be made on the basis of unsupported and uninvestigated statements by a neighbor, a friend of the family, or a social worker or probation officer employed by the court.

Most people do not realize that in many, if not most, juvenile courts in the United States there is often little practical difference between "delinquent" and "neglected" children. Their hearings may be held in the same room by the same referee or judge. They may be confined in the same detention or youth "home," and may have the same disposition as to placement: in a foster home, in an institution for children operated by one of the three major religious faiths or in a correctional institution for delinquents. In the years 1950–52, the most frequent placement of dependent and neglected children who required shelter care pending their court hearing was in boarding homes or homes of relatives and friends. However, 40 percent of those children were placed in detention homes, jails, or police stations with delinquents.[37]

The above-named types of placement raise a significant question as to the relation between legislative definitions and administrative definitions. In 40 per cent of the cases involving no delinquency, the status of *non-delinquent* nevertheless resulted in the same treatment accorded to *delinquents*. In those cases the legal categories of *dependent* and *neglected* were administratively redefined as being synonyms of the legal category *delinquent*. The Advisory Council of Judges asserts that in delinquency proceedings based on an alleged violation of law, "the courts quite uniformly hold that the probation report cannot be considered in adjudicating whether the violation was committed." [38] That assertion may correctly apply to some juvenile courts in recent years, but certainly not "quite uniformly" to the large, separate courts of the urban counties. One example will be sufficient here:

> Probably the most important function of the Probation Officer in terms of disposition of children's cases is his *pre-trial investigation*. . . . His function basically is to investigate and make a "family history," which includes personal histories of both parents, a health history of all members of the family, financial situation of the family, religious affiliation, home and neighborhood conditions, relationships among members of the family group, and attitudes toward present situation.[39]

No single one of the items mentioned in the above quotation, nor all of them together, have any relevance to the validity of the complaint that a boy, for example, snatched a purse, or burglarized a house, or stole an automobile. This is especially true

of the last item, "attitudes toward present situation." If he con-
fesses, a judge or referee is likely to think that the boy is co-
operative and guilty and therefore deserves another chance. If
he denies it he may be regarded as merely trying to conceal his
guilt and should therefore most probably, for his own good, be
committed to a correctional institution for juveniles. The probation officer also interviews the child and obtains a "delinquency
history." This consists of the charge, place of detention, the
group involved, the appearance, health, and personality of the
child, his educational and employment history, the child's attitude toward his present situation. In addition, "other agency
reports [are] submitted to the Juvenile Judge as aids in dispos-
ing of the matter in the best interests of the child." [40]

In order to serve the welfare of the child the data collected are
presented in a hearing conducted in "an informal and friendly
atmosphere." The result, it is claimed, will be that "the child will
then look upon the Court as someone who wants to help him,
and not necessarily punish him as a criminal." [41] One should not
be surprised to find such an unsophisticated statement in a law
review. Gilbert Geis has more than adequately demonstrated that
"a reading of the higher court decisions handed down by trained
jurists regarding juvenile court laws would make even the most
naive social worker blush uncomfortably with their free recourse
to ecstatic and unwarranted assumptions." [42]

The legal profession is not unified on the conception of the
juvenile court as a social agency. It has been said that to argue
that the child who is "adjudicated" a delinquent is not "punished" as the adult offender is, but provided with care, protection,
and treatment, is to make a distinction without a difference. The
sanctions employed by the juvenile court are essentially the same
as those employed by the criminal court. Principally they are
probation and institutional commitments. These juvenile-court
sanctions are indistinguishable from those of the criminal court,
even though the former are the result of "civil" rather than
"criminal" process. [43]

It is surely anomalous that civil process can in one instance—
the juvenile court—be used to impose criminal sanctions and in
another—white-collar crime—to avoid their imposition. White-

collar crime is the criminal violation by businessmen, of the laws regulating business, during the conduct of the business. The corporate executives of the electrical equipment industry, involved in the criminal violation of the anti-trust laws, referred to previously, are examples of white-collar criminals. The conviction of those men is one of the rare instances in which white-collar crime resulted in the imposition of criminal sanctions. Such offenders are typically subjected to civil process, which results in no stigma of being "criminal." [44]

The necessity for calling attention to these matters arises from the juvenile court's devotion to what is sometimes called "individualized justice" or "socialized justice." The objective of the court that operates as a social agency is not to ascertain whether the child committed any action for which he should be held, but rather to ascertain the causes of his behavior in order that he can be treated according to his needs. The noted juvenile court judge Paul W. Alexander has written of the "new concept of justice" that has developed in recent decades, and that "has been gaining rapid acceptance." The emphasis, he writes, is transferred from *what* the criminal did to *why* he did it, and from what society should do *to* the criminal to what it can do *for* him. Furthermore, the juvenile *"court doesn't have to find out whether the child is delinquent, but why."* [45] In a masterly understatement, Judge Alexander says that "this usually comes as something as a shock to laymen, lawyers, and most trial and appellate judges, and even to a new juvenile judge." Perhaps the shock occurs when the judge tries to comprehend how he can decide *why* a juvenile is delinquent without it first having been proved that he *is* delinquent. His question, "not whether but why?" has been asked by others, for example by Dr. Gustav L. Schramm, Judge of the Juvenile Court, Allegheny County (Pittsburgh):

> Juvenile courts are the least understood and the most misunderstood courts of our land. Their unique philosophy, procedures and approach are features that not all segments of the population, even of the legal profession of the bench, have fully perceived as yet. In our traditional courts the emphasis is on, "Did you or did you not?"; not on, "Why, under what circumstances, and what can be done to help?" [46]

The concern of the juvenile-court judges with *why* rather than with *whether* was stated some years before the development of reality therapy, discussed briefly in Chapter 3 in connection with the learning of a vocabulary of motives. Reference was also made there to sociologically based attempts to develop sociocultural environments conducive to the acceptance, by delinquents, of lawful conceptions of person, property, and the law. One can conclude that delinquents who have their behavior explained to them in courts that ask "Why," rather than "Whether" or "What," will tend to transmute the motives imputed to them into justifications for their misdeeds. And, following the reasoning of the judges, the justifications will absolve them of legal and moral responsibility for their offenses.

There is some concern in Australia that the juvenile court, functioning as a social agency, is leading to treatment without trial. Johnston states that this brings us closer to "1984":

> It is apparent to those who make contact with children's courts, and particularly to counsel accustomed to the adult courts' emphasis upon trial procedure, that the primary question asked in juvenile courts today is, "What treatment would be most beneficial to this child?", rather than, "Has this child committed an offense and so rendered himself liable to the sanction of the court?" Confidence in our treatment process is already leading to treatment without trial, undermining the rule of a rigid law, and bringing us closer to "1984." [47]

Mr. Justice John V. Barry of Victoria, in his report of the first United Nations Conference on the Prevention of Crime and the Treatment of Offenders (1955), wrote:

> The [non-punitive] theory of social defence may have a great deal to recommend it if applied wisely and judiciously, but if it be carried too far and used unselectively (and there is more than a little risk of its advocates doing so) it may produce a state of affairs very dangerous to the legitimate freedom of the individual.[48]

Canada is also experiencing some of the problems inherent in conceiving the juvenile court to be a social agency as well as a court of law. Canadian legislation is somewhat of a compromise between the English and American philosophies of the juvenile court. In his study of Canadian juvenile delinquency, Price states that for the English:

> the principles that govern the Juvenile Court way of dealing with the juvenile offender are these: one, that treatment, institutional or otherwise, should be directed exclusively to the individual's education and readjustment, and should be in no way dependent upon what the juvenile has done; and two . . . that, even within a comprehensive system envisaged for all juveniles in need of social and educational treatment, the principle of criminal responsibility still obtains. [Whereas] in the United States the Juvenile Court movement has developed differently, and children are regarded as exempt from criminal responsibility for their actions altogether. The English and American positions are different in this respect, and . . . Canadian legislation generally is something of a compromise between [them].[49]

The draftsman of the Juvenile Delinquents Act seemed to prefer the American philosophy of the juvenile court. He was, however, faced with a constitutional obstacle. In Canada the Provincial Legislatures have exclusive jurisdiction over the civil status of individuals. Therefore the Parliament of Canada does not have the power to enact the noncriminal status of juvenile delinquency, possessed by the several states of the United States. Since Parliament has exclusive jurisdiction with respect to criminal offenses, neither is it possible for a Provincial Legislature to enact laws on the basis of the American philosophy.[50]

The juvenile-court legislation is allegedly nonpunitive. Price, however, states that the very adjudication of delinquency itself is in fact punishment for an offense. He raises the further point of the potentiality for abuse. It may be said that, since the purpose of the juvenile court's action is to protect and benefit the child, its intervention is for the child's own good, and therefore abuse or possible abuse is not a problem. Price asks whether this is in fact a complete answer: "Where should the line be drawn when measures thought desirable in the protection of children seem to involve conflict with what have been regarded as accepted principles of social policy directed to the protection of the individual against arbitrary interference with liberty?"[51]

That the Canadian constitution, like other constitutions, written or unwritten, is a viable instrument is illustrated by a recommendation of the Canadian Corrections Association concerning the Juvenile Delinquents Act. A committee of the association recommends that

> The federal legislation should contain provision for those provinces which wish to do so to pass legislation to provide that any child charged with an offense may be dealt with under provincial legislation as neglected rather than as an offender. The Court should have authority to determine in any particular case whether proceedings are to be held under the federal delinquency legislation or under the complementary provincial legislation.[52]

That very thing has developed in Saskatchewan, if I interpret correctly some statements in recent publications of the provincial Department of Social Welfare and Rehabilitation. Under the heading "New Legislation," the *Annual Report* of that department for 1958–59 reads:

> It was decided that services to children should include services to delinquent children. This appeared to be a logical step because delinquent children require all the services which are offered to neglected or *potentially neglected children*. The only difference appears to be the manner in which these children are brought to the attention of the department, that is because their emotional disturbance or the neglect of parents have brought these children into conflict with the law.
>
> The part of the Corrections Act dealing with juvenile offenders has, therefore, been repealed and amendments made to The Child Welfare Act.[53]

On the basis of that *Annual Report* delinquency has been eliminated in the province by redefining it as a state of "neglect" or "potential neglect." One can predict that the acts previously qualifying young people as delinquents will not decrease in prevalence or incidence because their perpetrators are now covered by the Child Welfare Act. The equating of delinquency with neglect and *potential* neglect is now well established, at least officially: "Although the symptoms are different a child who commits a delinquency is a child with an emotional problem as is the neglected or potentially neglected child." [54] And in the *Annual Report* for 1959–60, one reads: "The emphasis in protection service is changing from gross neglect, such as ill treatment or malnutrition, to behavior problems shown by children. These problems are symptomatic of trouble ahead, if they are not treated early." [55] This statement certainly raises many questions. How is "behavior problem" defined, and by whom? On what moral and/or legal grounds is intervention to be undertaken? Will it be by employees of the department or of private social agencies? What is "treatment" and how early is "early"? Will it accelerate or impede the development of delinquent careers among adolescents?

It can correctly be said that "treatment" is one of the often-used but undefined terms in psychiatry, sociology, and social work. In one report this term or one of its synonyms was used at least thirty-four times in the first ten pages without once being defined.[56] One of the most useless of all possible conceptions holds treatment to be everything that happens to a person. An example is the statement that "in the institution [the Provincial Jail for Men], treatment includes every thing which happens to an inmate." [57] By the time the Annual Report, 1960–61, was published, gross maltreatment of children through neglect or purposive cruelty had practically disappeared, it was claimed. It also seems that any social organization larger than the family does not exist in the province, as far as the causation of delinquency is concerned. If I read the *Annual Report* correctly it is, on the whole, only immature and unstable parents who produce delinquents:

> Much more frequent are the conditions that arise from the immaturity or instability of parents who are unable or unwilling to discharge their responsibilities as parents; the Metis and Indians who cannot meet the standards imposed by society; and families whose children are emotionally disturbed or delinquent.[58]

One then encounters the following paragraph:

> Saskatchewan Boys' School, situated on the outskirts of Regina, provides a group living experience for boys who are delinquent or *potentially delinquent*. The school serves a dual purpose: It provides detention facilities for boys being held prior to court and accepts boys for treatment and training within the institution.[59]

The paragraph quoted is interesting for several reasons. It refers again to "potential delinquents," as several previous passages referred to "potentially neglected" children. They would include practically all, if not all, of the children in the province. No criteria of the "potentially delinquent" are listed, just as there are none for the "potentially neglected." Who is to decide which children are "potentially" delinquent? And in the absence of any overt delinquency, what action can be taken against them? What requires clarification is the statement, "Saskatchewan Boys' School . . . provides a group living experience for boys who are . . . potentially delinquent." This is a statement which says that the Boys' School has *potentially* delinquent boys among its inmates, as well as adjudicated delinquents. How is this possible? Could—or would—a magistrate be involved in the commitment of a boy who was, merely in someone's opinion, potentially delinquent? From my slight personal acquaintance I cannot conceive the possibility of this. Indeed, I think that the reverse would obtain, namely, a magistrate would demand the immediate release of a boy illegally confined. These *Annual Reports,* in revealing the trend of thought of legislatively influential people, indicate that the conception of "socialized justice" may be more advanced in Canada than is generally realized.

The elimination, through both legislation and administrative decision, of the distinction among the delinquent, the neglected, and the emotionally disturbed child reaches its finest flower and most perfect form in the practice of committing nonpsychotic delinquents to state mental hospitals for the insane. I quote from a study completed at Wayne State University in 1959:

> In recent years, there has been an increasing trend toward commitment of nonpsychotic delinquent children to state mental hospitals for detention purposes. It is not known, however, how widespread this practice is nationally, or what kinds of consequences occur within the mental hospital setting as a result of it.[60]

The author of the study found that 46 per cent of the inmates of seventeen mental hospitals in the northeastern United States were nonpsychotic delinquents. They could not have been committed without the signature of the juvenile-court judge and the attendant psychiatrist. The time of incarceration ranged from about two weeks to three years, with an average of about eighteen months. The nonpsychotic delinquents were subjected to psychotherapy, the average duration of the psychotherapeutic sessions being 44 minutes per week. As one superintendent of a mental hospital explained, "Some think we have the ability to help."

The committing of nonpsychotic delinquent Puerto Ricans to hospitals for the criminally insane had been protested a few years earlier by Wertham:

> The idea that Puerto Ricans are intellectually and emotionally different from and inferior to others, and consequently dangerous, is common. . . . I have encountered it again and again among professional workers: doctors, psychiatrists, psychologists, psychoanalysts, lawyers, clergymen, social workers, teachers. . . .
> . . . So it happens that Puerto Rican adolescents are wrongly diagnosed as schizophrenic and committed to state mental hospitals or called mentally defective and sent to institutions for the defective. Even though judicial notice has been taken of such falsely committed cases . . . the situation has not improved.[61]

It is thus that in recent years the distinctions between different classes of children are being progressively removed by administrative and legal action. Delinquent and nondelinquent, neglected and nonneglected, psychotic and nonpsychotic, actually delinquent and neglected, and potentially delinquent and neglected, tend to be classified as "disturbed" and therefore as "in need of help." [62] It may be that the trend I have been discussing reflects that arrogance and insensitivity to human values to which men who have no reason to doubt their own motives appear peculiarly susceptible.

The Attempt to Predict Delinquency

One other aspect of the trend under discussion should be mentioned briefly. This is the concern with the "delinquency prone" or "predelinquent" child, and the attempt to predict his delinquency. There is at least one universal complaint uttered by people who work with juvenile delinquents, from those employed by the federal government to those employed by private social-work agencies. It is that there is not enough trained personnel to deal properly with the problem of inadequate money and a dearth of correctional facilities of various kinds. Despite this, there is an ever-increasing concern with the attempt to detect the predelinquent before he has committed an overt act of delinquency and to subject him to intensive treatment in an attempt to prevent delinquency. As Riley has said:

> Before an acceptable definition of a delinquent is arrived at, social workers are concerned over the *predelinquent*. If we do not know what a delinquent is, what is a predelinquent? The idea seems to be that if we can do something now, before he is what the law describes as a delinquent, we can prevent him from becoming one. "Why wait until it is too late?" This is all the more confusing because the theory of juvenile court legislation is that when the state intervenes on behalf of a delinquent, he may be saved from becoming a criminal. It now appears that the state should intervene before the juvenile commits any wrong, because if left unprotected, he may commit one. This concept, of course, throws the need for a definition of a delinquent right out of the window.[63]

The most publicized attempt to detect the predelinquent "predicts" probable delinquency at about six years of age, or when the boy first enrolls in school. I refer to the instrument developed by Sheldon and Eleanor Glueck. The New York City Youth Board has been engaged in a test of the Glueck Social Prediction Table since September 1952. Its study began with an application of the tables to a sample of 220 boys when they first enrolled in school. The definition of delinquency used by the New York City Youth Board follows:

> Delinquency refers to repeated acts of a kind which when committed by persons beyond the statutory juvenile court age of sixteen are punishable as crimes (either felonies or misdemeanors)— except for a few instances of persistent stubbornness, truancy, running away, associating with immoral persons, and the like. Children who once or twice during the period of growing up in an excitingly attractive milieu steal a toy in a ten cent store, sneak into a subway or moving picture theatre, play hookey and the like and soon outgrow such peccadilloes are not true delinquents, even though they have broken the law.[64]

The New York City Youth Board, however, departed from its own definition, and included "school behavior," "antisocial behavior," "delinquent traits," and "mental illness" in its category of "delinquency." By so doing it was able to claim that 88.9 per cent of children acted as predicted.[65] "Antisocial behavior" and "delinquency traits" may be considered predictive of delinquency. But, as Elizabeth Herzog has indicated, the predicting of delinquency is precisely what the Glueck Prediction Scale purports to do: "Its efficacy, then, can hardly be judged on the basis of predicting *potential* delinquency." [66] The New York City Youth Board listed 76 children under "observed delinquency," with this expanded conception. Instances of mental illness and school behavior problems are even less justifiably included than are "antisocial behavior" and "delinquent traits." Thus, following Herzog, one can rework the Youth Board's original data. This shows the number of children classified as having a high probability of delinquency who are in the categories "unofficial delinquency" and "official delinquency." [67] The prediction was that 72 of the 220 children would be in one or the other of these two categories. Four years later, when the boys were nine and one-half to ten and one-half years of age, only nine had been classified as either officially or unofficially delinquent. All but one of the nine came from among those rated as having a greater than 50 per cent chance of becoming delinquent. But, since these nine comprise only one-eighth of those so rated, then for every one correctly predicted, eight were erroneously predicted, or "falsely branded," as Herzog puts it.

Seven years after the beginning of the study, when the children were twelve and one-half to thirteen and one-half years of age, the over-prediction of delinquency was still gross. Only one of every four boys for whom delinquency had been predicted in September 1952 was so classified at the end of 1959. Of the white boys for whom delinquency was predicted, only one in four was so classified; of Negro boys, the figure was two in every 7; and of Puerto Rican, the figure was four in five so classified.[68]

Such results hardly warrant the expenditure of large sums of money. Something more than money is of course involved in the use of the concept *predelinquent,* namely, the lives of the children so classified. The available evidence indicates that most of the children assigned a high probability score of becoming delinquent do not become so. That evidence indicates that large numbers of children should not be labeled "predelinquent." This is especially so because we are largely ignorant of the effects of such labeling. Some have argued cogently that it may facilitate the children's progress to delinquency. In evaluating both the New York City Youth Board and the Cambridge-Somerville studies, it can be seen that the errors in prediction are much greater for boys coming from families receiving public assistance than for boys from financially independent families.[69] Herzog has made the same point:

> These children are rated pre-delinquent because of their family misfortunes. All children whose families show [a high prediction of delinquency] are likely to be in need of services and should get them according to and because of their need. It seems unfair and unnecessary to compound their misfortunes by branding them on the basis of statistical computations which, however worthy the intentions, are "off the beam." [70]

Berkson has developed the thesis that the efficiency of a predictive device cannot be assessed by a single measure of effectiveness, such as the percentage of correct predictions, which the Gluecks and the New York City Youth Board use. He proposes measuring the efficiency of a device on the basis of utility and cost.[71] The utility of the Glueck Social Prediction Table is the percentage of delinquent boys correctly identified prior to their delinquency. It was found in 1957 that 8 of the 9 delinquents had been correctly identified in 1952, but at the cost of identifying a total of 72 as probable delinquents. Toby's study shows that at the end of 1959 the cost was overpredicting by four to one. By 1961, through revising its predictive instrument, the cost was overpredicting by two to one. The total number of predictions, correct and incorrect, and delinquent and nondelinquent, is not used in this conception of cost. One can, of course, also include in the cost the number of incorrect predictions of nondelinquency, as the Gluecks and others have. I have used "predictions of delinquency" rather than "total predictions" because the problem is the predicting of delinquency rather than of nondelinquency. Duncan has made the point that "the New York City Youth Board actually would have made far fewer incorrect predictions by simply assuming that none of the boys would become delinquent. . . ." [72] He questions whether an action-oriented agency attempting to prevent delinquency can afford such costs. Voss concludes that

> Systematic application of the Social Prediction Table to boys entering the first grade is highly questionable in the light of the accuracy of the predictions to date. The validity of the Gluecks' predictive instrument is still in doubt, and only an amazing reversal of the current results in the Youth Board investigation will validate the Glueck Social Prediction Table.[73]

Prigmore and Hakeem have recently concerned themselves with the problem of the reliability of the Gluecks' predictive scale. The studies discussed above have been concerned with its validity. Prigmore's research evaluated the reliability of the scale. One of his most serious criticisms is that Dr. Eleanor Glueck, one of the codevelopers of the scale, has been a rater or served as an advisor to the rater, in practically all of the validation studies attempted to this date, including that of the New York City Youth Board. A crucial methodological problem is whether raters other than she can arrive at the same judgments on the basis of common information about the parental factors included in the predictive scale. If they can, its reliability will be high and its value as a predictive instrument will be enhanced. If they do not, its value as a predictive instrument will be reduced. In the latter case, if it is still to be used in making decisions affecting the lives of boys, the reliability of the rating process will need to be improved.

Prigmore hypothesized that differences in the cultural backgrounds of the raters would result in differences in judgment when using the Glueck predictive scale; and he also predicted systematic differences in their judgments, on the basis of specific variations in their racial and regional backgrounds.[74]

Information on the Glueck factors was obtained from five juvenile probation officers in Baton Rouge, Louisiana, on sixty delinquent boys, white and Negro. The information, including the race of the boys, was given to eight raters, all of whom were middle-class, male social workers with a Master's degree in social work, employed in urban centers in the southern United

States. The raters comprised four groups: two Northern-educated whites, two Northern-educated Negroes, two Southern-educated whites, and two Southern-educated Negroes.

With respect to both white and Negro ratees, the expectations of Southern raters with racial background constant were greater than those of Northern raters. There was clear evidence that differences in cultural background account for different judgments regarding the Glueck scale, and that racial and regional differences will result in systematic differences in ratings.

The Glueck scale lacks rater reliability, and the complex, highly inferential Glueck factors, particularly those concerned with affection, lack reliability. The validity and reliability of a predictive instrument are closely related. Therefore the lack of rater reliability renders the validity of the Glueck delinquency prediction scale highly questionable. Prigmore concluded that the doubt as to both reliability and validity makes it unacceptable at present as an accurate and efficient instrument for delinquency prediction.[75]

Lopez-Rey analyzed the conclusions, data, and methodology of various experts on prediction. His conclusion was that their "probability and creditability" are barely superior to that of the predictions of the ordinary person in the conduct of his daily affairs:

> The statement, therefore, that delinquents are distinguishable because they are essentially mesomorphic, impulsive, extroverted, hostile, suspicious, stubborn, unconventional, adventurous, less methodical, and the like, cannot be considered as a law or as a base for prediction. . . . such an enumeration seems to prove the opposite of what was intended to be demonstrated, i.e., exceptional cases aside, delinquents and nondelinquents are very much alike physically, temperamentally, psychologically. . . .[76]

Toby concluded that "not a single validated example exists of successful early identification and intensive treatment programs." [77] And yet such claims as the following one by the Saskatchewan Provincial Department of Social Welfare and Rehabilitation are becoming more frequent:

> A result of the accelerated services to juveniles has been that

the police are also detecting incipient delinquents and referring these families for help before children actually come into conflict with the law. This has been helpful, because at this stage, the guidance of the child and casework with the families can control or alleviate the problem.[78]

It would be interesting to know what empirical evidence, if any, is possessed by that department to validate its claims and thus partially to justify its intervention in the lives of an unspecified number of families. The Gluecks also conclude that their Social Prediction Table is both reliable and valid. In discussing certain problems involved in identifying delinquents, Eleanor Glueck assumes that one basic problem is the wholly technical one of deciding when the state should intervene in the lives of families. She writes that

> [One] basic issue has to do with meeting the challenge of "doing something" following the identification of potential delinquents. The way points to the early treatment of families and children by the constituted agencies of society when the interpersonal relations between the parents and a particular child make him vulnerable to delinquency. The rationale for such intervention is embraced in the already accepted philosophy of "reaching out" casework and poses only the problem of the stage at which this "reaching out" is to be initiated, i.e., after signs of antisocial behavior have become clearly evident *or in advance of* them.[79]

There is indeed a basic issue involved in active intervention by the duly constituted agencies of society in the lives of families and children before the children engage in "antisocial" behavior. The issue is briefly stated in Allen's conclusion that the values of individual liberty may be imperiled by claims to knowledge and therapeutic techniques that, in fact, we do not know and by failure to concede candidly what we do not know. "At times," Allen says:

> practitioners of the behavioral sciences have been guilty of these faults. At other times, such errors have supplied the assumptions on which legislators, lawyers, and lay people generally have proceeded. Ignorance, in itself, is not disgraceful as long as it is unavoidable. But when we rush to measures affecting human liberty and human dignity on the assumption that we know what we do not know, or can do what we cannot do, then the problem of ignorance takes on a more sinister hue.[80]

Some Significant Positive Trends

To close on a critical and negativistic theme might seem to imply a pessimism I do not intend. The trends previously discussed seem to me to be sufficiently important to emphasize even at the expense of some of the significant positive ones. I can do hardly more than list some of the latter. One significant development is recent legislation involving the conception of the juvenile court and its procedures in the official handling of juveniles. As one analyst put it, the juvenile court is now in the third stage of a cycle of social reform: reforms, regrets, and revisions. In the New York Family Court Act, effective September 1, 1962, which can be taken as an example, there is a new and strong emphasis on due process of law. It therefore meets, in some respects, the previously stated objections to the juvenile court that is operated as a social agency. The act, in creating a new court with a new combination of jurisdiction, at the same time changed the procedures for the handling of juveniles. The family court now has jurisdiction over most matters relating to the family that come into court. It has jurisdiction over cases of neglect, custody, physically handicapped and mentally defective children, support cases, paternity proceedings, family offenses, the permanent termination of parental rights, adoption, and guardianship. And, most relevant to the present concern, it has jurisdiction over delinquency proceedings.

The principal characteristic of the New York Family Court Act, with reference to juvenile delinquency, is its emphasis on procedural rights, which is also present in the other jurisdictions of the court. The act explicitly establishes and distinguishes between two types of hearings, adjudicatory and dispositional. A 1963 amendment changed the name of "adjudicatory" hearings to "fact-finding" hearings. The establishing of the two types of hearings resulted from the decision of the act's draftsmen that the exercise of the court's power should depend on whether a given act or circumstance, selected by the legislature as sufficient ground for judicial action, has been specified. This legislative decision therefore excludes, in the adjudicatory hearing, reference to the young person's prior record, school reports, and the social investigation, as well as general evidence as to his charac-

ter and conduct. Such matters are reserved for possible consideration at the dispositional hearing. Thus the use of the court's
power does not turn upon the judge's opinion that the young
person before him has a "need for treatment" or is "in need of
help," regardless of whether he did what he was complained of
having done.

Only competent, relevant, and material evidence may be admitted in adjudicatory hearings, which are defined as hearings
"to determine whether the allegations of a petition . . . are supported by a preponderance of the evidence." Dispositional hearings, in contrast, are "to determine what order of disposition
should be made."

The New York Family Court Act also distinguishes between
juvenile delinquents and persons in need of supervision (PINS).
The former is "a person over seven and less than sixteen years of
age who does any act which, if done by an adult, would constitute a crime." The latter is a young person "who is an habitual
truant or who is incorrigible, ungovernable, or habitually dis-
obedient and beyond the lawful control of parent or other lawful
authority." The committee drafting the act resisted considerable
influence from many organizations interested in the welfare of
children, who wanted to raise the upper limit of juvenile delinquency from sixteen to seventeen or eighteen years. Young persons more than fifteen years old who have committed crimes
punishable by death or life imprisonment are not brought into
the Family Court unless a case involving such a person has been
referred to that court by a criminal court. The upper age limit
for persons in need of supervision is sixteen years for males and
eighteen for females. The older age limit for girls allows for the
supervision of sixteen- and seventeen-year-old runaways.

The two categories of young persons established in the act
have greatly reduced the definitions of juvenile delinquency that
were listed in the former penal law and Children's Court Laws of
New York, and that still mark the laws of practically all of the
other American states. The act, in addition, states the legislature's purposes and intention "to provide a due process of law
(a) for considering a claim that a person is a juvenile delinquent
or a person in need of supervision, and (b) for devising an ap-

propriate order of disposition for any person adjudged juvenile delinquent or in need of supervision." No such statement or one similar to it appears in any of the former laws. It establishes explicitly one of the conditions under which the law shall be interpreted: the majority decision in *People v. Lewis* is specifically set aside.[81] That decision had been basic to former Children's Court procedures; as recently as 1961, while the present Family Court Act was being drafted, a New York appellate court specifically refused to "re-examine the doctrine announced in the Lewis case." [82]

In *People v. Lewis* a divided court held that the legislature could employ great discretion in prescribing processes of law in juvenile cases, and the evidence of the commission of specified delinquent acts was only relevant as an aid to the Children's Court judge in ascertaining the reasons for the child's conduct and in deciding upon procedures for helping him. The majority opinion stated that the statute "clearly and unmistakably abolishes the distinction" between classes of children brought before the court by reason of neglect or delinquency, and that "the concept of crime and punishment disappears." [83] As the proceeding was not criminal, young Lewis had neither the right to nor the necessity for the procedural safeguards prescribed by constitution and statute in criminal cases. The dissenting opinion, in contrast, asked whether the constitutions of the United States and the State of New York apply to children or only to adults, so that "a child [can] be incarcerated and deprived of his liberty in a public institution by calling that which is a crime by some other name." The dissent also distinguished between continuing conduct that is not criminal but still harmful to the boy and the community, and the specific act and "charge of crime, called out of charity, 'juvenile delinquency.' " [84]

The above changes in the new Family Court Act are more than merely semantic differences from *People v. Lewis;* they are substantive. Related to them are provisions establishing law guardians and the right to remain silent. Lawyers, for a variety of reasons, have never played a large part in juvenile courts. The Family Court Act states a legislative conclusion "that counsel is often indispensable to a practical realization of due process of

law and may be helpful in making reasoned determination of
fact and proper orders of disposition." The act consequently
establishes a system of "law guardians" and expressly imposes on
the court the duty to inform respondents of their right to counsel. The costs of the law guardians are included in the budgets
of the Appellate Divisions. In cases of neglect, juvenile delinquency, and persons in need of supervision, the court also must
inform respondents of their right to be provided a law guardian
at public expense if they are unable to obtain a lawyer "by reason of inability to pay counsel or other circumstances." [85] The
New York City bar, according to Dembitz, was responsible for
this innovation:

> the bar became increasingly concerned with the lack of procedural
> protections in juvenile court in comparison to criminal or even civil
> cases; and this concern crystallized around the need for representa-
> tion. New York's new provision for the assignment of counsel
> emerged in large part from an experimental assignment project
> conducted with foundation funds by the New York Legal Aid
> Society under the leadership of the city bar association.[86]

New York and Oregon are the first states in the United States
to provide for the assignment of attorneys in every juvenile case
if the child or his parent requests counsel and cannot secure his
own. A number of other states are also supplying counsel in
juvenile cases, although on a less inclusive basis. California, for
example, directs the appointment of counsel in any case amounting to a felony, and in other cases leaves appointment to the
discretion of the judge. As recently as about 1955, lawyers were
almost unknown in juvenile court hearings; one estimate places
the maximum at one in every two hundred cases, even in metropolitan juvenile courts. The situation now presents a remarkable
contrast.

The Advisory Council of Judges of the National Council on
Crime and Delinquency has considered some of the problems and
trends involved in the right to counsel in juvenile court. It shows
that the number of appellate decisions upholding the right has
been increasing, and quotes approvingly from a 1960 California
study:

> We find no grounds to support the contention that the presence of

counsel will destroy the protective philosophy of the juvenile court or seriously alter the informality of proceedings. Where counsel has been employed in the juvenile court . . . judges . . . commented that attorneys perform a valuable service in safeguarding the minor's rights and in interpreting the reason for the court's disposition to the family.[87]

The above trends developed prior to the decision of the United States Supreme Court in *Gideon v. Wainwright* in 1963. Gideon was convicted of burglary in a Florida court, without the benefit of counsel, even though he had requested the court to obtain representation for him because he was indigent. His plea for counsel was rejected, he was forced to defend himself, and was convicted and sentenced to a term in prison. He finally managed to mail a writ to the Supreme Court, which ordered him retried. Supplied with a competent counsel, he was found not guilty and released after having served two years. In its decision, the court said:

> From the very beginning our state and national constitutions and laws have laid great emphasis on procedural and substantive safeguards designed to insure fair trials before impartial tribunals in which every defendant stands equal before the law. This noble ideal cannot be realized if the poor man charged with crime has to face his accusers without a lawyer to assist him.[88]

The decision has been carefully studied by many people interested in the juvenile court. The National Legal Aid and Defender Association and the National Council of Juvenile Court Judges cosponsored a conference at the University of Chicago in February 1964, to consider the implications of the decision for the juvenile court. One question discussed was whether the Supreme Court would, if a case were to be brought before it on appeal, decide that juveniles have a federal constitutionally provided right to counsel under juvenile court proceedings. The new and the old viewpoints were both represented. Arnold S. Trebach, administrator of the National Legal Aid and Defender Association, suggested that children appearing in delinquency proceedings in juvenile courts do have that constitutional right. His position met disagreement from Judge Daniel J. McNamara, senior judge of the Cook County (Chicago) Family Court, who is quoted as saying that "deprivation of a child's liberty is not to be considered as a means of punishment but rather a means of helping the child." [89]

The right to remain silent, which is analogous to the right against self-incrimination, is one of the most contentious issues of juvenile court justice: Since that court intends to help children, what rights that an adult has in a criminal proceeding should be accorded children in their court? The New York Family Court Act provides that the judge has the duty to advise the respondent of the right to remain silent, and provides further that it must be explained "at the commencement of *any* hearing." [90] The right therefore obtains in adjudicatory hearings, as well as in those which will commit children, place them, and determine the conditions of probation. Some of the objections to this section of the act seem to be complaints to the effect that it would inconvenience the court if the child had to be proven guilty.

Judge Smyth, for example, objects that formerly the Children's Courts of New York State, "backed by *People v. Lewis* . . . were enabled to practice the philosophy of help and understanding" in juvenile delinquency proceedings, in which warnings against self-incrimination were unnecessary. He is dismayed to find that "the benign provisions" of *People v. Lewis* have been replaced by the provision that "the respondent and his parent shall be advised of the respondent's right to remain silent." "Thus," the judge laments, "the clock is turned back sixty-three years and the practice of the fine philosophy . . . receives a body blow. . . . The judge will find it difficult to convince a boy and his family that he is a friend from whom nothing should be hid." [91] It seems, however, that the trend of legislation and opinion is definitely in the direction indicated by the Family Court Act.

The 1961 revision of Montana's Juvenile Court Act is quite different from that exemplified by California, New York, Oregon, and Rhode Island. Montana's act now contains the provision that "whenever the hearing in the juvenile court is had on a written petition charging the commission of any felony, persons having a legitimate interest in the proceedings, including responsible representatives of public information media, shall not be excluded from such hearing." In at least one of Montana's judicial districts juveniles so charged appear in open court and all the details of their trials may be published in all of the mass media, and some of them are. Under Montana's Juvenile Traffic Act, adopted as a means of reducing violations by offenders less than eighteen years of age, juveniles are also tried in open court, "and their driving mistakes are reported in embarrassing detail." It is claimed that a survey of the court records in the eighteen months following passage of the act (March 1961) revealed a decrease of 49 per cent in felony cases and 75 per cent in traffic violation cases.[92] To evaluate the validity of so startling a claim is impossible because of the complete absence of a description of the means used in arriving at the percentages.

It is useful to contrast briefly the Montana and New York acts. Both resulted in large part from criticisms of existing juvenile court laws and practices. The criticisms in Montana can be summarized as being in large part based on the charge of undue leniency. One result is that in that state juveniles can be and sometimes are now tried in a manner not greatly different from that of adults in criminal court. The judge metes out "large doses of publicity and punishment." Although the criticisms in New York were varied, there was a great concern with attempting to reconcile the conceptions of the juvenile court as a court of law and as a social agency. The New York act restored some semblance of constitutional rights for children in juvenile court, but without restoring the concepts of criminal trial and punishment to the proceedings. One can therefore still think of juvenile proceedings in New York as designed to protect the community through helping the child. Montana's act seems to revive the conception of punishment as constituting revenge and retaliation.

Another constructive trend of considerable importance involves attempts at delinquency control and prevention. There are so many that only a few can be mentioned. Projects to the number of 1,724 are listed in Volume IV (Winter 1963–64) of *Current Projects in the Prevention, Control, and Treatment of Crime and Delinquency*, published by the National Council on Crime and Delinquency, and are described in their practitioners' own words. Many are in the category of "action programs." The descriptions indicate that in many instances social action is untouched by either theory or data; however, there are also many instances, in which there is a direct concern with theory and a sophisticated attention devoted to problems of methodology.

Many of the works which I referred to or discussed in Chapter 3 indicate the kind of analysis of crime and delinquency that results from conceiving them to be sociocultural phenomena. One implication of that analysis is that sociocultural influences centering on the individual must positively influence him toward lawfulness if he is to be moved from crime or delinquency. Some attempts to implement that idea are well established; most are very recent. The oldest, continuously operating, and best known attempt—and in the opinion of many the best—to bring positively lawful influences to bear on the individual in a community that is high in delinquency is the Chicago Area Project, which developed from research on the epidemiology of delinquency and on the analysis of the sociocultural experience of children reared in neighborhoods with high rates of delinquency. It has demonstrated that residents of such neighborhoods are capable of collective action dealing with the problems of young people. That action, Kobrin concludes, has probably reduced delinquency in the program areas.[93] His conclusion is reasonable, but it seems too modest. There are now about fifteen similar projects in Chicago, established in areas marked by high rates of delinquency. The Chicago Area Project, as well as other activities to be mentioned below, are based in large part on the social-psychological conceptions of motivation and social role previously discussed. It will be recalled that the behavioral characteristics and social roles of the individual are, following this theory, considered to be the properties of groups and other sociocultural systems, and of relationships between individuals.

There are many other projects, some rural but most of them urban, directly concerned with juvenile delinquency. The listing of only a few is not intended to slight others. I have already referred to two examples of the former, the Vermont Youth Study and the Lane County (Oregon) Youth Project. The latter is particularly concerned with the causes of delinquency in rural and hinterland areas, and pays special attention to the changing economic and social character of rural life.

The Boston Delinquency Project, the "Midcity Project," conducted a program of delinquency control in a lower-class district of Boston during the years 1954–57. A major objective was to reduce the amount of delinquency engaged in by juveniles living in the area. Project method derived from a "total community" conception of the attack on delinquency, which has become very popular during the past decade, and is presently the basis, at least in part, of the fairly extensive delinquency-prevention programs of the President's Committee on Juvenile Delinquency and Youth Crime. The project executed action programs directed at three of the societal units widely agreed upon to figure prominently in the genesis and perpetuation of delinquency: the community, the family, and the gang. The programs were based on the assumption that delinquency engaged in by lower-class adolescents, whatever their personality characteristics, is in some significant degree facilitated by or actualized through the three structural features of the community listed in the previous sentence. Walter B. Miller, director of the Midcity Project, answered "No" to the principal evaluative research question: "Was there a significant measurable inhibition of law-violating or morally-disapproved behavior as a consequence of Project efforts?" [94]

The relative lack of success reported by the Midcity Project and the modest claims made by Kobrin for the Chicago Area Project are of importance in weighing the views of those who believe that a widespread and rapid change in the disapproved and illegal sociocultural behavior of the lower class can be achieved easily. Rev. Martin Luther King, Jr., seems to hold such a belief. In discussing the price for settling the debt that the United States owes the American Negro, he proposed the enactment of a Bill of Rights for the Disadvantaged:

> I am proposing that the United States launch a broadbased and gigantic Bill of Rights for the Disadvantaged.
> Such a bill would immediately transform the conditions of Negro life. The most profound alteration would reside not so much in the specific grants as in the basic psychological and motivational transformation of the Negro. I would challenge skeptics to give such a bold new approach a test for the next decade. I contend that the decline in school dropouts, family breakups, crime rates, illegitimacy, swollen relief rolls and other social evils would stagger the imagination. Change in human psychology is normally a slow

process, but it is safe to predict that when a people is as ready for change as the Negro has shown himself ready today the response is bound to be rapid and constructive.[95]

I do not want to be classed as one of Dr. King's "skeptics"; I could favor the introduction and passage of such a bill in the Congress. I would, however, justify it on the ethical or humanitarian ground that people ought to be able to live decently, simply because they are human beings. Such a bill could very well result in a drastic reduction of the "swollen" relief rolls. It could also result in the upward social mobility of those Negroes who presently are realistically oriented toward upward mobility but who cannot achieve it because of the difficulty of rising from unskilled and semiskilled jobs when possessing less than a high school education. Such a bill could make possible what the New York City colleges helped make possible for the children of the myriads of illiterate and semiliterate, unskilled, and non-English-speaking peasants who emigrated from eastern and southern Europe after 1880.

Such a bill, in brief, could result in a change in the class structure of the United States. The percentage of Negroes and whites in the lower class would be about the same, say, 40 per cent, of the population, rather than what it is estimated by some to be at present, about 80 per cent and 40 per cent, respectively. It is in this segment of the social structure that there is a marked concentration of "school dropouts, family breakups, crime rates, and illegitimacy." Some students of crime, delinquency, and family organization among the lower class, both Negro and white, have observed that an increase in their income and in the amenities of life during the past fifty years or more has not resulted in a proportionate decrease in their morally disapproved and illegal conduct. It may be expedient to justify a Bill of Rights for the Disadvantaged on the ground that it will drastically reduce crime and delinquency. Extensive experience with many projects, however, leads to the conclusion that it is a ground of dubious validity. Values must be changed; better housing, more income, better medical care, and the like, do not in and of themselves make it possible for people to change their values, even if they want to. Expectations of deliberately inducing rapid and widespread change in sociocultural conduct should, it seems, be quite modest.*

Examples of definite but limited expectations in the control and prevention of delinquency are provided by the recent "demonstration projects" financed partly by the President's Committee and partly by local communities. The President's Committee on Juvenile Delinquency and Youth Crime was established by an Executive Order on May 11, 1961. In September of that year the Congress enacted Public Law 87-274 which allowed the federal government to participate in a greater degree in the control and prevention of delinquency. The act allowed the federal government to do three things: (1) to provide assistance to communities in developing demonstration projects in the field of delinquency control and prevention, and in related services for youth; (2) to train personnel to work with young people in trouble; and (3) to evaluate and to disseminate the most effective means for using total community resources in the control and prevention of delinquency and in the expansion of opportunities for lower-class youth. The objective is to develop a nation-wide program that is locally based, and that is aimed at the prevention of delinquency and the amelioration of the social disabilities of lower-class youth.

I can refer only briefly to the demonstration projects, which focus on areas with high rates of delinquency by selecting crucial areas of the city for the development of action programs. The several demonstration projects in rural and hinterland areas such as Lane County, Oregon, are quantitatively different but qualitatively similar. These projects are sociologically oriented in their theoretical approach:

> Since causes of delinquency can, in large measure, be attributed to factors within the social system and are only partially psychogenic in origin, programs, mounted under the aegis of this federal program are not privileged to address individual symptoms but must be primarily focused on social causes. The overwhelming

---

* What is decent and what is moral is, of course, a matter of judgment, of values. I am assuming that my judgment of what constitutes being able to live decently, and of what decent and moral conduct is, does not differ significantly from Dr. King's judgment on these matters, although we do, however, differ significantly on the matter of religious values.

investment of resources in this country has been on programs for
control and individual treatment with relatively little to social
causation. Neither can isolated or specialized programs be charged
with solving the total problem of delinquency. The product of the
planning efforts developed under this program must be constructed
to achieve appropriate and simultaneous change in the many conditions identified as contributing to [delinquency].[96]

The general objective of the program to train personnel to
work with young people in trouble is to make possible the
development of a "comprehensive, coordinated community approach" to the prevention of delinquency; and to foster all that
that implies in terms of the development of programs designed to advance theory and research. Because of this com-
prehensiveness, Polk described the Juvenile Delinquency and
Youth Control Act of 1961 as "the most significant piece of youth
legislation that has come along in many many years, because in
the projects that have been developed, it elicits the mechanism
for change that is needed." [97] A new alliance between a uni-
versity-based research staff oriented toward theory and method,
and the community-based professional worker oriented toward
action has been formed. That alliance will presumably result in
advance both in theory and in action programs; but at the present
time that still remains to be seen. I should add that the phrase
"total community involvement" is inaccurate as applied to attempts to prevent or reduce delinquency and related problems,
when such attempts fail to articulate with the school system and
the economy, with the objective of meeting the problem of unemployment created by automation. The Midcity Project thus
was less than "total," and those sponsored by the President's
Committee are also, although they are admittedly much more
comprehensive than any previous ones.

One can only speculate at the time of this writing what effects
President Lyndon B. Johnson's program to eliminate poverty in
the United States will have on the incidence of crime and delinquency. They could be similar to those I suggested might result
from the passage of an Act to Aid the Disadvantaged. The President is, in effect, striving for such an act, although his program
would encompass also the population of a geographical region. If
that program is approved by the Congress, and appropriations are

voted for it, I foresee at least one major methodological problem in its operation. In several previous chapters I have made the point that people who are engaged in doing good for others sometimes act as if their moral judgments were scientific principles. They seem to believe that their value judgments are statements of sociocultural fact. The major problem to which I refer is that of maintaining the conception of poverty and its morally disapproved concomitants as being sociocultural phenomena. If the objective of the program becomes the rehabilitation of the poor, rather than the rehabilitation of the sociocultural processes that produce them, it will, I predict, fail. The poor—the poverty-stricken of the Appalachian region in particular—are no more psychiatric cases than are the delinquents, numbers racketeers, embezzlers, shoplifters, and those who use violence in interpersonal relations, discussed previously. It may be difficult to maintain poverty rather than mental illness or morality as the objective of the projected program.

One can draw a general conclusion from the recorded experience of the Chicago Area Project, the Midcity Project, and a number of others not mentioned by name. It seems that crime and delinquency will be with us for many decades and pretty much in their present proportions. In conformity with a secular or long-term trend, however, there may be some decrease in their rates. The many projects of the President's Committee may help to continue the trend.

Notes

Chapter 1

1. Edwin H. Sutherland, "Development of the Theory," in Albert K. Cohen, Alfred Lindesmith, and Karl F. Schuessler, eds., *The Sutherland Papers*, Bloomington: Indiana University Press, 1956, pp. 13–29; Edwin H. Sutherland and Donald R. Cressey, *Principles of Criminology*, 6th ed., New York: J. B. Lippincott Co., 1960, pp. 74–81.

2. See Charles Horton Cooley, *Social Organization*, Glencoe, Ill.: Free Press, 1956 printing, p. 5. See also Frank E. Hartung, "Common and Discrete Values," *Journal of Social Psychology*, 38, No. 1, 1953, pp. 3–22.

3. Daniel Glaser, "Criminality Theories and Behavioral Images," *American Journal of Sociology*, 61, 1956, pp. 433–44.

4. Daniel Glaser, "The Sociological Approach to Crime and Correction," *Law and Contemporary Problems*, 23, Autumn 1958, pp. 683–702, at p. 689.

5. See Herbert Blumer, "Attitudes and the Social Act," Presidential Address to the Society for the Study of Social Problems, Washington, D. C., September 1955.

6. Glaser, *op. cit.*, p. 689.

7. Karl Llewellyn, "Law and the Social Sciences—Especially Sociology," *Harvard Law Review*, 62, December 1949, pp. 1286–87.

8. Lawrence K. Frank, *Society as the Patient*, New Brunswick: Rutgers University Press, 1950.

9. Milton L. Barron, *The Juvenile in Delinquent Society*, New York: Alfred A. Knopf, 1954. Many similar titles could be listed for articles and books.

10. Marshall B. Clinard, *The Sociology of Deviant Behavior*, rev. ed., New York: Holt, Rinehart & Winston, Inc., 1962, pp. 74 and 76.

11. Mirra Komarovsky, "The Voluntary Associations of Urban Dwellers," *American Sociological Review*, 11, December 1946, pp. 686–98.

12. W. E. Mann, "The Social System of a Slum: The Lower Ward, Toronto,"

in S. D. Clark, ed., *Urbanism and the Changing Canadian Society*, Toronto: University of Toronto Press, 1961, pp. 57, 63.

13. W. I. Thomas and Florian Znaniecki, *The Polish Peasant in Europe and America*, New York: Alfred A. Knopf, Inc., 1918, p. 1128. Reprinted in part in Edmund H. Volkart, ed., *Social Behavior and Personality*, New York: Social Science Research Council, 1951, p. 233. See also W. I. Thomas, *The Unadjusted Girl*, Boston: Little, Brown & Co., 1923.

14. C. Wright Mills, "The Professional Ideology of Social Pathologists," *American Journal of Sociology*, 49, September 1942, pp. 165 ff.

15. Mabel A. Elliott, *Crime in Modern Society*, New York: Harper & Bros., 1952, pp. 94, 82. My italics.

16. *Ibid.*, p. 135.

17. Bernard Lander, *Towards an Understanding of Juvenile Delinquency*, New York: Columbia University Press, 1954, pp. 65, 89.

18. Statement by Robert K. Merton, in Helen L. Witmer and Ruth Kotinsky, eds., *New Perspectives for Research on Juvenile Delinquency*, Washington, D.C.: Government Printing Office, 1956, p. 39.

19. *Ibid.*, statement by Bernard Lander, pp. 55–56. My italics.

20. *Ibid.*, p. 55.

21. Statement of Hon. Samuel S. Leibowitz, Judge, Kings County Criminal Court, New York State. *Hearings* before the Subcommittee to Investigate Juvenile Delinquency of the Committee on the Judiciary, United States Senate, 86th Congress, 1st Session. February 12 and 13, 1959, p. 30.

22. The statement is printed in its entirety in the New York *Times* of November 19, 1961.

23. J. Edgar Hoover, "Who's to Blame for the Rising Wave of Crime?" *U. S. News and World Report*, January 1, 1962, p. 35.

24. William C. Kvaraceus, *Hearings, op. cit.*, 87th Congress, 1st Session, Part 9, March 9 and 10, 1961, p. 1594.

25. *Hearings, op. cit.*, 86th Congress, Part 4, September 23 and 24, 1959, pp. 465, 444. In the interview with J. Edgar Hoover, cited previously, it is stated as a fact that streets have become unsafe in many large cities: "There is another crime problem too. Streets have become unsafe in many of our large cities. What, in your opinion, is going to make it safe once again to walk on streets or use parks at night?" Mr. Hoover answered, in part, "Much of the blame for the dangers which lurk in the shadows along streets and in parks can be placed right at the feet of the citizens of the community. The disheartening truth is that too many of our citizens have become totally unconcerned about the safety and welfare of their fellow man." Hoover, *op. cit.*, p. 35.

Without meaning to deny the assaults, robberies, and other offenses committed on streets at night, two things should be noted. First, no evidence is cited, nor any source of any evidence, that streets have become less safe. Second, the question and its answer definitely imply that in some unspecified recent past the streets in large cities were safe and have now become unsafe. The implication is historically inaccurate, even though it is true that the streets of a given city may become less safe. For example, Agnes E. Meyer, the publisher of the Washington *Post*, says that fear haunts the citizens of the nation's capital. It is not safe to walk the streets at night . . . murder, rape, robbery, housebreaking, mugging—are at an all-time high. . . . Women remain at home in the evening because they are afraid to be out alone. The movies, and the department stores that are open on Thursday night have suffered a financial loss. When we pick up the morning paper we ask ourselves the question with which Western frontiersmen greeted each other every day— who got killed last night?

"The Nation's Worst Slum: Washington, D. C.," *Atlantic,* August 1963, p. 89.

   In contrast, the annual report of the United States Bureau of Prisons for 1963 says that

If we can believe Herbert Asbury in his book, *The Gangs of New York,* the hoodlum element of New York City was more numerous, better armed, and more powerful a century ago than it is today. The criminal and vice districts of New Orleans and San Francisco, according to the same authority are certainly a great deal tamer than they once were.

Federal Prisons: 1963, Washington, D. C., 1964, p. 4.

26. *Juvenile Delinquency: A Task Force Report,* submitted to Governor G. Mennen Williams, Lansing, Michigan, December 3, 1959, p. 19.

27. *Report on Services for Children and Youth with Emotional Difficulties and Behavior Problems,* Windsor: The Community Fund and Welfare Council of Greater Windsor, March 1961, p. 24.

28. I. Richard Perlman, "Delinquency Prevention: The Size of the Problem," *Annals of the American Academy of Political and Social Science,* 322, March 1959, p. 4.

29. *Hearings, op. cit.,* pp. 482–84.

30. *Ibid.,* p. 488.

31. William C. Kvaraceus, *The Community and the Delinquent,* New York: World Book Co., 1954, p. 36.

32. *Ibid.,* p. 41.

33. P. R. Mort and W. B. Featherstone, *Entrance and Promotion Practices in City School Systems,* New York: Teachers College, Columbia University, Bureau of Publications, 1932.

34. Harold F. Powell, "School Retardation," in *Clinical Psychology of Exceptional Children,* C. M. Louttit, ed., New York: Harper & Bros., 1957, pp. 142–58; and Harold F. Powell, "Social Adjustment as Related to Reading Disability," unpublished M.A. thesis, University of Michigan, 1943.

35. Daniel Schreiber has presented an adequate discussion of some recent studies of this in "Juvenile Delinquency and the School Dropout Problem," *Federal Probation,* 27, September 1963, pp. 15–19.

36. William F. Whyte, *Street Corner Society,* Chicago: University of Chicago Press, 1943.

37. Dr. Marjorie Rittwagen, as quoted by Virginia P. Held in *Hearings, op. cit.,* p. 476.

38. Walter B. Miller, "Implications of Lower-Class Culture for Social Work," *Social Service Review,* 33, September 1959, p. 223.

39. E. K. Wickman, *Children's Behavior and Teacher's Attitudes,* New York:

Commonwealth Fund, 1928. For a modified replication of Wickman's work see George A. W. Stouffer, Jr., "The Attitude of Secondary-School Teachers Toward Certain Behavior Problems of Children," *School Review*, 64, November 1956, pp. 358–62. See also P. M. Smith, "The School as a Factor," in Joseph S. Roucek, *Juvenile Delinquency*, New York: Philosophical Library, Inc., 1958, pp. 153–88.

An example of a teacher who believes this is the principal of an elementary school in the southwestern district of Detroit, located in a lower-class neighborhood. This principal has admonished the teachers in her school to think carefully before they fail any of their pupils. "You must ask yourself," she said to them, "when you are going to fail a pupil, 'Where did *I* fail *him?* What should I have done that I did not do?' " When a teacher in her school fails a pupil, the principal calls her into the office and asks the teacher to justify the failure. One result is that it is rare for a pupil in that school to fail, regardless of the low quality of performance. The promotion of pupils who are scholastic failures is euphemistically termed "social promotion."

40. For an excellent study of the sequences from juvenile delinquency to criminality, see Harold S. Frum, "Adult Criminal Offense Trends Following Juvenile Delinquency," *Journal of Criminal Law, Criminology and Police Science*, 49, May–June 1958, pp. 29–49; and his "Criminal Sequence Patterns," unpublished Ph.D. dissertation, Indiana University, 1952.

Sexual offenses and assaults against the person can properly, in my opinion, be part of the repertoire of a career delinquent, namely, one who makes the transition from delinquency as a game to delinquency for gain. Habitual drunkards should not be considered as having a "criminal career," as Walter Reckless properly observes, nor should narcotics addicts. Although the overwhelming proportion of criminal careers are those involving crimes of gain, mostly against property, the sexual offender who has developed the role of "compulsive criminal" for himself can, in my opinion, be regarded as a career criminal. See Walter C. Reckless, *The Crime Problem*, 3d ed., New York: Appleton-Century-Crofts, Inc., 1955, pp. 159 ff.

41. Walter Miller, *op. cit.*, and also his excellent study, "Lower Class Culture as a Generating Milieu of Gang Delinquency," *Journal of Social Issues*, 14, No. 3, 1958, pp. 5–19, at pp. 17–18.

42. Much of the large literature devoted to the analysis of the relationship between crime and socioeconomic class is scientifically worthless. The following are a few of the many good works that could be cited.

Wendell D. Baker, *A Study of Selected Aspects of Japanese Social Stratification: Class Differences in Values and Levels of Aspiration*, unpublished Ph.D. dissertation, Columbia University, 1956; Ely Chinoy, *The Automobile Worker and the American Dream*, Garden City: Doubleday Doran & Co., Inc., 1955; Albert K. Cohen, *Delinquent Boys: The Culture of the Gang*, Glencoe: Free Press, 1955; Albert K. Cohen and James F. Short, Jr., "Research in Delinquent Subcultures," *Journal of Social Issues*, 14, No. 3, 1958, pp. 20–37; Robert H. Guest, "Work Careers and Aspirations of Automobile Workers." *American Sociological Review*, 19, February 1954, pp. 155–63; H. T. Himmelweit, "Social Status and Secondary Education since the 1944 Act: Some Data for London," in D. V. Glass, ed., *Social Mobility in Britain*, London: Routledge and Kegan Paul, 1954; August B. Hollingshead, *Elmtown's Youth*, New York: John Wiley & Sons, Inc., 1949, pp. 83–147 and 360–88; Joseph A. Kahl, "Educational and Occupational Aspirations of

'Common Man' Boys," *Harvard Educational Review*, 23, No. 3, 1953, pp. 186–203.

Herbert H. Hyman, "The Value Systems of Different Classes: A Social Psychological Contribution to the Analysis of Classification," in Reinhard Bendix and Seymour M. Lipset, eds., *Class, Status and Power*, Glencoe: Free Press, 1953; Leonard Reissman, "Levels of Aspiration and Social Class," *American Sociological Review*, 18, April 1953, pp 233–42; Betty M. Spinley, *The Deprived and the Privileged*, London: Routledge and Kegan Paul, 1953.

Richard M. Stephenson, *Mobility Orientation and Stratification: A Study of One Thousand Ninth Graders*, unpublished Ph.D. dissertation, Columbia University, 1956; W. E. Mann, "The Social System of a Slum: The Lower Ward, Toronto," in S. D. Clark, ed., *Urbanism and the Changing Canadian Society*, Toronto: University of Toronto Press, 1961, pp. 39–69; and William F. Whyte, *op. cit.*, esp. "Part II, Racketeers and Politicians," pp. 111–252.

43. C. J. Eckenrode, "Their Achievement is Delinquency," *Journal of Educational Research*, 43, October 1950, pp. 554–60.

Chapter 2

1. Gina Lombroso Ferrero, *Lombroso's Criminal Man*, New York: G. P. Putnam's Sons, 1911, p. xiv.

2. *Ibid.*, p. xvi. Some students of Lombroso's work assert that he modified significantly his psychiatric conception of the criminal by making allowance for sociocultural influences on the individual's behavior. That is an incorrect interpretation. The above two quotations are from his summary of his theory, written just before he died. His last book, *Crime: Its Causes and Remedies* (Boston: Little, Brown & Co., 1913), also reveals that he retained his emphasis on pathological heredity.

3. J. A. E. Lacassagne, in *Revue Scientifique*, 1, No. 5, 1881, p. 683.

4. Charles Goring, *The English Convict*, London: His Majesty's Stationery Office, 1913. Goring worked on this monograph for twelve years.

5. *Ibid.*, p. 173.

6. William Healy, *The Individual Delinquent*, Boston: Little, Brown & Co., 1915. See also William Healy and Edith R. Spaulding, "Inheritance as a Factor in Criminality," *Bulletin of the American Academy of Medicine*, 15, April 1914, pp. 4–27.

7. Ernest A. Hooton, *Crime and the Man*, Cambridge: Harvard University Press, 1939; and also *The American Criminal: An Anthropological Study*, Cambridge: Harvard University Press, 1939.

8. The most careful evaluations of Hooton's two books are Sutherland, "The American Criminal and Crime and the Man," Albert K. Cohen, Alfred R. Lindesmith and Karl F. Schuessler, eds., *The Sutherland Papers*, Bloomington: Indiana University Press, 1956, pp. 273–78; Robert K. Merton and M. F. Ashley-Montagu, "Crime and the Anthropologist," *American Anthropologist*, 42, August 1940, pp. 384–408; N. S. Timasheff, "The Revival of Criminal Anthropology," *University of Kansas Law Review*, 9, February 1941, pp. 91–100; William H. Tucker, "Is There Evidence of a Physical Basis for Criminal Behavior?" *Journal of Criminal Law and Criminology*, 31, November-December 1940, pp. 427–37; James S. Wallerstein and Clement J. Wyle, " 'Biological Inferiority' as a Cause of Delinquency," *Nervous Child*, 6, October 1947, pp. 467–72.

9. The excellent and closely reasoned evaluation of Sheldon's work is in Edwin H. Sutherland, "Varieties of Delinquent Youth," in Cohen, Lindesmith, and Schuessler, *op. cit.*, pp. 279–90.

10. Cesare Lombroso, *The Female Offender*, New York: D. Appleton & Co., 1915, p. 55.

11. See the discussion of overlapping in George B. Vold, *Theoretical Criminology*, New York: Oxford University Press, 1958, pp. 43–156.

12. Goring, *op. cit.*, pp. 243, 248.

13. Henry H. Goddard, "A Measuring Scale for Intelligence," *Training School*, 6, June 1910, pp. 146–55; "A Revision of the Binet Scale," *Training School*, 8, September 1911, pp. 56–62.

Lewis M. Terman and others, *The Stanford Revision and Extension of the Binet-Simon Scale for Measuring Intelligence*, Baltimore: Warwick and York, Inc., 1919; Lewis M. Terman and Maud A. Merrill, *Measuring Intelligence*, Boston: Houghton-Mifflin Co., 1937; Lewis M. Terman, Chap. 5 of *Intelligence: Its Nature and Nurture*, Bloomington, Ill.: Public School Publishing Co., 1940; and Lewis M. Terman and Maud A. Merrill, *Stanford-Binet Intelligence Scale: Manual for the Third Revision Form L–M*, Boston: Houghton-Mifflin Co., 1960.

14. Charles Horton Cooley, *Human Nature and the Social Order*, 1st ed., New York: Scribners & Sons, 1902.

15. Some English biologists and biological psychologists continue to believe that their instruments used for estimating what has been learned do in fact measure accurately the hereditary capacity to learn. The fact is that no instrument used for estimating what has been learned—whether given the name "intelligence test" or any other name—can measure capacity to learn. A recent example of this English literature is P. B. Medawar, "Intelligence and Fertility," *The Future of Man*, New York: New American Library of World Literature, Inc., 1961, pp. 70–83, and the accompanying notes.

16. Lewis M. Terman, *The Intelligence of School Children*, Boston: Houghton Mifflin Co., 1917, p. 12.

17. Cohen, Lindesmith, and Schuessler, *The Sutherland Papers*; Leslie D. Zeleny, "Feeblemindedness and Criminal Conduct," *American Journal of Sociology*, 38, January 1933, pp. 564–76; Vold, *op. cit.*

18. The most adequate summary of the problem of intelligence and delinquency is to be found in Harry Manuel Shulman, *Juvenile Delinquency in American Society*, New York: Harper & Bros., 1961, pp. 354–75; and Martin H. Neumeyer, *Juvenile Delinquency in Modern Society*, 3rd ed., New York: D. Van Nostrand Co., Inc., 1961.

19. Sheldon Glueck uses the phrase "original nature." See "Theory and Fact in Criminology," *British Journal of Delinquency*, 7, October 1956, pp. 92–109.

20. "Bank Robbers—Why?" is the topic to which *The New Era*, 15, No. 2, 1961, is devoted. It is a study of 216 bankrobbers sentenced to a total of 3,956 years, who are serving their time in the federal prison at Leavenworth, Kansas. *The New Era* is the house organ of the convicts in that prison.

21. *Hearings, op. cit.*, 83d Congress, 2d Session, April 21–22, and June 4, 1954, pp. 81–83.

22. *Ibid.*, p. 158.

23. *Ibid.,* pp. 156–57.

24. *Ibid.,* p. 159.

25. *Ibid.,* p. 152. It would be interesting to know on what empirical or logical grounds Dr. Bender would except her "own three normal children" from the unqualified statement that in her medical opinion "there is no such thing as a normal child."

26. See the survey by Joseph T. Klapper, *The Effects of Mass Communication,* Glencoe: Free Press, 1962.

27. See, for example, *Hearings, op. cit.,* on television programs, April 6 and 7, 1955. Dr. Ralph S. Banay, research psychiatrist of Columbia University, is contradicted by Inspector Baker and Inspector Francis Davey of the Youth Bureau of the Detroit Police Department, and Dr. William Wattenberg found that delinquents and nondelinquents had the same favorite program—*I Love Lucy. Ibid.,* pp. 79 ff., and 57–58. Dr. Banay is of the opinion that "the adolescent mind" is a "delicately suggestible mechanism." *Ibid.,* p. 81.

28. See, for example, "Motion Pictures and Juvenile Delinquency," 122 pp., United States Senate *Report* No. 2055 (84th Congress, 2d Session), May 25, 1956, esp. pp. 8–18.

29. See, for example, *ibid.,* p. 20, which reproduces an editorial, "Prurient Motion-Picture Advertising in Times of Increased Sex Crimes," originally published in the *Journal of Social Therapy,* 1, April 1955, pp. 146–47, the official organ of the Medical Correctional Society.

30. See, for example, *Hearings, op. cit.,* March 9 and 10, 1961, esp. p. 1576, at which place the experts assembled by the National Council on Crime and Delinquency repeated what is pejoratively called the "imitation theory" of crime and delinquency.

31. "Juvenile Delinquency," 129 pp., *Report* No. 1953 of the Committee on the Judiciary, United States Senate, 86th Congress, 2d Session, June 15, 1960.

In the 87th Congress the subcommittee published "Effects on Young People of Violence and Crime Portrayed on Television," Part 10, *Hearings.* The hearings were held during June and July 1961, and January and May 1962, and published in 1963. In an excellent statement Professor Peter P. Lejins made the point, among others, that the television industry has no scientific basis for exonerating itself of the charge that television violence and crime fails to be reproduced in the subsequent behavior of children who witness it. "When a reputable social scientist makes the statement that there is no proof that a given program content is the cause of delinquent behavior, what he generally really means is that there is no proof either way—that no research means are as yet available to prove the situation . . . what science has said so far in its best researches is that it is impossible, to the satisfaction of the . . . scientific method, to prove a connection. But *that does not mean that it has been proven that there is no connection.* Pp. 1672–73; my italics.

Despite Dr. Lejins' statement, and two other good ones by Professors Albert Bandura and Ralph J. Garry, one wonders why the hearings were held and published. The 957 pages of the volume do not, in my opinion, advance our knowledge of the effects on the behavior of either young or old people of violence and crime portrayed on television.

Chapter 3

1. Robert K. Merton, Leonard Broom and Leonard S. Cottrell, Jr., eds., *Sociology Today*, New York: Basic Books, Inc., 1959. The index of this work shows that considerable space is devoted by various authors to such topics as anomie, conformity, consensus, and deviant behavior, but none to competition.

The index of the book edited by Talcott Parsons and Edward Shils, *Toward a General Theory of Action*, Cambridge: Harvard University Press, 1951, lists "competition" once. The word is used on p. 477, and is merely a casual and passing reference by a psychologist. The revised and greatly enlarged edition of Robert K. Merton, *Social Theory and Social Structure*, Glencoe: Free Press, 1957, fails to list "competition" in the subject index even once. This is also true of Albert K. Cohen, *Delinquent Boys*, Glencoe: Free Press, 1955; of Robert K. Merton and Robert A. Nisbet, eds., *Contemporary Social Problems*, New York: Harcourt, Brace & Co., 1961; of William C. Kvaraceus, *The Community and the Delinquent*, New York: World Book Co., 1954; of Sophia M. Robison, *Juvenile Delinquency*, New York: Henry Holt & Co., 1960; of Talcott Parsons, *The Social System*, Glencoe: Free Press, 1951, esp. Chap. 7; of Bernard Lander, *Towards an Understanding of Juvenile Delinquency*, New York: Columbia University Press, 1954, esp. Chaps. 5 and 6; and of Robert Dubin, "Deviant Behavior and Social Structure: Continuities in Social Theory," *American Sociological Review*, 24, April 1959, pp. 147–64.

Not even the publication of the National Education Association of the United States, *Delinquent Behavior: Culture and the Individual* (1959) has a reference to competition.

On the other hand, competition is discussed in Sutherland and Cressey, *op. cit.*, and in Donald R. Taft and Ralph W. England, Jr., *Criminology*, 4th ed., New York: Macmillan Co., 1964.

2. Richard A. Cloward and Lloyd E. Ohlin, *Delinquency and Opportunity*, Glencoe: Free Press, 1960, p. 183. They had discussed "criminal" and "conflict" cultures previously.

3. Clifford R. Shaw and Henry D. McKay, *Social Factors in Juvenile Delinquency: A Study of the Community, the Family, and the Gang in Relation to Delinquent Behavior*, for the National Commission on Law Observance and Enforcement, *Report on the Causes of Crime*, No. 13, Vol. II, Washington: Government Printing Office, 1931.

Frederic M. Thrasher, *The Gang*, Chicago: University of Chicago Press, 1927. Thrasher concluded that what the boy learns in the unsupervised gang or gang club usually takes three "general trends": personal habits, familiarity with techniques of crime, and a philosophy of life or an organization of attitudes facilitating further delinquency of a more serious type.

With the exception of techniques, my previous list of the learning of criminal conceptions of thought and action, a vocabulary of motives, and a self-conception seems not to differ substantively from Thrasher's "general trends." My later discussion indicates that that learning is not necessarily dependent upon boyhood membership in a gang.

4. Albert K. Cohen, *Delinquent Boys: The Culture of the Gang*, Glencoe: Free Press, 1955; and Albert K. Cohen and James F. Short, Jr., "Research in Delinquent Subcultures," *Journal of Social Issues*, 14, No. 3, 1958, pp. 20–37. Cohen and Short also have an excellent chapter on "Juvenile Delinquency" in Robert K.

Merton and Robert A. Nisbet, eds., *Contemporary Social Problems*, New York: Harcourt, Brace & World, Inc., 1961, pp. 77–126.

See also James F. Short, Jr., "Street Corner Groups and Patterns of Delinquency," A Progress Report from the National Institute of Mental Health Research Grant, M–3301, March 1, 1961 (mimeographed), 31 pp.

5. Cohen, *op. cit.*, p. 28.

6. *Ibid.*, p. 26.

7. William Healy and Augusta F. Bronner, *New Light on Delinquency and Its Treatment*, New Haven: Yale University Press, 1936, p. 205.

8. Paul W. Tappan, *Juvenile Delinquency*, New York: McGraw-Hill Book Co., 1949, p. 143. Henry D. McKay, "The Neighborhood and Child Conduct," *Annals of the American Academy of Political and Social Science*, 261, January 1949, p. 37.

9. Emanuel Celler, *Hearings, op. cit.*, September 23 and 24, 1959, p. 470.

10. Cohen, *op. cit.*, pp. 28–29.

11. Kenneth H. Rogers, *Street Gangs in Toronto*, Toronto: Ryerson Press, 1945, pp. 18–19, and passim. It is an episodic and, in some places, moralistic book.

12. Frederic M. Thrasher, *The Gang*, Chicago: University of Chicago Press, 1936, pp. 94–95.

13. Benjamin Fine, *1,000,000 Delinquents*, New York: World Publishing Company, 1955, pp. 36–38.

14. The following discussion draws on Gresham M. Sykes and David Matza, "Techniques of Neutralization: A Theory of Delinquency," *American Sociological Review*, 22, August 1957, pp. 664–70.

15. Clifford R. Shaw and Henry D. McKay, *op. cit.*, pp. 223–26.

16. Walter B. Miller, Hildred Geertz, and Henry S. G. Cutter, "Aggression in a Boy's Street-Corner Group," *Psychiatry*, 24, November 1961, pp. 291, 294.

17. This does not apply to "strict liability": "In problems relevant to criminal law, strict liability means liability to punitive sanctions despite the lack of *mens rea*," Jerome Hall, *General Principles of Criminal Law*, rev. ed., Indianapolis: Bobbs-Merrill Co., Inc., 1960, p. 325.

18. Sykes and Matza, *op. cit.*, p. 666, paraphrased. Following references to Sykes and Matza are to this study, pp. 667–70.

19. Nelson N. Foote, "Identification as a Basis for a Theory of Motivation," *American Sociological Review*, 16, February 1951, pp. 14–21, at p. 15.

20. C. Wright Mills, "Situated Actions and Vocabularies of Motives," *American Sociological Review*, 5, December 1940, pp. 904–13.

21. Kenneth Burke, *Permanence and Change*, rev. ed., Los Altos, Calif.: Hermes Publications, 1954, p. 11.

22. Richard Austin Smith, "The Incredible Electrical Conspiracy," *Fortune*, April 1961, pp. 132 ff., and May 1961, pp. 161 ff.

23. Virginia P. Held, "The Formless Years—What Can We do about 'J.D.'" *Hearings, op. cit.*, September 23 and 24, 1959, p. 474.

24. The author of the quotation was reared in a village in Iowa. Harold Dwight Eastman, "The Process of Urbanization and Criminal Behavior: A Restudy of Culture Conflict," unpublished Ph.D. dissertation, State Univerity of Iowa, 1954, p. 190.

25. William Glasser, "Reality Psychiatry: An Effective Treatment for Delinquents," Reference Bulletin No. 24, San Diego County Probation Department (mimeographed). Reproduced from a speech delivered before the National Institute on Crime and Delinquency, Seattle, during July 1962, p. 2.

Dr. Glasser is Consulting Psychiatrist at the Ventura School for Girls. Dr. Harrison is a psychiatrist at the Los Angeles Veterans Administration Neuropsychiatric Hospital. Both employ reality therapy exclusively in their respective institutions as well as in their private practice.

26. *Ibid.*, p. 3.

27. *Ibid.*, pp. 4–5.

28. *Ibid.*, p. 5.

29. *Ibid.*, p. 6. Somewhat parallel developments seem to have occurred independently of each other in psychiatry and sociology. Much of what Glasser and Harrison refer to as "reality therapy" has, as far as one can judge, been known for some years to sociology under the heading of "guided group interaction," and other names. Two examples of this concept and technique, and their application and development are the experimental project for the treatment of youthful offenders at Highfields, New Jersey, and "The Provo Experiment" with adjudicated delinquents in Provo, Utah. Both are explicitly based on the sociological theory of delinquency and crime, toward which "reality therapy" seems to have converged remarkably.

See Donald R. Cressey, "Changing Criminals: The Application of the Theory of Differential Association," *American Journal of Sociology*, 61, July 1955, pp. 116–20; Lloyd W. McCorkle and Richard Korn, "Resocialization within Walls," *Annals of the American Academy of Political and Social Science*, 293, May 1954, pp. 88–98; Joseph Abrahams and Lloyd W. McCorkle, "Group Psychotherapy of Military Offenders," *American Journal of Sociology*, 51, March 1946, pp. 455–64; Joseph Abrahams and Lloyd W. McCorkle, "Group Psychotherapy at an Army Rehabilitation Center," *Diseases of the Nervous System*, February 1947; Lloyd W. McCorkle, "Group Therapy in Correctional Institutions," *Federal Probation*, 13, June 1949, pp. 34–37; F. Lovell Bixby and Lloyd W. McCorkle, "Guided Group Interaction and Correctional Work," *American Sociological Review*, 16, August 1951, pp. 455–59; Lloyd W. McCorkle, "Group Therapy," in Paul W. Tappan, ed., *Contemporary Correction*, New York: McGraw-Hill Book Co., Inc., 1951, pp. 211–23; Lloyd W. McCorkle, Albert Elias, and F. Lovell Bixby, *The Highfields Story*, New York: Henry Holt & Co., 1958; H. Ashley Weeks, *Youthful Offenders at Highfields*, Ann Arbor: University of Michigan Press, 1958; Albert Elias and Jerome Rabow, "Post-Release Adjustment of Highfields Boys, 1955–57," *Welfare Reporter*, January 1960, pp. 7–11; LaMar T. Empey and Jerome Rabow, "The Provo Experiment in Delinquency Rehabilitation," *American Sociological Review*, 26, October 1961, pp. 679–96; LaMar T. Empey, "The Application of Sociological Theory to Sociological Problems," and the "Discussion" of Empey's paper by Edward J. Abramson, Gilbert L. Geis, and Harold Finestone, Annual Meeting of the Society for the Study of Social Problems, Statler-Hilton Hotel, Los Angeles, August 23–25, 1963; and Rita Volkman and Donald R. Cressey, "Differential Association and the Rehabilitation of Drug Addicts," *American Journal of Sociology*, 69, September 1963, pp. 129–42.

30. Fritz Redl and David Wineman, *The Aggressive Child*, Glencoe: Free Press, 1957, p. 261. My italics.

31. Marshall B. Clinard and Andrew L. Wade, "Toward the Delineation of Vandalism as a Sub-Type in Juvenile Delinquency," *Journal of Criminal Law, Criminology, and Police Science*, 48, January-February, 1958, p. 497.

32. John Barron Mays, *Growing Up in the City*, Liverpool: University of Liverpool Press, 1954, pp. 18–19.

33. Many sociologists would deny delinquents the comfort and support of this rationalization. An example is provided by J. P. Shalloo, who says, "The plain fact is that such vandals are fully aware of the nature of their actions and are as completely normal mentally as juveniles who do not engage in such conduct." He then refers to "incontrovertible evidence that such juveniles (delinquents) are not subnormal or abnormal." The overwhelming proportion of vandals, he asserts, "are as normal and as intelligent and resourceful as juveniles who find socially acceptable means of solving the problems that are an inherent part of the very trying process of growing up." J. P. Shalloo, "Vandalism: Whose Responsibility?" *Federal Probation*, 18, March 1954, pp. 6–8.

The same issue of *Federal Probation* contains a valuable symposium on vandalism, placing it with stealing in the cultural matrix of the versatility and meanness that characterize much of the delinquent subculture.

34. Shaw and McKay, *op. cit.*, p. 228.

35. *Hearings, op. cit.*, (1963), p. 1937.

36. "In many ways the inmate social system [of the prison] may be viewed as providing a way of life which enables the inmate to avoid the devastating psychological effects of internalizing and converting social rejection into self-rejection. In effect, it permits the inmate to reject his rejectors rather than himself." Lloyd W. McCorkle and Richard Korn, "Resocialization within Walls," *Annals of the American Academy of Political and Social Science*, 293, May 1954, p. 88.

37. Virginia P. Held, *op. cit.*, p. 475.

38. Statement of Bruno Bettelheim, *Hearings, op. cit.*, May 28 and 29, 1959, p. 187.

39. *Ibid.*, pp. 187–88.

40. *Ibid.*, p. 188.

41. Frank Gibney, *The Operators*, New York: Harper & Bros., 1960, p. 252.

42. Redl and Wineman, *op. cit.*, p. 195.

43. *Ibid.*, pp. 144–56.

44. John P. Clark, "Blame Acceptance Among Ohio Prisoners," unpublished Ph.D. dissertation, Ohio State University, 1960, chap. 1; and "Acceptance of Blame and Alienation among Prisoners," *American Journal of Orthopsychiatry*, 33, April 1963, pp. 557–61.

Since I did not read Dr. Clark's work until this manuscript had been written, I was unable to make adequate use of its considerable empirical data.

McCleery has shown that inmates in the incorrigible unit of prisons make use of the denial of responsibility, denial of the victim and condemnation of their condemners. See the discussion of "the Belief System" in Richard H. McCleery, "Authoritarianism and the Belief System of Incorrigibles," in Donald R. Cressey, ed., *The Prison: Studies in Institutional Organization and Change*, New York: Holt, Rinehart and Winston, Inc., 1961, pp. 290–302.

45. Walter C. Reckless, Simon Dinitz and Ellen Murray, "Self Concept as an Insulator against Delinquency," *American Sociological Review*, 21, December 1956, pp. 744–46; and "The 'Good' Boy in a High Delinquency Area," *Journal of Criminal Law, Criminology, and Police Science*, 48, June 1957, pp. 18–25; Dinitz, Reckless, and Barbara Kay, "Delinquency Proneness and School Achievement," *Educational Research Bulletin*, 36, April 10, 1956, pp. 131–36; "The Self Component in Potential Delinquency and Potential Non-Delinquency," *American Sociological Review*, 22, October 1957, pp. 566–70; Thomas G. Eynon and Walter C. Reckless, "Companionship at Delinquency Onset," *British Journal of Criminology*, 12, October 1961, pp. 162–70; Walter C. Reckless, "A New Theory of Delinquency and Crime," *Federal Probation*, 25, December 1961, pp. 42–46.

See also James F. Short, Jr., "Differential Association with Delinquent Friends and Delinquent Behavior," *Pacific Sociological Review*, 1, Spring 1958, pp. 20 ff.

46. Harwin L. Voss, "Insulation and Vulnerability to Delinquency: A Comparison of the Hawaiians and Japanese," unpublished Ph.D. dissertation, University of Wisconsin, Madison, 1961.

47. Frank R. Scarpitti, Ellen Murray, Simon Dinitz, and Walter C. Reckless, "The 'Good' Boy in a High Delinquency Area: Four Years Later," *American Sociological Review*, 25, August 1960, p. 558. See also Scarpitti's unpublished Ph.D. dissertation, "Differential Socialization: The Delinquent *Versus* the Non-Delinquent," Ohio State University, 1963.

48. Voss, *op. cit.*, p. 374. See also his "Ethnic Differentials in Delinquency in Honolulu," *Journal of Criminal Law, Criminology, and Police Science*, 54, September 1963, pp. 322–27.

49. Julian B. Roebuck, "The Negro Numbers Man as a Criminal Type: The Construction and Application of a Typology," *Journal of Criminal Law, Criminology, and Police Science*, 54, March 1963, pp. 48–60. For related and similar studies, see Julian B. Roebuck, "The Negro Drug Addict as an Offender Type," *Journal of Criminal Law, Criminology, and Police Science*, 53, March 1962, pp. 36 ff.; Julian B. Roebuck and Ronald Johnson, "The Negro Drinker and Assaulter as a Criminal Type," *Crime and Delinquency*, 8, January 1962, pp. 21–33; and Julian B. Roebuck and Mervyn L. Cadwallader, "The Negro Armed Robber as a Criminal Type: Construction and Application of a Typology," *Pacific Sociological Review*, 4, Spring 1961, pp. 21–26.

Although all of these studies confirm the theory being developed in these essays, only one can be discussed here.

50. Roebuck, "The Negro Numbers Man as a Criminal Type . . .", *op. cit.*, p. 59.

51. *Ibid.*

52. E. Franklin Frazier, *Black Bourgeoisie*, Glencoe: Free Press, 1957, pp. 127–28.

53. *Ibid.*, p. 211.

Chapter 4

1. This chapter is a revised and expanded version of a paper read in the Lane County Court House Auditorium to the Sixth Annual Juvenile Court Summer

Institute, sponsored by the Oregon Juvenile Court Judges Association and the University of Oregon, Eugene, August 15, 1963.

Other chapters of this book contain many references to Canada; this one does not. In my search of the literature I was unable to find published reports, or references to published reports, of studies of rural juvenile delinquency in Canada. In addition, correspondence with various Canadians knowledgeable in the field revealed no such studies. Dr. Helen C. Abell, of Ontario Agricultural College, has written to me that "Despite several years of research of a social economic nature in various parts of rural Canada, we have never gathered data on this matter of delinquency among the rural population." And, "Despite hundreds of personal interviews with sample surveys of the rural population the matter of rural juvenile delinquency has never been surveyed to my knowledge."

Professor P. J. Giffen of the University of Toronto stated that "there are, as far as I know, no published studies of Canadian rural delinquency. In fact the published matter on any aspect of delinquency in Canada is very meagre." Professor Rudolf A. Helling of Windsor University assured me that he knew of no such studies. Professor Richard Laskin of the University of Alberta wrote that according to his knowledge (which I may say is quite extensive) "the subject of rural or hinterland delinquency has not (or hardly been) treated by Canadian writers." Professor Denis Szabo of the University of Montreal wrote, "I am afraid you won't be able to find any Canadian references for your work on rural delinquency. To my knowledge very little significant research [on it] exists."

And finally, the Research Committee of the Ontario Department of Reform Institutions considered the matter. J. A. Graham, Deputy Minister, wrote on February 6, 1964, that "It was the opinion of the Members of this Committee that no study of juvenile delinquency in rural Canada has yet been made."

For the above reason the present chapter has only three brief references to Canada. I must thank my correspondents for their efforts on my behalf, and for permission to quote from their letters to me.

2. Thomas C. Esselstyn, "The Social Role of a County Sheriff," *Journal of Criminal Law, Criminology, and Police Science,* 44, 1953, pp. 177 ff.

3. Ralph W. England, Jr., University of Rhode Island, to Frank E. Hartung, February 28, 1958. Quoted with the writer's permission.

4. August B. Hollingshead, *Elmtown's Youth,* New York: John Wiley & Sons, Inc., 1949, pp. 389, 410.

5. Eastman, *op. cit.,* p. 114. See chap. 3, n. 24 above.

6. Nicolas Zay, "Gaps in Available Statistics on Crime and Delinquency in Canada," *Canadian Journal of Economics and Political Science,* 29, February 1963, pp. 84–85.

In 1958, a total of 3,917 informal cases was reported by the courts, while the total number of appearances resulting in the finding of delinquency was 11,391. Dominion Bureau of Statistics, *Juvenile Delinquency,* Ottawa, p. 9.

A comprehensive, brief review of previous studies of rural and small-town delinquency has been prepared by Kenneth Polk, "A Portrait of the Non-Urban Offender," a paper presented to the Annual Meeting of the Society for the Study of Social Problems, Statler-Hilton Hotel, Los Angeles, August 25, 1963. Polk uses the apt phrase, "hinterland areas," when he defines rural areas broadly, so as to include "small towns which are engaged in such extractive activities as mining, lumbering, fishing and similar industries . . . as well as rural farm areas."

Some other aspects of rural crime that could be studied are instances of arson, bombing, and vandalism committed by whites against Negroes and by Negroes against whites; criminal physical assaults upon and the murder of Negroes in some of the Civil War states, the Ku Klux Klan, "mortgage holidays" to prevent the auctioning of farms, illegal slaughtering of livestock, violations of laws and regulations controlling acreage, the cheating of sharecroppers, and the failure to pay state sales taxes on farm produce sold.

7. Eastman, *op. cit.,* p. 40.

8. Marshall B. Clinard, "Rural Criminal Offenders," *American Journal of Sociology,* 50, July 1944, p. 44. Reprinted in Marshall B. Clinard, *The Sociology of Deviant Behavior,* rev. ed., New York: Holt, Rinehart, & Winston, Inc., 1962, p. 258. My italics.

9. Eastman, *op. cit.,* p. 132. My italics.

10. H. S. Ferns, in a review of S. D. Clark, *The Developing Canadian Community,* in *British Journal of Sociology,* 14, December 1963, p. 384. See also: P. J. Giffen, "Canadian Criminal Statistics," in E. F. Beach and J. C. Weldon, eds., Canadian Political Science Association, Conference on Statistics, *Papers,* 1960, Toronto: University of Toronto Press, 1962, Table 13, p. 91.

A graphic description of the culture of violence in a small community (about 2,100 population) in southern Illinois is presented by Herman R. Lantz, *People of Coal Town,* New York: Columbia University Press, 1958.

11. Edmund de Schweinitz Brunner, *The Growth of a Science: A Half-Century of Rural Sociological Research in the United States,* New York: Harper & Bros., 1957, p. 110.

12. Otis Dudley Duncan and Jay W. Artis, *Social Stratification in a Rural Pennsylvania Community,* University Park: Pennsylvania Agricultural Experiment Station, Bulletin 543, October 1951.

13. Polk, *op. cit.,* pp. 12–13, and Table I.

14. Jerome Himelhoch, "History and Prospectus of the Vermont Youth Study," Progress Report No. 7, Goddard College, January 1962 (mimeographed), p. 3.

My statement of the relationship between delinquency and social class in the Vermont Youth Study is more emphatic and explicit than Professor Himelhoch presently states it. In a letter to me, dated January 14, 1964, he wrote that the correlation of delinquency and social class was limited to his preliminary study of convicted offenders. "My subsequent results," he continued, "based on several high school samples, show no correlations between self-reported delinquent acts and social class. My tentative conclusion at this stage of our research is that there are no class differences in law-breaking behavior in the communities I studied, but there *is* a definite tendency for lower-class youth and law enforcement officials to interact in such a way that official delinquency becomes concentrated in the lower class."

Himelhoch's reference to "self-reported delinquent acts" is methodologically significant. Such acts are discussed briefly in the next few paragraphs in the text above.

15. John P. Clark and Eugene P. Wenninger, "Socioeconomic Class and Area

as Correlates of Illegal Behavior Among Juveniles," *American Sociological Review,* 27, December 1962, p. 826.

Some similar studies are: James F. Short, Jr., "Differential Association and Delinquency," *Social Problems,* 4, January 1957, pp. 233–39; James F. Short, Jr. and F. Ivan Nye, "Reported Behavior as a Criterion of Delinquent Behavior," *Social Problems,* 5, Winter 1957–58, pp. 207–13; Robert A. Dentler and Lawrence J. Monroe, "Early Adolescent Theft," *American Sociological Review,* 26, October 1961, pp. 733–43.

16. Dentler and Monroe, *op. cit.,* p. 733; Polk, *op. cit.,* p. 14; Short and Nye, *op. cit.,* p. 207.

The self-report technique has several serious shortcomings, but it is unnecessary to enumerate them here.

17. From Hollingshead, *Elmtown's Youth,* 1949, to Robert J. Havighurst, Paul H. Bowman, Charles V. Matthews, and J. V. Pierce, *Growing Up in River City,* New York: John Wiley and Sons, Inc., 1962.

The same pattern can be inferred to have marked *Middletown,* the first and classic community study. This inference is based on a few direct and some indirect references. Robert S. and Helen M. Lynd, *Middletown,* New York: Harcourt, Brace & Co., 1929.

18. Eastman, *op. cit.,* pp. 155–56, and Tables 37 and 38. Table 38 includes only those boys who reported membership in a group that stole.

19. Hollingshead, *op. cit.,* pp. 414–36, esp. pp. 421–22. Early smoking was widespread among Elmtown's children.

20. Eastman, *op. cit.,* Table 34.

21. Polk, *op. cit.,* pp. 10, 13.

22. Hollingshead, *op. cit.,* p. 255 and chap. 8, "The High School in Action," pp. 163–203.

23. Matthews, *et al., op. cit.,* pp. 91, 94, 95.

24. Edward C. Devereux, Jr., Urie Bronfenbrenner, and John Harding, "Community Participation as a Research Problem," *Journal of Social Issues,* 16, No. 4, 1960, p. 1.

25. Jerome Himelhoch, Benjamin S. Brashears, Jr., and Joan R. Rayfield, "Hedonists and Moralists: Contrasting Cultures among Green Mountain Town Youth," Vermont Youth Study, Goddard College, January 1962, p. 2.

26. Jerome Himelhoch, "Statistical Analysis of Factors Relating to Juvenile Delinquency in Green Mountain Town," Vermont Youth Study, Goddard College, September 1960, p. A 4.

27. Hollingshead, *op. cit.,* pp. 398–399, 421–22. As we stated earlier, not all withdrawees, of course, are also delinquents.

28. Eastman, *op. cit.,* pp. 162–65.

29. *Ibid.,* p. 110.

In stating that delinquents seem to enjoy themselves in their delinquency, I have no intention of repeating or reviving Thrasher's tendency to romanticize the delinquent condition. See, for example, the chapters, "The Role of the Romantic" and "Wanderlust," in Frederic M. Thrasher, *The Gang,* Chicago: University of Chicago Press, 1927.

30. Talcott Parsons, "Psychoanalysis and the Social Structure," *Psychoanalytic Quarterly,* 19, 1950, p. 378. He has also written of "the overwhelming importance of infantile dependency. . . . on the whole compulsive independence (adolescent rebellion) is more common as a reaction formation against these passive dependency needs than the other way around," in *The Social System,* Glencoe: Free Press, 1951, p. 262. Parsons makes extensive use of the physical metaphor of the balancing scale in his analysis of human society. In common with many metaphorists, he seems to believe that his metaphor is in fact a veridical picture of human society.

The dispute over an alleged rebellious subculture is not confined to the American scene. It has also been asserted to exist in post-World War II Japan. But Vogel, after reviewing the data of various social surveys conducted in Japan, and on the basis of case studies taken in the area of Tokyo, 1958–60, concluded that "children are not rebelling." Also, "social research studies show virtually no major differences in attitudes between men and women regarding what rights and freedoms women should be allowed." Ezra F. Vogel, "The Democratization of Family Relations in Japanese Urban Society," *Asian Survey,* 1, June 1961, p. 19.

31. Ernest A. Smith, *American Youth Culture: Group Life in Teenage Society,* Glencoe: Free Press, 1962, p. 1. My italics.

32. James S. Coleman, *The Adolescent Society,* Glencoe: Free Press, 1961, p. 9.

Coleman is not wholly consistent. On p. 12 he writes, "Because adolescents live so much in a world of their own, adults remain uninformed about the way teen-agers spend their time, the things that are important to them, and the things that friends have in common." But on p. 34 he writes that "parents also want their children to be successful in the things that 'count' in the school, that is, the things that count in the eyes of other adolescents. And parents know what things count." There is no doubt, however, that the former quotation states Coleman's position.

33. *Ibid.,* pp. 164–65.

34. Seymour M. Lipset, *Political Man,* Garden City, N. Y.: Doubleday & Co., 1960.

35. Frederick Elkin and William A. Westley, "The Myth of Adolescent Culture," *American Sociological Review,* 20, December 1955, pp. 680–84; Hollingshead, *op. cit.,* p. 433.

36. Himelhoch, *op. cit.,* p. A5.

37. Eastman, *op. cit.,* pp. 240–41, 245–46.

Clinard undertook a replication of his original study in Sweden, in 1955. The replication confirmed the relation of criminal behavior to membership in a group of boys who stole; Eastman's study had shown the same thing. About two-thirds of the Iowan and the Swedish criminals belonged to such groups at one time or another. The similarity of these findings, Clinard remarks, is striking: "The claim that participation in delinquent groups is unique to American society was rejected, as there was no significant difference in such membership between the two samples. This is significant because contemporary Swedish criminological literature in general does not stress this factor, but instead emphasizes individual constitutional or psychological factors." Marshall B. Clinard, "The Relation of Urbanization and Urbanism to Criminal Behavior," in Ernest W. Burgess and

Donald J. Bogue, eds., *Contributions to Urban Sociology*, Chicago: University of Chicago Press, 1964, p. 556.

38. La Mar T. Empey and Jerome Rabow, "The Provo Experiment in Delinquency Rehabilitation," *American Sociological Review*, 26, October 1961, pp. 679–96.

39. Polk, *op. cit.*, p. 15.

40. Charles P. Loomis and J. Allen Beegle, *Rural Social Systems*, New York: Prentice-Hall, Inc., 1950.

41. Eastman, *op. cit.*, p. 162.

42. Marshall B. Clinard, *The Sociology of Deviant Behavior*, rev. ed.. New York: Holt, Rinehart & Winston, Inc., 1962, p. 213.

43. Eastman, *op. cit.*, pp. 112–14; 162–65.

44. Himelhoch, Brashears, and Rayfield, *op. cit.*, p. 3.

45. Matthews, *et al.*, *op. cit.*, p .69.

46. Himelhoch, Brashears, and Rayfield, *op. cit.*, p. 3.

47. Polk, *op. cit.*, p. 12.

48. *Ibid.*, p. 10.

Chapter 5

1. Norman Jaspan with Hillel Black, *The Thief in the White Collar*, Philadelphia: J. B. Lippincott Co., 1960.

2. *Ibid.*, p. 37.

3. *Ibid.*, pp. 92 and 26.

4. *Ibid.*, p. 93.

5. *Ibid.*, p. 26.

6. See Frank E. Hartung, "A Vocabulary of Motives for Embezzlers," *Federal Probation*, 25, December 1961, pp. 68–69.

7. For an enumeration of supposed exceptions to the theory of differential association, and a bibliography of the criticisms, see the article by Donald R. Cressey, "Epidemiology and Individual Conduct: A Case from Criminology," *Pacific Sociological Review*, 3, Fall 1960, pp. 47–58, esp. nn. 37–49.

8. Donald R. Cressey, *Other People's Money: A Study in the Social Psychology of Embezzlement*, Glencoe: Free Press, 1953, p. 20.

9. *Ibid.*, p. 30.

10. "Status-seeking, status-gaining, status-maintaining, irrespective of the unit, time and place is universal insofar as human relationships are concerned." Samuel Haig Jameson, "Principles of Human Interaction," *American Sociological Review*, 10, February 1945, pp. 6–7.

11. The following paragraphs are a brief summary of the complex third and fourth chapters in Cressey, *op. cit.*

12. Cressey cites other references. *Ibid.*, pp. 79, 173–74.

13. *Ibid.*, p. 84.

14. *Ibid.*, p. 96.

15. See a short bibliography for this in Sutherland and Cressey, *Principles of*

Criminology, 6th ed., pp. 219–20. The two brief quotations in this and the previous paragraph are from the same source. Their Chapter 12, "Processes in Criminal Behavior," presents a more detailed comparison of the life histories of the career delinquent and the trust violator.

McCleery has presented a vivid description of a different although related result of the continued private use of language that supports the present analysis of the vocabulary of motives. The thief in the white collar talks himself into a criminal violation of his position of financial trust. The isolated inmate in the incorrigible unit of a maximum security prison—which is physically separate from the other units—may talk himself into a mental hospital. The days and months during which his illusions are developed are seldom interrupted by contact with reality or by challenging skepticism. The isolate has no one but himself to convince that he is blameless and the victim of a complex plot.

McCleery says that

A fairly common product of this condition is a note written to the Warden [which] with minor variations, will express the idea that the inmate has complete power over the prison system. It will assert that unless the Warden stops "them" from trying to poison or hurt him, the inmate and God will destroy the system. If these notes find their way through official channels, the inmate may be transferred to a mental hospital where his condition is diagnosed apart from the situation that produced it. Prison inmates, however, recognize it as an extreme form of a common affliction they call "stir crazy." In its extreme form it manifests itself in the individual's not wanting to be released from prison, or from the incorrigible unit, or from his isolation cell. More rational inmates fear and resist going "stir crazy," but they do not resent it in others. They recognize it as a way of adjusting to confinement and distinguish it from the "cracking up" which comes with [the] inability to take punishment.

Richard H. McCleery, "Authoritarianism and the Belief System of Incorrigibles," in Donald R. Cressey, ed., *The Prison,* New York: Holt, Rinehart & Winston, Inc., 1961, p. 289.

16. For an example, see the New York *Times,* June 25, 1961, and the photograph accompanying the story, "14 Who Had no Cause for Crime in Court for 'Trial of Plenty.' "

17. Detroit *Free Press,* January 12, 1962.

18. Donald R. Cressey, "Role Theory, Differential Association, and Compulsive Crimes," in Arnold Rose, ed., *Human Behavior and Social Processes,* Boston: Houghton Mifflin Co., 1962, pp. 443–67.

19. John Dewey, "The Need for Social Psychology," *Psychological Review,* 24, July 1917, p. 276.

20. Barbara Wootton, *Social Science and Social Pathology,* New York: Macmillan Co., 1959, p. 249. Lady Wootton finds Cressey's article on the theory of differential association and compulsive crime, previously referred to, to be "convincingly argued." *Ibid.,* p. 234.

21. Michael Hakeem to Frank E. Hartung, February 2, 1962. Quoted with the writer's permission.

22. Gregory Zilboorg, *Mind, Medicine and Man,* New York: Harcourt, Brace & Co., 1943, p. 273.

23. Manfred S. Guttmacher, "The Psychiatric Approach to Crime and Correction," *Law and Contemporary Problems,* 23, Autumn 1958, p. 636.

24. As Wolfgang observes, even a cursory examination of the anthropological

and historical literature reveals that the motives for killing must be interpreted in terms of the culture, and particularly the value-system, within which the offender lives. Marvin E. Wolfgang, *Patterns in Criminal Homicide,* Philadelphia: University of Pennsylvania, 1958, p. 186. This is one of the outstanding works in the literature dealing with this topic.

See Jacqueline H. and Murray A. Straus, "Suicide, Homicide, and Social Structure in Ceylon," *American Journal of Sociology,* 58, March 1953, pp. 461–69; Murray A. Straus, "Childhood Experience and Emotional Security in the Context of Sinhalese Social Structure," *Social Forces,* 33, December 1954, pp. 152–60; Bryce Ryan, *Caste in the New Asia: The Sinhalese System,* New Brunswick: Rutgers University Press, 1953; Andrew F. Henry and James F. Short, Jr., *Suicide and Homicide: Sociological and Psychological Aspects of Aggression,* Glencoe: Free Press, 1954; Paul Bohannon, ed., *African Homicide and Suicide,* Princeton: Princeton University Press, 1960; and Cleobis Jayewardene, "Criminal Homicide: A Study in Culture Conflict," unpublished Ph.D. dissertation, University of Pennsylvania, 1960.

See also the studies by Arthur L. Wood, "A Socio-Structural Analysis of Murder, Suicide and Economic Crime in Ceylon," *American Sociological Review,* 26, October 1961, pp. 744–53, and *Crime and Aggression in Changing Ceylon,* Transactions of the American Philosophical Society, N. S., 51, Part 8, December 1961; and Edwin D. Driver, "Interaction and Criminal Homicide in India," *Social Forces,* 40, December 1961, pp. 153–58.

25. Marvin E. Wolfgang, "A Sociological Analysis of Criminal Homicide," *Federal Probation,* 25, March 1961, pp. 49–50. Wolfgang and Ferracuti estimate that "Probably less than five percent of all known homicides are premeditated, planned intentional killings, and the individuals who commit them are most likely to be episodic offenders who have never had prior contact with the criminal law. Because they are rare crimes often planned by rationally functioning individuals perhaps they are more likely to remain undetected." Marvin E. Wolfgang and Franco Ferracuti, "Subculture of Violence: An Interpretive Analysis of Homicide," *International Annals of Criminology,* 1962 (*ler semestre*), p. 54. Morris' data support their estimate. In his "study of something over 2,700 murders and non-negligent manslaughters (about one-third of all those that occurred in the United States between June 1, 1950, and May 31, 1951) . . . only thirty-seven were clearly planned or intended to gain economic, political, or other considered ends such as relief from suffering (as in so-called mercy killings) or even a planned vengeance." Albert Morris, *Homicide: An Approach to the Problem of Crime,* Boston: Boston University Press, 1955, pp. 14–15.

The hypothesis formulated above applies to the voluntary (nonnegligent) killer, and not to the relatively rare premeditating murderer. The hypothesis appropriate to the murderer who plans and deliberates is a modification of Cressey's hypothesis concerning the criminal violator of financial trust, as follows. A deliberate murderer is a person who conceives himself as having an interpersonal problem that he defines as nonshareable, is aware that the problem can be secretly resolved by killing the other person, and is able to apply to his own conduct in that situation verbalizations that enable him to adjust his conception of himself as a lawful or just person with his conception of himself as a killer. This hypothesis is, just as the other, in need of testing, although there is now enough data to warrant taking it seriously.

Psychiatric literature often refers to the several types of homicide. My study of it leads me to conclude that its concern is overwhelmingly with the voluntary or nonnegligent type. It is variously described as "murder without motive," or "murder due to senseless motives." One wonders, of course, what "senseless motives" can possibly be. That literature is practically worthless in testing any hypothesis about homicide because the mixture of statements of fact, theoretical interpretations, and speculation make it impossible to use the presumably empirical material. One example will have to do.

Karl Menninger and others published a study, "Murder without Apparent Motive: A Study in Personality Disorganization," *American Journal of Psychiatry,* 117, July 1960, pp. 48–53. They examined four men, three of whom faced execution and the fourth a lengthy prison term. They had previously been subjected to psychiatric examinations, and found to be sane. But some persons of financial influence had asked of each of them, "How can a person, as sane as this man seems to be, commit an act as crazy as the one he was convicted of?" The question implies that an act is in itself diagnostic of the actor's mental state.

The details of the homicides indicate that all four could properly have been charged with voluntary manslaughter rather than murder. None of the killings was premeditated, there was no financial or other monetary gain for the killer, and there was no accompanying crime. Each killing was quickly over. All four of the killers had previous records of some years' duration, of physical and even extreme violence against others. All four described parental violence during their childhood as a common and almost daily affair.

The reader is then informed that the Menninger team could not "reconstruct a rational motive" because no financial gain accrued to the killer, the homicides were unnecessarily violent (although no criteria of unnecessary violence were presented), the killers probably fantasied or actually observed the primal scene as something overwhelmingly violent and sadistic, three of the men had a history of stuttering during childhood, they all exhibited disturbances in the brittle quality of impulse control, and they revealed a severe ego deficiency which permitted impulse to flow directly into action and was therefore not easily shunted into thinking. Menninger also blurred the boundary between fantasy and reality in his interpretation of Rorschach and Thematic Apperception Tests. The killers, he continued, had shallow emotions regarding their own fate and that of their victims. Continuing the physical metaphor, he asserted that they had "an ego weakness that allowed the periodic breakthrough of intense aggressive impulses." They were unconsciously motivated

to be murder-prone in the sense of either carrying a surcharge of aggressive energy or having an unstable ego defense system that periodically allows the naked and archaic expression of such energy. The murderous potential can become activated, especially if some disequilibrium is already present, when the victim-to-be is unconsciously perceived as a key figure in some past traumatic configuration. The behavior, or even the mere presence, of this figure adds a stress to the already unstable balance of forces that results in a sudden extreme discharge of violence, similar to the explosion that takes place when a percussion cap ignites a charge of dynamite. (*Ibid.,* p. 52).

Metaphor remains metaphor, even when taken literally by its user. Metaphor is well established and acceptable in poetry, drama, and the novel. It decorates and entertains, and presents the reader with a problem to solve.

For another example of a similar psychiatric study, see Glen M. Duncan, *et al.,*

"Etiological Factors in First-Degree Murders," *Journal* of the American Medical Association, 168, November 29, 1958, pp. 1755–58.

26. Robert C. Bensing and Olive Schroeder, *Homicide in an Urban Community*, Springfield, Ill.: Charles C. Thomas, 1960, pp. 41, 105.

This concentration has also been found in Houston, Texas: Henry Allen Bullock, "Urban Homicide in Theory and Fact," *Journal of Criminal Law, Criminology, and Police Science*, 45, January–February 1955, pp. 565–75.

27. Goring, *op. cit.*, p. 248. The quick resort to violence in interpersonal relations had been institutionalized long before Goring wrote. More than a century ago Emerson wrote of the English,

The nation has a tough, acrid, animal nature, which centuries of churching and civilizing have not been able to sweeten. . . . The English uncultured are a brutal nation. The crimes recorded in their calendars leave nothing to be desired in the way of cold malignity. . . . The brutality of the manners in the lower class appears in the boxing, bear-baiting, cock-fighting, love of executions, and in the readiness for a set-to in the streets. . . . The costermongers of London streets hold cowardice in loathing: We must work our fists well! we are all handy with our fists.

English Traits (1856), in *Essays of Ralph Waldo Emerson*, New York: Book League of America, 1941, pp. 245–46.

"The lower the occupational status, the higher the homicide rate." Bensing and Schroeder, *op. cit.*, pp. 128–31.

28. Wolfgang, *op. cit.*, p. 50.

29. A presentation of the empirical and logical bases for the rejection of biological explanations of crime can be found in Taft and England, *op. cit.*

An epidemiological discussion of rates of crime is presented in Donald R. Cressey, "Crime," in Robert K. Merton and Robert A. Nisbet, eds., *Contemporary Social Problems*, New York: Harcourt, Brace & World, Inc., 1961, pp. 21–76.

30. Eleanor P. Wolf, "The Invasion—Succession Sequence as a Self-Fulfilling Prophecy," *Journal of Social Issues*, 13, No. 4, 1957, pp. 7–20; Morton Grodzins, *The Metropolitan Area as a Racial Problem*, Pittsburgh: University of Pittsburgh Press, 1958, p. 1; Chester L. Hunt, "Housing: The Northern Conscience and the American Dilemma," *Antioch Review*, 19, Winter 1959–00, pp. 509–21; and Commission on Race and Housing, *Where Shall We Live?* Berkeley: University of California Press, 1958.

31. Walter B. Miller, "Implications of Lower-Class Culture for Social Work," *Social Service Review*, 33, September 1959, p. 230. One study of a Georgia city of about 5,000 population showed about 89 per cent of the Negroes to be lower class, with about 26 per cent in the "upper lower" and 63 per cent in the "lower lower" class; the comparable percentages for whites are about 40, 30, and 10. Mozell C. Hill and Bevode C. McCall, "Social Stratification in 'Georgia Town,'" *American Sociological Review*, 15, December 1950, p. 724.

My estimate is that in 1950 about 73 per cent of Negro men and about 89 per cent of Negro women were in lower-class occupations in the United States, based on Brewton Berry, *Race and Ethnic Relations*, Boston: Houghton Mifflin Co., 1951, Table 9, p. 321.

32. Wolfgang, *op. cit.*, p. 50. Wolfgang and Ferracuti are attempting to specify operationally the content of the "subculture of violence." They have hypothesized

that it is possible to differentiate that subculture from the dominant system of values, to ascertain the quantity and intensity of the values in the subculture, and to locate ecologically the groups that observe and act on the value of violence. See Wolfgang and Ferracuti, *op. cit.*, and also Franco Ferracuti and Marvin E. Wolfgang, "Design for a Proposed Study of Violence: A Socio-Psychological Study of a Subculture of Violence," Social Science Research Center, University of Puerto Rico, Rio Piedras, Puerto Rico, August 1962 (mimeographed), 28 pp.

33. *Ibid.*, p. 52. See also Wolfgang, *Patterns in Criminal Homicide*, Tables 15 and 16.

34. Walter B. Miller, "Lower Class Culture as a Generating Milieu of Gang Delinquency," *Journal of Social Issues*, 14, No. 3, 1958, pp. 5–19, and Walter B. Miller, Hildred Geerth and Henry S. G. Cutter, "Aggression in a Boys' Street-Corner Group," *Psychiatry*, 24, November 1961, pp. 283–98.

35. Wolfgang, "A Sociological Analysis of Criminal Homicide," pp. 54–55.

36. Bensing and Schroeder, *op. cit.*, pp. 72–73.

37. Le Moyne Snyder, *Homicide Investigation*, Springfield, Ill.: Charles C Thomas, 1950, p. 8.

38. Perry B. Jackson, "Some Opening Thoughts," in Bensing and Schroeder, *op. cit.*, p. viii.

39. *Idem.*

40. A particular emphasis on culture, and perhaps the most extensive analysis of the relationship between crime and culture is to be found in Taft and England, *op. cit.* It is an analysis that can, in my opinion, be studied with considerable profit by the student of crime.

41. James F. Short, Jr., "Street Corner Groups and Patterns of Delinquency," A Progress Report from the National Institute of Mental Health Research Grant, M–3301, March 1961 (mimeographed), p. 9.

42. *Ibid.*, pp. 9–10.

43. *Ibid.*, p. 10.

44. Wolfgang, *op. cit.*, p. 55.

45. Gerald D. Robin, "A Study of Justifiable Homicide by Police Officers," Department of Sociology, University of Pennsylvania, n. d. (1962) (mimeographed).

46. *Ibid.*, pp. 26 ff. The cities are Boston, Buffalo, Milwaukee, Philadelphia, Washington, D.C., Cincinnati, Kansas City, Mo., Akron, Chicago, and Miami.

47. This case is summarized in Frederic Wertham, *The Show of Violence*, Garden City, N.Y.: Doubleday & Co., Inc., 1949, pp. 65–94.

48. Hannah Arendt, "Eichmann in Jerusalem: V," *New Yorker*, March 16, 1963, pp. 131–32; and *Eichmann in Jerusalem: A Report on the Banality of Evil*, New York: Viking Press, 1963, p. 253.

49. Herman Kahn, *On Thermonuclear War*, Princeton: Princeton University Press, 1960, pp. 30, 32, 36. "Few would contend that there is any plausible public policy which would justify ending life for everyone." (p. 29) Also see the Special Articles, "The Medical Consequences of Thermonuclear War," by a committee representing the Special Study Section of the Physicians for Social Responsibility (Boston), *New England Journal of Medicine*, 226, No. 2, May 31, 1962, pp. 1126–55.

See also the article by Everett C. Hughes, "Good People and Dirty Work," *Social Problems,* 10, Summer 1962, pp. 3–11. Hughes asked two sets of questions concerning the attempt by the Germans to extirpate the Gypsies, Slavs, and Jews. The questions may be personally disturbing to those people in any country, including the United States, who regard themselves as being decent and humane. One set concerns the good people who did not themselves perform that dirty work. The other concerns those who did. The two are not in fact separate, "for the crucial question concerning the good people is their relation to the people who did the dirty work, with a related one which asks under what circumstances good people let the others get away with such dirty actions (p. 4).

"Repeated calculations" by top United States military officers, says Fryklund, "produced a small library of war-game results which added up deaths and industrial damage and stated the presumed outcome of various nuclear wars that could be fought with existing plans." One such game calculated that 75 million Russians and 110 million Americans died, but that only one-half of the industry of both countries was destroyed. Richard Fryklund, *100 Million Lives,* New York: Macmillan Co., 1962, pp. 23–24, 4. Premier Krushchev also has spoken of a Russian pre-emptive first strike in a speech to the Supreme Soviet, January 14, 1960. Quoted in Fryklund, p. 90.

50. Leonard D. Savitz, "Crime and the Negro: A Critical Review of the Literature," Philadelphia, Department of Sociology, Temple University, 1962 (hectograph). This study was undertaken at the request of the Commission on Human Relations of the City of Philadelphia.

51. E. Eames, "Race and Criminal Statistics," A Report Prepared for the Philadelphia Fellowship Commission, 1958 (dittoed). My summary.

52. Ira DeA. Reid, "Race and Crime," *Friends Journal,* 3, November 30, 1953, pp. 772–74.

One study relevant to the thesis that crime is a sociocultural phenomenon, and to the above hypothesis concerning the murderer, has not yet been referred to. Shannon showed that great differences in the spatial distribution of the rates of crime persist over time. Subcultural variations of a sectional character, he concluded, are probably responsible for the sectional patterns of crime. He showed that the rates for murder and nonnegligent homicide, and for aggravated assault, are persistently higher in the southeastern United States. Over the years the following states have had the highest rates of homicide: Virginia, Mississippi, Florida, North Carolina, Alabama, Georgia, Texas, and Tennessee. The same states, with the exception of the last two, have the highest rates of aggravated assault.

Since Shannon's study was concerned with states and sections, it cannot be compared with the statistical work performed in such limited areas as cities: for example, the work in Chicago by Clifford Shaw, Henry D. McKay, Solomon Kobrin, and others. It is nonetheless significant in that, first, it demonstrates the temporal and spatial stability of the distribution of gross rates of crime, especially the three mentioned in the previous paragraph. Second, it shows that those crimes are concentrated in the sections of the United States with seemingly the most highly developed subculture of violence, embracing both races and all social classes. Third, it shows that those crimes are least frequent in those sections where the subculture of violence is least developed, namely, New England, the

Middle Atlantic and the west North Central States. Lyle W. Shannon, "The Spatial Distribution of Criminal Offenses by States," *Journal of Criminal Law, Criminology, and Police Science*, 45, September–October 1954, pp. 264–73.

Almost all of the studies cited above are largely statistical in character. There is also a large body of discursive literature that is anecdotal and descriptive. The journals of the various state historical societies, as one example, are replete with such studies. They are important because they depict in a manner impossible in quantitative studies, the quality of their subject-matter. A good example of such studies is Jack Kenny Williams, *Vogues in Villainy: Crime and Retribution in Ante-Bellum South Carolina*, Columbia: University of South Carolina Press, 1959.

The book is concerned almost exclusively with white citizens. Slaves and "free blacks" were tried by special minor courts and punished according to particular written and unwritten codes. Williams shows that the criminals were a diverse aggregation of male and female, ranging in age from early childhood to near senility, in education from illiterate to college graduate, in intelligence from insane (idiot?) to brilliant, and financially from the poverty-stricken to the reasonably rich. Some of them were men and women of eminent social background.

The two prominent characteristics of the crime and retribution of the period are the pervasiveness of violence throughout the class structure, and the upper-class basis of the criminal law. The book shows that the upper-class white South Carolinian was very democratic: he discriminated against everyone else, whether slave, freedman, or white lower class. Williams quotes one writer as saying that "people of quality" were so devoid of compassion that they "thanked God and took heart when one poor-white killed another" (p. 23). The South Carolinian of 1790–1860 was certainly not less prone to commit physical violence than is the one of today, Williams writes, and he was not less prone to violate the code of conduct between the sexes: "He fought, murdered, raped, and swindled about as much as his presentday counterpart; and this despite nostalgic claims which are sometimes made by those who derive their impressions of ante-bellum society from sentiment and tradition" (p. 136).

Vance and Wynne make the point that folk rationalizations in the southern United States condone and prescribe violence outside the law: "Men bent on lynchings in our southern states operate in public for both private and public vengeance, openly defy both the law and its representatives, but conform to the demands of the folk ways. Because of the strength of these folk ways, lynchers are rarely brought to trial even when known to the community." Rupert P. Vance and Waller Wynne, Jr., "Folk Rationalizations in the 'Unwritten Law,'" *American Journal of Sociology*, 39, 1934, p. 484.

Texas is an example of a state in which murder is justified on the ground of "a higher morality" than the law:

There is no better law than the unwritten law—the proof is that it doesn't have to be written. It springs spontaneously to the hearts and minds of honest honorable men. . . .

The result of all this shooting—and I believe that Texas has more of it than any other state in the Union—is to minimize the rotten plots of indecent or moneyminded citizens. I believe there is greater security and respect for the home here and less need to get seventeen lawyers and examine a contract between honest men than anywhere else under the sun. . . . Texas cannot help feeling that if you object to our shooting under those conditions you must be one of the sort we'd "get."

Chester T. Crowell, "Six Shooter Ethics," *Independent,* December 5, 1912. Quoted in Vance and Wynn, *op. cit.,* p. 489.

In a more current statement, Robert Wallace, in answering the question "What Kind of Place is Dallas?" (*Life,* Jan. 31, 1964, p. 69), replied, in part, that one of its characteristics,

indeed a characteristic of the state as a whole—is the local habit of going armed, of carrying pistols in pockets or the glove compartments of cars. An accurate estimate of the habit's extent is not possible, because firearms may be purchased by any adult in the city and no permit is required. But one University of Texas professor has noted that "about half the boys and perhaps one third of the girls have weapons with them at the university. Normally about 25% of the gunowners in my classes admit to carrying pistols." Rabbits and beer cans are on the receiving end of much of this gunfire, but it is also true that Dallas has a much higher murder rate than the supposedly gangster-ridden cities of New York or Chicago.

In 1962 the rate of murder and nonnegligent manslaughter was 41 per cent greater in Dallas than in Chicago and 98 per cent greater than in New York City. The rates in 1962 for these offenses, per 100,000 population, in selected Standard Metropolitan Statistical Areas were: Boston, 2.4; Chicago, 7.0; Dallas, 9.9; Detroit, 4.3; Fort Worth, 9.6; Los Angeles, 4.5; New York, 5.0; San Francisco, 4.3. *Uniform Crime Reports,* 1962, Washington, D. C.: United States Department of Justice, 1963, Table 4.

Another excellent study of institutionalized violence is Paul M. Angle's *Bloody Williamson: A Chapter in American Lawlessness,* New York: Alfred A. Knopf, Inc., 1952.

53. Frank E. Hartung, "Observation: A Social Psychological Analysis," Detroit: Wayne State University, 1961 (mimeographed).

54. See also Kenneth Burke, "On Interpretation," in *Permanence and Change,* rev. ed., Los Altos, California: Hermes Publications, 1954, pp. 5–66.

55. My discussion of the "self" and of "self-conception" throughout this book has drawn more from Charles Horton Cooley, "The Social Self—1. The Meaning of 'I'; 2. Various Phases of 'I'," *Human Nature and the Social Order,* 1956 printing, Glencoe: Free Press, pp. 168–263, than from George Herbert Mead, *Mind, Self and Society,* Chicago: University of Chicago Press, 1934.

These two books contain what are in many respects still the best analyses of problems relating to the self, role, and identification.

56. Frank E. Hartung, "A Critique of the Sociological Approach to Crime and Correction," *Law and Contemporary Problems,* 23, Autumn 1958, p. 734.

57. Wootton, *op. cit.,* pp. 234–35.

58. Frank E. Hartung, "Sexuality," *Dictionary of the Social Sciences,* New York: UNESCO, 1964.

59. Frederic Wertham, "The Psychiatry of Criminal Guilt," in Edmond N. Kahn, ed., *Social Meaning of Legal Concepts,* No. 2; "Criminal Guilt," New York: New York University School of Law, 1950, pp. 153–69. Wertham also states (pp. 164–65): "I have never seen a murder or suicide in a case of obsessive-compulsive

neurosis. The two psychiatrists who have made the greatest contribution to the study of obsessive-compulsive neurosis, Pierre Janet and Freud, have also seen no such case."

See also Henry A. Davidson, "Irresistible Impulse and Criminal Responsibility," *Journal of Forensic Sciences*, 1, January 1956, 1–18; and Jerome Hall, *General Principles of Criminal Law*, 2d ed., Indianapolis: Bobbs-Merrill Co., 1960, p. 488.

60. A. A. Milne, "Lines and Squares," *When We Were Very Young*, New York: E. P. Dutton Co., 1924, p. 12. Quoted with the permission of the publishers.

61. Hall, *op. cit.*, p. 488; Wertham, *The Show of Violence*, pp. 13–14.

62. Isaac Ray, *A Treatise on the Medical Jurisprudence of Insanity*, 5th ed., 1871, pp. 239–43.

63. *Ibid.*, p. 246.

64. F. C. Redlich, "The Concept of Health in Psychiatry," Alexander H. Leighton, *et al.*, eds., *Explorations in Social Psychiatry*, New York: Basic Books, Inc., 1957, p. 140.

65. *Report* of the Royal Commission on the Criminal Law Relating to the Criminal Sexual Psychopath, Ottawa: The Queen's Printer, 1958, p. 22.

66. *Ibid.*, p. 21.

67. Cressey, *op. cit.*, p. 456.

68. Franz Alexander and Hugo Staub, *The Criminal, the Judge, and the Public*, rev. ed., Glencoe: Free Press, 1956, p. 146.

69. Leland E. Hinsie and Robert Jean Campbell, *Psychiatric Dictionary*, 3d ed., New York: Oxford University Press, 1960, p. 414.

70. *Uniform Crime Reports*, 1960, Washington: Government Printing Office, Table 19, p. 94.

71. Eleanor Touroff Glueck, "Efforts to Identify Delinquents," *Federal Probation*, 24, June 1960, p. 53.

72. Dorwin Cartwright, "Achieving Change in People: Some Applications of Group Dynamics Theory," *Human Relations*, 4, 1951, pp. 381–92.

For a more extensive discussion of this point than I can give here, see Donald R. Cressey, ed., *The Prison: Studies in Institutional Organization and Change*, New York: Holt, Rinehart & Winston, Inc., 1961, pp. 5–10.

73. Albert J. Reiss, Jr., "The Social Integration of Queers and Peers," *Social Problems*, 9, Fall 1961, p. 102.

74. *Ibid.*, p. 119.

Chapter 6

1. Ernest Hilgard, *Unconscious Processes and Man's Rationality*, Urbana: University of Illinois Press, 1958, pp. 5, 17.

2. Kingsley Davis, "Mental Hygiene and the Class Structure," *Psychiatry* 1, January 1938, pp. 55–65.

3. Barbara Wootton, *Social Science and Social Pathology*, New York: Macmillan Co., 1959, p. 214. One should, in my opinion, study the whole of Chapters 7 and 8, "Social Pathology and the Concepts of Mental Health and Mental Illness," pp. 203–26, and "Mental Disorder and the Problem of Moral and Criminal Responsibility," pp. 227–67.

4. Orville R. Gursslin, Raymond G. Hunt, and Jack L. Roach, "Social Class and the Mental Health Movement," *Social Problems*, 7, Winter 1959–60, pp. 210–18.

5. For an historical perspective and a comparison of the mental health movement with the early Christian church, see John R. Seeley, "Social Values, the Mental Hygiene Movement and Mental Health," *Annals of the American Academy of Political and Social Science*, 286, March 1953, pp. 15–25.

6. Kingsley Davis, "The Relation of Means to Ends: The Problem of Rationality," and "Religious Institutions," in *Human Society*, New York: Macmillan Co., 1949, pp. 128–33, 509–45, and *idem*.

7. According to Davis, four "persistent causes of error" and "constant sources of nonrational conduct" are superempirical ends, haziness of the ends, ignorance, and normative restrictions. *Ibid.*, pp. 128–33.

8. *Ibid.*, p. 131.

9. The most recent authoritative statement of action theory continues the judgment of lower-class behavior and values in terms of upper-class values. According to Pitts's analysis of "Deviance and the Maintenance of Conformity," illness, error, crime, and sin are deviations from, and even pathological forms of, middle-class conformity. Jesse R. Pitts, "Introduction" to "Personality and the Social System," in Talcott Parsons, Edward Shils, Kaspar D. Naegele, and Jesse R. Pitts, eds., *Theories of Society*, Glencoe: Free Press, 1961, pp. 701–16. Error and illness are said to be two forms of deviation that apparently derive exclusively from failures to reach efficiency and/or effectiveness. An adaptive failure of the personality is "the failure to transform the organism and the personality into role facilities, motivational and non-motivational: this would be *illness*, either physical or mental" (p. 701). It should be noticed that no lesion is required in this conception of mental and physical illness. Crime is so defined as to be jurisprudentially and sociologically useless: "Nonreciprocity is defined as *crime* of varying seriousness" (p. 702). Almost any behavior that does not adhere to the values of action theory is deviant (p. 708). Indeed, one unstated premise of Pitts's entire discussion is that there is a single system of values in the United States. It is by definition therefore that behavior and values from which the values of action theory differ, are classified as deviant or pathological by action theory.

10. *Ibid.*, pp. 128, 510, 526, 542. It is necessary to read Davis' discussion "The Relation of Means to Ends," pp. 128–33, and his chapter "Religion," pp. 509–48, for oneself in order to capture the intellectual quality resulting from the confining of rationality to means and ends.

11. *An Introduction to Social Psychology*, 5th ed., Boston: John M. Luce & Co., 1919, pp. 44 and 379.

12. *Ibid.*, p. 378.

13. Morris Ginsberg, "Is Reason the Slave of Passions?" *Plain View*, 9, 1955, p. 227.

14. Davis, *op. cit.*, pp. 516, 540, 129.

15. Edward B. Tylor, *Primitive Culture*, London: Henry Holt & Co., 1871, Vol. 1, pp. 22–23; Vol. 2, p. 447.

My comments should not be interpreted as a defense of religion. The distinction between superstition and religion depends, it seems, on one's own religion; other beliefs are superstitious. To avoid any religious discrimination on my part, I use "superstition" broadly, so as to include all religions.

16. Davis, *op. cit.*, p. 133.

17. Marie Jahoda, *Current Concepts of Positive Mental Health,* New York: Basic Books, Inc., 1958.

18. Jack R. Ewalt, "Staff Review," in Gerald Gurin, Joseph Veroff, and Sheila Feld, *Americans View Their Mental Health,* New York: Basic Books, Inc., 1960, p. x. My italics. See also *Action for Mental Health: Final Report of the Joint Commission on Mental Illness and Health,* Letter of Transmittal by Kenneth E. Appel and Leo H. Bartemeier, New York: Basic Books, Inc., 1961.

19. Wootton, *op. cit.*, pp. 203–26.

20. Stanley S. Marzolf, "The Disease Concept in Psychology," *Psychological Review,* 54, July 1947, 211–21; J. Mayone Stycos, "A Consideration on Methodology in Research on Mental Disorder," *Psychiatry,* 12, August 1949, 301–11.

21. Thomas S. Szasz, "Growth and Structure of the Myth," *The Myth of Mental Illness,* New York: Paul B. Hoeber, Inc., 1961, pp. 21–72.

22. *Ibid.*, p. 43.

23. Thomas S. Szasz, "Acquittal by Reason of Insanity," and "The Hospitalized Mental Patient's Fight for Freedom," in *Law, Liberty, and Psychiatry,* New York, Macmillan Co., 1963, pp. 138–46 and 169–81.

24. F. C. Redlich, "The Concept of Health in Psychiatry," in A. H. Leighton, John A. Clausen, and Robert N. Wilson, eds., *Explorations in Social Psychiatry,* New York: Basic Books, Inc., 1957, p. 139. See also Jahoda, *op. cit.*

25. *Ibid.*, pp. 152, 153. For the value statements about mental health made by middle-class psychiatrists to middle-class people who were the only ones to understand them, see: F. S. Redlich, A. B. Hollingshead, *et al.*, "Social Structure and Psychiatric Disorders," *American Journal of Psychiatry,* 109, December 1953, pp. 729–34, and F. C. Redlich and E. Bellis, "Social Class Differences in Attitudes toward Psychiatry," *American Journal of Orthopsychiatry,* 25, No. 1, 1955, pp. 60–70.

26. Karl A. Menninger, *The Human Mind,* 3d ed., New York: Alfred A. Knopf, Inc., 1946, p. 2.

27. Leo Srole, Thomas S. Langner, Stanley T. Michael, Marvin K. Opler, and Thomas A. C. Rennie, *Mental Health in the Metropolis,* New York: McGraw-Hill Book Co., Inc., 1962, pp. 395–96.

28. For an analysis of why they *had* to make these claims, in terms of their criteria of mental health, see Frank E. Hartung, "Manhattan Madness: The Social Movement of Mental Illness," *Sociological Quarterly,* 4, No. 3, July 1963, 261–72.

29. Heinz Hartmann, "Towards A Concept of Mental Health," *British Journal of Medical Psychology,* 33, 1960, pp. 243 and 247–48. See also his book, *Psychoanalysis and Moral Values,* New York: International Universities Press, 1960.

Fordham also writes that "There is at present no agreement about the nature of mental health. Perhaps there never will be. . . ." Michael Fordham, "Ego, Self, and Mental Health," *British Journal of Medical Psychology,* 33, 1960, p. 249. And Culpin, in an historical study, concludes that "Here, then, is a terminology of inexactitudes." Millais Culpin, "The Conception of Mental Disorder," *British Journal of Medical Psychology,* 35, 1962, p. 73.

30. I am indebted to Professor Robert L. Stewart, of Central Michigan University,

for reminding me of the distinction between mental disease conceived as an entity based on the medical analogy, and conceived as sociocultual behavior classified according to the observer's unstated social-class values.

Chapter 7

1. Melanie Klein, *The Psycho-Analysis of Children,* London: Tavistock Publications, 1954; *Contributions to Psycho-Analysis,* 1921–1945, London: Hogarth Press, 1948; and *Narrative of a Child Analysis,* New York: Basic Books, Inc., 1961, pp. 198, 289, 339, 424.

Winnicott says that "the infant aims at breaking ruthlessly through into the mother to take out of her everything that is felt there to be good. . . ." Donald W. Winnicott, "Psycho-Analysis and the Sense of Guilt," in John D. Sutherland, ed., *Psycho-Analysis and Contemporary Thought,* London: The Hogarth Press, 1958, pp. 23–24.

2. In addition to Freud's works referred to above in the text, see his discussion in *A General Introduction to Psychoanalysis,* New York: Garden City Publishing Co., 1938 ed., pp. 288–96.

3. *Ibid.,* pp. 288–96. See also Gregory Zilboorg, "Instincts and their Manifestations" and "Varieties of Human Aggression," in *Mind, Medicine, and Man,* New York: Harcourt Brace & Co., 1943, pp. 72–108 and 225–45.

4. Sigmund Freud, "The Psychology of Women," Chap. 5 of *New Introductory Lectures to Psychoanalysis,* New York: W. W. Norton & Co., 1933.

5. Theodor Reik, *Ritual: Psychoanalytic Studies,* with a Preface by Professor Sigm. Freud, London: Hogarth Press and the Institute of Psychoanalysis, 1931, p. 132.

6. Redlich, *op. cit.,* p. 144.

7. I have not placed Sir Russell's statement within quotation marks, as I wrote it while listening to him during an interview on radio Station CBE, Windsor, February 26, 1961.

8. Redlich, *op. cit.,* p. 144.

9. Harry Stack Sullivan, *Conceptions of Modern Psychiatry,* with a critical appraisal by Patrick Mullahy. Reprinted from *Psychiatry,* 3, February 1940, and 8, May 1945.

More particularly, see Sullivan, *The Interpersonal Theory of Psychiatry,* ed. H. S. Perry and M. L. Gawel, New York: W. W. Norton & Co., 1953.

10. August B. Hollingshead and Frederick C. Redlich, *Social Class and Mental Illness,* New York: John Wiley & Sons, Inc., 1958, pp. 11–12.

11. William A. White, *Crime and Criminals,* New York: Macmillan Co., 1933, p. 49.

12. William A. White, *Insanity and the Criminal Law,* New York: Macmillan Co., 1923, p. 20.

13. White, *Crime and Criminals,* pp. 160–61.

14. David Abrahamsen, *The Psychology of Crime,* New York: Columbia University Press, 1960. See my review of this book in the *American Sociological Review,* 26, June 1961, 480–81. Abrahamsen first made this statement in his *Who Are the Guilty? A Study of Education and Crime,* New York: Columbia University Press, 1952, p. 125. See the review of this book by Donald R. Cressey,

Journal of Criminal Law, Criminology, and Police Science, 43, January–February 1953, pp. 649–51.

15. Franz Alexander and Hugo Staub, *The Criminal, the Judge, and the Public: A Psychological Analysis*, rev. ed., with new chapters by Franz Alexander, Glencoe: Free Press, 1956, pp. x, xi.

See my review of this book in *Social Problems*, 5, Spring 1958, pp. 364–65.

16. Walter Bromberg, *Crime and the Mind: An Outline of Psychiatric Criminology*, Philadelphia: J. B. Lippincott Co., 1948, pp. 19, 20, 25, 178.

17. Benjamin Karpman, "Criminality, Insanity and the Law," *Journal of Criminal Law and Criminology*, 39, November–December 1949, pp. 584, 605–6; and Benjamin Karpman, "Criminal Psychodynamics: A Platform," *Archives of Criminal Psychodynamics*, January 1955, I, p. 96.

18. Karl A. Menninger, *op. cit.*, pp. 460, 449.

19. Karl A. Menninger, "Medicolegal Proposals of the American Psychiatric Association," *Journal of Criminal Law and Criminology*, 19, September–October 1928, p. 373.

20. Philip Q. Roche, "Criminality and Mental Illness—Two Faces of the Same Coin," *University of Chicago Law Review*, 22, 1954–55, pp. 320–24. My italics.

21. Roche, *op. cit.*, p. 323; and Henry Maudsley, *Responsibility in Mental Disease*, London: D. Appleton & Co., 1874, p. 34. Roche, who cites Maudsley's work in his *The Criminal Mind*, does not refer to him when stating the peculiar doctrine that they have in common.

22. Ernest Jones, M.D., *Essays in Applied Psycho-Analysis*, Vol. 2, London: The Hogarth Press, 1951, pp. 227–28.

23. *Ibid.*, pp. 229, 230, 228.

24. Hilgard, *op. cit.*, p. 17.

25. Jerome Hall, Review of Manfred S. Guttmacher and Henry Weihofen, *Psychiatry and the Law*, New York: W. W. Norton & Co., 1952, in *Iowa Law Review*, 38, June 1953, p. 687.

26. One of the best historical discussions is in Arthur E. Fink, *Causes of Crime: Biological Theories in the United States, 1800–1915*, Philadelphia: University of Pennsylvania Press, 1938. The title of this book works an injustice on its scope, because it includes continental European writings as well as American.

Zilboorg claimed that the irresistible impulse was first postulated in 1578 by Johann Weyer: "Such progressive and humanistic concepts as that of the 'irresistible impulse' were fully and clearly stated by Weyer" in 1578. Gregory Zilboorg, *A History of Medical Psychology*, New York: W. W. Norton & Co., 1941, p. 243.

Zilboorg used as his source the 1885 reprinting of Weyer's two-volume work, *Histoires, disputes et discours des illusions et impostures des diables, etc.* He cites no page to substantiate his conclusion that Weyer was referring to the same thing that contemporary psychiatrists refer to when they use the concept *irresistible impulse*. Two superior graduate students, to each of whom I had given the same assignment, unknown to the other, were unable to locate the passage in Weyer that would justify Zilboorg's claim for the existence of the alleged "progressive and humanistic concepts" in 1578.

27. Isaac Ray, *A Treatise on the Medical Jurisprudence of Insanity*, 5th ed., 1871, pp. 257–58.

28. Friedrich Albert Lange, *Geschichte der Materialismus,* 1905 ed., Vol. 2, pp. 427–28; and *The History of Materialism,* London: Kegan Paul, Trench, Trubner & Co., 1925, Vol. 3, pp. 121–22.

29. George Combe, *A System of Phrenology,* 4th ed., Cooperstown, N.Y.: H. and E. Phinney, 1843, p. 38.

Perhaps no other single event brought the phrenological doctrine of moral insanity to the attention of the public more than the trial of Charles J. Guiteau for the murder of President James A. Garfield, in 1881. The trial centered on the question of his responsibility: Was he sane or insane at the time of the murder? It became a crucial question as to whether a disease-entity such as moral insanity existed. Some psychiatric witnesses for the defense testified that insanity can exist in the absence of delusion, hallucination, or illusion. Many psychiatric witnesses for the prosecution testified that "moral insanity" was only another name for wickedness, and that Guiteau was sane and therefore responsible. Moral insanities, they testified, were only crimes. That is, what to some people was kleptomania was in fact only larceny; what to some was dipsomania was in fact only excessive drinking; and what to some was pyromania was in fact only arson.

30. Ray, *op. cit.,* p. 215.

31. Having written my comments about phrenology and psychiatry before reading Benjamin Pasamanick's delightful article, "An Obscure Item in the Bibliography of Isaac Ray," *American Journal of Psychiatry,* 111, September 1954, pp. 164–71, I was unable to make as much use of it as I should have liked to. See also Winfred Overholser, "Isaac Ray," in Hermann Mannheim, ed., *Pioneers in Criminology,* Chicago: Quadrangle Books, Inc., 1960, pp. 113–34; and Owsei Temkin, "Gall and the Phrenological Movement," *Bulletin of the History of Medicine,* 21, No. 2, 1947.

32. David Hume, *A Treatise of Human Nature,* L. A. Selby-Bigge, ed., p. 415.

33. Edwin A. Sutherland, "The Diffusion of the Sexual Psychopath Laws," *American Journal of Sociology,* 56, September 1950, pp. 543–54; and "The Sexual Psychopath Laws," in Albert K. Cohen, Alfred Lindesmith, and Karl F. Schuessler, eds., *The Sutherland Papers,* Bloomington: Indiana University Press, 1956, pp. 185–99.

34. *Commonwealth v. Mosler,* 4 Pa. 264 (1846).

35. Zilboorg, *op. cit.,* p. 564. My italics.

36. Henry Weihofen, *Mental Disorder as a Criminal Defense,* Buffalo: Dennis and Co., Inc., 1954, p. 97.

37. Alfred Lief, ed., *The Commonsense Psychiatry of Adolph Meyer,* New York: McGraw-Hill Book Co., 1948, p. 39.

38. *American Journal of Insanity,* 38, 1881–82, p. 425.

39. Henry A. Davidson, "Irresistible Impulse and Criminal Responsibility," in Richard W. Nice, ed., *Crime and Insanity,* New York: Philosophical Library, 1958, p. 35. See, also, Henry A. Davidson, *Forensic Psychiatry,* New York: Ronald Press, 1952, pp. 11 ff.

40. Manfred S. Guttmacher and Henry Weihofen, *Psychiatry and the Law,* New York: W. W. Norton & Co., 1952, pp. 56–57. My italics.

That their prediction was correct seems indicated by the following figures applying to the federal district court of the District of Columbia. After July 1, 1955, anyone acquitted in any criminal trial by reason of insanity is automatically and mandatorily committed to St. Elizabeth's Hospital, the District's mental institution. The rule is that if some evidence has been introduced, by either the prosecution or the defense, that the defendant has a mental illness or a mental defect, and the prosecution or the defense has failed to overcome this evidence in proving his mental capacity beyond a reasonable doubt, he shall be acquitted by reason of insanity, and committed to St. Elizabeth's with no terminal date on his sentence. As the rule operates,

even if an individual is acquitted by reason of insanity, there is no finding that he is presently insane or presently mentally ill. There is no finding that he is presently socially dangerous. There is no finding that he is in need of institutional mental care at the present time [and] his acquittal by reason of insanity is not based on an affirmative finding that he was at the time of the crime insane.

As to those acquitted and committed under the rule,

it is well to realize that prior to *Durham* [July 1, 1954] probably less than 1 per cent of the cases tried in our [District of Columbia] criminal court resulted in a verdict of not guilty by reason of insanity. And immediately following that *Durham* decision, the percentage did not substantially increase. However, by the fiscal year 1957 the percentage was 1.5; in fiscal 1959 it went up to 6.7; and in fiscal 1960, 8.7; and in the first six months of fiscal 1961 (July 1–Dec. 31, 1960), 14.2; and in the month of February of this year (1961), 25 per cent of all cases tried resulted in verdicts of not guilty by reason of insanity.

Since the mandatory commitment is not dependent on the alleged offense, those who commit the "less dramatic" ones, to use Guttmacher and Weihofen's phrase, from drunkenness to the writing of bad checks, predominate in number.

The case of *Lynch v. Overholser* showed that

in the District of Columbia, we are confronted with a situation that is unique in the Nation. An insanity defense can be foisted upon a reluctant and competent defendant in criminal proceedings . . . the roles in [the *Lynch* case: Frederick C. Lynch v. Winfred Overholser, Habeas Corpus No. 130–60, U.S. District Court for the District of Columbia] were reversed, and both the roles of the defense and the prosecution were turned topsy-turvy in a scene which seems almost like out of Alice in Wonderland.

Instead of the defendant presenting evidence that he was not guilty by reason of insanity, the prosecution did so. On this evidence . . . the court entered a judgment of acquittal by reason of insanity, and ordered the defendant committed to a mental hospital until such time as he was certified as no longer mentally ill, or likely in the foreseeable future to be dangerous to himself or others.

Lynch had been charged with overdrawing his bank account by $100 and failing to make restitution within five days.

[His case] is significant for the fact that [it] appears to endow the Government with the right of foisting an insanity defense upon an unwilling and competent defendant upon any charge. The life-long liberty of any citizen brought into open court upon nothing more serious than a traffic ticket may be put into jeopardy. The consequences in the District of Columbia are particularly serious, in view of the fact that the court of appeals, under the *Durham* rule, has made it plain that any kind of mental disease and not just a psychosis is a legally sufficient mental disease for the assertion of the insanity defense.

It is not farfetched, therefore, to envision a situation in which honest psychiatric testimony is presented that a parking violation is attributable to the tension generated by a mild and perhaps very widespread mental disorder which is susceptible to psychotherapy.

We inquire in deadly seriousness, which of us could stand such scrutiny?

We submit with all the influence at our command, that if the doctrine of the *Lynch* case were to prevail as a result of legislative inaction, the specter of arbitrary hospitalization would cast a pall on customary American freedom, at least in the District of Columbia.

The quotations are, respectively, from the statements by Lawrence Speiser, Oliver Gasch, and Richard Arens, attorneys practicing in the District, in *Constitutional Rights of the Mentally Ill*. Hearings before the Subcommittee on Constitutional Rights of the Committee of the Judiciary, United States Senate, 87th Congress, 1st Session, May 2, 4, and 5, 1961: Part 2—Criminal Aspects, pp. 552 and 568; and March 28, 29, and 30, 1961: Part 1—Civil Aspects, pp. 207–9.

41. Maudsley, *op. cit.*, p. 139.

42. Jerome Hall, "Psychiatry and Individual Responsibility," *Yale Law Journal*, 65, December 1956, p. 775; and "The Purposes of a System for the Administration of Criminal Justice," a lecture delivered at Georgetown University Law Center, October 9, 1963.

43. Sir Norwood East, *Society and Its Criminals*, London: Blakiston's Sons & Co., 1951, pp. 20–21.

44. Weihofen, *op. cit.*, p. 84.

45. *Ibid.*, p. 67.

46. Sheldon Glueck, *Crime and Correction*, Cambridge: Addison-Wesley Press, 1952, p. 153.

47. Sheldon Glueck, *Law and Psychiatry: Cold War or Entente Cordiale?* Baltimore: Johns Hopkins Press, 1962, pp. 47–48. The first criticism, published in his first book, *Mental Disorder and the Criminal Law* (Boston: Little, Brown & Co., 1925) was quoted by Judge Bazelon in *Durham v. United States,* 214 F. 2d 862 (D. C. Cir. 1954).

48. Glueck, *Law and Psychiatry*, pp. 50–52, 57.

49. Zilboorg, *op. cit.*, p. 416.

50. Jerome Hall, "Responsibility and Law: In Defense of the McNaghten Rules," *American Bar Association Journal*, 42, 1956, pp. 917–19.

51. Guttmacher and Weihofen, *op. cit.*, p. 410.

52. *Federal Prisons*, 1961, Bureau of Prisons, Department of Justice, Washington, D. C.

53. *United States v. Pollard*, 171 F. Supp. 474, at p. 481.

54. *Ibid.*, p. 481.

55. *Ibid.*, p. 479.

56. *Ibid.*, p. 480.

57. *Ibid.*, pp. 480–81.

58. *Ibid.*, p. 481. The material within the last quotation marks is from Manfred S. Guttmacher and Henry Weihofen, *Psychiatry and the Law*, New York: W. W. Norton & Co., 1952, p. 413.

59. *Pollard v. United States*, 282 F. 2d 450 (1960) and 285 F. 2d 81 (1960).

60. 282 F. 2d 450 (1960), pp. 454–55. My italics.

61. *Ibid.*, p. 462. My italics.

62. *Ibid.*, p. 464.

63. 285 F. 2d 81 (1960), p. 84. In his dissent, Judge Simons accepted Judge Levin's findings of fact. He wrote:

they substantially sustain his conclusion that the Appellant [Pollard] was sane when he committed the crimes charged. Particularly am I unable to entertain the concept that the Appellant wished to be apprehended, while at the same time yielding to an irresistible impulse to commit the crimes and to escape detection and apprehension. I would sustain the conviction.

282 F. 2d 450 (1960), p. 464.

64. *State v. Felter*, 25 Iowa 67, 82 (1868). Quoted from Glueck, *op. cit.*, p. 52.

65. 285 F. 2d 81 (1960), p. 82.

66. *Smith v. United States*, 36 F. 2d 548, 551 (1929).

67. 282 F. 2d 450 (1960), p. 457. My italics.

68. One is reminded of Richard T. La Piere's excellent analysis of the subversion of American character, *The Freudian Ethic*, New York: Duell, Sloan and Pearce, 1959, esp. Chaps. 2, 3, and 7.

69. Edward Glover, "Medico-psychological Aspects of Insanity," *British Journal of Psychology*, 23, No. 1, 1932, p. 165. A few pages before, Glover had said of "the normal person" that his " 'normality' represented a victory over an original state of madness." A few years later Ruth Benedict, in the last pages of her *Patterns of Culture* (1934), developed the thesis that "ordinarily the most bizarre of the psychopathic types of the period" are those who most faithfully conform to the norms of their society. Roszak more recently made the point that "Freud . . . became progressively more aware that 'normalcy' may actually be the socially acceptable form of psychic sickness. Man, Freud concluded, is the neurotic animal; the disease is of his nature. . . . What historians may really be studying, not occasionally but at all times, is diseased matter." Theodore Roszak, "The Historian as Psychiatrist," *The Nation*, 195, No. 17, November 1962, p. 343. Ostrow insists that the difference between normal and pathological human behavior is only one of degree, not of kind. Mortimer Ostrow, "War and the Unconscious," *Bulletin of the Atomic Scientists*, 19, January 1963, p. 27. Ostrow is committed to what he calls "classical, authentic, psychoanalytic psychology."

In addition to believing that normality is madness, Glover is convinced that general practitioners and surgeons practice magic rather than medicine, and are psychotic to boot. From his "point of view the conduct of the general physician borders on the pathological. . . ." Any pointed effort by the physician to exclude psychiatric factors "constitutes a 'pathological' manifestation." The persistence with which psychiatric factors in treatment

are plastered with the labels of organic therapy shows a lack of reality feeling which at first sight seems little short of psychotic. But the general physician is not strictly speaking psychotic in this respect: his lack of reality feeling approximates more closely to that exhibited by cases of conversion hysteria. For example, when a childless woman states her psychological requirements in terms of amenorrhoea, the general physician enters into her conspiracy by attributing her condition to, shall we say, bloodlessness. But he is not content with endorsing this symptomatic disguise; he plays up to the situation by administering by mouth or by injection some drug in the potency of which he has profound conviction. Fortified by the rationalizations of scientific diagnosis, he initiates or carries through symbolic ceremonials of impregnation, showing that while he accepts his patient's conversion mechanism at her own valuation, he can return a Roland for her Oliver. Stripped of their rationalizations, his therapeutic convictions are seen to be of a magical order. Irreproachable as his organic diagnostic methods may be in their own sphere, they have been exploited on this occasion to endorse the therapy of white magic, although the recovery of his patient, should that ensue, is regarded as a tribute to scientific method. This latter assumption is not merely a venial expression of pride: it is an essential part of the system by which he screens from himself his thaumaturgic proclivities. He is of course not limited to this one form of defence: the aspersions cast by general physicians on the scientific validity of psychological [that is, psychiatric] methods illustrates the operation of another defence mechanism, viz., projection of the self-criticism engendered by their own psychological myopia.

Edward Glover, "The Psychology of the Psychotherapist," *British Journal of Medical Psychology*, 35, Part 1, 1962, pp. 47–48.

70. Manfred S. Guttmacher, *Model Penal Code*, Tentative Draft No. 4, 1955, p. 175. His statement fails to refer to even one of those psychiatrists, including those with forensic experience, who find the McNaghten Rules adequate and reject the hypothesis of the irresistible impulse.

The American Law Institute seems to have depended primarily on this brief memorandum by Guttmacher for its "Model formulation" on "Mental disease or defect excluding responsibility," which reads: "A person is not responsible for criminal conduct if at the time of such conduct as a result of mental disease or defect he *lacks substantial capacity* either to appreciate the criminality (wrongfulness) of his conduct or *to conform his conduct to the requirement of law."* Model Penal Code, Proposed Final Draft No. 1, 1961. The portion I have italicized "excludes" one from responsibility for his conduct by reason of an irresistible impulse, but without naming that concept.

Wechsler, who since 1952 has been Chief Reporter for the Model Penal Code, has referred to a feature of its provision on responsibility that he thinks "worthy of attention." The drafters of the Code deliberately formulated the statement on mental disease or defect "without, of course, attempting to define these terms in general." This is another instance in which the concept "mental disease," the use of which may have grave consequences for individual and community, is deliberately undefined but employed as if its users know what it means. See Herbert Wechsler, "On Culpability and Crime: The Treatment of *Mens Rea* in the Model Penal Code," *Annals of the American Academy of Political and Social Science*, 339, January 1962, p. 38.

71. Manfred S. Guttmacher, "The Psychiatrist as an Expert Witness," *University of Chicago Law Review*, 22, 1955, p. 326.

72. Thomas S. Szasz, "The Myth of Mental Illness," *American Psychologist*, 15, No. 2, 1960, pp. 113–18; and "The Uses of Naming and the Origin of the Myth of Mental Illness," *American Psychologist*, 16, No. 2, pp. 59–65.

73. Guttmacher, *op. cit.*, pp. 327–28. My italics.

74. Philip Q. Roche, *The Criminal Mind*, New York: Grove Press, 1958, p. 182.

75. *Ibid.*, pp. 187, 185.

76. *Ibid.*, p. 185.

77. Maudsley, *op. cit.*, p. 151.

78. Roche, *op. cit.*, p. 185.

79. Karl A. Menninger, "Psychiatry and the Law: A Dual Review," *Iowa Law Review*, 38, No. 6, 1952, p. 702.

80. *Ibid.*, pp. 701–2.

81. Roche, *op. cit.*, p. 260. Also see pp. 266, 270.

82. Gregory Zilboorg, *Mind, Medicine and Man*, New York: Harcourt, Brace & Co., 1943, p. 274.

On the other hand, Guttmacher says that "one of the greatest difficulties in psychiatry is its esoteric vocabulary." "The Psychiatric Approach to Crime and Correction," *Law and Contemporary Problems*, 23, Autumn 1958, p. 636.

Frankel says that "Freudian doctrine, for example, provides a language for saying silly things in an impressive way [and] Freudian language offers a way of inflating the importance of findings that are merely banal." Charles Frankel, "The Status of Freud's Ideas," in Sidney Hook, ed., *Psychoanalysis, Scientific Method and Philosophy*, New York: New York University Press, 1959, p. 327.

83. Jerome Hall, *General Principles of Criminal Law*, 2d ed., Indianapolis: Bobbs-Merrill Co., Inc., 1960, pp. 483–85. I am repeating Hall's thesis, which seems to me valid.

84. Sigmund Freud, *Collected Papers*, Vol. 2, London: Hogarth Press, 1924, pp. 277, 282. See also the definitions of "principle," "reality," and "reality-testing" in Leland E. Hinsie and Robert J. Campbell, eds., *Psychiatric Dictionary*, 3d ed., New York: Basic Books, Inc., 1960.

85. Franz Alexander and William Healy, *The Roots of Crime*, New York: Alfred A. Knopf, Inc., 1935, p. 276.

86. Freud, *op. cit.*, Vol. 4, p. 147.

87. For the recognition given to the social event as distinguished from the nature-event, Hall lists the following references as examples: Richard Sterba, *Introduction to the Psychoanalytic Theory of the Libido*, New York: Nervous and Mental Disease Publishing Co., 1942, p. 68; Franz Alexander, *The Psychoanalysis of the Total Personality*, New York: Nervous and Mental Disease Publishing Co., 1930, pp. 125–26; R. Laforgue, *The Relativity of Reality*, New York: Nervous and Mental Disease Publishing Co., 1940, pp. 37, 39, 49–50; A. A. Brill, *Freud's Contribution to Psychiatry*, New York: W. W. Norton & Co., 1944, p. 155; Sigmund Freud, *op. cit.*, Vol. 4, p. 18.

88. Brill, *op. cit.*, p. 169, Laforgue, *op. cit.*, p. 37, and Sandor Ferenczi, "Stages in the Development of the Sense of Reality," *Contributions to Psycho-Analysis*, Boston: Richard C. Badger, 1916, pp. 233–34.

89. Freud, *op. cit.*, Vol. 2, p. 279, and 250–51, 271.

90. Freud states that "the ego takes a perception for real if its reality is vouched for by the mental faculty which ordinarily discharges the duty of testing the reality of things." Sigmund Freud, *Group Psychology and the Analysis of the Ego*, London: International Psychoanalytic Press, 1922, p. 77. See also Paul Schilder, *Introduction to a Psychoanalytic Psychiatry*, New York: Nervous and Mental Disease Publishing Co., 1928, p. 19.

91. "Now conscious thought by means of speech signs is the highest accomplish-

ment of psychical apparatus, and alone makes adjustment to reality possible. . . ." Ferenczi, *op. cit.*, p. 195. Edward Podolsky writes that "intelligence is the capacity for acquiring, absorbing and using knowledge of reality," in "Psychoanalytical Views of Intelligence," *Psychoanalytical Review*, 28, No. 3, 1941, p. 359. Also see Franz Alexander, *Fundamentals of Psychoanalysis*, New York: W. W. Norton & Co., 1948, p. 85.

92. Robert Wälder, "Das Freiheitsprobleme in der Psychoanalyse und das Probleme der Realitäts—prüfung," *Imago*, 20, No. 4, 1934, pp. 467–84. Hall uses "apprehension" in his translation, but I think that "comprehension" is more accurate.

93. Hall, *op. cit.*, p. 485. I have not pursued Professor Hall's reference to Erskine in this quotation, as being not relevant here.

94. Max Grünhut, *Penal Reform: A Comparative Study*, London: Oxford University Press, 1948, p. 429.

95. Weihofen, *op. cit.*, pp. 95–96.

96. Guttmacher and Weihofen, *op. cit.*, p. 409.

97. Hall, *op. cit.*, p. 489.

98. After a brilliant critique of the psychiatric approach to crime and correction, Hakeem concluded:

Psychiatric testimony should not be admissible in court. The courts have traditionally followed the principle that expert testimony and evidence that purport to be scientific will not be admissible unless their reliability and validity have been amply tested and unless substantial agreement among the appropriate experts has been demonstrated. When it comes to psychiatric testimony, the courts are acting in heedless disregard and flagrant violation of this eminently sound principle. It should be unmistakably clear on the basis of the evidence adduced here . . . that psychiatrists have not attained the level of competence and scientific reliability and validity necessary to make their testimony eligible for serious consideration by the courts. Nor should it be looked upon as a sound basis for coercive decisions, judicial or correctional. The courts should not allow psychiatric testimony to be heard, irrespective of whether the psychiatrists are partisan or court-appointed, attached to a court clinic or to a hospital.

Michael Hakeem, "A Critique of the Psychiatric Approach to Crime and Correction," *Law and Contemporary Problems*, 23, Autumn 1958, p. 681. Also see Thomas S. Szasz, *Law, Liberty, and Psychiatry*, New York: Macmillan Co., 1963.

99. Hall, *op. cit.*, p. 470.

100. Edward L. Thorndike, *Man and His Works*, Cambridge: Harvard University Press, 1943, p. 133. See especially n. 64, p. 471, in Hall, *op. cit.*

101. Edward C. Jandy, *Charles Horton Cooley: His Life and Social Theory*, New York: Dryden Press, 1942, p. 157.

Chapter 8

1. William L. Kolb, "Images of Man and the Ordering of Sociological Data," paper read at the annual meeting of the American Sociological Association, Statler-Hilton Hotel, New York City, August 31, 1960; and "Images of Man and the Sociology of Religion," *Journal for the Scientific Study of Religion*, 1, October 1961, pp. 5–29.

2. Francis A. Allen, "Criminal Justice, Legal Values and the Rehabilitative Ideal,"

Journal of Criminal Law, Criminology, and Police Science, 50, September–October 1959, p. 230.

3. Aldous Huxley, *Brave New World Revisited,* New York: Bantam Books, Inc., 1960 printing, p. 26.

4. David Abrahamsen, *The Psychology of Crime,* New York: Columbia University Press, 1960.

5. *Ibid.,* p. 322.

6. *Idem.* My italics.

7. *Uniform Crime Reports*–1960, U.S. Department of Justice, Washington, D.C.: Government Printing Office, 1961, p. 31.

8. Alan Barth, *The Price of Liberty,* New York: Viking Press, 1961, pp. 42–43.

9. Justice William O. Douglas, "Vagrancy and Arrest on Suspicion," address to University of New Mexico Law School, Albuquerque, New Mexico, March 10, 1960. Quoted in Barth, *op. cit.,* p. 43.

10. Caleb Foote, "Safeguards in the Law of Arrest," *Northwestern University Law Review,* 52, March–April 1957, p. 16.

11. *Ibid.,* p. 29.

12. Detroit *News,* January 14, 1961.

13. Barth, *op. cit.*

14. National Commission on Law Observance and Enforcement, Report No. 11, *Lawlessness in Law Enforcement,* Washington, D.C.: Government Printing Office, 1931, p. 1.

15. *Ibid.,* p. 190.

16. The Detroit *News,* April 12, 1963, p. 8 B. President John F. Kennedy's appointment of Commissioner Edwards to the U.S. Sixth Circuit Court of Appeals was confirmed by the U.S. Senate, December 16, 1963.

The policy of equal enforcement and improved community relations may have another result. It may have the long-run effect of reducing the conflict in Detroit between the police and the courts on the relationship between the criteria for arresting and the criteria for charging and convicting. The police may disagree with the prosecutor or the court, by regarding as unacceptable to them the criteria applied by the latter in charging or adjudicating an arrested person. "This conflict, particularly between police and judiciary, is most evident in Detroit." Wayne R. LaFave, "The Police and Nonenforcement of the Law," 1962 *Wisconsin Law Review,* pp. 104–37; 179–239, at p. 123. Another relevant and important study by LaFave is "Detention for Investigation by the Police: An Analysis of Current Practices," *Washington University Law Quarterly,* June 1962, pp. 331–99. Professor LaFave's studies are based on his participation in the analysis of the American Bar Foundation's Survey of the Administration of Criminal Justice in the United States.

See also Claude R. Sowle, ed., *Police Power and Individual Freedom: The Quest for Balance,* Chicago: Aldine Publishing Co., 1962. This book deals with four areas of the administration of criminal law in which debate has become most heated: arrest and detention, search and seizure, police interrogation, and self-incrimination. These were chosen by Northwestern University School of Law as the principal topics for discussion at its International Conference on Criminal Law Administration, 1960.

17. *The Detroit School-Community Behavior Project,* Detroit Board of Education and Detroit Commission on Children and Youth, rev., August 1960, p. 1.

18. *Report on Services for Children and Youth with Emotional Difficulties and Behavior Problems,* Windsor: Community Fund and Welfare Council of Greater Windsor, March 1961.

19. *Ibid.,* p. 7.

20. *Ibid.,* p. 17 and *passim;* 32.

21. *Ibid.,* pp. 13, 24–26, 32, 33.

22. *Ibid.,* pp. 42–44; 64. My italics.

23. Lyle W. Shannon, "The Problem of Competence to Help," *Federal Probation,* 25, March 1961, p. 32.

24. *Ibid.,* pp. 32–34.

25. *Ibid.,* p. 35.

26. Donald R. Cressey, "The Nature and Effectiveness of Correctional Techniques," *Law and Contemporary Problems,* 23, Autumn 1958, pp. 754–71.

27. Helen L. Witmer and Edith Tufts, *The Effectiveness of Delinquency Prevention Programs,* Washington: Government Printing Office, 1954, p. 47.

28. Paul W. Tappan, *Crime, Justice and Correction,* New York: McGraw-Hill Book Co., 1960, p. 394.

29. *Comparative Survey of Juvenile Delinquency,* Part I: North America, rev. ed. By United Nations, Department of Economic and Social Affairs, New York: United Nations, International Documents Service, Columbia University Press, 1958, p. 108. The data for this report was obtained by Dr. Paul W. Tappan, who also wrote the text.

30. Paul W. Tappan, Statement and Testimony in "The Effectiveness of the Juvenile Court System in the District of Columbia," *Hearings* of the Subcommittee to Investigate Juvenile Delinquency of the Committee on the Judiciary, U.S. Senate, 86th Congress, 1st Session, February 12 and 13, 1959. Washington: Government Printing Office, 1960, pp. 15–21.

31. Roscoe Pound, "Foreword" in Pauline V. Young, *Social Treatment in Probation and Delinquency,* 2d ed., New York: McGraw-Hill Book Co., 1952.

32. Dissenting opinion of Mr. Justice Musmanno, *In re Holmes,* 379 Pa. 599, 613; 109 A.2d 523, 529 (1954).

33. Matthew J. Beemsterboer, "The Juvenile Court: Benevolence in the Star Chamber," *Journal of Criminal Law, Criminology, and Police Science,* 50, 1960, p. 464.

34. Lawrence Speiser, *Hearings, op. cit.,* January 4–5, 1960, pp. 1242–49.

35. Gilbert Geis, "Publicity and Juvenile Court Proceedings," *Rocky Mountain Law Review,* 30, February 1958, pp. 25–26.

36. Some examples are: Bertram M. Beck, "Juvenile Delinquency," *Social Work Year Book,* 1955, New York: American Association of Social Workers, 1955, pp. 301–2; Herbert A. Bloch and Frank T. Flynn, "The Juvenile Court: Background, Philosophy and Structure," Chap. 12 of *Delinquency,* New York: Random House, Inc., 1956; Chief Justice Cobb of the Court of Domestic Relations of New York City, "Social and Legal Aspects of the Children's Court," quoted in *Comparative Survey of Juvenile Delinquency,* rev. ed., n. 60; Lewis Diana, "The Rights of

Juvenile Delinquents: An Appraisal of Juvenile Court Procedures," *Journal of Criminal Law, Criminology, and Police Science,* 47, No. 5, 1957, pp. 561–69, and "What is Probation," *Ibid.,* 51, No. 2, 1960, pp. 189–208; Ralph W. England, Jr., "What is Responsible for Satisfactory Probation and Postprobation Outcome?" *Ibid.,* 47, No. 6, pp. 667–76; Richard R. Korn and Lloyd W. McCorkle, "The Juvenile Offender," in *Criminology and Penology,* New York: Henry Holt & Co., Inc., 1959; Sol Rubin, *Crime and Juvenile Delinquency,* New York: Oceana Publications, Inc., rev. ed., 1961; Paul W. Tappan, *Juvenile Delinquency,* New York: McGraw-Hill Book Co., 1949, pp. 195–223 and 289–309, and *Crime, Justice, and Correction,* New York: McGraw-Hill Book Co., 1960.

Also see the chapter on the juvenile court in Robert G. Caldwell, *Criminology,* New York: Ronald Press Co., 1956, pp. 359–85.

37. Children's Bureau, Department of Health, Education and Welfare, *Juvenile Court Statistics, 1950–1952,* Washington: Government Printing Office, 1954, p. 5.

38. *Procedure and Evidence in the Juvenile Court,* Advisory Council of Judges of the National Council on Crime and Delinquency, New York: National Council on Crime and Delinquency, 1962, p. 57. This short but excellent work reflects some of the current thought regarding the dilemma of the juvenile court in retaining its social philosophy, informality, and friendly atmosphere, while at the same time avoiding the risk of a casual disregard of the rights of the child and his family, which can be preserved only by retaining protective legal safeguards.

39. Ronald J. Harpst, "Practice in Cuyahoga County Juvenile Court," *Cleveland-Marshall Law Review,* 10, September 1961, pp. 514–15. My italics.

40. *Ibid.,* p. 515.

One need not insist, Allen shows, that the hearsay rule in all its rigor be bodily transported into juvenile court proceedings:

> The essential point is that, before the child can properly be subjected to the drastic powers of the court, more than rumor and gossip is required to establish his legal eligibility for such treatment. . . . restrictions must be placed on the use of social case work reports when the issue is whether the child committed the acts charged against him. If such reports are to be employed at all for this purpose, counsel for the child should be given the names of those supplying information to the investigator and should have the right to call such persons into court for cross-examination.

Francis A. Allen, "The Borderland of the Criminal Law: Problems of 'Socializing' Criminal Justice," *Social Service Review,* 32, June 1958, p. 118.

The Advisory Council of Judges is opposed, writing that "the latter procedure is not, however, judicially approved for the adjudicative stage of the proceedings." Advisory Council of Judges, *op. cit.,* pp. 64–65.

41. Elaine J. Calumbro, "Evidence in Cuyahoga County Juvenile Court," *Cleveland-Marshall Law Review,* 10, September 1961, p. 529.

Although the Advisory Council of Judges disapproves the use of probation reports in the adjudicative phase, it does, of course, recommend their use in disposition. It seems to approve limited disclosure of such reports to the child or his parents or counsel, and of examination of the probation officer: ". . . disclosure and examination must not be carried to the point that they interfere with securing expert opinion or defeat therapeutic considerations." Advisory Council of Judges, *op. cit.,* p. 60.

The first point seems to have no validity. The second, supposed danger to therapeutic considerations, must be countered with the point that fairness to the child requires disclosure of the diagnosis or recommendations to the child's counsel or parents, if desired by the latter.

The above quotation reveals that the conception of the juvenile court as a social agency is dominant among the judges on the advisory council. Their position seems to assume that (1) expert opinion drawn upon by them is scientifically valid; (2) the judge knows what therapy or treatment is, and (3) therapy is always good and that it is effective. All three points are open to serious question.

42. Geis, *op. cit.*, p. 10. Geis's point is relevant to the decision of the appellate court in *Pollard v. United States.*

43. Paul W. Tappan, "Legal Aspects of Juvenile Delinquency," *American Law Institute Proceedings,* 20, 1955, and Eleanor A. Blackley, "Treatment Practices in Juvenile Court," *Cleveland-Marshall Law Review,* 10, September 1961, p. 533.

44. Edwin H. Sutherland, *White Collar Crime,* New York: Holt, Rinehart & Winston, 1961 edition. See also Marshall B. Clinard, *The Black Market,* New York: Rinehart & Co., 1952, and Donald J. Newman, "White Collar Crime," *Law and Contemporary Problems,* 23, Autumn 1958, pp. 735–53.

See also my "Law and Social Differentiation," unpublished Ph.D. dissertation, University of Michigan, 1949; "White Collar Offenses in the Wholesale Meat Industry in Detroit," *American Journal of Sociology,* 56, July 1950, pp. 25–35; "Common and Discrete Group Values," *Journal of Social Psychology,* 38, January 1953, pp. 3–22; "White Collar Crime: Its Significance for Theory and Practice," *Federal Probation,* 17, June 1953, pp. 31–36.

45. Paul W. Alexander, "Of Juvenile Court Justice and Judges," *1947 Yearbook of the National Probation and Parole Association,* New York, 1948, pp. 189–93. Alexander held the same position in 1960. See his "Constitutional Rights in Juvenile Court," American Bar Association *Journal,* 46, November 1960, pp. 1206–10, and "The Fable of the Fantastic Delinquents," *Federal Probation,* 24, March 1960, pp. 13–17.

46. Gustav L. Schramm, "Philosophy of the Juvenile Court," *Annals of the American Academy of Political and Social Science,* 261, January 1949, p. 107.

The same sentiment was expressed by a graduate of the Harvard Law School, who at the time was Judge of the Municipal Court of Philadelphia, vice-chairman of the Pennsylvania Council of Juvenile Court Judges, and a member of the executive committee of the National Association of Juvenile Court Judges. Judge Winnet wrote, "The offense itself is of secondary importance. It is regarded as symptomatic of the underlying personality maladjustment." Nochem S. Winnet, "Fifty Years of the Juvenile Court: An Evaluation," American Bar Association *Journal,* 36, March 1950, p. 363. It is important to realize that no juvenile-court judge specifies what he means by such terms as "underlying" and "personality maladjustment."

47. Stanley W. Johnston, "Justice or Correction? Changing Emphases in Penology," University of Western Australia *Law Review,* 5, December 1960, pp. 91–92.

48. That the concept of "social defense" constitutes a clear and present danger to the freedom of the individual is shown in the study by Shlomo Shoham, "The Prevention of Crime as Conceived by the International Congresses and Meetings

on Criminal Policy," *International Annals of Criminology*, 1962, *ler semestre*, pp. 123–38. He shows that Lombrosian psychiatrists and sociologists, and contemporary (psychoanalytic) psychiatry meet and merge in the concept of "social defense." They would substitute the psychiatrist's non-appealable judgment for the rule of law.

49. Ronald R. Price, Secretary of the Committee on Juvenile Delinquency, Department of Justice, Ottawa, "Juvenile Delinquency: A Canadian Dilemma," an address to the Biennial Fall Institute of the British Columbia Corrections Association, November 2, 1962, p. 9.

50. *The Juvenile Court in Law*, 4th ed., Ottawa: The Canadian Welfare Council, 1952, p. 2. The original edition of this booklet was written by the late William Louis Scott.

51. Price, *op. cit.*, p. 17.

52. It is unnecessary to present here either an analysis or a summary of the philosophy of the juvenile court in all of the major countries that have established it. That task has been partially performed by Tadeusz Grygier, in "The Concept of the 'State of Delinquency' and Its Consequences for Treatment of Young Offenders," a lecture sponsored by the Law School, the Department of Sociology and Anthropology, the School of Social Work, and the Delinquency Control Training Center, of Wayne State University, February 13, 1963.

Grygier shows that juvenile delinquency was abolished *by law* in Soviet Russia. The behavior that was delinquent was of course not eliminated; the concept "juvenile delinquency" was merely removed from the statute books. Eliminating the legal concept "delinquency" by means of enacting a law, while at the same time leaving the behavior of delinquents untouched may seem to some people to be double-talk. Grygier remarks that although the present year is only 1963 in the Christian era, many aspects of the 1984 style of double-talk are already with us in many countries, expressing the contemporary philosophy of juvenile-court justice. Those countries include Poland, the Federal Republic of (West) Germany, Switzerland, Denmark, Greenland, Canada, the United States of America, England, and Sweden. This is an incomplete listing. In the United States, Massachusetts was among the first of the states to shift its policy from the correction of offenders to that of treating them before they were convicted.

Detention of children who have not been found guilty of any offense, if custody would be likely to do them good, has recently been suggested in England. The Report of the Committee on Children and Youth (H. M. S. O., 1960, known as the Ingleby Report), concluded, "In practice it is becoming more and more difficult to distinguish between punishment and treatment" (par. 110). This was not new. The Curtis Committee of 1946 stated that "it is often an accident whether a child is brought before the Court for an offence or as a neglected child, and it is accordingly appropriate that the same methods of treatment should be equally available in either case" (par. 38).

53. *Annual Report, 1958–59*, Department of Social Welfare and Rehabilitation, Province of Saskatchewan, Regina, p. 22.

54. A. M. Nicholson, Minister, Department of Social Welfare and Rehabilitation, *Social Welfare in Saskatchewan*, Regina, 1960, p. 17.

55. *Annual Report, 1959–60*, Department of Social Welfare and Rehabilitation, Province of Saskatchewan, Regina, p. 22.

56. *Juvenile Delinquency: A Task Force Report,* submitted to Governor G. Mennen Williams, Lansing, Michigan, December 3, 1959.

57. *An Interpretation of Group Counselling,* Provincial Jail for Men, Corrections Branch, Department of Social Welfare and Rehabilitation, Regina, Saskatchewan, April 22, 1958, unnumbered, but p. 9. Written by F. E. A. Ewald, G. J. March, R. J. Thelander, J. Ursan, G. W. Russon.

58. *Annual Report, 1960–61,* Department of Social Welfare and Rehabilitation, Province of Saskatchewan, Regina, p. 22.

59. *Ibid.,* p. 25. My italics.

60. Juanita L. Hall, "The Use of State Mental Hospitals as a Placement Resource for Nonpsychotic Delinquent Adolescents," unpublished Master's thesis, Wayne State University, 1959, p. 1.

61. Frederic Wertham, *The Circle of Guilt,* New York: Rinehart & Co., Inc., 1956, pp. 133–34.

62. Allen, *op. cit.,* p. 232.

63. Ralph J. Riley, "Who Is a Juvenile Delinquent?" *Federal Probation,* 22, June 1958, p. 20. Mr. Riley is Chief Administrative Officer, Family Court of Cook County, Chicago.

64. *An Experiment in the Validation of the Glueck Prediction Scale: Progress Report* from November 1952 to December 1956. New York City Youth Board, Research Department, July 1957, p. 23.

65. *Ibid.,* Table XI.

66. Elizabeth Herzog, *Identifying Potential Delinquents,* United States Children's Bureau, Washington: U. S. Government Printing Office, 1960, p. 2.

67. New York City Youth Board, *op. cit.,* Tables V and VIII.

68. The figures have been computed from Jackson Toby, "Early Identification and Intensive Treatment of Predelinquents: A Negative View," *Social Work,* 6, July 1961, Tables 4 and 5. Toby's figures are unfortunately not strictly comparable to those in New York City Youth Board, *op. cit.,* although he did obtain them from the Board.

69. Toby, *op. cit.,* p. 13.

70. Herzog, *op. cit.,* pp. 3–4.

It should be added that the Gluecks disagree with the viewpoint expressed by Dr. Herzog:

The fears expressed in some quarters that the use of our Social Prediction Table would unjustly "stigmatize" innocent children as delinquents are, in our opinion, unfounded. . . . The prediction device is not some gadget to be applied by anybody untrained in the assessment of child-parent relationships. It is an instrument to be used only by those who have had sufficient training in its employment.

Sheldon and Eleanor Glueck, "Potential Delinquents can be Identified: What Next?" *British Journal of Criminology,* 4, January 1964, pp. 224–25.

Since writing the above comments I have had a chance to read *Delinquency Prediction: 1952–1960, A Progress Report,* issued by the New York City Youth Board, October 1961. This prediction is methodologically and conceptually no better than the ones discussed above, and may be worse, because 76 white non-Jewish boys have been added to the sample, and the prediction scale has been changed from 5-factor to a 2-factor device. Although its title is *Delinquency Prediction*, the report repeatedly insists that the Youth Board has an instrument "which is the most sensitive for the early detection of *potential* delinquents" (p. 14; my italics). In addition, *nine years after its first prediction* of potential delinquents, the Youth Board reworked its data and reduced the 1952-predicted potential delinquents to 37 in number (p. 14)! But on p. 20 the number given is 36.

The report then states: "We find that of the 36 boys predicted delinquent, 19 are already persistent delinquents, and 2 additional boys are exhibiting serious predelinquent behavior" (p. 20). Several comments must be made concerning that statement. First, the Youth Board seemed seriously disturbed by its gross over-prediction as indicated by Herzog and Toby, and others not named here. Second, the statement made in October 1961, that 36 boys were predicted delinquent is misleading because it states that the number of 36 is in actuality a *prediction*. It is in fact nothing more than a post-diction, made possible by questionable statistical manipulation. Third, the statement that "19 are already persistent delinquents" is for several reasons misleading and less than candid: (a) the 19 include both "unofficial" and "official" delinquents, with the former said to have engaged in "delinquent-like behavior," which is undefined; (b) the latter also includes boys who have engaged in "delinquent-like behavior" and *who have not been adjudicated delinquent;* (c) both categories include boys whom the Youth Board would classify as "schizoid" or "psychotic." Fourth, the Youth Board means by the term "predicted delinquent" nothing more than that it has "predicted potential delinquency."

Let it be granted for the sake of argument that after nine years of study the Youth Board did predict delinquency for 36 boys in its sample, and that 19 of them were in fact delinquent. It was still overpredicting by about 100 per cent.

71. Joseph Berkson, " 'Cost Utility' As a Measure of the Efficiency of a Test," *Journal of the American Statistical Association,* 42, June 1947, pp. 246–55.

72. Otis Dudley Duncan, "Review of *Predicting Delinquency and Crime,*" *American Journal of Sociology,* 65, March 1960, p. 538.

73. Harwin L. Voss, "The Predictive Efficiency of the Glueck Social Prediction Table," *Journal of Criminal Law, Criminology, and Police Science,* 54, December 1963, pp. 421–30, at p. 430. Voss discusses both the 2-factor and 3-factor tables in the Youth Board's *Delinquency Prediction, 1952–1960, A Progress Report,* whereas I referred only to the 2-factor device in footnote 70, above.

74. Charles S. Prigmore, "An Analysis of Rater Reliability on the Glueck Scale for the Prediction of Delinquency," unpublished Ph.D. dissertation, Department of Sociology, University of Wisconsin, 1961. Also see Charles S. Prigmore, "An Analysis of Rater Reliability on the Glueck Scale for the Prediction of Juvenile Delinquency," *Journal of Criminal Law, Criminology, and Police Science,* 54, March 1963, pp. 30–41.

75. The above research is summarized in Project No. 693, "An Analysis of Rater Reliability on the Glueck Scale for the Prediction of Juvenile Delinquency"; Personnel: Charles S. Prigmore, Michael Hakeem, in *Current Projects in the Prevention, Control, and Treatment of Crime and Delinquency,* Winter, 1962–63; New York: National Council on Crime and Delinquency, 1963, pp. 246–47.

76. Manuel Lopez-Rey, "Some Misconceptions in Modern Criminology," in Gerhard O. W. Mueller, ed., *Essays in Criminal Science*, South Hackensack, N. J.: Fred B. Rothman & Co., 1961, p. 22.

Lopez-Rey's conclusion is similar to an earlier one arrived at by Vold. The latter analyzed the theories and data concerning the alleged physical types of criminals, theories of feeblemindedness and psychopathy, and theories that causally related personality to criminality. Vold found that "in all of these comparisons there is a great sharing of common personality characteristics with notions of 'deviant personality' limited strictly to relatively obscure statistical findings in terms of probability; otherwise, delinquents and nondelinquents are much more alike than different." George B. Vold, *Theoretical Criminology*, New York: Oxford University Press, 1958, p. 130.

77. Toby, *op. cit.*, p. 13.

78. *Annual Report, 1959–60*, Department of Social Welfare and Rehabilitation, Province of Saskatchewan, Regina, p. 22.

79. Eleanor Touroff Glueck, "Efforts to Identify Delinquents," *Federal Probation*, 24, June 1960, p. 56. My italics.

The Gluecks' Social Prediction Tables have been the subject of considerable discussion, from which acrimony has not been absent. For a bibliography of many of the adverse and laudatory evaluations, see Sheldon Glueck, "Ten Years of *Unraveling Juvenile Delinquency*: An Examination of Criticisms," *Journal of Criminal Law, Criminology, and Police Science*, 51, September 1960, nn. 61–82; Frank E. Hartung, "A Critique of the Sociological Approach to Crime and Correction," *Law and Contemporary Problems*, 23, Autumn 1958, nn. 2–21; and Voss, *op. cit.*

80. Allen, *op. cit.*, p. 230.

81. 260 N. Y. 171, 183 N. E. 353 (1932).

82. *People v. James*, 9 N. Y. 2d 82, 211 N. Y. S. 2d 170, 172 N. E. 2d 552 (1961).

83. *People v. Lewis*, 183 N. E., 354.

84. *Ibid.*, p. 356.

85. New York Family Court Act, pars. 241, 243, 249.

86. Nanette Dembitz, "Ferment and Experimentation in New York: Juvenile Cases in the New Family Court," *Cornell Law Quarterly*, 48, Spring 1963, p. 509.

87. *Report* of the Governor's (California) Special Study Commission on Juvenile Justice, Part I, November 1960, p. 27. Quoted in *Procedure and Evidence in the Juvenile Court*, Advisory Council of Judges, *op. cit.*, p. 44.

As Paulsen has said, "A judge's performance (and that of his staff) will be much more alert and careful under the gaze of a lawyer than otherwise." Monrad G. Paulsen, "Fairness to the Juvenile Offender," *Minnesota Law Review*, 41, 1957, p. 571.

88. *Gideon v. Wainwright*, 83 S. Ct. 792 (1963), at 797.

89. New York *Times*, March 1, 1964. The news account also stated: "A recent study showed that, in the 75 largest American cities, including New York, Chicago and Los Angeles, lawyers were involved in only 5 per cent of such actions." That seems to be a high percentage. Most of the lawyers, I think, come into juvenile court only when the county prosecutor has petitioned the juvenile court to waive its jurisdiction of the young person to the adult criminal court, because

a felony has been committed. The parents or guardian may secure counsel to argue against such petitions, only a minority of which are granted.

90. New York Family Court Act, par. 741.

91. George W. Smyth, "New Family Court Act of the State of New York," *Crime and Delinquency*, 8, October 1962, pp. 412–13.

92. *The Reader's Digest*, April 1964, p. 126.

93. Solomon Kobrin, "The Chicago Area Project: A 25–Year Assessment," *Annals of the American Academy of Political and Social Science*, 322, March 1959, pp. 19–29. See also Anthony Sorrentino, "The Chicago Area Project after 25 Years," *Federal Probation*, 23, June 1959, pp. 40–45.

94. Walter B. Miller, "The Impact of a 'Total Community' Delinquency Control Project," *Social Problems*, 10, Fall 1962, p. 187. Miller will explicate the components accounting for the limited impact of the project's efforts in a forthcoming book, *City Gangs*. The explanatory analysis will develop the thesis that culturally derived incentives for engaging in violative behavior were far stronger than any counter incentives the project brought to bear. That explanation is derived from a general theory of gang delinquency whose leading principle is that patterned involvement in violative behavior by gangs of the Midcity type occurs when four cultural components are concurrently present: maleness, adolescence, urban residence, and low-skill laboring class status. Miller, "The Impact of a 'Total Community' Delinquency Control Project," *op. cit.*, pp. 191–92.

95. Martin Luther King, Jr., "Why We Can't Wait," *Life*, May 15, 1964, p. 100. This article is an excerpt from *Why We Can't Wait*, New York: Harper & Row, 1964.

96. Hyman Frankel and Sanford Kravitz, "Federal Program for Delinquency and Control," in National Council on Crime and Delinquency, *Current Projects in the Prevention, Control, and Treatment of Crime and Delinquency*, 2, Winter 1962–63, p. 14.

97. Kenneth Polk, in *Hearings* of the Subcommittee on Employment and Manpower of the Committee on Labor and Public Welfare, United States Senate, Eighty-eighth Congress, First Session, August 13, 1963, p. 158.

Index

Abell, Helen C., 277
Abrahams, Joseph, 274
Abrahamsen, David, 186, 220–22, 225–26, 293, 302
Abramson, Edward J., 274
Action theory, 168–73
Adjudication, of delinquency, 234–35; hearing, gossip and hearsay, 251–52
Adolescent subculture, in Japan, 280n; hypothesis of rebellious, rejected, 111–14
Advisory Council of Judges, 236, 254, 304–5n, 309n
Alexander, Franz, 164, 186, 214, 290, 294, 300–1
Alexander, Paul W., 238, 305
Allen, Francis A., 220, 250, 301, 304, 307, 309
Angle, Paul M., 289
Anomie and alienation, as reciprocal rejection, 105–8
Antiscientific position, and irresistible impulse, 197–98
Appel, Kenneth E., 292
Arendt, Hannah, 152, 286
Arens, Richard, 297
Aristotle, 39; intellect derogated by, 170–71
Artis, Jay W., 278
Asbury, Herbert, 267
Ashley-Montagu, M. F., 269

Baker, Inspector, 271
Baker, Wendell D., 268
Banay, Ralph S., 271
Bandura, Albert, 271

Barron, Milton L., 20, 265
Barry, Justice John V., 239
Bartemeier, Leo H., 292
Barth, Alan, 222, 224, 302
Bazelon, David, 209, 297
Beach, E. F., 278
Beaser, Mr., 50
Beck, Bertram M., 303
Beegle, J. Allen, 117, 281
Beemsterboer, Matthew J., 303
Behavior, "wrong," and psychiatric treatment, 212
Behavioral problems, 176
Bellis, E., 292
Bender, Lauretta, 48–51, 76, 271
Bendix, Reinhard, 269
Benedict, Ruth, 298
Bensing, Robert C., 285–86
Berkson, Joseph, 247, 308
Berry, Brewton, 285
Bettelheim, Bruno, 79–80, 275
Bill of Rights for Disadvantaged, 259–61
Bixby, F. Lovell, 274
Black, Hillel, 125, 128, 281
Blackley, Eleanor A., 305
Bloch, Herbert A., 303
Blumer, Herbert, 265
Bogue, Donald J., 281
Bohannon, Paul, 283
Bordua, David J., 62
Boston Delinquency Project, 259
Bowman, Paul H., 279
Brain, Russell, 184, 293
Brashears, Benjamin S. Jr., 279, 281
Brill, A. A., 300
Bromberg, Walter, 187, 294
Bronfenbrenner, Urie, 279

Bronner, Augusta F., 273
Broom, Leonard, 272
Brunner, Edmund de Schweinitz, 278
Bullock, Henry Allen, 285
Burgess, Ernest W., 280
Burke, Kenneth, 64, 273, 289
Burton, Mrs., 127

Cadwallader, Mervyn L., 276
Caldwell, Robert G., 12, 304
Calumbro, Elaine J., 304
Campbell, Robert J., 290, 300
Capen, Nahum, 194
Cartwright, Dorwin, 165, 290
Celler, Emanuel, 273
Charcot, Jean Martin, 175
Chicago Area Project, 258
Children, delinquent and lawful, 249;
   delinquent, dependent, and neglected,
   235–36, 241–43; imprisonment, 256
Chinoy, Ely, 268
City streets, 26, 266–67n
Clark, John P., 84, 275, 278
Clark, S. D., 266, 269, 278
Clausen, John A., 292
Clergy, 182–84
Clinard, Marshall B., 20, 93, 100, 119,
   265, 275, 278, 280–81, 305
Cloward, Richard A., 55, 272
Cobb, Chief Justice, 303
Code, conventional, 60–61
Cognition, 154–55
Cohen, Albert K., 56–57, 93, 111, 115,
   265, 268–70, 272–73, 295
Coleman, James S., 112–13, 280
College boys, 35
Combe, George, 194–96, 295
Commonwealth v. Mosler, 197
Competence to help, problem of, 229–30
Competition, as social process, 54–55
Compulsive actions, absent in crime,
   161; harmless and individual, 160–61;
   diagnosis of, 161–63
Compulsive crime, normal conduct,
   133–66
Compulsive criminal, 137–66; Chris-
   tian witch, 155–56; corporeal exist-
   ence of, 155–56, 160; postulate in
   psychiatry, 155
Conduct, in psychiatry, 214–15; groups
   and personal relationships, 165–66,

258; repetition of, 157; results from
   decisions, 209; scientific explanations
   of, 69–72; as self-diagnostic, 192–93,
   197, 211–12
Conformists, as psychopaths, 298n
Conformity, in social service, 229; study
   of, maximized, 54–55
Conscience, possessed by every child, 71
Consensual validation, absence of, 127,
   133, 158, 209
Cooley, Charles Horton, 17, 44, 265,
   270, 289, 301
Cooney, John Russell, 128
Corner boys, 34; classification of, 35
Cottrell, Leonard S. Jr., 272
Cressey, Donald R., 13, 15, 37, 128–29,
   131–32, 134, 138, 163, 230, 265, 272,
   274–75, 281–83, 285, 290, 293, 303
Crime, biological explanation of, 38–46,
   143; deliberate, 18–19; genesis of, as
   emotion, 199–201; as mental illness,
   181–217; irrational and rational, 56–
   58, 163–64; normal sociocultural phenomenon, 17; and psychiatry, 213;
   racial differences, 143; rural, 278n;
   and social class and social organization, 143–47; as social disorganization, 19–25; and sociocultural learning and
   symbolism, 37–53; distribution of
   rates, 287–88n; and unconscious motivation, 198–201; and sociocultural
   conditions, 143
Criminal, as adaptive and conservative,
   46–47; contemporary handling of, 26;
   "compulsive," as social role, 156–58;
   new, enemy of human race, 152–53;
   as sick, 185–90
Criminal conduct, 36
Criminal-sequence patterns, 268n
Criminal violation of financial trust,
   129–34
Criminality, not innate, 38–46; role of
   group in learning, 47–52
Criminally insane, 211
Cronkite, Dean F. C., 9–10
Crowell, Chester T., 289
Cuelenaere, J. M., 10
Culpin, Millais, 292
Cutter, Henry S. G., 273, 286

Davey, Francis, 271

Davidson, Henry A., 198, 290, 295

Davis, Kingsley, 167–70, 173, 290–92

Delinquency, as positive achievement, 20, 30, 36, 55–84; aleatory component of, 147–48; attempt to predict, 244–50, 309n; rural and urban in lower class, 102; legal redefinition, 241–43, 306; and failure in school, 30–33; as game and career, 65; as irrational conduct, 56–58, 110; irresponsible use of term, 227–28; as conduct, 57–58; mechanistic explanation of, 65–72; nonfinancial, 57–58; as normal sociocultural phenomenon, 17; overprediction of, 246–48, 307–9n; proof of, unnecessary for adjudication of, 253; psychiatric and sociological conceptions, 62–64, 110; not romanticized, 279n; as social institution, 26; sociocultural setting of, 102–8; "two-strikes" theory of, 28–29, 66; rural, hinterland, and urban: as recreation, 57, 110, 121–23; essentially same, 93–99, 123; quantitative differences between, 123

Delinquent, 133–36; conventional values, 61; hedonist, 108–18; innocent victim, 67; passive subject, 65–72; selection of victims, 60

Delinquent subculture, 55–62; rural and hinterland, 110–18

Delinquents, state mental hospitals, 243–44

Delusions, 162–63

Dembitz, Nanette, 254, 309

Dentler, Robert A., 279

Determinism, psychic, 203

Detroit schools, General Continuation Training Program, 61–62; Job Upgrading Program, 62; retarded pupils, 30–31; "social promotion," 268

Devereux, Edward C. Jr., 279

Dewey, John, 157, 282

Diana, Lewis, 303

Differential association, theory of, 15; and "atypical" offender, 125–66; as integrative, 16; and self-conception, 85–88; criticisms of, 129; "compulsive," forcible sexual, and white-collar criminals, 125–36, 133–66, 159–60

Dillan, Chief Justice, 206

Dillinger, John, 38

Dinitz, Simon, 84–85, 87, 276

Dipsomania, 295n

Disjunctive theory of self, 191–217 *passim;* in federal court decisions, 208

Douglas, William O., 223, 302

Driver, Edwin D., 283

Dryden, John, 184

Dubin, Robert, 272

Due process, in juvenile court, 252

Dumas, Alexandre, 132

Duncan, Glen M., 284

Duncan, Otis Dudley, 247, 278, 308

Durham v. United States, 210–11, 296–97n

DuWors, Richard E., 10

Eames, E., 154, 287

East, Sir Norwood, 199–200, 297

Eastman, Harold Dwight, 93–94, 96, 98, 100, 102–5, 108–10, 114–15, 117, 119, 273, 277–81

Eckenrode, C. J., 269

Edwards, George, 225–26, 302

Efficiency, class basis of, 189; of means, and reason, 169

Eichmann, Adolf, 139, 152

Eisenhower, Dwight D., 26

Elias, Albert, 274

Elkin, Frederick, 113–14, 280

Elliott, Mabel A., 22, 266

Elmtown's Youth, 95–117 *passim*

Emerson, Ralph W., 285

Empey, LaMar T., 116–17, 274, 281

Ends and means, subject to reason, 172–73

England, Ralph W. Jr., 12, 94, 272, 277, 285–86, 304

Esselstyn, Thomas C., 94, 277

Evil conduct, equated with mental illness, 178

Ewald, F. E. A., 307

Ewalt, Jack R., 175, 292

Exculpation, and compulsion, irresistible impulse, and temporary insanity, 159; and irresponsibility, extended to recidivists, 198–99

Experts, confusion of, 173–79

Eynon, Thomas G., 276

Faculties, independently functioning, 193–95; in modern psychiatry, 196

Family, and delinquency, 47–48; Freudian drama of, 182–84
Featherstone, W. B., 31, 267
Feld, Sheila, 292
Ferenczi, Sandor, 300–1
Ferns, H. S., 99, 278
Ferracuti, Franco, 283, 285–86
Ferrero, Gina L., 269
Fine, Benjamin, 273
Finestone, Harold, 274
Fink, Arthur E., 294
Flynn, Frank T., 303
Foote, Caleb, 223, 302
Foote, Nelson N., 273
Fordham, Michael, 292
Frank, Lawrence K., 20, 265
Frankel, Charles, 300
Frankel, Hyman, 310
Frazier, E. Franklin, 91, 276
Freud, Sigmund, 39, 171, 175, 182–84, 213–14, 290, 293, 298, 300
Frum, Harold S., 268
Frustration, 16; crime and delinquency, 25–36, 53–62; upper-class interpretation of, 33–35
Fryklund, Richard, 287

Gall, F. J., 194
Galton, Francis, 40
Ganey, J. Cullen, 64
Gang delinquency, 103–4
Gangs, 272n
Garfield, James A., 295
Garry, Ralph J., 271
Gasch, Oliver, 297
Gawel, M. L., 293
Geel Officer Kruppke!, 79
Geertz, Hildred, 273
Geis, Gilbert, 235, 237, 274, 303, 305
Germans, and dirty work, 287n
Gibney, Frank, 81, 275
Gideon v. Wainwright, 255, 309n
Giffen, P. J., 277–78
Ginsberg, Morris, 170, 172, 291
Glaser, Daniel, 18, 265
Glass, D. V., 268
Glasser, William, 69–71, 274
Glover, Edward, 208, 298–99
Glueck, Eleanor T., 42, 165, 245, 247–50, 290, 309

Glueck, Sheldon, 42, 200, 209, 245, 247–50, 270, 297–98, 309
Glueck, Sheldon and Eleanor T., 42, 245, 247–48, 250, 307
Glueck Social Prediction Table, 245–50, 307–8
Goddard, Henry H., 44, 46, 270
"Good Boy," 85–88
Goring, Charles, 40–44, 46, 143, 269–70, 285
Graham, J. A., 277
Gray, John P., 198
Greeth, Hildred, 286
Grodzins, Morton, 285
Group, role in learning criminality, 47–52
Growing Up in River City, 102–21 passim
Grünhut, Max, 215, 301
Grygier, Tadeusz, 306
Guest, Robert H., 268
Guillotin, Dr., 176
Guilt, of "compulsive" criminal, 157; delinquent, 58–60; embezzler, 136
Guiteau, Charles J., 196, 198; trial of, 295n
Gurin, Gerald, 292
Gursslin, Orville R., 291
Guttmacher, Manfred S., 141–42, 198, 200, 209–12, 216, 282, 294–97, 299–301

Habit, distinguished from compulsion, 157
Hazing, 73–75
Hakeem, Michael, 12, 140, 248, 282, 301, 308
Hall, Jerome, 129, 161, 190, 199–200, 213–16, 273, 290, 294, 297, 300–1
Hall, Juanita L., 307
Harding, John, 279
Harlow, Harry F., 18
Harpst, Ronald J., 304
Harrington, G. L., 69–70, 274
Hartmann, Heinz, 178, 292
Hartung, Frank E., 265, 277, 281–82, 289, 292, 309
Havighurst, Robert J., 279
Healy, William, 41–42, 214, 269, 273, 300

Held, Virginia P., 66, 267, 273, 275
Helling, Rudolf A., 10, 277
Henderson, George, 12
Henry, Andrew F., 283
Herzog, Elizabeth, 246–47, 307–8
Highfields, New Jersey, 274n
Hilgard, Ernest R., 18, 190, 290, 294
Hill, Mozell C., 285
Himelhoch, Jerome, 94, 100, 109, 117, 121, 278–81
Himmelweit, H. T., 268
Hinsie, Leland E., 290, 300
Hinterland area, defined, 277–78n
Hollingshead, August B., 94, 104, 106, 113, 117, 185, 268, 277, 279–80, 292–93
Homicide, 149–50; "higher morality," 288–89n
Homicide, criminal, degrees of, 142; rates, 142; in Dallas, Texas, 289n; motives for, 283n; premeditated, author's hypothesis of, 283n; psychiatric literature on, 283–85n; author's hypothesis of, 140–51 *passim;* as socioculturally normal, 140–54
Homosexuality and role-playing, 165–66
Hook, Sidney, 300
Hooton, Ernest A., 41–42, 269
Hoover, Herbert, 26
Hoover, J. Edgar, 24–25, 266
Hughes, Everett C., 287
Hull, Clark L., 18
Hume, David, 196, 295
Hunt, Chester L., 285
Hunt, Raymond G., 291
Huxley, Aldous, 220, 302
Hyman, Herbert H., 269

Identification, differential, 18, 156–57
Impulse, controlled and uncontrollable, 163
Incredible Electrical Conspiracy, 64–65
Individual responsibility, and psychiatry, 176, 190
Individual rights and rehabilitative ideal, 219–63
Innovation, misleading use of term, 54
Insanity, possible, with reason unaffected, 193; scarcity of, 141; verdict, 295–97n
Instinctivist doctrine, 172

Integrative theory, 191–217, 219, 298n
Intellect, during insanity, 192, 196, 200–11 *passim*
Intelligence tests, 43–45
Interaction, symbolic, 15
Intervention, crime or delinquency, 242, 250; mass psychiatric proposed, 221–26; reasons for, 226, 245
Iowa State Reformatory, 68–69
Irrationalism, 167–73
Irresistible impulse, absence of evidence of, 207–8; American Law Institute, 299n; recurrence, 204–5; issue of, 216–17; methodological problem, 162, 192, 197; concept of, 97, 190–201; disjunctive theory of self, 191; legal issue of, 161; medico-legal theory of, 161–63; and observer's repugnance, 77; Canadian psychiatrists, 163
Itschkies, 60

Jackson, Perry B., 146, 286
Jahoda, Marie, 175, 292
James, Robert L., 10
Jameson, Samuel Haig, 281
Jandy, Edward C., 217, 301
Janet, Pierre, 290
Jaspan, Norman, 125–28, 281
Jayewardene, Cleobis, 283
Johnson County, Iowa, juvenile court, 67–68
Johnson, Ronald, 276
Johnston, Stanley W., 239, 305
Jones, Ernest, 180, 204
Junior Outlaws, a juvenile gang, 60–61
Justice, socialized, 238, 243
Juvenile court, procedural safeguards in, 230–39; in Australia, 239; in Canada, 230, 239–41; cross-examination of informants, 304n; dilemma of, 304n; as child-guidance agency, 230–44 *passim;* child's counsel, 305n; guilt of child irrelevant in, 305n; and other agencies, 219–44; public hearings in, 235–36, 256–57
Juvenile Court Summer Institute, 12, 276n
Juvenile delinquency, legal definition, 306n

Kahl, Joseph A., 268

Kahn, Edmond N., 289
Kahn, Herman, 153, 286
Karpman, Benjamin, 187–88, 294
Kay, Barbara, 276
Kennedy, John F., 302
Khrushchev, Nikita, 287
King, Martin Luther Jr., 259–61, 310
Klapper, Joseph T., 271
Klein, Melanie, 293
Kleptomania, as larceny, 295n; social class basis of diagnosis, 127, 162–64; social role, 157–59
Kobrin, Solomon, 93, 258–59, 287, 310
Kolb, William L., 219, 230, 301
Komarovsky, Mirra, 21, 265
Korn, Richard R., 77, 274–75, 304
Kotinsky, Ruth, 266
Kravitz, Sanford, 310
Kretschmer, Ernest, 42
Kroeber, A. L., 44–45
Kvaraceus, William C., 29–30, 266–67, 272

Lacassagne, J. A. E., 269
LaFave, Wayne R., 302
Laforgue, R., 300
Lander, Bernard, 22–23, 266, 272
Lane County (Oregon) Youth Study Project, 93–123 *passim*, 258
Lang, O. E., 10
Lange, Friedrich A., 195, 295
Langner, Thomas S., 292
Language, private use of, by embezzler, 129–36; compulsive criminal, 155–59; isolated prisoner, 282n
Lantz, Herman R., 278
La Piere, Richard T., 298
Larceny, not female problem, 164–65
Laskin, Richard, 12, 277
Law, and psychiatrists, 181–90; dispute between, in 19th century, 199; and psychology, 216
Law enforcement, equality of, 302n; and irresistible impulse, 201–17; U.S. constitutional value, 224
Learning, capacity for unmeasurable, 270n; symbolic, 16; in crime, 11, 13–14, 53–92
Leibowitz, Samuel S., 23, 28–29, 66, 143, 266
Leighton, Alexander H., 290, 292

Lejins, Peter P., 271
Levin, Theodore, 202–5, 298
Lief, Alfred, 198, 295
Lindesmith, Alfred R., 265, 269–70, 295
Lipset, Seymour M., 269, 280
Llewellyn, Karl, 19, 265
Locke, John, 172
Lombrosian psychiatry, 269n
Lombroso, Cesare, 38–43, 270
Loomis, Charles P., 117, 281
Lopez-Rey, Manuel, 249, 309
Louttit, C. M., 267
Lower class, and middle-class values, 59
Loyalty, appeal to higher, 81–82, 127
Lynch v. Overholser, 296–97n
Lynd, Robert S. and Helen M., 279

McAllister, Thomas, 201–2, 205–6
McCall, Bevode C., 285
McCleery, Richard H., 275, 282
McCorkle, Lloyd W., 77, 274–75, 304
McDougall, William, 171–72
McKay, Henry D., 55, 57, 93, 110, 272–73, 275, 287
McNaghten Rules, 209n; criticized for intellectualism, 199–200, 212; psychotic defendant not responsible under, 198; irresistible impulse as substitute, 192; slippery slope, 138
McNamara, Daniel J., 255
McRuer, James Chalmers, 163
Madmen, no lesion of understanding, 212
Man, as irrational, 54, and rational, 173; Judeo-Christian and psychiatric philosophy of, mutually exclusive, 181–84
Mann, W. E., 265, 269
Mannheim, Hermann, 295
March, G. J., 307
Martin, W. M., 9
Marzolf, Stanley S., 292
Mass media in crime and delinquency, 48–52
Matthews, Charles V., 279, 281
Matza, David, 60, 62, 65, 75, 77, 81, 273
Maudsley, Henry, 189, 199, 212, 294, 297, 300
Mays, John B., 275
Mead, George H., 289
Medawar, P. B., 270
Menninger, Karl A., 177, 188, 206, 212–13, 284, 292, 294, 300

Mental disease, behavior socioculturally, 292–93n; without definition, 299n; moral values, 177–79; proposal to abandon concept, 175; without impairment of intellect, 162

Mental health, and happiness, 168; Sunday school sermon, 177–78; social movement, 167–79

Mental illness, defined, 179; everyone has, 188; in mental functioning, 189–90; moralistic accusation, 174–75; myth of, 175–76; undefined, 174–75

Mental normality, as madness, 208

Mentally ill, psychiatrists and treatment, 213

Merrill, Maud A., 270

Merton, Robert K., 54–55, 266, 269, 272–73, 285

Metaphor, 284n; in psychiatry, 159, 210, 284n

Meyer, Agnes E., 266

Michael, Stanley T., 292

Miller, Walter B., 60–61, 93, 110, 144–45, 148, 150, 259, 267–68, 273, 285–86, 310

Mills, C. Wright, 266, 273

Milne, A. A., 290

Mitigation, 208

Mobile Mental Hygiene Clinics, 221, 226

Model Penal Code, 209–10

Monroe, Lawrence J., 279

Montana Juvenile Court Act, 256–57

Moral conduct and mental health, 178

Moral (partial) insanity, defined, 195–96; irresistible impulse, 197–201; as wickedness, 295n

Moral situations, knowing and understanding, 208–9

Moral values, disguised, 28

Morris, Albert, 283

Mort, P. R., 31, 267

Motive, 63–65, 82, 131–32, 154, 159–60, 165, 258

Motives, vocabulary of, 19, 37; appeal to higher loyalty, 81–82, 127–28; attributed to others, 56–58, 145–47, 202 ff.; to self, 202–3; criminal and embezzler, 136; condemnation of condemners, 77–81; denial of injury, 72–75; denial of responsibility, 65–72, 128; denial of victim, 75–77; in embezzlement, 127–

33; beyond delinquency, 83–84; learning criminal, 58 ff.; of numbers racketeer, 89–90; of prisoners, 84; self-conception, 53–55; supplied by legal authorities, 62–84; in white-collar crime, 125–36

Mueller, Gerhard O. W., 309

Mullahy, Patrick, 293

Murder, supposed motiveless, 192–93

Murderer, mental normality of, 152–53

Murray, Ellen, 276

Musmanno, Justice, 231, 303

Naegele, Kaspar D., 291

Napoleon, 179

Narcotics addiction, 55

Negroes, civil rights of, 76–77

Neumeyer, Martin H., 270

Newman, Donald J., 305

New York City Youth Board, 245–50, 307–8n

New York Family Court Act, of 1962, 251–57, 310

Nice, Richard W., 295

Nicholson, A. M., 306

Nisbet, Robert A., 272–73, 285

Normal conduct, 215

Normality, 298n

Numbers racketeer, 88–92

Nuremberg Trials, 152–53

Nye, F. Ivan, 279

Ohlin, Lloyd E., 55, 272

Operators and Corruptibles, 81

Opler, Marvin K., 292

Orexis, and cognition, 170

Ostrow, Mortimer, 298

Overholser, Winfred, 295

Parsons, Talcott, 112, 272, 280, 291

Pasamanick, Benjamin, 295

Passions, 196

Pathology, 192

Paulsen, Monrad G., 309

Pearson, Karl, 40

Perlman, I. Richard, 267

Perry, H. S., 293

Phrenology, in law, 207; in modern psychiatry, 193–96, 207, 295n

Physicians and surgeons, 298–99n

Pierce, J. V., 279

Pinel, Philippe, 176, 212
Pitts, Jesse R., 291
Plant, James S., 67
Plato, 12, 39
Podolsky, Edward, 301
Police, brutality, 225–26; illegal arrest practices, 222–26; and prosecutor, disagreements between, 302n
Polk, Kenneth, 12, 94, 100, 105, 116–17, 122, 262, 277–79, 281, 310
Pollard v. United States, 201–8, 297–98n
Pound, Roscoe, 231, 303
Powell, Harold F., 32, 267
Predelinquent, concept of, 245–50
President's Committee on Juvenile Delinquency and Youth Crime, 261–62
Price, Ronald R., 240, 306
Prigmore, Charles S., 248–49, 308
Procedural rights, in 1962 N.Y. Family Court Act, 251 ff.; in criminal court, 255; in juvenile court, 253–54
Proscription list, 221, 227–28
Prosser, R. R., 163
Provo (Utah) Experiment, 116–121 *passim;* 274n
Psychiatric diagnosis, class basis of, 175, 185, 211; conflicts in, 151–52; disorganized state of modern, 210–11
Psychiatrist, visions of, 38–39; responsibility for releasing, 213; as expert on mass media, 48–51
Psychiatry, and born criminal, 38–45; problems in living, 176; conflict within, 211; women as inferior in, 39–40
Psychoanalysis and social psychology, 217
Psychology, faculty, 170; contemporary, man as irrational in, 167; feeblemindedness and crime, 40–45
Psychosis, 179
Punishment, desire for, 203–6
Punitive decisions, 221–22
Pyromania, as arson, 295n

Rabow, Jerome, 274, 281
Rational person, 200
Rationality, 174
Rationalization, 62–84
Ray, Isaac, 162–64, 193–94, 196, 211, 290, 294–95

Rayfield, Joan R., 279, 281
"Reality principle," 213–15
Reality therapy, 69–72
Reason, attack on, 167, 189; derogated, 170–72, 193–201; and responsibility, 167–79; slave of passions, 196; unimpaired during insanity, 196, 200–1, 295n
Reciprocal rejection, social process of, 77–81, 106–8
Reckless, Walter C., 84–85, 87, 268, 276
Redl, Fritz, 71, 83, 275
Redlich, Fredrick C., 163, 177, 185, 290, 292–93
Rehabilitative ideal, 220
Reid, Ira DeA., 154, 287
Reik, Theodore, 183, 293
Reiss, Albert J. Jr., 165–66, 290
Reissman, Leonard, 269
Religion, evolution of as rational process, 173; and mental health, 168
Rennie, Thomas A. C., 177, 292
Responsibility, denial of, 127, 135, 220
Right, to counsel and in juvenile court, 253–56
Right from wrong, delinquent knows, 71; test, rejected by psychiatrists, 213
Riley, Ralph J., 245, 307
Rinehart, D. R., 94
Rittwagen, Marjorie, 267
Roach, Jack L., 291
Robin, Christopher, 161
Robin, Gerald D., 149, 286
Robison, Sophia M., 272
Roche, Philip Q., 188–89, 211–13, 294, 299–300
Roebuck, Julian B., 88–92, 276
Rogers, Kenneth H., 273
Role-playing, and compulsive crime, 155–60
Role-taking, deficiency in, 77, 139–40, 151, 160
Roosevelt, Franklin D., 26
Roszak, Theodore, 298
Roucek, Joseph S., 268
Rubin, Sol, 304
Rural and hinterland delinquency, 93–125
Russon, G. W., 307
Ryan, Bryce, 283

Saskatchewan, Province of, 241–43, 249–50

Savitz, Leonard D., 153, 287

Scarpitti, Frank R., 87–88, 276

Schilder, Paul, 300

Schmideberg, Melitta, 66, 78

Schmitt, C. H., 10

Schramm, Gustav L., 238, 305

Schreiber, Daniel, 267

Schroeder, Olive, 285–86

Schuessler, Karl F., 265, 269–70, 295

Scientific principles, 161–62, 168–69, 177–79

Scott, William L., 306

Seeley, John R., 168, 291

Selby-Bigge, L. A., 295

Self, disjunctive and integrative theories of, 170, 190–201; consequences of, 201–8

Self-conception, 18, 37; of delinquent, 65–72, 86, 118–23; difficult to modify, 87–88; of embezzler, 134–35; of "good boy," 85–87; limited by sociocultural experience, 165–66; of numbers racketeer, 89–90

Self-consciousness, role of personal pronouns in, 156

Self-conversation, 129, 133, 136, 158, 282n

Self-preservation, irresistible impulse, 204–5

Self-reporting, technique of, 85, 101–2, 278–79n

Senn, J. N., 163

Shalloo, J. P., 275

Shannon, Lyle W., 12, 229, 287–88, 303

Shaw, Clifford R., 55, 93, 110, 122, 272–73, 275, 287

Sheldon, William H., 42, 270

Shils, Edward, 272, 291

Shoham, Shlomo, 305

Short, James F. Jr., 56, 115, 147–48, 150, 268, 272–73, 276, 279, 283, 286

Shulman, Harry M., 270

"Sickness," 213

Simons, Charles, 205, 298

Smith, Ernest A., 111–12, 280

Smith, P. M., 268

Smith, Richard Austin, 273

Smith v. United States (1929), 206–8, 298n

Smyth, George W., 256, 310

Snyder, Le Moyne, 286

Social class, 143, 285n; rural delinquency, 99–102; violence in England, 285n

Social defence, 239, 305–6

Social organization, 17, 25

Social participation, 20–21, 104–8, 113

"Social promotion," in school, 268n

Sorrentino, Anthony, 310

South Carolina, crime in ante-bellum, 288n

Sowle, Claude R., 302

Spaulding, Edith R., 269

Speiser, Lawrence, 232–33, 235, 297, 303

Spence, Kenneth W., 18

Spinley, Betty M., 269

Spontaneous conduct, 97–98

Srole, Leo, 292

State v. Felter, 298n

Staub, Hugo, 164, 186, 290, 294

Stephenson, Richard M., 269

Sterba, Richard, 300

Stewart, Robert L., 292

Store-hopping, 56

Stouffer, George A. W. Jr., 268

Straus, Jacqueline H., 283

Straus, Murray A., 283

Strict liability, 129, 273n

Stycos, J. Mayone, 292

Sullivan, Harry Stack, 185, 190, 203, 293

Superman Comics, 49, 76–77

Suspicion, arrest for, 222–26

Sutherland, Edwin H., 15, 17–18, 37, 42, 45, 65, 94, 128, 134, 197, 265, 269–70, 272, 281, 295, 305

Sutherland, John D., 293

Sweden, group delinquency in, 280n

Sykes, Gresham M., 60, 62, 65, 75, 77, 81, 273

Symbolic communication and compulsive crime, 139–41

Symbolism, 18; and sociocultural learning, and crime, 37–92

Szabo, Denis, 277

Szasz, Thomas S., 175–76, 179, 292, 299, 301

Taft, Donald R., 272, 285–86

Tappan, Paul W., 57, 110, 230, 232, 273–74, 303–5
Techniques of neutralization, 62–63
Temkin, Owsei, 295
Terman, Lewis M., 44–46, 270
Testimony, psychiatric, excluded from court, 301n
Thelander, R. J., 307
Thermonuclear war, 153, 287n
Thomas, W. I., 21, 266
Thorndike, Edward L., 216, 301
Thrasher, Frederic M., 55, 62, 110, 272–73, 279
Timasheff, N. S., 269
Toby, Jackson, 247, 249, 307–9
Tolman, E. C., 18
Treatment, 242; psychiatric, undefined, 221
Trebach, Arnold S., 255
Trends, some positive, 251–63
Tucker, William H., 269
Tufts, Edith, 303
Tylor, Edward B., 173, 291

United States v. Pollard, 201–8, 297n
Ursan, J., 307

Value judgments, 162–63
Values, discontinuity of, 114
Vance, Rupert P., 288–89
Vandalism, conception of, 77; definition of, social context, 72–73; as rational conduct, 120
Vandals, 275n
Vermont Rural Youth Project, 93–123, 258
Veroff, Joseph, 292
Vicious circle, 192–93, 206, 212; and irresistible impulse, 163
Violence, on television, 271n; subculture of, 144–51, 285–86n; interpersonal, 143, 151, 154; sociocultural phenomenon, 98–99, 140–55; rural and urban, 96–98; institutionalized in southern U.S., 287–89n
Vogel, Ezra F., 280
Vold, George B., 45, 270, 309
Volkart, Edmund H., 266
Volkman, Rita, 274
Voss, Harwin L., 85, 87–88, 248, 276, 308–9

Wade, Andrew L., 275
Wälder, Robert, 301
Wallace, Robert, 289
Wallerstein, James S., 269
Wattenberg, William, 271
Wechsler, Herbert, 299
Weeks, H. Ashley, 274
Weihofen, Henry, 197–200, 210, 212, 215–16, 294–97, 301
Weldon, J. C., 278
Wenninger, Eugene P., 278
Wertham, Frederic, 48–49, 161, 244, 286, 289–90, 307
Westley, William A., 113–14, 280
Weyer, Johann, 294
White, William A., 186, 293
White-collar crime as a disease, 127–28
White-collar thief, 125–36
Whitman, R. L., 163
Whyte, William F., 267, 269
Wickman, E. K., 35, 267–68
Williams, D. Colwyn, 10
Williams, G. Mennen, 267, 307
Williams, Jack Kenney, 288
Wilson, O. W., 226
Wilson, Robert N., 292
Windsor, Ontario, Community Fund, 27, 227–29
Wineman, David, 71, 83, 275
Winnet, Nochem S., 305
Winnicott, Donald W., 293
Witmer, Helen L., 266, 303
Wolf, Eleanor P., 143, 285
Wolfgang, Marvin E., 142–45, 148–50, 282–83, 285–86
Women, inferior to men, 39
Wood, Arthur L., 283
Woods, Hon. Mervyn J., 10
Woods, Mervyn J. (Mrs.), 10
Wootton, Barbara, 138, 158, 167, 175, 219, 282, 289–90, 292
Wyle, Clement J., 269
Wynne, Waller Jr., 288

Young, Pauline V., 303

Zay, Nicolas, 96, 277
Zeleny, Leslie D., 45, 270
Zilboorg, Gregory, 141, 193, 197, 200, 213, 282, 293–95, 297, 300
Znaniecki, Florian, 21, 266